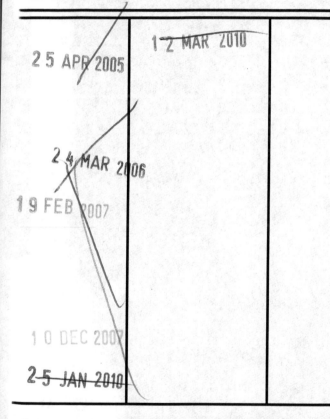

Creative
and Mental
Growth

Plate 1.
*"I Can Stand on My Head,"
painted by a five year old girl.
Young children paint and draw
from their own experiences,
reflecting their exuberance and
joy of living.*

SEVENTH EDITION

Creative and Mental Growth

Viktor Lowenfeld
W. Lambert Brittain

*Macmillan
Publishing Co., Inc.*
NEW YORK

*Collier Macmillan
Publishers*
LONDON

Macmillan Publishing Co., Inc.
866 Third Avenue, New York, New York 10022

Collier Macmillan Canada, Inc.

Library of Congress Cataloging in Publication Data
Lowenfeld, Viktor.
   Creative and mental growth.

   Bibliography: p.
   Includes index.
   1. Art—Study and teaching.   2. Creation (Literary, artistic, etc.)   3. Children as artists.   4. Artists—Psychology.   I. Brittain, W. Lambert.   II. Title.
N350.L62   1982   707   81-8356
ISBN 0-02-372080-8   AACR2

Printing: 2 3 4 5 6 7 8   Year: 2 3 4 5 6 7 8 9 0

PREFACE

This book is about children, from the child who is just beginning to walk, to the young adult who is taking his place as a mature member of our society. The book is concerned with children's art, their creativity, and their social and intellectual development. It was designed particularly for teachers and parents and others who are interested in understanding the interrelationship between cognitive development and creative and artistic expression. This field is an exciting one, for the expression of growing children is constantly changing, reflecting their interests, emotions, and intellectual awareness. I hope I have captured some of this excitement, because I would like to share with the reader some of the insights, respect, and inspiration that I have felt in putting together this edition.

Parents and teachers are crucial beings in the lives of children. It is primarily through them that values are established, intellectual processes are stimulated, and positive reactions to the environment are supported. This book should provide the means for parents and teachers to understand the importance of creative expression and to realize that creativity and art are a vital part of the learning process. It is not the product that concerns us, it is not the picture or the properly executed clay piece or the construction made from wood that should concern us. Rather it is the value of these experiences to the child that is important. If the youngster has increased in awareness of the environment, has found joy in developing skills, has had the opportunity to express feelings and emotions, then we have succeeded. The field of art is constantly changing, and the laborious learning of particular techniques or skills that seem to be presently in vogue may be meaningless to youngsters and no longer in vogue ten years from now. It is not these transient skills that are important, but rather the development of a sensitive, creative, involved, and aware child that is the goal of this book.

For those who have had the opportunity to read earlier editions of this work, several changes can be noted. The chapter which is concerned with the development of aesthetic awareness has been moved to an early section of the text. It deserves a place with the other important factors that give a basis for understanding and planning experiences with children. Essentially, the book is in three parts. The first part deals with the general factors involved in working with children; the second part focuses specifically on the developmental stages and concerns revolving around the actual teaching or working with children up through the age of twelve; the third section begins with a general introductory chapter and then deals primarily with the art of older children and young adults.

There have been many new sections added to the present edition, and some sections have been reworded or clarified. Additional illustrations have been added to point out the great variation that exists in children's drawings. The final chapter has been expanded, and illustrations have been added to provide information for psychologists who wish to compare the artistic development of children with various other manifestations of behavior. The reader will note a number of references to new research studies. It is gratifying to know that the art of children has become of great interest to psychologists, sociologists, anthropologists, and others who are concerned with the behavior and development of children.

Although it has been over twenty years since Viktor Lowenfeld died, his impact on the field of art education is still being felt. His philosophy is as fresh today as it was thirty years ago. I have tried to emphasize the uniqueness of every child and to stimulate adults to provide the physical and psychological environment to make children's lives richer and more meaningful. I have been fully supported in this task by Mrs. Viktor Lowenfeld and by Dr. John Lowenfeld. I am grateful for their confidence.

To the many people who have helped to make this new edition possible, I express my thanks. It is to the children who served as willing subjects for experiments and who provided many illustrations that I owe the most gratitude. It is they who have taught me the importance of creativity. My graduate students, my undergraduate classes, and my colleagues, both here at Cornell and elsewhere, have freely commented on sections of the previous edition. I have taken their suggestions seriously, and this new edition reflects some of their input.

I am grateful to Veronica Terrillion for allowing me to photograph her sculpture which is seen in Figure 8. Also, Jason Seley was kind enough to share with me his bumper sculpture in Figure 58. I have had pleasant discussions with Peter Wilson regarding the relationship between map reading and drawing ability; I am indebted to him for Figures 59 and 130.

Many teachers have shared with me the drawings and paintings that they have collected from their classes. This book could easily double in size if I allowed myself to yield to the temptation to include a larger fraction of the art products available. I do owe special thanks to Marlene Ginsburg for Figure 64, to Irene Russell for Figure 74, to Yu-Chin Chien and Anne Liebermann-Lloyd for Figure 86, and to Marjorie Martin for Figure 138. Pat Bechtold was a valuable source, providing Figures 30, 203, 212, 213, and 215, as well as Plates 31 and 32.

Jane Hooper helped gather a large number of drawings on the topics "Eating" and "Rain." This includes Figures 29, 133, 134, 153, 177, 179,

184, 190, 195, 196, and 206. Also I wish to thank Gordon Myer for Figure 210, Brian Dean for Plate 8, and Jean Holland for Plates 19 and 24.

In addition, I have had the help of fellow photographers; I wish to thank Barrett Gallagher for Figures 54, 83, 90, and 214; Jack Grant for Figures 75, 163, and 178; Lynn Haussler for Figures 79a, b, and c; Jean Warren for Figure 116; and the photo science studios at Cornell for Figure 71.

Several research projects have provided the background information for parts of the present volume. The Cornell research project in early childhood education was responsible for Figure 4, and the Cooperative Research Project #6-8416, U.S. Office of Education, was responsible for Figure 52. Also, many museums and art collections helped with illustrative material. I wish to thank them for their help and cooperation, particularly the Danish National Museum for Figure 45; Mr. Roger Hardley, Curator of Australian Ethnography, Queensland Museum, for Figure 46; the Herbert F. Johnson Museum of Art, at Cornell University, for Figures 47, 48, and 51; the Ithaca College Collection for Figure 56; the Australian National Museum for Figure 186; and the Indiana University of Pennsylvania for Plate 20.

In the sixth edition I made a comment in the preface that I would be glad to hear from anyone who had questions about the text or had information to share. I had not realized that so many people read a preface. I was surprised that many took me up on my suggestion, and it has been a source of satisfaction to know that I have been able to communicate on a more personal level with many who have read the previous edition. If you have questions, comments, or find some sections of the present edition confusing or in disagreement with your thoughts, I would be delighted to hear from you. It is from your comments that I can and will make changes so that future readers will have a better understanding of the importance of creative activities for children.

W. Lambert Brittain
Department of Human Development
and Family Studies
Cornell University
Ithaca, New York 14853

CONTENTS

take notes

10

**Art in the
Secondary
School
315**

11

**The Age of
Reasoning**
*The Pseudo-
naturalistic
Stage, Twelve
to Fourteen
Years*
353

12
The Period of Decision
Adolescent Art in the High School, Fourteen to Seventeen Years
389

13
Summary
423

Bibliography
435

Index
451

XIV

COLOR PLATES

Creative and Mental Growth

The Importance of Art for Education

The Meaning of Art Activities

Art is a fundamental human process. Every society, from the most primitive to the most sophisticated, has expressed itself through art. But more important, every person has put thoughts and emotions into an art form. Art is a personal and satisfying activity at any age, for although the arts are responsible for a greater awareness of the external world, it is also the arts that give vent to the emotions, the joys and fears of life. Young children use art as a means of learning, through the development of concepts which take visible form, through the making of symbols which capture and are an abstraction of the environment, and through the organization and positioning of these symbols together in one configuration.

Art is a dynamic and unifying activity, with great potential for the education of our children. The process of drawing, painting, or constructing is a complex one in which the child brings together diverse elements of his experience to make a new and meaningful whole. In the process of selecting, interpreting, and reforming these elements, he has given us more than a picture or a sculpture; he has given us a part of himself: how he thinks, how he feels, and how he sees.

Formal education is tremendously important when we realize that our children—from the age of five or six to sixteen, eighteen, or beyond—are forced by law and job requirements to spend ten, twelve, sixteen, or even twenty years behind school doors. That is a severe sentence just for being born a child. Yet the serving of this sentence is supposed to qualify a youngster to take his place as a contributing and well-adjusted member of society. From some points of view education has done its task; looking around us today, we can see great material gains. But serious questions can be raised about how much we have been able to educate beyond the making and consuming of objects. Have we in our educational system really put emphasis upon human values? Or have we been so blinded by material rewards that we have failed to recognize that the real values of a democracy lie in its most precious asset, the individual?

In our present educational system most emphasis has been put upon the learning of factual information. To a great extent the passing or failing of an examination or of a course, or the passing on to the next grade, or even the remaining in school depends upon the mastery or memorization of certain bits of information that are already known to the instructor. The function of the school system, then, would seem to be that of producing people who can file away bits of information and can then repeat these at a given signal. Once the student has achieved a certain competency at producing the proper bits of information at the correct time, he is considered ripe for graduating from school. What is most disturbing is that the skill in repeating bits of information may have very little relationship to the "contributing, well-adjusted member of society" we thought we were producing.

Mankind will not be saved by merely developing a good creative art program in public schools; but the values that are meaningful in an art program are those which may be basic to the development of a new image, a new philosophy, even a totally new structure for our educational system. More and more people are recognizing that the ability to learn differs from age to age and from individual to individual and that this ability to learn involves not only intellectual capacity but also social, emotional, perceptual, physical, and psychological factors. The process of learning is very complex and there may, therefore, be no single best teaching method. Our tendency to concentrate on developing the capacity to regurgitate bits of information may be putting undue emphasis on only one factor in human development, the one that is measured by intelligence tests. Intelligence as we now test it does not encompass the wide range of thinking abilities that are necessary for the survival of mankind. The abilities to question, to seek answers, to find form and order, to rethink and restructure and find new relationships, are qualities that are not generally taught; in fact, they seem to be frowned upon in our present educational system.

It may be that one of the basic abilities that should be encouraged in our public schools is the ability to discover and to search for answers, instead of passively waiting for answers and directions from the teacher. The experiences central to an art activity require self-direction. This is equally true of a nursery school child experimenting at the easel and of a college student painting a picture that necessitates mixing colors and inventing new forms.

We learn through our senses. The ability to see, feel, hear, smell, and taste provides the contact between us and our environment. But the process of educating children can sometimes be confused with teaching certain limited, predetermined responses, and the curriculum in public schools tends to be little concerned with the simple fact that man, and the child too, learns through these five senses. The development of perceptual sensitivity, then, should become a most important part of the educative process. Yet in most areas other than the arts, the senses are apt to be ignored. The greater the opportunity to develop an increased sensitivity and the greater the awareness of all the senses, the greater will be the opportunity for learning.

One of the basic ingredients of a creative art experience is the relationship

Figure 2.
*For children, art is an engrossing
activity which utilizes their
knowledge, observations, and
experiences.*

between the artist and his environment. Painting, drawing, or constructing is a constant process of assimilation and projection: taking in through the senses a vast amount of information, mixing it up with the psychological self, and putting into a new form the elements that seem to suit the aesthetic needs of the artist at the time. If we look at formal education, we realize that the transmission of knowledge rests upon 26 letters and 10 numerals. These are merely tools to use in the pursuit of knowledge, and are not in themselves learning.

THE MEANING OF ART ACTIVITIES   5

Figure 3.

The interaction of children with their environment provides the means for the development of thinking. These children are learning by firsthand experience about the crunch and smell of fall leaves.

These 36 abstract figures are manipulated and reshuffled from kindergarten through college. The development of mental growth, then, tends to become an abstract function as these figures take on different and more complicated meanings. However, it is not the knowledge of these figures or the ability to rearrange them that make for mental growth, but rather understanding what these figures mean. Being able to assemble letters in proper sequence to spell *rabbit* does not constitute an understanding of a rabbit. To really know a rabbit a child must actually touch it, feel its fur, watch its nose twitch, feed it, and learn its habits. It is the interaction between the symbols, the self, and the environment that provides the material for abstract intellectual processes. Therefore, mental growth depends upon a rich and varied relationship between a

THE IMPORTANCE OF ART FOR EDUCATION

child and his environment; such a relationship is a basic ingredient of a creative art experience.

Factual learning and retention, unless exercised by a free and flexible mind, will benefit neither the individual nor society. Education has often neglected those attributes of growth that are responsible for the development of the individual's sensibilities, for his spiritual well-being, as well as for his ability to live cooperatively in a society. The growing number of emotional and mental illnesses in this nation, coupled with our frightening hesitation to accept human beings as human beings regardless of nationality, religion, race, creed, sex, or color, are vivid reminders that education so far has failed in one of its most significant aims. While our high achievements in specialized fields, particularly in the sciences, have improved our material standards of living, they have diverted us from our emotional and spiritual values. They have introduced a false set of values, which neglect the innermost needs of an individual. Art education, as an essential part of the educative process, may well mean the difference between a flexible, creative human being and one who will not be able to apply his learning, who will lack inner resources, and who will have difficulty relating to his environment. In a well balanced educational system, the total being is stressed, so that his potential creative abilities can unfold.

The Meaning of Art for Children

Art is not the same for a child as it is for an adult. Although it may be difficult to say just what art means for any particular adult, usually the term "art" has very definite connotations. Among them are museums, pictures hanging on walls, disheveled painters, full-color reproductions, attics with northern exposure, models posing in the nude, a cultural elite, and generally a feeling of an activity that is removed from the real world of making a living and bringing up a family. Somehow art is supposed to be "a good thing," and art books on the coffee table or "good" pictures for the walls of one's home ought to bring some kind of elevating spirit into life. But for the common man art may be like taking a dose of medicine. Art for the adult, at any rate, is usually concerned with the area of aesthetics or external beauty.

Art for the child is something quite different. For a child, art is primarily a means of expression. No two children are alike, and, in fact, each child differs even from his earlier self as he constantly grows, perceives, understands, and

Figure 4.

These are four drawings of a man done by Rachel, a kindergarten child, over a short period of time. Part A shows a five year old's concept of a man. Note the lack of arms; but Rachel does include a head, body, and legs with toes. In B Rachel has drawn much more, and her concept of a man now includes arms with hands and fingers. The toes are now attached to a foot and buttons have appeared. In C the single line previously used for legs and arms is now double, as if the limbs had volume. Note the hat that does not rest on the head but floats above it. The final drawing D shows a rather complex and complete drawing, much more typical of a six year old.

A   B

interprets his environment. A child is a dynamic being; art becomes for him a language of thought, and as he grows his expression changes.

Sometimes teachers, intrigued by the beauty of children's drawings and paintings, will save these paintings and admire them as examples of true spontaneous art. Occasionally they go a step further and suggest the proper colors or correct forms. Although they profess enthusiasm for the freshness and directness of children's paintings, some teachers impose their own color schemes, proportions, and manner of painting upon children. From this discrepancy between the adult taste and the way in which a child expresses himself arise most of the difficulties that prevent children from using art as a true means of self-expression.

If it were possible for children to develop without any interference from the outside world, no special stimulation for their creative work would be necessary. Every child would use his deeply rooted creative impulses without inhibition, confident in his own means of expression. Whenever we hear children say, "I can't draw," we can be sure that some kind of interference has occurred in their lives. This loss of self-confidence in one's own means of expression may be an indication of a withdrawal into one's self. Often the mis-

THE IMPORTANCE OF ART FOR EDUCATION

C　　　　　　　　　　　　　　　　　　D

take is made of evaluating children's creative work by how the product looks, its colors and shapes, its design qualities, and so forth. This is unjust, not only to the product but even more to the child. Growth cannot be measured by the tastes or standards of beauty that may be important to an adult. However, art has been traditionally interpreted as relating mainly to aesthetics, and this concept has in some cases limited the opportunity for art to be used in its fullest sense. In art education the aesthetic quality of the final product is subordinated to the creative process. It is the child's process—his thinking, his feelings, his perceiving, in fact, his reactions to his environment—that is important.

Every child, regardless of level of development, should first of all be considered as an individual. Expression grows out of, and is a reflection of, the total child. A child expresses thoughts, feelings, and interests in drawings and paintings and shows knowledge of the environment in his creative expressions. A ten year old who is concerned with the mechanical operation of parts, gears, levers, and pulleys will work through these relationships in his drawings. Note the intense concentration shown in Figure 5. Much thought and planning have gone into the details of the operation of the airplane that the boy is drawing. In Figure 6 the wings and the joining of the various struts have

Figure 5.
The concentration of this ten year old boy is typical of a child who is confident of his own creative ability.

Figure 6.
This plan for a working model of an airplane, drawn by a ten year old boy, shows his thinking through of the functions of the various parts and an inventive awareness of mechanical details.

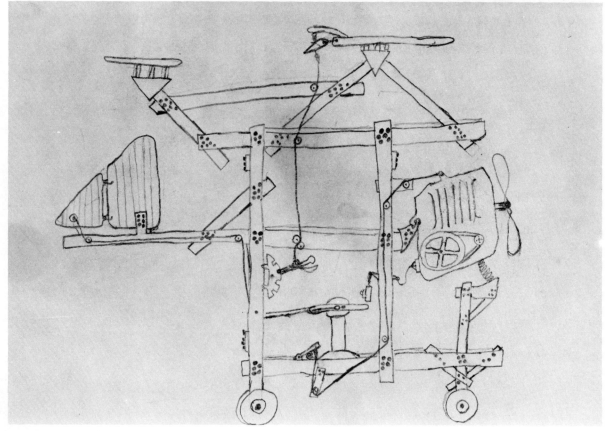

THE IMPORTANCE OF ART FOR EDUCATION

been thought through in detail. Notice the mechanism for adjusting the rudder. It is irrelevant that this looks little like an adult concept of a plane. Each child reveals his interests, capabilities, and involvement in art, although these may in some cases bear little relationship to "beauty."

Occasionally we hear of a child who is outstanding in art. This may be a child who performs in ways that are neat and proper, who satisfies the artistic likes of the teacher. Sometimes a child who is frustrated in school subjects such as reading, writing, or arithmetic may turn to art for a release from frustrations, because in art there is no right or wrong answer. Both of these children may get a great deal of satisfaction from drawing, and if they are rewarded for their efforts, they will certainly continue to try to gain recognition. However, it may be a youngster who is silent and withdrawn who most needs the opportunity for art expression. A teacher who has certain tastes and artistic standards may find it difficult to understand that these standards are irrelevant for the self-expression of youngsters.

Although the artistic standards of the teacher must be subordinated to the needs of children in art education, this does not mean that the paintings or drawings by children cannot have great beauty in themselves. Rather, it is through the process of art that art itself unfolds. If we were to focus on the art product, we would be concerned primarily with the making of beautiful objects rather than with the effects that making has upon children. Art education, therefore, is primarily concerned with the effect that the process has on the individual, whereas the so-called fine arts are more concerned with the resulting products.

Every school, not only in kindergarten and elementary classrooms but also in the secondary school, should try to encourage each youngster to identify with his own experiences and help him to go as far as he can in developing concepts that express his feelings and emotions, and his own aesthetic sensitivities. We should never be satisfied with the stereotyped response or with the unfeeling or automatic drawing, since this indicates that the child is showing insensitivity to his own feelings and experiences. It is more important that we stimulate and make meaningful the relationship between the youngster and his own environment; an adult concept of what is important or beautiful must not be imposed.

The essential ingredient is the child, a child who has feelings, emotions, love, and hate, and who has no need for the stick figure that may be taught in first grade, or the abstract design that is taught in junior high school. His individual expression is just as important to him as the artist's creation is to the adult. The teacher should recognize that his or her own learning experiences will avail children nothing, for it is the children's learning that is important in the educational process. It is not the adult's answer but the child's striving toward his own answer that is crucial.

The Senses As Basic to Learning

It is only through the senses that learning can take place. This may sound like an obvious statement; however, its implications seem to be lost in our educational system. It may be that education merely reflects the changes in our society, for people seem to be relying less and less on actual sensory contact with their environment. They are becoming passive viewers of their culture rather than active makers of it. Football games are watched, not played. Music has become a soothing background syrup in the shopping center rather than an opportunity for actual involvement. The television has become a mass means of distraction in which the viewer's only involvement is that of turning the *on* or *off* switch. Even groceries come packed in their own sterile plastic containers, removed not only from touch but also from smell.

Schools have done little to educate these senses that are our only avenue to learning. Although a number of activities are included at the nursery school level that involve manipulation and movement, most of these activities are taught as ends in themselves. The purpose seems to be to develop particular skills so that these can be checked off as having been taught, rather than utilizing them as a means to expression. The first grade teacher is satisfied when children learn how to manipulate scissors, but the possibilities of using scissors creatively are limited. The farther up the educational ladder we go, the farther removed children become from relying on their own senses, until a good deal of learning becomes not only vicarious, but also abstract in nature.

Our forefathers were in daily contact with their environment. Not only did they build their own homes and grow their own food, but they also made their own music and art. Even in the last fifty years there have been dramatic changes. The local hardware store has lost its bin of nails, sacks of grain and seed are no longer available to run one's fingers through, and the grocery store no longer smells of freshly ground coffee or oranges that have gotten a little too old. The smell of freshly baked bread or the taste of one's own homemade root beer are sensory experiences that have almost disappeared. It is encouraging to observe an increased awareness of nature, particularly among our young people. Our national parks attract increasing numbers of visitors. Possibly the

THE IMPORTANCE OF ART FOR EDUCATION

Figure 7.
*Blackeyed peas in an open
container create an interesting
pattern. Prepackaged
merchandise, each item in its own
sterile plastic pack, has removed
the senses of touch and smell from
many of the goods we buy.*

greater interest in camping and backpacking is a result of the urge to experience the senses more fully.

There is little opportunity today for youngsters to dam up a stream, dig a tunnel to China, or build a tree house. The complete involvement of oneself in a project of a purely physical, sensory nature is rapidly disappearing. Paint-by-the-number kits and preplanned, precut projects have made art sterile. A family may now be more concerned about selecting the proper decorator for their living room than with expressing their own likes and dislikes, or interests.

Touching, seeing, hearing, smelling, and tasting involve the active participation of the individual. There is evidence that even the young child needs to be truly encouraged to see, touch, or become involved in his environment. In a case of sensory deprivation, a youngster may be isolated from external stimulation. It is not just a question of the presence of sounds, or of having things available to touch and see; it is the stimulation of the interaction between the youngster and the environment through the senses that makes the difference between the child who is eager to explore and investigate that environment and one who retreats from it. Obviously, deprived youngsters can come from what might be called affluent surroundings. Even if a child's basic physical needs are met, he may nevertheless be seriously deprived in other areas of development. For example, in families where constant status seeking

THE SENSES AS BASIC TO LEARNING

13

is a consideration, children may be ignored or considered merely as objects to be displayed at appropriate times. Apparently this type of behavior is also seen in the animal kingdom, for it has been observed that, when animal parents are occupied with status seeking pursuits, they neglect their offspring (Morris, 1969).

One observational study of young deprived children reported that these youngsters were not alert to, or even responsive to, the teacher's spoken directions, or to a display of colored paper, scissors, and paste set out for them. Although the children were constantly scanning the environment, these objects failed to attract their attention (Malone, 1967). It is obvious that for young children the senses are extremely important, but in later years too the development of refined sensory experiences should be a continuing process. Art education is the only subject matter area that truly concentrates on developing the sensory experiences. Art is filled with the richness of textures, the excitement of shapes and forms, the wealth of color, and youngster and adult alike should be able to receive pleasure and joy from these experiences.

Auditory sensitivity means detailed listening, not just hearing; visual sensitivity means an awareness of differences and details, not just recognition; the same is true for touching, and for all sensory experiences. We are living in a time in which mass production, mass education, and mass seeing and experiencing have suppressed the sensitive relationships of the individual. Art education has the special mission of developing within the individual those creative sensitivities that make life satisfying and meaningful.

Self-identification and Self-expression

People today have to a great extent lost their ability to identify with what they do. Few of us can point to our own contribution to society. Technology has made man little more than a machine. The worker often is not a part of the planning or design of the product; the job no longer requires a skilled or able workman, but a reliable employee. In some instances, mechanization of production has reached the point where the operators may neither see the product nor work on it directly. A study of the organization of the factory—an organization that made workers feel isolated, dominated, detached, and discontent—was made by Blauner (1964). His data show that this is not necessarily true of

Figure 8.
Few people have the freedom to build statues on their front lawns. In this life-size, painted concrete equestrian statute, an elderly woman's artistic expression is reflected through her creative manipulation of the material.

all occupations; those that entail a good deal of craftsmanship and personal involvement have more satisfactions to offer to workers than mere money. This dehumanization of the worker is of great concern to many, and there is a call for a new basis for the organization of the workplace which would allow for an increase in the quality of life for the worker (Heisler, 1977; Trist, 1978; Wilson, 1978). Sometimes the demands of a job and what the worker expects may lead to serious conflict, and the results reduce the worker's self-initiative (Gowler and Legge, 1978). But worker satisfaction and involvement in a job are apparently directly related to how important he feels his skills are, how varied the tasks he performs are, and how much he can learn on the job (Rousseau, 1977).

When work is only a means of survival, the rewards and satisfactions of life are sought in entertainment or diversions. The questions "Who am I? Where am I going? What do I stand for?" reveal a serious dilemma. It is not only youth who are searching for identity. Although no one is happy to become a number, we are all rapidly becoming merely a series of numbers for the purposes of tax deductions, bank collections, vehicle identifications, insurance payments, mail delivery, licensing skills, and even hospitalization. It may not even be possible to build one's own woodshed or porch without approval from the local zoning board. Restrictions on one's creative productions are legalized pressures for conformity; no innovations are allowed; different is wrong. In spite of restrictions, a few people have been able to assert their own individuality and build some remarkably ingenious structures (Boericke and Shapiro, 1973; Moholy-Nagy, 1976; Wampler, 1977). These houses have often required great effort and sacrifice, but show that man is capable of creative effort in spite of restrictions and pressure to conform. In a democratic society it is essential that the individual be able to know what he thinks, say what he feels, and help remake the world around him.

Our educational system has done little to change the increasing loss of identity with oneself. Rewards are given for neat papers, for correct answers, for recalling the proper information. Little is done to stimulate the child to find the rewards from within the learning process: to find satisfaction in solving his own problems, to take pleasure in developing greater knowledge and understanding for its own sake, or to measure success or failure in areas of importance to the self.

To a great extent our educational system is geared toward measurable academic skills. Here learning can be measured easily, but this is defining learning in a very narrow sense. Learning does not merely mean the accumulation of knowledge; it also implies an understanding of how this knowledge can be utilized. We must be able to use our senses freely and creatively and develop positive attitudes toward ourselves and our neighbors for this learning to become effective. Children rarely have the opportunity to share ideas and develop attitudes about themselves and others. Although from the outside the school may look like a center of learning, this learning takes place in isolated cells, with fifth graders rarely seeing a kindergarten child except when passing in the halls. Adults are excluded, and except for the teachers many children see no adults for hours at a time. For a fifth grader, the world is largely made up of

Plate 2.
"Man," painted by a five year old boy. A painting by a young child is usually direct and uninhibited. Here red, blue, yellow, and green are boldly used for the figure with no attempt at naturalism.

Plate 3.
*"I Am Putting on My Sweater,"
drawn by a seven year old boy.
This picture might mistakenly be
considered that of a child who has
problems, because he has
apparently scribbled over his own
face and body with a green
crayon. However, it actually is a
drawing of getting dressed and
putting a sweater on over his
head.*

Plate 4.
*"I Have a Loose Tooth," drawn
by a six and a half year old girl.
Here a girl shows that she has a
loose tooth. The exaggerated size
of the mouth and great number of
teeth show how important this
experience was.*

Figure 9.
The opportunity for young children to draw or paint provides a basis for developing a self-concept.

other fifth graders. Bronfenbrenner (1970) has warned that, when children have contact only with their agemates, they have no opportunity to learn culturally established patterns of cooperation and mutual concern. He sees the likelihood of a very unfortunate outcome: increased alienation, indifference, antagonism, and violence.

No art expression is possible without self-identification with the experience expressed as well as with the art material by which it is expressed. This is one of the basic factors of any creative expression: it is the true expression of the self. The art materials are controlled and manipulated by one individual, and the completed project is his. This is as true at a very young age as it is for adult artists. It is individuals who use their art materials and their form of expression according to their own personal experiences. Because these experiences change with growth, self-identification embraces the social, intellectual, emotional, and psychological changes within the child.

There is also a need for the ability to identify with others. In a peaceful society that combines humans of different heritages, it is essential to be able to identify with those we fear, those we do not understand, or those who appear strange to us. Scientifically we have made great gains, but socially we no longer know our immediate neighbors, and are unable to communicate with them peacefully. It is only through self-identification that we can begin to identify with others. As a child identifies with his own work, as he learns to appreciate and understand his environment by becoming involved in it, he develops the attitude that helps him understand the needs of his neighbor. The process of creation involves incorporating the self into the activity; the very act of creation provides understanding of the process that others go through in facing their own experiences. To live cooperatively as well-adjusted human beings and to contribute creatively to such a society become most important objectives for education.

The term "self-expression" has often been misunderstood. Self-expression is giving vent in constructive forms to feelings, emotions, and thoughts at one's own level of development. What matters is the mode of expression, not the content. It is important to mention this, because one of the greatest mistakes that can be made in the use of the term "self-expression" is to think of it in terms of an unstructured or uncontrolled emotion, or, on the other hand, to consider it as mere imitation.

The very young child expresses himself freely through babbling or crying. This may be a truer means of self-expression than a higher form of art, if that work of art is dependent on others or upon imitations of a scene or content that is not relevant to the person producing it. Technical perfection bears little

SELF-IDENTIFICATION AND SELF-EXPRESSION

19

relationship to self-expression; the production of technically excellent art products may be far removed from the real expressive needs of the producer.

There is great satisfaction in expressing one's own feelings and emotions in art. Even the very young child who knows nothing about the technical difficulties in pencil rendering, or the various gradations of graphite hardness, can get great satisfaction from making a scribble with a soft pencil. He is expressing his own importance through his own means, and the satisfaction he derives from his achievement is self-evident. The self-confidence that can develop from this type of expression provides the basis for more advanced levels of art.

This area of discussion is closely related to the development of self-concept. The individual's own expression is of prime importance, and art probably contributes as much to this area of development as to any other. It has been recognized that young children need to see themselves as being worthy to deal with the complex environment in which they find themselves. In a longitudinal study of sixth graders in Australia (Williams, Poole, and Lett, 1977), those children who were in the top 5 percent on a creativity test were higher in self-esteem than less creative children. This is also true of older children, although the self-concept of ability and attitudes toward achievement are much harder to change as the child grows older. One study attempted to change the self-concept of a group of ninth grade low achievers. Their parents were involved in helping to change that image; as the self-concept of the ninth graders improved, their academic achievement improved (Brookover, 1967). The relationship between creativity and ego development in college populations has been studied by Phillips (1973) and by Workman and Stillion (1974); both studies found a significant correlation between creativity and a positive self-perception. A basic goal of art education is to develop in the child the ability to create a product using whatever skills one has, without having to follow a pattern or methods prescribed by others, and without having to rely on external rewards for satisfaction.

The Meaning of Art for Society

Art is often considered the highest form of human expression. It is certainly true that art is something that is cherished, sometimes valuable for the collector, and can even be stolen for ransom. Art is also a reflection of the society that creates it. The art of ancient Greece or Egypt tells us a great deal about the society in which it was produced. It is a little difficult to evaluate the present

THE IMPORTANCE OF ART FOR EDUCATION

forms of art within our own society; although art critics enjoy tackling this task, the artists themselves seem to be less interested in the meaning of the art they produce.

For some people the field of contemporary art is a mystery. Apparently it has broken away from past traditions, and to some extent it seems more closely related to smashed automobiles or the stacked soup cans on the grocer's shelf. At times it may resemble some of the bad dreams one does not speak about, or the nonsensical play of lights and forms. For many people today's art is distant from their interests and far removed from the refined cultural taste supposedly associated with "art." It may seem especially unrelated to the scientific world in which we live.

Snow (1961) has written about these two extremes within our society: the artistic, literary pull on one side as against the scientific on the other. However, it is interesting that art and science have somehow managed to keep forms that parallel the advanced state of knowledge in each area (Cassidy, 1962). The dissolving of space in science has been matched by the dissolving of space in paintings. Einstein's theory of relativity and the nonobjective movement in art developed about the same time. Although few people today claim to be scientific experts, many believe in the value of advanced scientific experimentation. There is growing concern over the sources of energy and the preservation of natural resources; society eagerly awaits the dissemination of the latest scientific information. Most scientific reference books have been overtaken by new and pertinent data (Mitton, 1977). At the same time, most people claim to know what they like in art and doubt the value of new experimental art forms. It seems strange to realize that one segment of our society is given approval, but another segment is condemned for its investigations. The physical scientist has gained control over parts of his environment through experimentation and manipulation of symbols. The artist also must come to grips with mass, energy, and motion, but in his field attitudes and values also play a part. Both scientist and artist continually try to fathom the unknown in their search for truth.

Art can have meanings within our society other than as the highest form of expression. It can be used in the most crassly commercial fashion to advertise, promote, and sell a variety of products, candidates, and ventures. Many would object to calling this art, but its use of color and form and concern about audience impact makes it a very evident part of our culture. It may be that this type of art is more truly representative of our culture than the art that is being produced for the connoisseur. It could be interesting to look at our society from the point of view of an archaeologist a few thousand years from now and

Figure 11.

The teacher can do much to encourage sensitivity to detail. The radiating design quality, the arrangement of seeds, the moisture, and the surprising beauty to be found in small things may be seen in a slice of orange.

guess at the kind of society he might piece together from the variety of art forms found in the drugstore, automobile showroom, or airport novelty shop.

Somebody has to worry about the future of our country. With poorly designed "builder" houses, glaring neon signs, big billboards proclaiming the virtues of particular kinds of beer, and local streams being used as garbage dumps, the prospects for the future beauty of the earth look very dim. Most schools do nothing about the problem of deciding what the world that we and our children are going to live in will look like. The art teacher, the biology teacher, and a few concerned individuals may be able to enlist the aid of the young people who look with anger at the degradation of our common inheritance. Politicians can no longer afford to ignore group protests that call attention to loss, blight, and waste. There are increasing numbers who would like to preserve and protect our environment. Examining our surroundings in de-

THE IMPORTANCE OF ART FOR EDUCATION

tail, seeing beauty not only in the spectacular but also in the smallest growing things, is not limited to any one field. But art experiences can bring new realizations of this environment, evaluations based on reasons other than economic. The conservation of our resources depends in part on the sympathetic preservation of that which is beautiful, that which has intrinsic value, and that which is reusable in other forms.

Art ability has often been considered something one is born with, something that comes intuitively to a sensitive individual. There has been serious questioning whether art can really be taught. But there are also people who feel that art is so vital to our society that we must begin early in our educational system to teach good taste and to develop habits of care in selecting objects from the environment. Both of these views seem too extreme. On the one hand is the opinion that nothing can be done to encourage or stimulate youngsters in their art experiences; it is almost as if a magic spark from heaven somehow alights on the chosen few. The other extreme tries desperately hard to develop a curriculum that, through proper rewards and appropriate disciplinary action, makes youngsters conform to the standards of the teacher. Somehow excluded from both views is the individual who should be free to reject or accept, to formulate opinions, and to evolve new directions, but who should *not* be free to be a passive bystander in our society.

Art can play a meaningful role in the development of children. The focus of teaching is the developing, changing, dynamic child who becomes increasingly aware of himself and his environment. Art education can provide the opportunity for increasing the capacity for action, experience, redefinition, and stability needed in a society filled with changes, tensions, and uncertainties.

The Meaning of the Art Product

There are many ways of looking at children's drawings. Probably most adults see children's art as being interesting, exciting, and colorful examples of self-expression. Often the product appeals to adults because it exhibits a certain magnetism, possibly reflecting one's own childhood, or possibly inducing a certain amount of envy of the freedom and spontaneity that is apparent in the product. This is particularly true of the work of young children. Older children may develop a technical skill and begin to develop a naturalistic representation which can sometimes be admired for the interesting solution to a visual problem or for the skill in mastering a particular procedure.

Professionals in the field of art and psychology often look at art from different points of view. Sometimes the art product is seen as a reflection of the inner personality of the child, as an indication of the child's development, or possibly as a reflection of the achievement of the student toward the goals set by the teacher. In any case, here the end product is considered important. Probably most important is the frame of reference that the examiner brings to this task. A clinical psychologist, a parent, and a teacher will all see different things in the same representation—this can sometimes be confusing. What may seem a wonderful picture to one, may seem merely a symptom of behavior to another, or may seem a failure to the third. Maybe we should be more specific.

1. One method of looking at children's drawings and paintings is called the psychoanalytic approach. In this format, the viewer is usually the one who has some background in clinical psychology. A drawing or painting is used as a projective technique in which the child paints or draws what is important to him, and each line or space is looked at in terms of its relationship to the whole painting. Particularly interesting to this type of viewer is the drawing of the human figure. How the arms are drawn, the size of the body in comparison to the rest of the figure, and the number of buttons on the shirt or dress is sometimes felt to be important. The central concern of the clinical psychologist is to develop a healthy person. The art, then, is a means of discovering the internal conflicts and disturbing experiences which influence the child's development. It is assumed that there is constantly conflict between the self and the environment and that the ways in which these conflicts are resolved determine a child's personality.

The drawing or painting activity is also considered therapeutic. That is, the child usually paints freely the events and problems that have caused conflicts. The ability to put these on paper and to see these things in context with other parts of the child's environment serves as a catharsis. The child is usually encouraged to act out or to paint those things that seem to be most important to him, and the verbalization of these activities is supposed to provide good therapy. The product then becomes important, not only as a record of the problems and conflicts the child is facing, but also as a record of progress toward the healthy personality.

There has been a great deal written on the use of art as a projective measure in helping to understand the problems faced by children and adults. However, there is much inconsistency in the method of interpreting drawings even by those who are supposed to be expert in the field. There is no standard system of scoring drawings, and much of the interpretation is intuitive. In prac-

Figure 12.

An adult might see this second grader's drawing as being full of aggression, with a large axe form, a hanging child, and a youngster shielding his eyes. Actually, it is a drawing of favorite activities, such as climbing a rope and riding a bicycle, with only the necessary parts of the tree shown. The child's regular schema for a man did not provide two hands for riding the bicycle, so one arm extends over the head to the other handlebar.

tice, drawings are often used as one part of a battery of information that helps the experienced clinician obtain a broader understanding of a client. But this is no area for the uninitiated to tread; it is thin ice for the best clinician, since it is difficult to distinguish between the drawings of emotionally disturbed children and normal children of a younger age (Blum, 1979).

Sometimes children's drawings are analyzed by individuals with little or no background in understanding children's art; the results would be quite funny if these people were not sometimes taken seriously. Often what happens is that the individual will see forms or shapes in children's drawings that have meaning to the person looking at the drawings, though not to the child who drew them. To some extent we get a better understanding of the person making these interpretations than we do of the child who made the picture.

2. Another and diametrically opposed view of children's art is exemplified by the behavioral psychologist. In looking at children's drawings and paintings, he may see entirely different configurations than the clinical psychologist. The behaviorist is more concerned with the activities of the child that are reinforcing and shaping behavior. Basically, he believes that the environment is primarily responsible for the making of the child. As we change or build the environment in different patterns, the child will change and will reflect the experiences that he has had. The child's drawings, therefore, will also change and reflect his thinking processes. It would be necessary, then, to

THE MEANING OF THE ART PRODUCT

determine what would be important for the child to learn and then to set up the conditions for that learning to take place. The drawing becomes an indication of the child's understanding of the task at hand. Often this task is not known to the child, but the success or failure of the youngster's achievements is measured against a pre-established criterion, which may be called the development of perceptual skills, the realization of color harmony, the development of spatial relationships, the awareness of proportion, or some other name. In each case, the goal is quite clear to the advisor, and the program toward its successful completion is laid out in advance. Usually the child has little voice in these goals.

If we look at the art product to determine how well a child has achieved some predetermined instructional objectives in art, we must make some sort of evaluation; the objectives must be measurable. Has the child achieved greater use of color in drawings? Has perspective been understood and used correctly? However, this way of examining the product means that the process of painting must be dissected into fragments, and the real meaning of expression becomes lost. Examining the art product for the acquisition of particular skills assumes that these skills are somehow necessary to further expression; it also assumes that the teacher knows what these skills are and how to put them into proper sequence so that the learner can develop competency. A kindergartener draws with freedom and spontaneity, with all the ability and skill needed; it is not until the child has been in the educational system for a number of years that this freedom is lost. It will not be the skills the youngster lacks, but the urge and desire to paint directly and freely, without fear of evaluation, and without being told to improve his or her color sense or to learn the rules of perspective.

The person who determines what another must learn and how this learning must take place, looks at the art product primarily to see if these predetermined goals have been attained. The teacher is asking if there is evidence of successful teaching methods; the behavioral psychologist is looking for changes in attitude or behavior. This approach is certainly different from that of the clinical psychologist, but no more valid.

3. A third way of looking at children's drawings is the developmental approach. Here the drawing or painting is examined from the point of view of seeing how the child measures up to what is expected of him at any particular age. It is assumed that the child is basically a changing, moving person who follows a predetermined growth pattern, although this pattern varies considerably. Each stage of development follows the preceding one in logical sequence and each stage is a springboard for the next. To some extent the developmental psychologist has very little influence over the way in which the child behaves

THE IMPORTANCE OF ART FOR EDUCATION

artistically. The drawing or picture will reflect the particular stage of development that the child has reached; although the youngster can be encouraged to expand or enlarge the painting, the way in which it is painted or the concept that the child is trying to portray will not change. The feeling is that the child cannot change until he is ready, and that is predetermined by his developmental level. When he says his paintings do not look right or when he is dissatisfied with the method of representation, a child is at a transitional stage and is ready to be helped but cannot be pushed into the next stage of development.

A teacher who adheres to a strict developmental approach to viewing children's art may feel that the best thing to do is to stay out of the way. Besides providing materials and a place to work, there may be little left for this teacher, since the art product's appearance is essentially out of both the teacher's and the child's control. However, all children do not arrive at the same concept of their environment at the same time. If every child were preprogrammed to develop artistic concepts at a set rate, then environmental influences would seem to play but a minor role. However, such is not the case, and psychological literature is filled with evidence that changes in the environment can drastically affect the rate of growth but not its pattern. This theory needs further discussion, but not in relation to ways of interpreting the art product.

4. A fourth approach to looking at children's art is often relegated to an art teacher. Sadly enough, this approach has the least amount of excitement in it. Here the basic assumption is that children need to develop a vocabulary, both verbal and pictorial, upon which they can build their expression. The role of the art teacher seems to be that of providing the materials, developing tasks which will be executed by the child in mastering certain artistic skills, and motivating the child so that the drawing and painting activities continue. The art activities become sequential in that they build upon one another from the point of view of artistic achievement and not from the point of view of the child's development. Teachers who favor the mastery of skills before the development of expression feel that it is necessary to teach how to use a brush, to clean off the excess paint, and to control the quality of line before real expression can take place with that material. For older children, it apparently is necessary to teach linear perspective and a good pencil technique so that these may be used for the expressive needs of the child. Also, certain awareness of the use of materials is important, so a progression of materials is presented to be mastered by children. For example, the nursey school teacher may feel it important that a child should be able to use tempera paint, some simple drawing instruments, and paste. The junior high student will have copper embossing, styrofoam

carving, simple weaving techniques, the use of pen and ink, and possibly some design principles to master. The high school student will be concerned with etching, throwing clay on the wheel, using the air gun, and mastering acrylics or oils. The art product in these cases becomes a record of the youngster's preparation and his success in achieving certain levels of proficiency within the realm of school art.

Figure 13.
The child has discovered how to manipulate scissors. The task she has set for herself requires concentration and the achievement is a source of satisfaction.

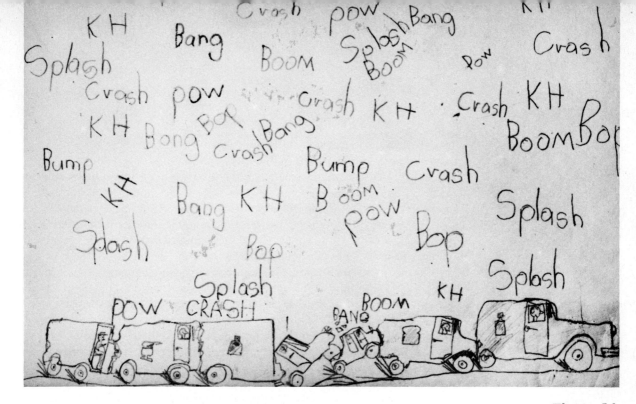

Figure 14.
A seven year old boy saw a traffic accident which distressed him. This is one of several drawings he made in the days that followed.

Which of the above is the "correct" way of looking at children's art is not the basic question. Obviously the training and background of the adult will influence the perception of what the product signifies. Also, the differences between these four ways of looking at the art product have been artificially stressed, maybe unduly so; however, it is probably important to bear in mind that these ways of looking at children's products can influence the way we treat the product and motivate the child and can affect the rewards or praise that we may distribute. It is important to know where we stand in relationship to these theories and goals.

One important factor to be kept in mind is that creative work must be understood individually. We can only appreciate the significance of creative work by understanding the child and seeing his picture as part of his life. For example, it may happen that a child portrays an emotional event that has great personal significance, such as a fire that has burned down his house or an accident in which he was involved. To the adult these may be ordinary paintings; they may even be ugly from an aesthetic point of view. Yet the work produced may be an important resolution within the child's own life; to direct attention only to the painting and to be concerned only with technical abilities would be an injustice. It is also true that an insignificant and timidly executed work may provide insight for the teacher so that activities can be planned that will give the child the opportunity to develop confidence in his expression. Each art work must be considered on its own merits, and this is true for all levels of teaching.

Children's creative works not only differ from one individual to another; great differences can be seen from one stage of development to another. An experience that is meaningful to a child of twelve may be meaningless to a child of seven. It is not the content that becomes the important consideration in children's drawings, but the way in which youngsters portray this content. A child will draw and paint from what he is. These feelings, desires, thoughts, and explorations with paint and subject matter will all appear in the painting. Particularly a young child, but to some degree everyone, paints in a direct manner with no thought of hiding or concealing true feelings.

For the child, the value of an art experience is in the process. In the discussion of the importance of the art product we have been concerned primarily with the adult, what the drawing, painting, or three-dimensional construction means for the viewer. To examine the picture without understanding what the child's intention was, to make assumptions about personality from one example of art work, or to assess competence in art on the basis of what is included or omitted from the product, does both the product and the child an injustice. To say that this child has weaknesses or that that one has strengths, based upon one teacher's opinion, helps neither the child nor the teacher. If the purpose is to understand the child and to give support for his expression, to find out how we can involve him more fully in life, then it is a legitimate one for teachers. The preschool child may not recognize his own painting the next day. However, the high school student looks at his painting with a very critical eye; his purpose is quite different. But for both, the excitement of painting is in the subjective reaction to the world, in displaying on the painting surface the thoughts and sensitivities that are part of creative and intellectual growth.

Understanding Growth and Development

2

Art as a Reflection of Development

The art products of children tell us a great deal. The child reveals himself directly and without fear. Art for him is more than a pastime; it is a meaningful communication with himself; it is the selection of those parts of his environment with which he identifies, and the organization of these parts into a new meaningful whole. It is important for his thinking processes, for his perceptual development, for his emotional development, for his increasing social awareness, and for his creative development. It is obvious that correcting drawings or imposing particular demands that have no meaning for the child serves no purpose and may instead establish a pattern of dependency upon the adult for direction and support.

Knowledge is usually thought of as flowing from the teacher to the student. The teacher has the responsibility for organizing the environment, providing the instructional materials, deciding upon the best method of conveying the appropriate information, and developing a curriculum which supposedly covers the syllabus materials. The child, on the other hand, is usually the one who is graded on his acquisition of this knowledge and on his ability to deal with the structure of the classroom in a socially acceptable way. The students' responses are judged as though they were signs of growth, although they may be primarily mimicking the teacher's own values.

Art can bring a new dimension into this organization, a dimension that is concerned with the psychological processes that occur and are experienced and developed in the youngster, while involved in learning. This may be a high-level intellectual process quite akin to the thinking carried on by adults at the frontiers of our knowledge. Art provides the youngster with a wide range of possibilities. Growth is not limited to the areas that have been predetermined by the educational system. The manner of seeking answers and finding solutions reflects the child's growing ability to deal with a diverse range of possibilities constructively in his creative activities.

The study of children's art can be fascinating. Through an understanding of the way a youngster draws and the methods he uses to portray his environment, we can gain insight into his behavior and develop an appreciation of the complex and varied ways in which children grow and develop. Working with children in the area of art necessitates both an understanding of the various developmental stages and a thorough knowledge of the possibilities for growth. Such awareness is necessary for the teacher to determine to what extent the youngster can comprehend and utilize the art experience.

Subject Matter in Art

Art is not the same type of subject matter as arithmetic. In arithmetic, as in many other subject matters areas, the teacher plans gradations in the difficulty and amount of new material presented so that the youngster can properly grasp and deal with the content involved. In art, however, there is no external subject matter that needs to be presented in small doses. Subject matter in creative activities has a different meaning from that in other fields. The same content is used in art by the very young child as is used in art by the professional artist. A man can be drawn by a five year old child or by a sixteen year old youth. The child will draw a head and legs, and this will be satisfying; the sixteen year old will represent the man with a conscious consideration of size and proportion, and include all of the visible body parts. The difference between the two drawings is not in the subject matter but rather in the manner in which it is represented. What changes is the subjective relationship between man and his environment. It is this subjective relationship that becomes important and not the drawing itself.

The content, such as trees, houses, plants, flowers, and people, will vary depending upon who is doing the drawing. For the five year old a tree has a trunk and something indefinite on top; a ten year old would draw the tree with branches to climb on; the sixteen year old would draw the tree as part of the environment, with concern for proper proportions. It is the same tree, but what has changed is the subjective relationship of the people to the tree. The tree, as in the example of the man, is understood in different ways and therefore will be drawn in quite different ways. It would be beyond the comprehension of the five year old to draw a tree in all its details as part of the environment. To say which tree is better would be ridiculous. For each youngster, we have a tree that is symbolic of his relationship to the subject matter. For the sixteen year old to draw like the five year old would be as unnatural as it would be for the five year old to draw like the sixteen year old. In a sense there is no subject matter in art, only different ways of portraying the artist's relationship to objects, people, feelings, and emotions about the world.

The drawing by a five year old does not really represent his knowledge of a man. Every five year old knows that we have fingernails if his attention is directed toward them, but no average child of this age ever draws fingernails. The child draws his subjective experience of what is important during the act of drawing. He draws only what is actively in his mind. Therefore the drawing gives us an excellent record of the things that are of importance to the child during the drawing process. A child knows a great deal more in a passive way than he ever uses. Part of a teacher's responsibility is to make this knowledge more active.

34   UNDERSTANDING GROWTH AND DEVELOPMENT

Each child draws his environment differently from any other child. The sixteen year old, for example, may be concerned about distances and sizes and his role in society; his mental and emotional growth are reflected in the way he portrays these differences. The five year old, however, experiences everything through himself; his spatial relations are limited to his own immediate surroundings, which he can touch, feel, or experience kinesthetically.

Subject matter is really not important in children's drawings; it is how this subject matter is portrayed that becomes important. Knowledge of the changes in drawings that appear at various developmental levels and of the subjective relationship between the child and his environment are necessary to an understanding of the growth of creative activities.

Developmental Stages in Art

As children change, so does their art. Children draw in predictable ways, going through fairly definite stages, starting with the first marks on paper and progressing through adolescence. It is sometimes difficult to tell where one stage of development stops and another begins. That is, growth in art is continuous and stages are typical midpoints in the course of development. Not all children move from one stage to another at exactly the same time; except for the abnormal or exceptional child, these stages follow one another, however, and a description of each is valuable in understanding the general characteristics of the child and his art at any particular time.

The very young child begins drawing by making random marks on paper. This stage is usually referred to as the *Scribbling Stage.* These random marks become much more organized and controlled, but it is not until about the age of four that youngsters make any recognizable objects in their drawings. Therefore we can say that the scribbling stage usually lasts from two to four years of age. Even scribbles go through various stages of development, from random marks to controlled scribbles. Sometimes parents try to teach youngsters at this stage of development how to draw something like an apple. It is a mystery to the child that these marks drawn by the well-meaning parent can have any relationship to a real apple. This can be a frustrating experience for both parent and child, whereas the scribbling activity in itself is usually pleasurable; having an adult interested usually makes it even more interesting to the scribbling child. Apparently paying attention to scribbling, and providing opportunities to draw and encouragement in using materials, can speed up development, but not very much. At any rate, the child tends to scribble until he is about four, and he seems to have a good time doing it.

The next stage is usually referred to as the *Preschematic Stage,* where the child makes his first representational attempts. This stage usually starts at about four years of age and lasts to around seven. Here the child draws the typical head-feet representation of a man, and begins to draw a number of other objects in his environment with which he has had contact. These figures or objects appear somewhat randomly placed on paper and can vary in size considerably. These first representational attempts provide an opportunity for adults to converse with children about their drawings, and usually children of this age are eager to explain and show what they have done without self-consciousness.

The next stage is the *Schematic Stage,* which starts somewhere around seven and lasts until about nine years of age. Here the child develops a definite form concept. His drawings symbolize parts of his environment in a descriptive way; the child usually repeats with some variation the schema that he has developed for a person again and again. It is at this time that one interesting characteristic of children's drawings appears: the child arranges the objects he is portraying in a straight line across the bottom of the page. The house is followed by the tree is followed by the flower which is next to the person who may be next to a dog which is the end of this picture. These works of art look quite decorative.

It is usually the first three stages of development that attract the enthusiasm of adults, who admire the freshness and the spontaneity of children's drawings. However, this spontaneous and fresh method of painting comes naturally to children; possibly adults wish that they too could enjoy the freedom of childhood, forgetting that growing is not always full of joy and happiness.

By the time a child reaches the age of nine he is entering the *Stage of Dawning Realism* that lasts from nine to twelve years. Here his peers become so important that this is sometimes referred to as the Gang Age. The drawings by a child of this age still symbolize rather than represent objects. The youngster is much more aware of himself and this awareness shows in his drawings. They are more detailed than his earlier work, and objects are no longer placed in neat rows across the bottom of the page. He is becoming interested in detail and no longer makes the large, free drawings that he made at a younger age. Not only is he beginning to draw smaller, but he is no longer eager to show his drawings and explain them; in fact he hides them from adult observation. The youngster is much more conscious of himself as a member of society and this is reflected in his art work.

Somewhere around the age of eleven or twelve the youngster becomes increasingly aware of his natural surroundings, and he begins to worry about such things as proportion and depth in drawings. This stage is referred to as

Figure 17.

(Left) This house, drawn by a five year old girl, shows an awareness that the house encloses space, with people indoors, drapes at randomly placed windows, and a chimney on top. (Below) Here a fourth grader has drawn herself jumping rope in the yard of her house. Everything is lined up along the bottom of the paper: the tree with its round top which is symbolic of leaves, the girl rigidly looking straight forward, and the house with the important details of chimney, front door, garage door, and, of course, the TV antenna. (Opposite) A ninth grade boy has included a great deal of detail in his drawing of a downtown brick building. His observations of his neighborhood are combined with an active imagination and a sense of humor to produce a visually pleasing picture.

Jump Rope

the *Pseudo-Naturalistic Stage,* the stage of reasoning. There is a great deal of self-criticism, and drawings are now hidden in notebooks or are attempts at cartoons. The drawing of the human figure shows a great deal of detail and, as might be expected, an increase in the awareness of sexual characteristics. There is also a greater awareness of differences and gradations in color, although some youngsters are not able to develop this visual awareness. For some, this stage marks the end of their artistic development and we often find that adults, when asked to draw something, will make a drawing that is very typical of the twelve year old.

ART AS A REFLECTION OF DEVELOPMENT

Figure 18. (*Opposite*)

For young children, scribbling is a purposeful activity. Painting provides the ideal opportunity for the manipulation and enjoyment of color.

At about the age of fourteen, or later, youngsters are at the age of development where a real interest in visual art can take place. They develop a conscious awareness of art and are often eager to develop artistic skills. Some high school students gain great competency in mimicking art forms or styles that may be currently in vogue, and some youngsters develop what might be thought of as a talent for portraying their visual environment. This age is also somewhat shallow in its artistic form, particularly if the perfected style or technique has been laboriously copied from elsewhere. To some extent, the natural development of a youngster does not extend beyond this stage, but it is possible now to develop artistic skills consciously.

Apparently these developmental stages are fairly consistent with all children, wherever they happen to be. This is especially true of the beginning stages of representation before his culture influences a child in his artistic development. What he draws will differ, depending upon the environment in which he lives and the drawing instrument that is used, but all children scribble until about the age of four; the period of first representational attempts will continue until about six or seven regardless of where the child lives.

It also appears that instruction in drawing does not have much influence upon these stages. This is particularly true of young children, but by the time the youngster is eleven or twelve, some effects of training can be seen in the quality of his work. In encouraging children to look for information about contours of objects or patterns such as angles and curves, Salome (1965) found that this training had no influence over the drawings of fourth grade youngsters but apparently made some improvement in the drawings of fifth graders. However, in an experiment with fifth graders, Neperud (1966) found that only girls of high intelligence were able to profit from instruction that emphasized visual elements.

A number of studies have attempted to document the various developmental stages in children's growth. These sometimes give different names to the stages, such as calling the scribbling stage a stage of manipulation, and so forth, but there is general agreement as to the stages themselves. Lark-Horovitz and Norton (1959) found that these drawing characteristics varied more as children grew older and that it was sometimes difficult to tell where one stage of development started and another stopped. Applegate (1967) found that those children who were higher in the stage of development than their chronological age would indicate were generally higher in mental age, whereas children lower in intelligence drew according to their mental age rather than chronological age. It is to be anticipated, therefore, that the developmental stages as listed above are primarily for normal children.

Significance of the Developmental Stages

Before examining the various developmental stages in more detail, it is probably important to emphasize the significance of these stages and to give some rationale for their importance in the whole educative process. Although separate stages can be identified, actually the stages fuse into one another, as children reorganize their thinking abilities and begin to form new relationships with their environment.

It is easier to see the changes in children's drawings as they grow than it is to explain why these changes occur. Children do not attempt to copy nature as adults know it. There is no straight-line progression from a very poor drawing or the scribble that a young child makes of an object to an advanced likeness such as an adolescent youngster might draw. Lewis (1963) gathered drawings from children from kindergarten through eighth grade in which they represented, among other things, a house. She found that kindergarten children actually drew a house that was more naturalistically correct than did children in older grades up through fourth. Children in the first, second, and third grades were concerned about drawing several sides of the house, which it would be impossible to view naturally. Obviously youngsters are not trying to portray their environment in a natural way. It is not that they are unable to do this because they lack the competency or coordination, but apparently that they are satisfied with their own means of representation.

We may well have been led down the wrong road by comparing children's drawings to nature. Drawing is a process that a child uses to signify and reconstruct his environment; the process of making a drawing is much more involved than a mere attempt at visual representation. That is, the child may be acting out or moving part of his environment around, and the parts are merely symbolized by whatever happens to be satisfying enough to connote the image or object. Looking at children's drawings from this point of view, it becomes apparent that the youngster himself is actually involved in every drawing. He is a spectator and an actor at the same time.

For example, drawings by five year old children have no space relationship except from the self. The five year old draws the objects around him and the finished picture looks as if the youngster had placed objects randomly around the page. By the time a child is seven he begins to put the objects that he is drawing in a line, but each of these objects is drawn facing the child himself, as if they were lined up to be seen. These objects do not relate to each other but rather to the child artist himself. It is not until about the age of nine that we find drawings in which objects relate to each other rather than to the viewer. About the age of twelve or so, the picture starts to become a representation of space and objects within that space.

Drawings give a good indication of the child's growth, moving from an egocentric point of view to a gradual awareness of the self as part of a larger environment. Even the scribbling child's drawing of undefined shapes may be self-portrayal. Possibly the first man symbol is really not a man at all, but a representation of the self that slowly begins to take on the meaning of any person.

Piaget (1959), in studying children's thinking, discovered that there were stages in development that closely parallel the stages of development mentioned above. The first stage, which lasts until about the age of two, he calls the *Sensory-motor Period,* and this is followed by a *Preoperational Period* which lasts until about the age of seven, followed by a stage of *Concrete Operations* which lasts from about seven to age eleven. Another stage begins at age eleven or twelve and is usually called *Formal Operations.* Piaget, with his collaborators, has produced a tremendous amount of material which supports the proposition that the child thinks in quite different ways from an adult. It is not necessarily poorer reasoning or lack of education that makes the child a child. According to Piaget, these stages are indications of ways in which children typically deal with information, and these modes of thinking actually prevent certain kinds of learning. A well-known example of this is the experiment in which a child views water being poured from a squat beaker into a tall one, and he believes that the water increases in quantity through some trick; and in pouring it back, the child believes the quantity has suddenly diminished. It is not until after the age of six or seven that a child will realize that the volume of water does not change.

Although Piaget's stages are for intellectual development, it is not surprising to find the same stages in art. When asked to draw the level of water in a container which was tipped at different angles, children from four to seven

represented the water as parallel to the base of the container, whatever its position. Only after the age of eight did children represent the water level as being constantly horizontal (Piaget and Inhelder, 1967). This experiment was duplicated (Maxwell et al., 1975) to try to teach this concept to eight to ten year olds, but the children's drawings improved only minimally.

Several studies have given support to the theory that young children cannot visualize a scene from a vantage point other than their own. One experiment (Coie et al., 1973) had children look at a model of several small houses. Then a doll was moved to a location away from the child, who was asked to pick out from a series of photographs what he thought the doll would see. This task was almost impossible for the five year old to accomplish. Usually the child selected photographs that looked liked what he himself saw.

However, the responses improved up to the age of eleven, which was the oldest group tested. But even here there were errors. The same stages of development can be seen in children's drawings. The young child draws everything in relation to himself. It would almost appear that the child has no concept of space removed from himself; that is, he is egocentric and is not able to take another's point of view, although photographs and three-dimensional drawings utilizing perspective have certainly been a part of his environment. It is not until the Gang Age, about nine years, that we find drawings beginning to have a life in themselves; that is, action can take place within the drawing and people can begin to look at each other or go into the house or observe the scenery without having to stand at attention for the observer.

Drawings may reflect the ability of children to deal with parts of their environment in a very practical way. The teaching of particular skills becomes meaningful only when the child can use this information. For example, a five year old does not put shadows in his drawings. To try to show him that shadows exist, to teach him methods of shading and how a shadow is cast, would be meaningless. Lee (1968) asked youngsters of a variety of ages to make an actual shadow using rings of various sizes placed in front of a light. Younger children were unable to deal with the problem and believed that the bigger the ring the bigger the shadow, regardless of where this ring was placed. It was not until the age of eight that the youngsters began considering distance from the light as influencing the size of the shadow. At the age of thirteen both the dimension and distance factors were considered, but it was not until the age of seventeen that even half of the youngsters could verbalize the operating principles involved.

Drawing and other art activities obviously are not merely the results of manipulative skills. The ability to do certain tasks that require manual dexterity can often be accomplished fairly early in life, but the concepts that children draw do not reflect the eye-hand coordination that one might expect. The young child who threads the needle for grandmother may have a great deal of coordination; however a drawing by this child will clearly reflect his stage of cognitive development and can easily be distinguished as the work of a child. For teachers to be concerned with manipulative skills, symbol development, or mastery of various materials puts the emphasis on the products of learning rather than on the process. For children, art is a way of learning and not something to be learned.

It seems that some things can not be taught until a child is cognitively able to grasp the concepts. Brittain (1969) attempted to teach preschool children the simple task of copying a square. Although he tried to do this with a

Figure 21.

Art is a way of learning, as relationships are figured out during the act of drawing. A challenging activity, it must be meaningful for the youngster.

variety of means, thoroughly saturating nursery school children with the square concept, he was not able to improve their square making ability. However, at the age of four, children that he worked with did accomplish the task of copying a square successfully. Those children who were not so lucky as to be taught square making abilities also accomplished the task successfully at the age of four. The ability of children from five to eleven years to perform visual, haptic, and kinesthetic tasks was tested and reported by Birch and Lefford (1967). Intersensory organization was explored, as well as controlled motor performance, spatial orientation, and discrimination of form. As much growth in the ability to perform tasks with geometric shapes occurred between ages five and six as between six and eleven. In the developing child there is a continual growth of interrelation among the separate sensory systems, and it was determined that increases in the accuracy of intersensory judgment continue to age eleven.

It is possible to look at children's growth in art as being a process of organizing thoughts and representing environment in such a way as to give us an

UNDERSTANDING GROWTH AND DEVELOPMENT

understanding of the development of thinking. It seems clear then that these developmental stages are not merely developmental stages in art, but are developmental stages in the whole growth pattern and that the art product is merely an indication of this total growth. Actually, the art activity may *be* growth in itself.

Although the developmental stages are always found in the same sequence, the inference should not be made that this sequence cannot be accelerated or retarded. Heredity undoubtedly plays a part in this, but the environmental influences are those that can be altered and enriched, and it is this aspect that is of crucial importance to the teacher and parent.

The Importance of the Art Experience

Unusual children require unusual amounts of time to follow the sequence. Some may seem stalled on one stage for an indefinite length of time, as is often the case with retarded children. Gifted children may go quickly through these stages. Just why this is so is apparently tied up with the whole process of cognitive development: progression through the sequence follows intellectual growth. Harris (1963) has substantial documentation for the validity of the Draw-a-Man Test as an indicator of mental age.

Sometimes children are taught by teachers or parents to draw particular symbols that are more typical of later developmental stages. A frequent symbol is the stick figure, though sometimes an outline form or even a method of drawing a house or cat is shown to and mastered by a child at an early age. Occasionally the seven or eight year old can even master a good reproduction of a box in perspective, but in all these cases, the symbol is drawn automatically without a real understanding of the reasoning involved.

It should be emphasized that learning takes place in the context of that which is known. The brain assimilates new information which is only understood in relation to information it has already processed. An eight year old child who is drawing a baseline can not be suddenly shown the theory behind three point perspective and be expected to gain any understanding of the concepts involved. A nursey school child who is drawing a head–feet representation of a man will not understand the rationale behind the dictum that a person should be seven heads tall. Even showing illustrations, measuring an adult head and showing that it will go into the length of the body seven times, would have no effect upon the nursery child's drawing. In these examples, the adult does not take into consideration the abilities of the child to understand the concepts involved.

Some biologists have established basic nutritional needs for the physical development of children. Psychologists have also established certain needs for the proper psychological development of children. In these lists there does not appear the need to draw and paint. Apparently somebody overlooked the importance of this area. Every child draws; every child, given the opportunity, loves to paint. No motivation is necessary for young children; it seems to be a natural form of learning. The activity varies in length and in intensity, depending upon the child and the particular time of day and other circumstances. But there seems to be a need to draw: a need to represent parts of the environment that the child has come in contact with, a need to put down his own thoughts, a need to clarify the relationship between objects and people, a need to express himself in a tangible way. The role of a teacher of art is more than to make it possible for this to happen; rather, it is the teacher's role to provide the circumstances, the motivation, the materials in such a way that the experience has to happen.

It is important to start where the child is and to broaden his store of experiences. Except in special cases, there is no reason for praise since the experi-

Figure 22.
The teacher needs to support the student, who works toward his own goals in planning and carrying out his own project.

Plate 5.

"Mother Is Picking Tulips," drawn by a seven year old child. At this age objects are placed on a base line across the bottom of the page. Notice how the flowers remaining to be picked are large and stereotyped in form, whereas the picked ones are much smaller.

Plate 6.

"We Are Playing on the Playground," drawn by an eight year old girl. This picture is unusual because it departs from the base line concept. The children standing in a circle are represented according to the child's experience of a circle, rather than perceived visually. There is a schema for running and a separate one for standing.

Plate 7.
*"I Caught a Fish," drawn by a
five and a half year old girl. The
five year old child has an
interesting space concept. Here a
girl stands on a dock symbolized
by the line encircling the figure,
the steps behind her are in the
upper corner, and the fish are
shown swimming around in a
mass of water at the bottom of
the page.*

ence itself is rewarding. The scribbling child should have the attention of an adult and the paper and drawing tools to perform his work; the older child should have the opportunity to talk about what he has done and have a listener who is sympathetic to his artistic problems. The teenager who is having a problem with his wood project ought to have someone to ask if there might be other ways of accomplishing his aims; the young adult who is developing artistic skills should have a teacher to help him set new artistic goals.

The developmental stages then take on a great deal of meaning when we realize that the educative process is something that goes on in the child's thinking and not in a teacher's list of potential artistic accomplishments, regardless of how enthusiastic a teacher may be about these goals.

Art as a Basic Means of Learning

Usually when one talks of the basics in learning, what comes to mind is reading, writing, and arithmetic. In fact, the three areas have sometimes become so important in the thinking of non-educators that the mastery of these areas by children is confused with learning. Reading, writing, and arithmetic are merely tools to use in the learning process. A child needs to be curious; a child needs to seek answers and to pursue the acquisition of information at his own level of understanding. Seeking help in the written word can sometimes be of value in this search for knowledge; sometimes the use of numbers can supply answers; the communication of thoughts, feelings, and emotions can sometimes be put into words. However, unless reading, writing, and arithmetic are important and useful to a child, they are but meaningless symbols to be manipulated and remain within the confines of the classroom.

Actually, there is very little known about how children learn to read. Most of the reading methods presently available are those devised and supported by publishing houses. In fact, there is even some problem in defining what reading is. Too often we look upon the mere recognition of letters or words, or the verbalization of these symbols, as being reading. However, reading implies much more than recognition, and even more than understanding the particular meaning of each word. Reading should be able to evoke thoughts, to raise questions, and to be open to interpretations. What is read needs to be assimilated, and should be related directly to the experience of the child so the meaning can be evaluated in terms of his or her own experiences.

Figure 23.
This nursery school boy is working diligently, making his own symbols for letters, a first step in learning how to write. He already has a rough notion of the letter E, but with numerous horizontal lines.

Reading is much more than a recognition game. Merely translating the observed symbol into sound is not a sign of literacy.

Writing can sometimes become a meaningless activity for children. The physical problems of trying to copy or trace the written word are tremendous. This is particularly true of the young child who is beginning to write his name. An examination of any college graduate's handwriting will quickly reveal that skills learned in the elementary grades relative to making letters with a nice, round hand have been forgotten. It seems almost as though there is an inverse relationship between education and the ability to write legibly. This is not to

UNDERSTANDING GROWTH AND DEVELOPMENT

suggest that the time spent teaching young children how to write is wasted; rather, the time is an imposition on both teachers and children, and particularly for the less coordinated may cause anxiety and negative feelings about school. Even in the upper grades where children are writing compositions, too often the grammar and proper spelling are checked but the content ignored. The ability to communicate with others, the ability to confront oneself with one's own thoughts and to organize and put these on paper in a logical manner are all important parts of the educational process. Somehow the usual writing skills do not seem to incorporate these factors.

Arithmetic fares no better. The young child can recognize the numeral 5, but the parent or teacher does not know what meaning this has for the child. For example, a 5 can be an interesting shape, somewhat like a curled up snake, and one must be careful not to confuse it with another curly one, the 2. On the other hand, the 5 may be part of a series falling between 4 and 6. There seems to be some order in numbers, and the 5 is sort of the middle one. Possibly the child sees 5 as a quantity. It is about as many marbles as he can hold at one time or as many peas as will fit on a spoon. Possibly 5 is merely a symbol which he recognizes as the location on the dial of his favorite TV program or the number over his classroom door.

Meaningless drills often are part of the method of teaching these skills. Prepositions may be memorized, poems may be recited, or arithmetic tables may be learned by rote. Except for escaping the wrath of the schoolteacher, these seem to be of little value outside of school. Few of us can remember how to divide by fractions, and fewer of us ever use that skill in our daily activities. To think that reading, writing, and arithmetic have become so important in the learning process is to confuse the tools with the objectives.

Some school systems have a yearly reading ability test. On the basis of this test, children are called overachievers or underachievers, or are earmarked as reading at grade level. Teachers whose classes fall below the norm are sometimes admonished to spend more time on the reading program. What is ironical about all of this is that there is serious question whether reading tests actually test reading skills (Livingston, 1972). Different reading tests will give different answers, and there is little experimental information to show that these tests are valid. In other words, they may not be measuring what they claim to measure, and the youngster who does poorly on one of these tests may be subjected to a remedial program based upon the notion that there are certain elements of language behavior that can be identified and corrected. But the success of any remedial program can be seriously questioned (Hammill and Larsen, 1974).

Most parents and many teachers do not view art as a subject matter to be mastered. Occasionally there is a teacher who feels that art needs to have the same basis in the curriculum as reading, writing, or arithmetic. The thought is that there are certain fundamentals that need to be learned, such as working with particular materials, learning the principles of design, memorizing the names of great artists, and mastering complex procedures. The mastery of these artistic gimmicks is of no more value to a child than is the time spent on learning to divide by fractions: interesting information for the moment, but quickly forgotten once the youngster closes the classroom door.

If we really expect to develop an inquiring mind in a child, one that is eager to tackle the problems of today, a mind that is flexible, inquisitive, and seeks for solutions in unusual ways, then the attention that we have paid to the so-called basic learning areas may be ill-placed. The arts can play a tremendous role in learning and may be more basic to the thinking processes than the more traditional school subjects. Every drawing, whether by a scribbling child or a high school student at the peak of learning efficiency, demands a great deal of intellectual involvement.

When a young child moves from the scribbling stage, about the age of four, to the stage of making his first representations, he develops a symbol or symbols for parts of his environment. For example, the head-feet symbol stands for a man. In attempting to represent what he has seen and experienced, he produces an image that is more faithful to his thoughts than to his perceptions. He remembers this image and is able to reproduce it as a symbol in context with other symbols. And it is the child's individual reaction to things around him and his own personal form of categorizing, cataloging, and organizing the objects and things that are of importance to him.

It is not until a child is able to make and reproduce the symbols at will that he can begin to understand that other people have also made symbols. A three-humped line followed by a circle with a tail and a two-humped line also can stand for a man. The ability to understand these more complex symbols as part of reading comprehension must follow the development of the child's own symbolic discoveries.

Although the early symbols by children tend to be isolated and somewhat randomly distributed on the drawing surface, within a year's time the symbols begin to relate one to another and are usually drawn in reference to a continuous baseline. This organizational ability is one which is continuous, and evolves from a mere placing of one object next to another as in a series, to a much more complex relationship where objects overlap and begin to have depth at about the age of eleven or twelve. This manipulation of symbols in

Figure 24.
*A vital learning environment,
with flexible use of space,
stimulates the thought processes of
inquiring minds. The continuous
process of problem solving in art
requires intellectual activity.*

relation one to another which still retain their meaning although moved up or down, left or right, is a method of thinking which is akin to algebraic reasoning. This type of thought process cannot be imposed from without, but develops through the child's manipulation of his own mental images.

It is becoming more and more evident that the manipulation of forms and shapes relevant to the child's own experiences is a necessary prerequisite for the utilization of words and numbers. It is amazing that in some circles

ART AS A BASIC MEANS OF LEARNING

art may be considered an educational frill, whereas it is a fundamental catalyst in the thinking process and development of cognitive ability in children.

Art as a Means of Understanding Growth

The picture that a youngster draws or paints is much more than markings on paper. It is an expression of the total child at the time he was painting. Sometimes children can become very engrossed in art, and the product may have a real depth of feeling and completeness; at other times the activity may be merely an exploration of a new material, but even in this case the picture shows the youngster's eagerness or hesitation in attempting a new task. Although it is stating the obvious to say that no two children are alike, it is also true that of thousands of drawings by children, no two are ever alike. Each drawing reflects the feelings, the intellectual capacities, the physical development, the perceptual awareness, the creative involvement, the aesthetic consciousness, and even the social development of the individual child. Not only is each of these areas reflected in the drawing that a youngster does, the changes as the child grows and develops are also clearly seen. In order to better understand and evaluate the importance of these changes, the significance of the different components of growth should be understood.

Emotional Growth

A drawing can provide the opportunity for emotional growth, and the extent to which this is accomplished is in direct relation to the intensity with which the creator identifies with his work. Although this is not easily measured, the degrees of self-identification range from a low level of involvement with stereotyped repetitions to a high level where the creator is truly involved in portraying things that are meaningful and important to him and where, particularly in young children, he appears in the picture himself. It is here that there is the best opportunity for emotional release.

Frequent stereotyped repetitions are apparently seen only in drawings by children who have developed rigid patterns in their thinking. In a case study, Lowenfeld (1957) drew some conclusions about a girl with whom he had extensive contact. He felt that every adjustment to a new situation implies flexibility—flexibility in thinking, flexibility in imagination, and flexibility in action. In this severe case of emotional maladjustment there was real difficulty in

Figure 25.
*Children who feel secure are not
easily distracted by their
surroundings and are confident in
their artistic expression.*

adjustment to new situations. In her drawings she felt most secure by repeating the same meaningless, stereotyped schema of a figure. Such stereotyped rigid repetition expresses the lowest type of emotional involvement.

At certain stages of development the youngster may spontaneously repeat forms to insure his mastery over these forms. The flexible use of a symbol can be readily seen by changes and modifications. A youngster drawing a flower garden will include flowers in a variety of positions, some tall, some short, some bent over, and maybe one that has been broken or stepped on. However, the stereotyped repetition of a flower is repeated in a meaningless way without any involvement or new experience shown on the part of the youngster. This may be an escape from facing a world of experiences and may in fact be satisfying to the individual who made it.

An emotionally unresponsive child may express his detached feelings by not including anything personal in his creative work. "There is a tree, there is a house." Nothing is included that will indicate his relationship to these objects. He is merely passively representing objects. This detached art expression shows neither action nor variety, but rather indicates only enough to signify an object. Figures usually are not included, but if they are they show no action. The experienced artist may also show this lack of involvement in repeating a technically proficient piece of art or a certain mannerism without any changes or involvement of the self. He too is caught in the stereotyped repetition of his own techniques.

With the direct inclusion of the self, the child actually participates in his drawing; he may appear directly in his creative work or he may represent someone with whom he identifies. The tree he draws is a particular tree, the house is no longer any house but has certain characteristics that were important to him in the act of drawing. He closely identifies with his drawings and is free to explore and experiment with a variety of materials. His art is in a constant state of change and he is neither afraid of making mistakes nor worrying about the grade he might receive on this particular project. The intensity of involvement provides for emotional growth.

Intellectual Growth

The intellectual development of children can be readily seen in their drawings. How aware the child is of his surroundings, the amount of knowledge that is actively at his disposal, and his ability to portray his relationship to his environment are all indicators of his intellectual development. As a child grows, his use of details and awareness of his environment both change. A child who lags behind in developing concepts and awareness of his environment may show a lack of intellectual growth. For example, a child who draws like a five year old when he is actually seven may in fact have the intellectual abilities of a five year old in spite of his chronological age. But there may be other factors involved. Sometimes it may be merely a lack of involvement in a particular drawing. Or there may be emotional restrictions which block the child's expression. However, usually a drawing full of details, reflecting a child's awareness of his world at his level of development, indicates a child of high intellectual ability.

Intelligence is usually defined as the ability to think in rational ways, to deal effectively with one's environment, and to learn the kinds of things ex-

pected in school. Most children, before they are finished with the public schools, will have taken several group administered and at least one individually administered intelligence test. These tests basically assess the way in which children respond to particular verbal, spatial, memory, and problem-solving tasks as compared to other children the same age. So a normal IQ score of 100 indicates that a child responds to these questions in about the same way as an average child of the same age.

If a child has difficulty communicating to an adult, because of language differences or because of some verbal handicap, a drawing test is often used. The best known measure of mental maturity is the Draw-A-Man Test (Harris, 1963). Children are provided a pencil and a sheet of white paper and told to make a picture of a man, to make the very best picture that they can, and to make the whole man, not just his head and shoulders. The finished drawing is scored basically on the number of details included and is compared with the typical drawing for any particular age.

The relationships between intelligence tests are reasonably high. Apparently, the development of artistic ability closely parallels a child's intellectual growth up to the age of ten years (Burkhart, 1967). The importance

Figure 27. (Opposite)
This is a pencil drawing by a six year old boy who has watched his father mow the lawn.
Notice how very much aware he is of the sound, of the grass ahead of the mower that still
needs to be cut, and of the mechanical features of the mower. See too that the boy identifies so
closely with his father that he puts his own sneakers on him, with the important laces he has
just learned to tie.

that parents and sometimes teachers place upon intelligence tests is often not warranted. Environmental conditions, social factors, and emotional and psychological variables can all affect a child's intellectual functioning. For most children, however, intellectual ability remains fairly stable. But sometimes a child may seem to have special talent in art and not score very highly on the standard intelligence tests. In this case, the drawing itself should be looked upon as the valid measure of a child's functioning. Sometimes certain personality or behavioral traits will have negative influence or depress a child's score in the usual testing situation. How a child reacts to adults, his feelings about himself, or his nervousness in a test-taking setting all can be negative factors. A study that compared scores on individually administered intelligence tests with a drawing test (Lewis and Livson, 1980) found that eight year old children who did better on the Draw-A-Man Test than on the other test measures tended to be more withdrawn, shy, and unsure. Those children who did better on a more conventional test were more open, verbal, and socially alert. The quiet child who has artistic talent is showing his intelligence clearly. This is not to suggest that anyone can estimate a child's abilities merely by looking at his drawings. However, a sensitive teacher can gain insight and an understanding of some of the problems a child himself may not be able to deal with by realizing that drawings and paintings reflect the child's thinking process.

Although drawings can reflect a child's intellectual growth, drawings can also stimulate and encourage that growth. Everyone functions with a storehouse of passive knowledge, that knowledge which we use to move from place to place, to recognize objects and people, and to provide us with the necessities of life. However, few of us take active notice of a particular tree, the arrangement of food on our plates, the shape of the crack in the sidewalk in front of us, or even the number of buttons on the coat which we may put on daily. When a child draws a picture, these details become important and he becomes actively aware of his environment; the tree becomes a particular tree in front of his house, and even the number of buttons on his shirt can become important. Art can contribute a great deal to intellectual growth.

Physical Growth

Physical growth in a child's creative work is seen in his ability for visual and motor coordination, in the way he controls his body, guides his line, and performs skills. The changing physical growth can be easily observed in children at the scribbling stage, when the marks on the paper change from a few random marks to a controlled scribbling within a relatively short period of time. Also the desire to make more refined and minute changes in sculptural form can develop motor skills very rapidly at the junior high school level.

UNDERSTANDING GROWTH AND DEVELOPMENT

Not only the physical involvement in creative activities, but also the conscious and unconscious projection of the body indicate physical growth. This projection of the self into the picture is usually referred to as body imagery. Essentially, the physically active child will portray active physical motions and he will develop a greater sensitivity to his physical achievements. Often the unconscious presence of muscular tensions or body feelings will also be portrayed. Sometimes children with impairments will project these into their creative work. The ear that aches or the knee that has been scraped will be given emphasis. Continued overemphasis or omissions of body parts may be tied to the physical condition of the individual.

Perceptual Growth

The cultivation and growth of the senses is an important part of an art experience. This is of vital importance, for the enjoyment of life and the ability to learn may depend upon the meaning and quality of the sensory experiences. In creative activity the increased perceptual growth can be seen in a child's increasing awareness and use of a variety of perceptual experiences. Visual observation is usually the most emphasized in an art experience, with a developing sensitivity toward color, form, and space. Young children's paintings indicate enjoyment and recognition of color, whereas on the advanced level the ever-changing relationships of color in different lights and atmospheric conditions can be stimulating. Perceptual growth is a growing sensitivity to tactile and pressure sensations, from the mere kneading of clay and touching of textures to sensitive reactions to clay modeling in sculpture and the enjoyment of different surface and textural qualities in a variety of art forms.

Perceptual growth also includes the complex area of space perception. A young child knows and understands the immediate area around him, which has significance to him. As he grows the space around him grows and the way he perceives it will change. Auditory experiences are often included in art expression ranging from mere awareness of sounds to sensitive reactions to musical experiences. Kinesthetic experiences that range from simple uncontrolled body movements to highly developed coordination can also be seen as the basis for a variety of art forms. Space, shape, colors, textures, kinesthetic sensations, and visual experiences include a great variety of stimuli for expression. Children who are rarely affected by perceptual experiences show little ability to observe and little awareness of differences in objects. Awareness of variations in color, differences in shapes and forms, smoothness and roughness, sensitivity to light and dark, are all part of the creative experience. Inability to utilize perceptual experiences may indicate a lack of growth in other areas. The teacher may play an important part in developing in youngsters the eagerness to see and feel and touch their surroundings, and in providing a wide range of experiences in which the senses play an important part.

Social Growth

The social growth of youngsters can readily be seen in their creative endeavors. Drawings and paintings reflect the degree of identification the child has with his own experiences and the experiences of others. The very young child begins to include people in his drawings as soon as he leaves the scribbling stage. Usually, in fact, the first recognizable object drawn by a child is a person. As the child grows, his art reflects his growing awareness of his social environment. As he develops a greater awareness of people and their influence on his life, these assume a large percentage of his subject matter content.

The art process itself provides a means of social growth. Expressing the self on a sheet of paper also means viewing that expression. This viewing and looking at one's own work and one's own ideas is a first step in communicating these thoughts and ideas to others. Art has often been thought of primarily as a means of communication, and as such it becomes a social rather than a personal expression. The drawing can then become an extension of the self out into the world of reality as it begins to encompass others in the viewing of the subject matter. This feeling of social consciousness is the beginning of a child's understanding of the larger world of which he is a part.

The development of social awareness goes on also in the portrayal of parts of our society with which the child can identify. This includes those

RELATION.   SENSITIVE

forces that are established to preserve society itself. Drawing the fireman, the road crew repairing a hole, the nurse helping people in the hospital, or the policeman giving directions, all provide stimulus to develop this social awareness. The arts can also contribute, through cooperative work, a greater awareness of each individual's contribution to a large project. This is particularly effective when the opinions of peers are sought and when the need is developed for social interdependence.

For older children, the art of other cultures provides a means by which a society or a people can be felt and understood; the values of one generation can have some influence on the next, as when watching Grandfather work at woodcarving, or a neighbor doing intricate needlework, preserving the traditions of her native country. Studying the variety of contemporary art from today's cultures can give indications of the attitudes and feelings of these people. One such investigation, examining the drawings by children from a variety of societies, indicated that group values can readily be seen in children's drawings of men (Dennis, 1966).

Figure 28.
Art may provide the opportunity for social interaction with peers. Developing an awareness of others and their creative efforts can be an important part of an art experience.

It is important to stress the significance of the individual's ability to live cooperatively in his society. This ability cannot be developed unless the child learns to assume responsibility for the things he is doing, is able to face his own action, and by doing so identifies with others. Creative activities provide an excellent means for taking this important step.

Aesthetic Growth

Aesthetic growth is often considered the basic ingredient of any art experience. Aesthetics can be defined as the means of organizing thinking, feeling, and perceiving into an expression that communicates these thoughts and feelings to someone else. The organization of words we call prose or poetry, the organization of tones we call music, the organization of body movements is usually referred to as dance, and the organization of lines, shapes, color, and form makes up art. There are no set standards for aesthetics; rather, the aesthetic criteria are based on the individual, the particular work of art, the culture in which it is made, and the intent or purpose behind the art form. There is a tremendous variety of organization in art. Aesthetic form is not created by the imposition of any external rule, but rather a creative work grows by its own principles.

In the creative products of children, aesthetic growth is shown by a sensitive ability to integrate experiences into a cohesive whole. This integration can be seen in the harmonious organization and expression of thoughts and feelings through the lines, textures, and colors that are used. Young children organize intuitively, whereas those in the secondary school can find pleasure in the conscious manipulation and organization of spatial relationships in paintings. Each art material has different demands in terms of its aesthetic use; a block print, for instance, presents an entirely different concept of organization from a fine line drawing.

Aesthetics is also intimately tied to personality. Painters are recognized by their organization of colors and forms; a Van Gogh can be picked out anywhere by one who is familiar with his style of organization. The organizational framework used to portray experiences in art can often give an indication of some of the unconscious ordering that is unique for each person. Lack of organization or the disassociation of parts within a drawing may often be an indication of a lack of integration within the individual. One of the methods sometimes used to assess the value of therapy with psychotic patients is a study of the cohesiveness of organization in the drawings they produce.

Education has been thought of as the cultivation of expression in an organized manner. That is, it is the organization of words to make verbal communication, the organization of numbers or symbols to develop mathematical

drainage

Figure 29.
"It's Beginning to Snow," shows a simple, direct organization of space, resulting in a satisfying representation which conveys a child's feelings about the holiday season.

thinking, and the organization of images to make the arts. Education can therefore be looked upon as the development of aesthetic behavior. The thesis that art should be the basis of education has been pursued in depth by Herbert Read (1958). The thought that some balance and organization must be built into the educational system could be reflected in the development of courses in the humanities, such as those that are offered in several school systems. Aesthetic development is certainly an integral part of education.

Creative Growth

Creative growth starts as soon as the child begins to make marks. He does this by inventing his own forms and putting down something of himself in a way that is uniquely his. From this simple documentation of oneself to the most complex form of creative production there are many intermediary steps. Within the drawings and paintings of children, creative growth can readily be seen in an independent and imaginative approach to the work of art. Children do not have to be skillful in order to be creative, but in any form of creation there are degrees of emotional freedom: freedom to explore and experiment, and freedom to get involved. This is true both in the use of subject matter and in the use of art materials.

The literature on creativity has grown tremendously in the last few years. This area is becoming of increasing concern, both to educators and to researchers. Art experiences have always been considered the basis of creative activity within the schools. However, an awareness of this literature avails us nothing unless we can relate it directly to the individual child. We will go into detail later about the importance of creativity for art. For now it is sufficient to say that every art product, if it is truly the work of the youngster, is a creative experience in itself.

Those children who have been inhibited in their creativity by rules or forces unrelated to themselves, may retreat or resort to copying or tracing. They may quickly adopt styles from others, constantly ask for help, or follow examples of work that has been produced by their peers. Needless to say, the mere command to stop copying and become creative accomplishes nothing. Creativity cannot be imposed but must come from the child. This is not always an easy process, but the development of creative abilities is essential in our society. Both the process and the product reflect the youngster's creative growth.

RELATED ACTIVITIES

1   Observe the changes that take place in art expression by collecting drawings from children from kindergarten through high school age. Trace the development of the representation of a single object, such as a tree. Notice how the subject matter does not change, but the *manner* of representation changes as the child changes.

2   Observe a class of fifth grade children as they draw. Notice which ones are restless, easily distracted, uncertain, or asking adults for approval.

Compare the art products of these children with those of the youngsters who appear to be very involved in their work and self-sufficient. Look for stereotypes, inclusion of the self, simple objective reports, rich detail, action of the figures, and aesthetic quality. What conclusions can you make?

3   Work with a class of third grade youngsters. Plan one lesson emphasizing environment: trees, homes, school, and so forth. Plan a second lesson that emphasizes the imaginative: dreams, make-believe animals, strange creatures. Do the same children seem to enjoy both lessons?

4   Plan a lesson which includes drawing people; carry it out with kindergarten, second grade, and fourth grade children. Use the same materials and paper size for all classes. Compare the finished products and note the differences in developmental levels.

5   Collect drawings from a kindergarten class and list the various methods of portrayal of sensory experiences. Check especially for symbols for sounds and movements.

6   In second and sixth grade classes, pour colored water into a large jar while children watch. Give each child a sheet of paper on which are drawn two outlines of your empty demonstration jar, one vertical and one tipped at about a 45 degree angle. Ask the children to draw the water level in the vertical jar, and then as it would appear if the jar were tipped. How many children in each grade showed the water level the same in both jars? Do not try to correct the drawings.

The Development of Creativity

3

The Importance of Creativity

The development of creative thinking has tremendous importance for us, both as individuals and as a society. It offers a change from what is and has been, to what might be or what is yet to be discovered. The term *creativity* may have become too popular, for it is applied like sparkling paint to book titles, do-it-yourself projects, or performance groups. The definition of creativity depends upon who is doing the defining. Often researchers are rather narrow in their definition, stating that creativity means flexibility of thinking or fluency of ideas; or it may be the ability to come up with new and novel ideas, or to see things in new relationships or to think in ways that are different from other people. Usually creativity is thought of as being constructive, productive behavior that can be seen in action or accomplishment. It does not have to be a unique phenomenon in the world, but it does have to be basically a contribution from the individual.

Creativity has been considered the opposite of conformity, but this may not always be true. We have to conform a great deal in our society to rules and regulations that mean safety for ourselves and others. This kind of conformity, conformity to rules of physical behavior, is basic to society so long as these rules are able to be changed by those affected. There is another whole area of conformity, that of mental conformity, that may be of danger to our society. We need to differentiate between these two. This may be a difficult thing for young children to do, but as adults we must be sure that the pressures of conformity are limited to those areas that are necessary for the sake of society. One of the difficult tasks of a teacher of young children is to provide socially acceptable ways in which children can use and be encouraged to use their creative abilities while keeping to a minimum the areas in which they will have to conform.

Probably the most crucial time in the encouragement of creative thinking is when the child is beginning formal schooling. It is here that initial attitudes are established, all too seldom with the realization that school can be a fun place where the individual's contribution is welcome and where changes can be sought and made. Very young children have a freedom to act without regard for the amount of knowledge mankind has already amassed about such an action. Children learn to walk without an intellectual understanding of the motor control involved. What a person knows or does not know may bear no relationship to creative action. Children create with the aid of whatever knowledge they happen to have at the time. The very act of creating can provide new insights and new knowledge for further action. Probably the best

Figure 31.
Construction with large blocks in nursery school can develop in unexpected ways. Active participation in such activity is a form of creative problem solving.

preparation for creating is the act of creation itself. Waiting to act until a good factual preparation can be obtained, or stopping children from creating until they know enough about the subject to act intelligently, may inhibit action rather than promote it. Giving the child opportunities to create constantly with the knowledge he currently has is the best preparation for future creative action and thinking.

A second crucial period is in early adolescence, when attitudes are formed that remain into adult life: feelings of personal worth and assessments of one's place in the larger world. It is important for these young people to know that they can have an effect upon their environment and that their ideas and thoughts are valued. The pressures for conformity are severe; the slightest deviation from the norm may be ridiculed. Creativity at this age needs to be supported; the youngster who enjoys the arts or sees the world in a different way may need the encouragement and reassurance of an adult.

Creativity does not just happen. It is an essential part of the learning process, but there are many elements to consider in planning class activities. These include the environmental factors over which the teacher has direct control: the physical structure of the room, the materials, and also the psychological environment, which may be much more important. Another factor is that of the social values involved. At certain ages the youngsters will become more dependent upon peers for direction and approval than upon the teacher. Another variable is the personality of each child. In addition there is the problem of developing skills by which creativity can become unleashed. It is this last area that is emphasized in most books and texts, but the teaching of skills or the development of competencies in art will bear little relationship to the de-

THE DEVELOPMENT OF CREATIVITY

velopment of creativity unless all the factors considered above are involved in the planning process.

At one time distinct stages were suggested for the development of creative thinking. These consisted of an initial stage called *Preparation,* followed by a thinking period called *Incubation,* which was background for the next stage of *Illumination,* which was followed by a period called *Verification.* These stages were looked upon as sequential, and the school's role seemed limited to the initial stage of preparation only. Now it is outmoded to think of creativity in so limited a format. Rather, creativity is more closely related to thinking abilities and to attitude development. If there is any justification for saying that these four steps exist in the creative process, then they would have to be varied considerably to include both the many periods of illumination that a nursery school child goes through in building with blocks and the one sudden illumination that results in an invention by a research engineer. It is probably best to think of creativity as a continual process for which the best preparation is creativity itself. In fact, there is real joy in discovery—which not only is its own reward but provides the urge for continuing exploration and discovery.

Creative and Intellectual Behavior

Every child is born creative. The urge to explore, to investigate, to discover, is not limited to human behavior, but is experienced by the whole animal kingdom. There have been numerous studies of rats showing that, given a chance, a rat will investigate an unknown maze, explore a new box, or go down a pathway which has been altered in some way. Harlow (1965) has demonstrated that monkeys can and do learn to solve mechanical puzzles when no motivation is provided other than the presence of the puzzle; monkeys will look through a window, put sticks together, explore a new trinket, all motivated by curiosity alone. Harlow says the monkey is actually a very incurious, nonmanipulative animal as compared to man, and the only justification for using monkeys in these experiments is that we have more monkeys available for research than children.

We should not be troubled about motivating children for creative behavior; what we should be aware of are the psychological and physical restrictions that the environment puts in the way of the developing child to inhibit his own natural curiosity and exploring behavior. The preschool child is full of questions, and hardly a parent exists who has not become tired of the question "why?" Yet, our school system is so organized that, just a few years later, the child has little opportunity to ask questions; it is now the teacher who asks. "Did you finish your homework? What is the answer to the fourth problem on page 27? Who can list three causes for World War I? Why are you late for class?" And so on and so on. It is possible for art to fall into the same trap. "What are the principles of design? What are hue, intensity, and value? List three outstanding painters of Renaissance art. What is the solvent for oil paints?" And so on and so on. Picasso, Magellan, and dividing by fractions are all in the same boat. It is not surprising that under these conditions children need to be encouraged to be inquisitive, since this is a skill that has not customarily been developed. But the asking, curious, creative individual must be a goal of our educational system.

Sometimes intelligence and creativity are confused. The problem is compounded by the fact that creativity is usually considered an attribute that has positive value; because intelligence is also valued highly, these two are often put together. Generally speaking, creativity may have little to do with intellect.

Figure 32.

Fluency of ideas can be seen in drawings, as in this one by a six year old girl. She has indicated the motion as she swings and has shown variety in the trees and flowers in her surroundings.

The intelligence test is only an approximation of one small part of the total functioning of the mind. In some cases the individual who scores well on IQ tests may also do well on tasks of creativity; in other cases there may be no relationship. Wallach and Kogan (1965) demonstrated that traditional measures of intelligence do not measure the same thing as what they call associative creativity, the latter being measured in a game-like, nonevaluative manner. Although they studied fifth grade children, other work (Wallach and Wing, 1969; Ward, 1969) has found generally the same distinction between creativity and intelligence in both younger and older children. McKinney and Forman (1977) found that even at second grade level there is a clear distinction between creativity and intelligence.

Intelligence tests stress convergent thinking, with a correct response already determined. This is the ability which seems important for success in school. On the other hand, creativity tests attempt to measure divergent thinking, where there is no single correct answer. Divergent ability includes thinking of a great number of different answers, or thinking of different methods or approaches to problems, or thinking of the unusual or novel. Possibly we have given intelligence too narrow a definition, for both intelligence and creativity are part of the cognitive processes. There seems to be evidence that although creativity and intelligence can be tested separately, both are important. The intelligent child may be able to memorize factual information, deal with numerical problems, and quickly master written material, yet may have difficulty when asked to go beyond the known, to formulate questions, to find ways of seeking new knowledge. The creative child has to be smart enough to deal with his creativity in constructive ways. It has been estimated that the most productive people in our society are not necessarily the most intelligent.

One theory about the structure of people's intellectual functioning supposes that there are five different operations in the mental process: cognition, memory, convergent production, divergent production, and evaluation (Guilford 1964). Creativity would be considered a divergent production. The creative arts are extremely important in our educational system if only because they stress divergent thinking, and any number of possible solutions to problems or any number of outcomes in painting or drawing can be correct. An art teacher's open-ended questions to stimulate divergent thinking might be, "Which colors make you feel sad? How would you feel if you were purple? Which color would you like to be?" The importance of teaching toward divergent thinking is stressed by Burkhart (1962, p. 27): "The value of the divergent question is that it requires the student to look at a content area from a variety of viewpoints and to participate in an imaginative way in answering the question."

By way of direct contrast, in a lesson on color, children might be asked questions that are factual and demand specific convergent answers such as, "What are the primary colors? What are the secondary colors? Give an example of a split-complementary color scheme."

In some cases, teachers may try to justify the importance of art by stressing its academic aspects. Although there are many areas in the school's program that attempt to stimulate children's intellectual development, a prime purpose of the arts is to develop the creative domain. It makes no difference whether this creativity will be used in the arts or sciences. The creative elements in cognitive development cannot be left to chance.

Schools and Creativity

Creative growth seems to operate on a different set of patterns than do other areas of behavior. We are all familiar with the healthy child of about four who has a vivid imagination and a great deal of curiosity about things around him. Some researchers have found, however, that by the time the child is eight or nine he seems much less creative, and again in the seventh and eighth grades there is a dip in creative growth (Torrance, 1962; Kincaid, 1964). We have to be careful not to assume that children are creative in the same way that adults are, but even so, these leveling-off periods seem to exist. There is some evidence that these plateaus may be related to the plateaus between growth spurts of the brain. Certainly the demands of parents, teachers, and peers may put a high value on conforming behavior at these times. There is no doubt that parents considerably squelch what might be thought of as childish behavior and insist that their teenage son or daughter stop being "silly."

It is sometimes said that the public school discourages creative thinking, but the school has many tasks and we might be better justified in saying that creative thinking is not very high on the list of most teachers' objectives. Some research indicates that teachers do not like the creative child (Getzels and Jackson, 1962). There is reason to believe that the sweet, conforming child is rewarded in the classroom to the disadvantage of the development of imagination and creative thinking. This can happen in art classes too. The home influence is a significant factor in encouraging the development of creative thinking (Weisberg and Springer, 1967), but society in the form of parents, teachers, or peers undoubtedly rewards certain types of behavior at certain ages, and maybe this is why creative behavior develops in such an uneven pattern.

Figure 33.
*Children develop imaginative
ideas in an atmosphere that
encourages creativity. The
classroom situation must be
flexible enough to allow
youngsters the freedom to express
their own ideas.*

Creativity needs to be nurtured in a particular kind of environment. The "anything goes" atmosphere is apparently just as negative an influence as the authoritarian atmosphere where individuals are completely dominated. In reviewing research on differences in open and traditional classrooms, no remarkable increase in creative skills for children taught in open classroom settings is found. Although popular philosophy seems to expect that a lack of traditional structure might encourage greater flexibility of thinking, apparently it is not the classroom structure as much as the nature of the student-teacher interaction that is important. However, in a study of 13 urban Head Start classes (Huston-Stein, Friedrich-Cofer, and Susman, 1977), it was found that high levels of adult direction produced conformity when adults were present. In less structured classes, they found more pro-social behavior and more imaginative play,

SCHOOLS AND CREATIVITY

which they felt is a necessity for promoting the overall cognitive and emotional development of young children. A creativity enrichment program in the informal setting of a summer camp in Israel (Goor and Rapoport, 1977) measurably enhanced the creativity of young adolescents; four months later the improvement was still evident.

The Measurement of Creativity

Probably at one time or another every person has made a judgment about who is a creative individual. Almost any teacher can tell you who the creative person is in his class, but sometimes it may be difficult to distinguish whether the youngster who was identified as creative in one class would also be identified as the creative child in another. We may get some of the terms confused, particularly since creativity is usually seen in a positive light and therefore is sometimes associated with responsiveness, or just looking awake. The youngster who is bored, gazes out the window, is unruly, or just talks too much may be thought of as creative if the teacher in charge sees creativity in a negative light. At any rate, almost any teacher does measure creativity but usually by his own standards.

Relying on the advice of some 87 teachers and counselors, Torrance (1967) lists some specific kinds of behavior which he thinks are indicators of creative talent. Some of these are: the student can occupy his time without being stimulated; he goes beyond assigned tasks; he asks questions beyond the single why or how; he comes up with different ways of doing things; he is not afraid of trying something new; and he enjoys drawing designs and pictures even while the teacher is giving a lecture or directions. Also he is observant, does not mind the consequences if he appears to be different, and enjoys experimenting with familiar objects rather than just letting things be.

If it is possible to think of some actions of children as being creative, and if we can describe them so that everyone understands what these actions are, then it would be logical that these attributes could be tested. This has been done, and there are several tests for creativity that have been used for a number of years. One of the reasons these tests have been developed is to encourage the creative individual to get the training and background needed to contribute to society. Sometimes the motivation is a little more shortsighted than this, because some companies want to know who among their personnel are creative people, so that these people can be freed of routine tasks and can utilize their creativity for the company's benefit. Also, if one wonders if creativity can be increased, it is nice to have some sort of measure available to check any increase; and for this, some sort of creativity test would be necessary.

One of the most commonly agreed upon components of creative thinking is the ability to produce a large number of ideas. This is usually referred to as a "fluency factor." A simple way to test for this is to ask "How many uses can you think of for a brick?" Some responses might be: use it as a paperweight on a desk, use it to hold down the lid of a garbage can, warm it and use it as a bedwarmer, use it to hold down newspapers in the wind. The more ideas one can put down on paper, apparently the more fluent one is, which may relate to one part of creative thinking.

Another factor usually considered is the ability to shift easily from one type of thinking to another, or to be flexible in one's thinking patterns. If we look at the list given for the uses of a brick above, it seems that three of the four suggested uses utilized the weight of the brick only. Possibly the person responding was just stuck in a rut. An additional factor often considered part of creative thinking is the ability to come up with unusual or remote ideas, which is often referred to as an originality factor. Looking back at our brick example, it seems like an unusual response to warm a brick and use it for taking the chill off sheets, but this might be a good use. If we had a lot of people responding to our question on uses for a brick, it would be fairly easy to find the unusual or infrequent responses and to select the person who seems to have greatest originality. A number of other factors are often looked for in a testing situation: one is seeing relationships where others might miss them, another is being able to elaborate on or embroider an idea, and a third is being sensitive to problems or seeing ways of improving or changing a situation or an object.

Creativity tests do not have to be verbal. In fact, there is an advantage in having both verbal and nonverbal tests. A nonverbal or figural test for fluency may be to ask someone to see how many objects he can make using a circle. A sheet of paper with a whole lot of circles on it would be the test sheet; this could be scored quite easily for fluency, by the number of circles used; for flexibility, seeing how many different ways these circles have been utilized; and for originality, by seeing who used the circles in the most original manner. Probably the most prolific designer of such tests has been Guilford (Guilford, 1968). Many of the tests for creativity have stemmed from research that was done with college and professional people. Others have contributed a great deal to the literature on measurement (Barron, 1963; Mednick and Mednick, 1964; Torrance, 1962). In fact, the list of instruments useful in studying creative behavior is lengthy, including such diverse methods as self-description, personal

NAME Beckwith Harriet
(Last) (First)

In five minutes see how many objects you can make from the circles below.
A circle should be the main part of whatever you make. With a pencil add lines to
the circles to complete your picture. Your lines can be inside the circle, outside
the circle, or both. Try to think of things that no one else will think of. Make as
many things as you can and put as many ideas as you can in each one. Add labels
or titles if the identity of the object is not clear.

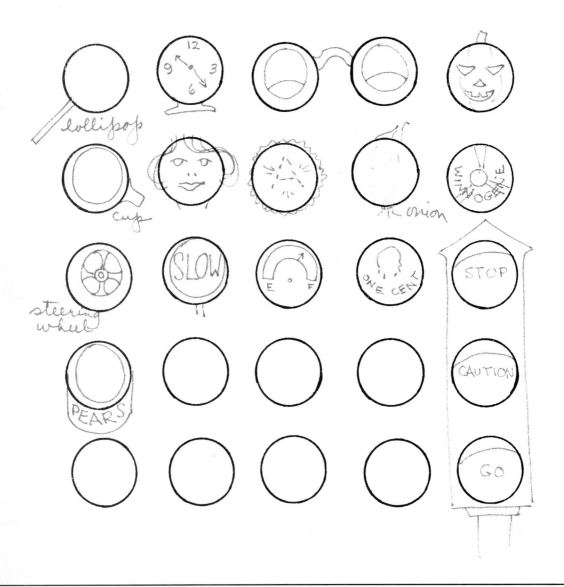

opinions, making up problems, playing with toys, or drawing completion (Davis, 1971; Kaltsounis, 1971; Kaltsounis, 1972).

There has been some criticism about the use of creativity tests in the classroom. Some of it stems from a doubt that a child can be creative in a school environment using tools which are usually considered school tools. Another more serious consideration is whether we want to give a child another score to carry around. Schools may feel it wise to locate the most creative children and give them special treatment. There would be some advantages in finding out who the least creative child in a class is, so that we could devise methods to encourage him to explore his environment, to become more flexible in his thinking, and to be more fluent in his thoughts. We will discuss methods which might be helpful shortly.

Other criteria of the creative behavior of children are less tangible and therefore a little more difficult to measure. One of these can be thought of as the openness of the individual toward the unknown or the new. This is more than just being curious since it connotes a whole way of looking at the world, of being receptive to things outside the self, of being acutely aware of things and sensitive to change. Another area that is difficult to measure is that of psychological health; Maslow (1962) has termed this self-actualization; a self-actualized individual is secure in himself, cares little about mundane things, is basically motivated, and has no illusions about his own capabilities.

Some schools have attempted to include creativity as an area to be assessed along wih intelligence, motor skills, sight, and hearing. A few colleges have tried using such tests as part of entrance requirements, particularly for people in the arts. But there are many problems. Hattie (1977) mentions some of them: that creativity is not unidimensional; age differences are important; scoring procedures differ; and effects of stress or other conditions have not been standardized. It seems that there is a long way to go before creativity testing is part of standard procedures.

It is just as well that testing for creativity is a complex matter. Otherwise every report card would probably have a space to mark in a grade for "creativity," and each grade school teacher might be responsible for teaching this area along with reading, writing, and developing mathematical skills. Can you imagine a class with one youngster who could not go to recess until he has thought of twelve uses for a coat hanger? Or a class memorizing an assembled list of six fundamental principles in the creative process? Or a youngster failing an examination because he could not think of a word which relates slugger to belfry and ball? At the same time, this lack of ease in measurement may be one reason creativity has not been considered an essential part of the curriculum.

But things are changing and it is comforting to know that creativity is being considered in some areas as a necessary part of the development of thinking.

Methods of Developing Creative Potential

There have been many attempts recently to develop programs designed to increase creative potential. There is evidence that these programs do increase the creative responses of individuals if they are tested on material similar to that on which they have been practicing. However, there seems to be less evidence that this increase lasts over a long period of time. Since most of these programs are a conscious effort at changing one's thinking patterns, it follows that one needs to be rewarded for this thinking. Sometimes in a school setting these kinds of rewards might be rather hard to find.

Recently there have been some programs designed primarily for the elementary school which are supposed to increase the creative abilities of children. Although some of the theories behind these programs are similar to those for adult programs, the procedures are quite different. One rather elaborate program (Williams, 1972) consists of several books, tape cassettes, and posters for teachers to utilize. The program is divided into three groups, the first being designed for the college instructor who is preparing future teachers, the second group of materials is designed to be used by people in the training program, and the third group of materials is designed for use in the classroom with children. The program assumes that many innovative procedures have remained untried because teachers just do not understand how to use them. Certainly this criticism could not be leveled here. A broad approach to creativity is emphasized, with children carrying out many activities in many areas. Suggestions are offered for ways to plan a lesson which emphasizes eight traits: fluency in thinking, flexibility, originality, elaborative thinking, risk taking, complexity, curiosity, and imagination. Although the arts are utilized in this program, its objectives are to increase the creativity of individuals in the whole learning process. Obviously, with such a step-by-step procedure, not very much is left to the teacher's imagination.

Another program designed primarily for the upper elementary school leaves the teacher out entirely. This is a programmed learning series of fifteen lessons in cartoon form. The authors (Covington et al., 1972) have bypassed

Plate 8.
*"Playing on the Sidewalk,"
drawn in crayon by an eight year
old girl with a high degree of
creative awareness. Young
children do not copy that which is
before them; rather, they
reorganize meaningful parts and
ignore the irrelevant, to portray a
particular moment of importance.*

Plate 9.
*"Swimming in the Pool,"
painted by a young Japanese
child, who shows all the activity
at the crowded pool. The creative
urge to find significance in one's
actions and to adjust, adapt, and
organize these into a single
framework is a cognitive process
which is basic to learning.*

Plate 10
"Leaves," painted by an adolescent, is a free interpretation of leaves and greenery, evoking the essence of a forest. The adolescent is able to abstract from nature and enjoys making new forms.

Figure 35.
Painting is in itself a creative learning process, in which each youngster develops unique methods of organization, elaborates on his own theme, and derives satisfaction in the process.

the teacher and designed comic books for children to read at their own pace. The youngsters follow the cartoon characters, Jim and Lila and their Uncle John, a high school teacher and detective, through a number of problem solving processes in which the student is supposed to analyze the given information and to come up with possible solutions to some rather interesting little stories. As is customary, the publishers are very enthusiastic about selling these materials; at least this is one way of making creativity come to the attention of

METHODS OF DEVELOPING CREATIVE POTENTIAL

Figure 36. (*Opposite*)
These children are concentrating on the gestures of an adult and closely following the pantomime, which may be variously interpreted, depending upon the subtlety of motions and creativity of the beholder. Many common activities that take place daily can be the starting point for increasing children's creative thinking.

classroom teachers. However, there is little evidence that a packaged program can merely be inserted into the curriculum to make the children more creative, productive, original thinkers.

It might be helpful to examine a few programs that were designed for adults, with the idea that some of the suggested methods might be adapted for use with a secondary school population. These programs vary considerably, from those that operate with a group of people for reenforcement of ideas and support for members, to programs that are designed for an individual to take steps to improve his own creative power.

Probably the best known creativity workshop operates on a group basis with what might be called a brainstorming method. Parnes (1967) lists several principles underlying his particular method. One principle is the development of many ideas and solutions to a given problem. This means thinking up a large number of possible alternatives with the rationale that the more solutions suggested, the greater the chances that one might be original. Parnes' second principle is deferred judgment; this suggests that, when one is working on a particular problem, judgment is withheld so that many ideas are generated without any immediate attempt at evaluation or at finding a quick solution to the problem. His third underlying principle is the formation of remote associations. Some things habitually go together such as salt and pepper, snow and ice, and so forth. To help break down these patterns, unusual combinations of words are used to force workshop members to think of new verbal relationships; such words might be wind and book, water and dust, or tree and gas tank. In the evaluation process, judgment is also deferred until all of the criteria are established and a final solution can be arrived at.

Another approach to the development of creative thinking has been called synectics (Gordon, 1961; Prince, 1970). This approach, differing considerably from the preceding one, emphasizes the use of metaphor or analogy. Speculation is encouraged and the emotional component is considered more important than the intellectual, with far-out, irrational thoughts encouraged and care taken in the group interaction that no thoughts are squelched or left unexamined. The synectics approach has been used primarily in solving some of the problems in industry, with some success. The role of the leader is important since careful probing and constant encouragement seem crucial for uninhibited thinking.

Still another approach has been an individual one, with an emphasis on particular exercises and games (Kirst and Diekmeyer, 1973). The plan calls for spending a half hour each day doing the variety of interesting experiments and filling in exercises which, it is assumed, will develop flexibility, originality,

Figure 37.
The role of the teacher is not passive. Encouraging the child's thinking, and not expecting a predetermined answer or solution, gives the child the greatest opportunity to develop his creativity.

inventiveness and adaptability. An emphasis is put on fun and loosening up the thinking process.

There are other approaches to developing creative thinking, some of which are clearly designed to make money off the unsuspecting noncreative individual who has dreams of becoming an artist or plastic surgeon. But, it would be entirely possible to develop a program for oneself or for a class utilizing some of the basic underlying principles. Each age has unique characteristics which make it a distinct population, and starting a conscious program of de-

THE DEVELOPMENT OF CREATIVITY

veloping creative thinking could be a lot of fun and very rewarding. Obviously the leader, or teacher, is an extremely important part of the whole procedure. Important aspects of developing children's creative thinking are encouraging each member to participate, withholding judgment, stimulating and rewarding unusual thinking, and promoting the seeing of relationships between ideas as they grow into one another. Making pictures out of unusual words, in which the picture and the word must say the same thing, pasting together unusual captions on illustrations, putting together parts of animals to make the best animal in the world, or making a machine that does not do anything—such projects can develop a thinking process in which the unusual or original becomes acceptable. What would the world look like if you were a frog, or as big as an ant, or a tree in a windstorm? Suppose the world were turned inside out, or plants started to walk around, or you were really a red crayon! The list of interesting possibilities is endless, and students are usually eager to engage in fantasy, speculate on problems, and develop new ways of looking at the world.

One feature that pervades all of the commercial programs attempting to develop creative thinking is that the process is external; that is, problems are devised for adults to solve, children are seduced into learning through cartoon characters, exercises are figured out by someone else to be completed, and so forth. In art, however, the process is intrinsic; that is, the problem is not from outside the youngster, but originates within him. Finding methods in three-dimensional materials to express an emotion, thinking of ways to make something look smooth and syrupy, finding a system of having something recede into the distance, or even struggling to make initial images, are all problems that originate within the youngster himself. This is not to suggest that the above programs have no value. Making creativity an essential part of the curriculum is important, and every teacher would probably be more successful if arithmetic, social studies, or writing could be seen as a creative activity.

It is even possible to improve one's own creativity on a self-instruction basis. At least one study (Huber, et al., 1979), using programmed instructional materials with fourth, fifth, and sixth grade students, found that verbal creativity scores improved as compared with a group that followed a regular school program. However, it apparently is possible to improve creative responses by merely telling children to be creative, something which may not be asked of students very often. Children at both the elementary and secondary level scored higher on an unusual uses test when it was labeled a creativity exercise than they did when the same test was labeled a word exercise (Speller and Schumacher, 1975).

It is important to develop creativity at a young age. It may be that the attitude of being creative—finding the unknown challenging, coming up with many thoughts and ideas, looking for differences and similarities, having unique and original thoughts—is established early in life. At least it appears that these attitudes, once established, tend to be continuing. One research investigation (Kogan and Pankove, 1972) looked at the creativity of tenth grade students. These tenth graders had been tested on some of the same measures five years earlier when they were in fifth grade. Although there was some variability in the individual scores, the report states that there was great stability in the level of productivity and uniqueness. Another study (Torrance, 1972) attempted to discover whether young people, identified as creative during their

Figure 38.
An interested adult encourages inquiring minds by helping these nursery school children plant seeds. Curiosity is natural and should be supported at an early age.

high school years, become productive, creative adults. Some 392 high school students had taken a battery of creativity tests; twelve years after graduation they were again contacted and asked what they were doing and where they had been. Their achievements were analyzed by judges on a ten point scale. The young people who were identified as creative during their high school years had become productive, creative adults. In addition, Torrance found that these creative high school students tended to develop careers which involve detours for relevant reasons. Most of them included study or work in a foreign country; many chose unusual occupations compared to those who had scored low on the creative scale. If these studies are an indication, it will be interesting to see how those children who have been identified as creative will contribute to our society in another fifty years or so.

Probably the most important consideration in this area is to provide a model for the youngster to emulate. By model, of course, we are referring to the teacher. Although it is well accepted that art teachers value independence in thinking more than teachers in other fields (Davis and Torrance, 1965), there is pressure for teachers to conform to the school standards of behavior. Youngsters need an opportunity to see teachers who admit that they do not know, who are willing to accept the thoughts of others, who can enjoy life and like having others enjoy theirs, who have many ideas and the flexibility to allow children to have their own, and who accept every youngster on his own worth. Such attributes would make the art teacher an important person in the classroom, even if he were never to teach art.

Art and Creativity

As much as we might like to think of art and creativity as being the same, it seems that this connection can not be left to chance. Sometimes the way art is taught may negate creativity, or possibly teaching for creativity might negate art. However, experiments have been done, focusing upon methods of teaching art, which may help insure that both creativity and art are fostered.

Some art programs are designed to give students a great variety of experiences with many materials, whereas others prefer to have students concentrate on a few materials that are explored more fully. Those who favor the "breadth" approach feel that the variety of materials accommodate the different interests of students and keep their attention; the "depth" approach advocates feel that concentration on a few materials leads to sequential learning.

A study of this problem of breadth versus depth was carried out with ninth graders over a period of a year (Beittel, Mattil et al., 1961). Three classes were given a battery of pre-tests; then for a year one class was taught art with only a breadth approach, one class was taught art with a depth approach, and one class was taught with what was their usual manner. Paintings were collected throughout the year and judged. Another battery of post-tests were given to the ninth graders at the end of the year. The results favored the depth approach class, in both aesthetic sensitivity and spontaneity. The breadth approach is popularly supposed to encourage a spontaneous approach to art, but it actually lost ground. The control class was judged the poorest group of all. The report concludes that, in spite of some restless demand for variety from students, it seems wiser to begin early with a depth oriented program.

A similar study was done with college students (Davis, 1969). Here a test on eight factors of creative thinking and some measures of art attitude and aesthetic quality were used before and after a semester of either a breadth or depth curriculum. The results were somewhat inconclusive, but the greatest amount of growth was in nonverbal originality in the depth group, with some other advantages comparable for both groups.

And a third study on this topic (MacGregor, 1967), using four classes in a high school, found advantages for the depth approach. One class was restricted in both subject matter and media, one was restricted in neither, and the other two classes were restricted in either subject matter or materials. Again, with judges and tests, the results showed the greatest gains in the group that was most restricted.

Although the depth approach to teaching art has support, the vast majority of programs, particularly in the elementary school, are basically breadth programs, with one project following another, week by week. Brittain (1969) even found the same pattern common at the nursery school level: clay work, followed by pasting, followed by string painting, and so on. The rationale usually given for such an approach is that students need to know how to use materials before they can create with them. The danger is that students may begin to feel that art is nothing more than a series of little projects or a series of experimentations with materials, bearing little relationship to expression or creativity. Kern (1978) makes an appeal for shifting the emphasis in school art away from the cafeteria approach. He feels learning in the arts involves the mastery of complex skills. "None can be learned in an hour, a day, or a week and real mastery requires a lifetime."

The concern for externals, for the product, may be a factor if a teacher feels insecure in art. There are numerous articles and books showing step-by-

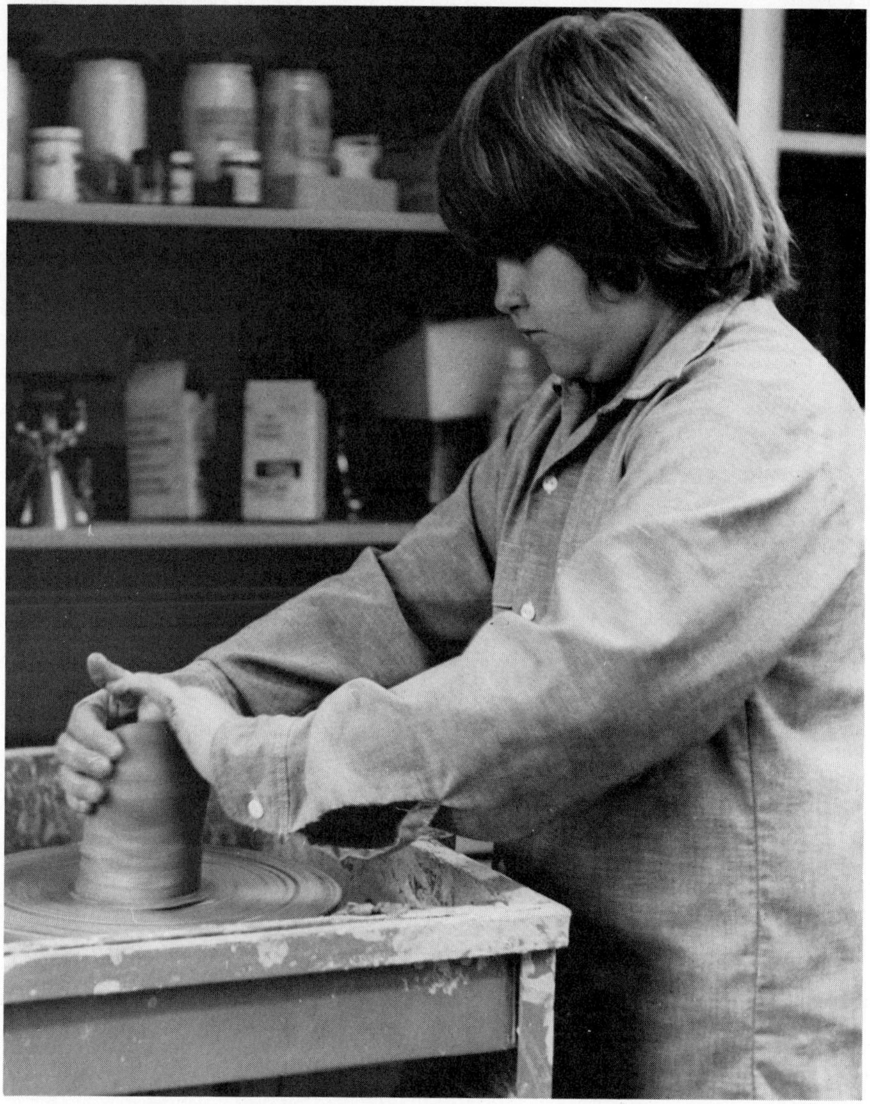

Figure 39.
*In order to create with clay, a
child needs a depth of experience
during which he can develop a
sensitivity to the material.*

step methods for doing innumerable projects. Certain teachers have an empty
feeling, not knowing what to do for art this week. Other teachers are motivated by generosity, feeling that children must not be deprived of any opportunities to experience art materials—with the thought that "more must be
better." The goal of art should not be the development of the teacher's creativity, but the youngsters'. Fluency of ideas, flexibility of approaches, originality
of responses, and seeing new relationships are apparently not nurtured by a
smorgasbord of art projects.

ART AND CREATIVITY

89

Sometimes the art product—the painting, sculpture, or whatever—is regarded as an isolated work of art to be examined, admired, or evaluated on its own merits. The artist is somehow forgotten except as he receives the reflected glory or scorn, but his comments, his thoughts, or even the process which he went through to produce the product, is really not asked for. Is a creative painting produced by a creative artist? In our concern for the creative process and the emphasis on developing creative thinking, are we able to say that the art products produced by creative people will be judged better or more original? As part of a larger study (Csikszentmihalyi and Getzels, 1971), 31 college art students were observed during the process of producing a still life. The finished products were judged by experts, and there was a close relationship between those products judged as being original and the discovery oriented behavior of the artist. But there was not the same relationship of originality to craftsmanship.

Figure 40.
Perseverance and determination seem important in carrying out plans in the wood shop. Children learn much about the nature and special qualities of wood during the process of creating three-dimensional forms.

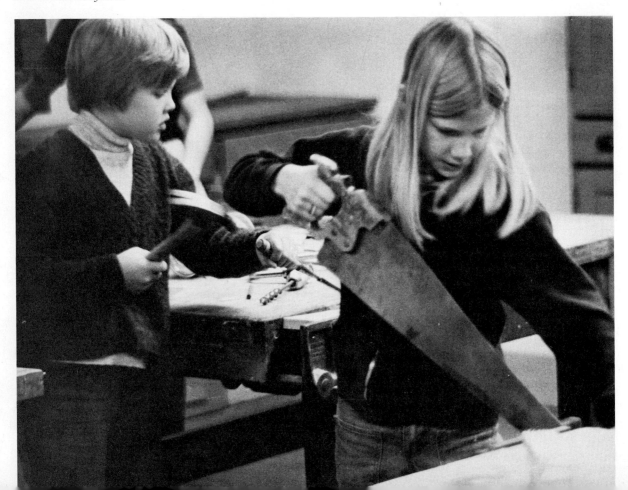

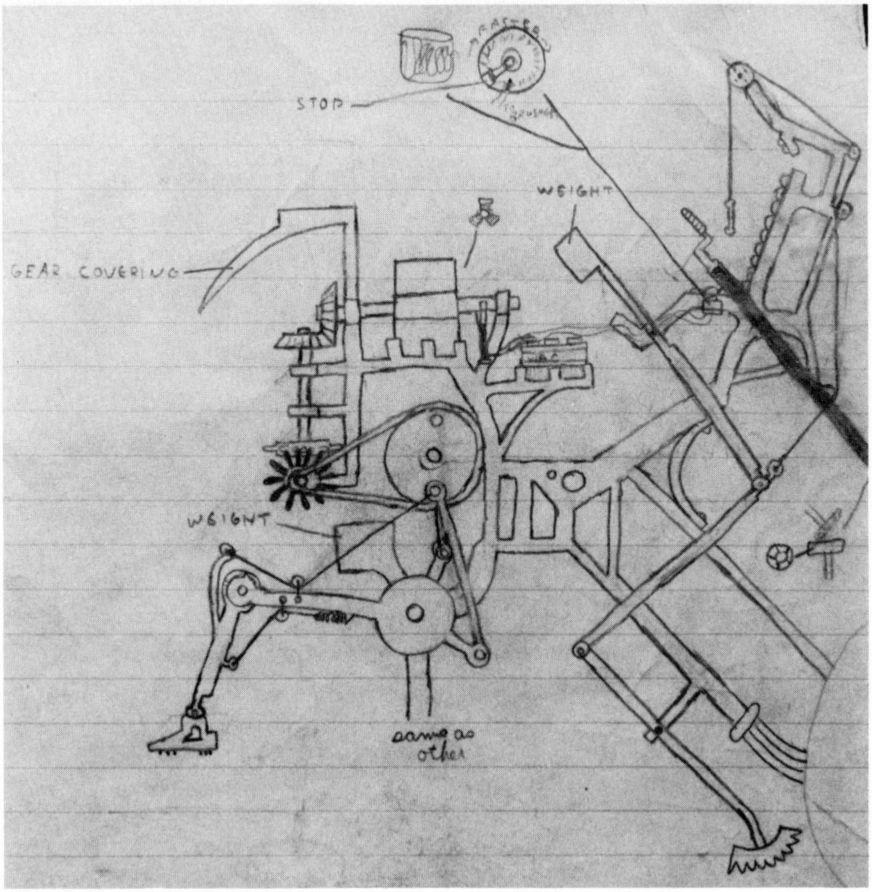

Figure 41.
*This drawing is of a machine
that walks, an idea which a
creative ten year old boy spent a
great deal of time developing.
This is as legitimate an art
activity as producing a still life or
making an abstract design.*

Another study of art students in training has been reported by Barron (1972). Students in art school were interviewed, given a number of psychological tests, and their art work was examined. The data indicated that art students as a group were higher in flexibility and were less well socialized, more impulsive, and more unconventional than the general population. Michael (1970) sent questionnaires to 350 recognized artists in several fields of art: painters, sculptors, weavers, jewelers, potters, and so forth. In analyzing their replies, Michael found that over 90 percent of the respondents felt that they are concerned with society and what goes on in the world, that the process by which they create is flexible and ideas are developed while working, that the product grows by constantly shifting and relating various elements, and that they do not try to identify with any particular art movement or approach.

It seems that to be a creative artist one must be a creative person. The students at art school and the professional artists have a behavioral approach to living that can only be termed creative. But all artists are not necessarily creative people. There are a lot of jobs that are certainly art related that call for merely technical skill. And there are a lot of other fields of creative endeavor in the sciences, medicine, mathematics, and so forth that can lay claim to the need for creative thinking. Art experiences may be just as important for students going into these areas as into the arts.

Summary

Art and creativity have always been closely entwined. For years the art program in the public schools has been the bastion of creativity, and often art experiences and creative activity have meant the same thing. However, with the increasing interest in creativity and the great number of research studies in this area, it is becoming quite clear that it is possible to have an art program in the schools that is not automatically creative in nature. Creativity is becoming of vital concern to many people; we need to understand the process involved in developing the creative thinking abilities of children. There is no doubt that this area will be of increasing concern in the future as society turns toward the unknown, and schools will of necessity have to teach not only what is known but also teach *toward* what we do not know. Art can play an important part in this field. In fact, it has been suggested (Hoffa 1964) that intensive experience in the arts should be a basic tool of education to promote creative thinking.

Creativity, and how best to promote it, is of interest to increasing numbers of people. Society values what Morris (1969, p. 37) has called " . . . man's insatiable curiosity, his inventiveness, his intellectual athleticism." According to Stenhouse (1967, p. 10), ". . . it is pre-eminently the task of education so to induct people into culture that their personal freedom and creativity are preserved and indeed enhanced."

RELATED ACTIVITIES

1 Observe a nursery school child and a senior high school student in their drawing activity. Do their approaches to art indicate any differences in their apparent levels of creativity? Is one age more creative than the other?

2   Observe several junior high school non-art classes. Notice differences in the ways the teachers accept creative behavior, such as when a student asks probing questions, wants to become involved in related or tangential activities, comes up with different ways of doing things, enjoys experimenting, is not satisfied with easy answers, and questions the text.

3   Observe an elementary school class. How much pressure for conformity is there, such as rote memorization and all children doing the same things at the same time, even trips to the drinking fountain? In rooms with pressure for conformity, are there also duplicated sheets for the children to color, or drawings that all appear very similar?

4   List some suggestions for encouraging creative thinking in a second grade class. Be specific in telling how this could be accomplished in reading, arithmetic, and art.

5   Have a college class select from their members the most creative individuals. Is there general agreement on who these creative persons are? What were the criteria on which selections were made?

6   Observe an elementary class for several sessions and list the number of opportunities for developing divergent thinking. Compare this with the number of times thinking is directed toward one "right" answer.

The Development of Aesthetic Awareness

4

The Meaning of Aesthetics

The development of aesthetic awareness is a basic part of art education. Growth is on an ever-changing continuum, and this is very true in the area of aesthetics. The organization of our thinking abilities, the development of our perceptual abilities, and the close relationship to our emotional capabilities can be considered aesthetic growth. There is no formula for aesthetic growth. Aesthetic education does not take place simply by a teacher's criticism or guidance when an individual makes his art product. It is a much larger task and may bear little relationship to making a student aware of the principles or rules for organizing a work of art. Such matters as proportion, balance, and rhythm are often regarded as part of the understanding that a student should develop in relation to his own work of art and to the art work of others. However, there is no set of rules that can be readily applied to individuals, and aesthetic growth does not happen merely by applying rules that are external to an individual. Developing aesthetic awareness means educating a person's sensitivity toward perceptual, intellectual, and emotional experiences so that these are deepened and integrated into a harmoniously organized whole.

Aesthetic development cannot be separated from creative development. Both are bound up with the whole process of growing, and are influenced by all of the variables from our environment that make us different personalities. In a broad sense, aesthetic education deals with a vast spectrum of experiences in art, including the production of art forms. Some definitions include the observation and understanding not only of art but also of nature, or at least those parts of nature that can be called beautiful. However, in a narrower sense, aesthetics refers only to the perception and appreciation of art. The development of aesthetic awareness is usually seen in a harmonious organization of parts, and this organization changes with age in the same way that other changes can be seen in growth. Aesthetics has little to do with sentimentality on the one hand or the accumulation of factual knowledge on the other. The gushy comment—"I just love modern art, don't you?"—probably shows as little aesthetic awareness as does the shrewd appraisal of the work of art from the point of view of its value on the market today. Aesthetics is an active perceptual process; it is the interaction between an individual and an object which provides a stimulating harmonious experience.

Any creative activity originates in a person, utilizing a multitude of cognitive and sensory perceptions. In the process of creating a picture, for example, an artist paints from his conscious awareness and his unconscious or preconscious motivations; he selects the forms and colors which will make up his final painting. In the process, however, the artist may pause and say to himself, "That is not right." Here the interaction between the painting and the artist takes on new meaning, for he has made a judgment about the organization and found it not to his liking. Therefore, it is easy to see that creative expression and aesthetic awareness are closely entwined.

It is possible to get overzealous about the importance of developing aesthetic awareness. We must remember that this is something that cannot be imposed from without. Aesthetic education must not become indoctrination. The need for developing an understanding and an appreciation of those things around us must come from the person himself. There is no evidence that aesthetics can be easily measured, or that absorbing the vocabulary of aesthetics will refine one's tastes, make one a better person, or even help in the selection of a necktie. To quote Herbert Read (1966), "We have to live art if we would be affected by art. We have to paint rather than look at paintings, to play instruments rather than go to concerts, to dance and sing and act ourselves, engaging all our senses in the ritual and discipline of arts."

Art Appreciation

Closely related to our discussion is the role that art appreciation plays in the development of aesthetic awareness. Somehow the question of taste enters into the discussion, and it may be that taste is something that can be learned. As the student develops the ability to make selections, based upon some criteria that have been established by art authorities, we assume that he is developing good taste; high school students are able with enough encouragement to be selective if they are properly rewarded. This may have very little to do with aesthetic awareness. Obviously we all have different tastes, but there should be no justification for arranging these on a scale from good to bad. Good taste could probably be defined as what the art critic would select, so the uneducated individual would undoubtedly be thought to have little or no taste. But, of course, this is also tied up with culture, and it is quite obvious that we are not treasuring the same qualities in objects that our grandparents did. Each era has its own peculiarities, and these cultural differences play havoc with establishing rules for good taste. "A thing of beauty is a joy forever" is a saying rarely heard today in our rapidly changing culture.

More important than these considerations is the fact that youngsters do not react to the environment in the way that adults do. Children's drawings

THE DEVELOPMENT OF AESTHETIC AWARENESS

ART APPRECIATION

differ considerably from one age to the next, and there is good reason to believe that the objects they appreciate also vary. A ten year old boy will have developed a natural appreciation for stones, frogs, rusty bolts, and other strange assortments of objects that probably mean a lot more to him than the painting that hangs in a museum.

Discussions of art appreciation are often concerned with the principles of design. These are not always given the same names, but are essentially concerned with the surface pattern of a picture; such words as harmony, balance, rhythm, unity, center of interest, and so forth are often mentioned. There is often the notion that learning these particular words bears some relationship to developing an awareness of the good and bad qualities to look for in paintings, and that therefore an appreciation of art will result.

Eisner (1966) gave a 60 item test dealing with information about art terms, art media, artists, and art history to secondary school students in several states and to some elementary education college students. He found that although there was some gain in knowledge with grade level, only about half the items were answered correctly in secondary school, with girls scoring somewhat better than boys. Eisner lamented the fact that 38 percent of his students thought that Picasso and Matisse worked in the seventeenth or eighteenth century; about a third knew what value or hue meant. Undoubtedly there is a need to understand terms if one is going to use them, and an exposure to art should increase a knowledge of such terms, but it would be a big mistake to confuse the learning of these terms with an appreciation of art.

Sometimes the history of art is considered an avenue to developing the aesthetic tastes. But there is no genuine history of art; rather, there are historians who have selected art objects from those that have remained from a society and collected these together in such a way that others look upon these examples as typical of a period in history. Which of these examples are shown depends to a great extent upon the art historian. Similarly, the history of the American Revolution can be seen quite differently by an historian who is writing a textbook for the American public schools than by an historian whose purpose is to show the influence of British naval power upon the development of Europe. Hieronymus Bosch is much more popular today than he was fifty years ago. And it is certainly the art historian who has rescued Van Gogh from obscurity. To some extent, then, a study of the history of art can provide the opportunity to follow the development of art styles as seen by an authority, but it does not necessarily provide us with an appreciation of these styles, nor does it automatically develop an aesthetic awareness of objects outside the realm of art history.

THE DEVELOPMENT OF AESTHETIC AWARENESS

Some art educators would no doubt argue that the art appreciation of individuals needs to be cultivated and taught by those who are somehow wise and educated. This goes against the basic assumption of democracy, in which every person, unless previously intimidated, is usually a strong defender of his own views and tastes.

Culture and Aesthetic Awareness

It might be interesting to contemplate what a future archaeologist would think about our society if he uncovered it a thousand years from now. Art has been thought a good indicator of the values and attitudes of the society in which it was made. Today we cherish the remnants of past societies' art forms, and from these we draw conclusions about the particular society in which these forms were found. The Greek temple is very different from the Gothic cathedral, yet each of these forms expresses and represents its own culture.

Certainly the Gothic cathedral style would be uncovered a thousand years hence, housing our churches and some of our institutions of higher learning. These Gothic structures would, of course, be false façades, made of steel and covered over to look like Gothic cathedrals. There would be Greek temples, too, though somewhat altered, housing what might be government operations. Once again, however, these buildings would not be honest representations but rather duplicates from a past culture that considered these buildings an important part of their society. It may be somewhat symbolic to see governmental functions housed in buildings that are more representative of a bygone age.

The archaeologist a thousand years from now would certainly be confused. He would find homes which were also false façades. Many of them would be built in a style which was popular in the eighteenth century, but for some reason were duplicated like stereotyped patterns for twentieth-century people, complete with big chimneys and small panes of glass. No, not big chimneys, but plywood cubes stuck on these houses to simulate chimneys, and not small panes, but plastic inserts that could be removed easily when the windows were to be washed. Inside, the homes would be even more confusing. The dining room might look surprisingly like a seventeenth century French room, with a chandelier and a table with built-in worm holes. But the chandelier would really be made for electricity and the furniture would have been mass produced. The styles of the living room and the bedroom, too, would be from an earlier era. The kitchen and bathroom would have the most modern of appliances, although sometimes hidden under an "old" cooktop or pseudo-Roman sculptured fixtures.

Undoubtedly our archaeologist would think that there was something wrong with a society where an individual could walk from one century to another by merely going from one room to the next. Apparently, the occupants of these homes had an unaware acceptance of these stereotyped patterns as symbols of a security that was not present in the culture itself. However, science was evidently an important element, since the range, refrigerator, and dishwasher were of the latest design. The occupants of these homes would seem to have been schizophrenic, escaping into a world of meaningless resurrected patterns.

There would be some contemporary buildings in existence, and the most forward-thinking architects would have been utilized for building airports, sports arenas, and factories. These, the archaeologist would undoubtedly feel, were representative of the civilization. Apparently, he would conclude, this strange culture that he had unearthed had no confidence in their institutions, but a stronger belief in transportation, physical competition, and industrial power. Evidently, the individual was inclined to hide from the society and felt more comfortable in taking refuge in past periods. Even in the smaller examples of the art forms, the vase and bottle, the same discrepancy was seen. The most attractive plastic bottles were produced by industry and used for dispensing soap, shampoos, and lotions; whereas the vase selected by the homemaker was a piece of glass pseudo-styled as a sixteenth century hobnailed goblet in which flowers were displayed. Floor coverings, scientifically durable and easy to clean, simulated stone or wood and the "solid" brick wall was made of plastic.

The archaeologist would probably be right in his opinion of our society. This is not just a question of aesthetics, because his uncovering of our art in museums would only make him sure that the artists of our time had turned their backs on the society in which they lived, and were either poking fun at the society from which they had removed themselves or had become so self-centered and individualistic that they too had lost contact with their own society. The prospect of teaching what is "good taste" in a society as confused as ours seems a little ridiculous.

Aesthetics and Society's Values

Not too long ago the prospect of gracious living was an objective to strive for. Just what gracious living meant was apparently a stereotype in itself. Expensive accessories and pseudo-styled furniture were part of the scene; undoubtedly, shutters at the window and an antique knocker at the door were there too. Dinner would be by candlelight with soft music, with modern art looking down from the wall.

Young people today are certainly questioning this as an ideal, but many educators still look upon the gracious-living model as the one they want to impose upon all children as a goal in life. This becomes particularly absurd when we realize that many parts of our society may have goals of their own, especially those persons who still retain some of their customs and traditions from Asia, Europe, Africa, or South America. Many children within our society come from environments that are both dreary and depressing, and the image of gracious living is unattainable and bears no relationship to their own existence.

Art was originally an integral part of society, and the aesthetic properties of an object were no more important than its function. The task of the artist was largely to decorate shrines, homes, and public buildings, to fashion utensils and ornaments, to record historic events, and the like (Dissanayake, 1980). However, a century ago aesthetics began to be considered an element in art aside from its function. Quackenbos (1871) felt that the purpose of art was to excite the imagination with the novel, the wonderful, the picturesque, the sublime, and the beautiful.

Aesthetics must be removed from the good, the true, and the beautiful. The development of aesthetic awareness must be much more concerned with the individual and not with the imposition of ideas, terms, or certain learnings, regardless of how well intentioned these learnings might be. It becomes very

Figure 45.
This Byzantine mosaic is bold in its style, with a strong linear quality. Its purpose was to give a message to the viewer.

apparent that we cannot teach aesthetic values unless we are aware of the individual and his cultural environment. As a society we have inherited a good deal of our feelings about art from European traditions. One of the most influential books dealing with the story of art (Gombrich, 1978) barely touches upon art outside that framework, and then only as it influenced the European tradition. Yet art and aesthetics are universal. The cultures of Africa, the societies of the Near East, the varied populations of the Far East, the Aboriginals in Australia, the native North and South Americans, have all developed aesthetic standards for art, value systems which are basically different from that which is reflected in our teachings.

Changes in Aesthetic Taste

It is fairly obvious that standards of beauty are constantly changing. A car that is ten years old has no particular value, either for its aesthetic appeal or for its functional use. However, a thirty year old car takes on quite a different appeal and can suddenly be cherished. In the same way, the severity of architectural design that was popular a few years ago is becoming softened, and an interest in patterns and textural qualities is beginning to reappear. The taste and aesthetic standards of our time are undoubtedly influenced by many variables, and trying to put these into a context that can be explained to students in school presents a difficult problem.

It is revealing to look at the textbooks on art education that were published fifty years or more ago. Some of the problems seen at that time are still with us, but the examples of good art and the type of pictures that were supposed to interest children in grade school seem a little ridiculous to us today. However, art education was thought to be a means of elevating the thinking of every person, with the assumption that somehow an understanding of art would make people happier and better. As Nichols (1877, p. 153) put it, "Men are usually selfish because they see so little. Teach them to observe, to compare, and they will discover the good and the beautiful rather than the bad and ugly; for there is nothing evil in itself, but only that which the mind conceives in its ignorance." In a *Manual of Drawing,* Thompson (1895) was quite certain how to produce the good and the beautiful. Beauty was considered as perfect form, with the principal sensuous elements being regularity, variety, and harmony. Thompson's examples of beauty seem a little strange in today's world. Wilson (1899) published a picture series for use in elementary schools that

Figure 46.
This Australian Aboriginal wooden shield shows an aesthetic concern, completely apart from the formal teaching of design. The urge to decorate is universal.

Figure 47.
Educators seem to change in what they feel are appropriate pictures for young children to appreciate. "The Goose Girl," painted by Bouguereau, was typical of the pictures selected for study by children at the turn of the century. (Collection, Herbert F. Johnson Museum of Art, Cornell University.)

attempted to aid teachers in imparting to children a true appreciation and love for paintings by the world's great masters. In the preface to this series, James Hopkins, who was then director of drawing in the Boston Public Schools, said that picture study should be taken seriously: "The effort is not for amusement, entertainment, or decoration alone; it has an aim and a purpose larger, broader, and more dignified than any of these." The pictures Wilson selected for the children to admire, however, are rarely seen any more, and in some cases even the artist himself has passed into oblivion.

We can be amused at earlier attempts at developing aesthetic awareness in children by trying to establish methods for teaching the good, the true, and the beautiful; however, the uncomfortable thought creeps in that, maybe fifty or sixty years from now, our attempts to impress upon children the beauty of a Picasso, Chagall, or Klee will also be viewed as mildly amusing.

Changes constantly occur in the art field, and a sudden interest in assemblages gives way to an art that capitalizes on optical illusions. This may be followed by the enlarging or endless duplication of everyday items from the grocery store, which in turn is supplanted by other, newer interests, such as earth sculpture or a self-destroying art form, which is followed by kinetic art or light displays, in turn succeeded by multimedia shows, accidental art, art deco, or duplicator art. This is not to say that these art forms are merely styles that change like the seasons, but rather that the teacher of art may be viewing art from the narrow perspective of his own background and training. The excitement he feels about a new art form may not be shared by his students, particularly when yet another direction in art is promoted by the popular magazines and he becomes suddenly old-hat in his ideas.

A development of self-awareness on the part of students, in fact, may be more important in the long run than the appreciation of any particular style of art. Honesty in design and excitement in art are important qualities which can be felt only through the self. Art is a reflection of today's world that can provide a direction for the future; students need to be able to evaluate change and be curious about the unfamiliar.

Aesthetic Development

A fifth grade teacher was standing in the front of her room looking through a large stack of paintings, which had just been picked up off the floor where they had been drying. She was saying how much her children enjoyed their art experiences, that is, all but one child, "The one in the back row that needs the haircut," she said, nodding toward one boy who looked as if he could stand a bath. She began thumbing through the paintings. "Aren't some of these lovely?" Most of them looked tightly drawn and carefully colored. Suddenly she came upon one that was full of color, painted very directly, and apparently with a lot of feeling. It was a large head outlined in strong purple with a red background, looking somewhat like one of Rouault's paintings. She looked up and, shrugging her shoulders, said, "See, always this crude scribbling, no talent at all."

It was fairly obvious that this teacher had certain likes and dislikes in art, which she was using to evaluate the children's work. The fact that the boy needed a haircut and a bath may also have influenced her judgment. However, she was imposing her own tastes and aesthetic values upon these youngsters, and in so doing was undoubtedly having an impact upon their own values. Another teacher might not have been as outspoken or might have selected another picture to decry. There is no doubt that the aesthetic values of our society are transposed to youngsters either directly or indirectly.

Probably our teacher would have been just as much at fault if she had selected the boldly painted head as an outstanding example of art and displayed this for the class to see. Our society has changing values in art; standards of goodness or badness may not be important, but what may be vital is the development of children's aesthetic awareness, based upon open flexible minds rather than upon some changing aesthetic standard which may not be appropriate twenty years from now. We should be much more concerned with the fifth grader himself, for he might be the one to direct our society to a new and different form of beauty that may break away from our own narrow definitions.

The Preschool Child

During the first couple of years of life a child discovers a great deal about his environment. He does this by examining everything that he can touch; he explores it not only by sight but also handles and tastes everything that he can. He enjoys the opportunity to rattle, move, or put together any object that he can manipulate. He often shows preferences even at this early age for certain toys or dolls. Language is used primarily to communicate his basic needs for food or for attention.

At about the age of three the child can select an object from a series. It is possible for him to select a square from a series of geometric forms although he cannot draw or copy a square until a year later (Brittain, 1969). There is no evidence to indicate that practice in perceiving shapes is of any value to the

THE DEVELOPMENT OF AESTHETIC AWARENESS

Figure 48. (Opposite)
"Migration," by Rauschenberg. The artist in today's society has turned away from tradition. Although the artist is making a serious statement, many members of our society look upon such paintings as worthless. (Collection, Herbert F. Johnson Museum of Art, Cornell University.)

preschool child, for he does not improve particularly in ability to select objects or shapes even after being given practice in this task. Even extensive help in showing youngsters how to draw a square does not improve their square-drawing ability.

When the preschool youngster looks at pictures, he is eager to point out those objects that he recognizes, but this may be quite different from getting an understanding of the picture itself. At the age of four or five years children can identify familiar objects in pictures but they enumerate them one after another and do not relate them to one another in any way; not until age seven do children attempt coherent, logically related interpretations (Vernon, 1965).

Figure 49.
Young children's sensitivity to their environment includes curiosity about how things look, smell, feel, taste, and sound. Onions are more than a food, since youngsters are intrigued by their ball-like quality and the noise made by their dry skins.

The preschool child learns in an active way rather than in a passive way. That is, his actual interaction with his environment, his touching, seeing, manipulating, are all part of his total development, and his cognitive and perceptual growth are closely entwined. The preschool child has little concept of time; to a great extent, the world has little past or future; rather, it is. Often the child will express strong preferences, but these preferences change rapidly and the nursery school teacher will sometimes find that she is hated one moment and loved the next. Pictures on the wall are not art in the usual sense to the preschool youngster. Art is what he himself makes. However, the nursery school child usually does not remember his own drawings or paintings after a few hours, and it could not be expected that he can develop any learning abilities in terms of aesthetic awareness as adults understand it. It may well be that sensitivity toward living is based on the continual interaction that a child has with his environment. The degree to which this interaction is encouraged and stimulated can be an element in developing the urge and attitude toward exploring and investigating other forms and in voicing preferences or being able to discriminate differences more easily at a later age. The preschool child is probably at the most crucial age for the development of a sensitivity toward living.

The Elementary School Child

There are great changes in physical and mental development from the time the youngster is in kindergarten until he arrives at the sixth grade. The changes apparent in a child's creative art as he matures are also evident in his aesthetic development. Most first grade youngsters can give simple descriptions of pictures, naming the objects that are pointed out to them, if these are recognizable as objects, and can identify colors if they are not too subtle. However, the description is limited to the objects in a painting and does not extend to any interaction between objects. That is, the first grader is able to identify things he recognizes but not the mood or atmosphere, nor is he able to discuss the message that a particular painting might have. It is not until later that a picture can be seen to have a story or interaction within the frame itself. Vernon (1965) indicates from her research that it is not until ten or eleven years of age that children can interpret what is happening in a picture, what the people are doing, and so forth. This inability to see relationships roughly parallels the ability in drawing, for the first grader will draw objects, but these objects are related in his pictures only by being placed one beside the other, and it is not until about ten or eleven that overlapping begins to appear.

Children in the elementary school do not recognize paintings or other works of art in the same way as adults. Although adults may enjoy the work of a particular painter, such as Picasso or Cezanne, because of the particular style or the colors, tonal quality, or atmosphere, this is not true for children. A study by Gardner (1970) found that first, third, and sixth grade children were generally insensitive to the painting styles of various artists. However, ninth graders did significantly better in selecting another painting from several shown that was like the ones that they had just seen. The younger children tended to match paintings by subject matter, such as a little boy or a church which happened to appear in one of the sets. Most children, up through sixth grade, are insensitive to line variation or shading in drawings (Carothers and Gardner, 1979). In a study including a group of nineteen year old students, the conclusion was drawn that only in the adolescent and postadolescent years do a majority of children give responses which reveal their awareness of the formal aspects of paintings (Gardner and Gardner, 1973).

Ample evidence indicates that it would be a difficult task to develop in elementary school children an awareness of stylistic differences in paintings. No doubt, with proper rewards and proper punishment, such stylistic differences could be mastered by fifth and sixth grade children. Probably aesthetics would be lost in the process. There seems to be no reason why this area of learning cannot be postponed until the age of twelve or thirteen when such learning becomes easier. This does not mean that aesthetics as such should be ignored in the elementary school; rather, a different kind of program should be developed, and this will be discussed later.

An adult concept of aesthetics has no meaning for very young children. A nursery school child is not aware of the aesthetic qualities of, for example, a lamp. A lamp is to turn on when it is dark. Lamps look like the lamp in his house, his lamp that he can turn on by pulling the chain. When he encounters a lamp that is quite different—one with a large translucent shade instead of the small metal bulb cover and a button to push to turn it on—he may be surprised to find that it, too, is a lamp. This discovery stretches his concept of "lampness." If the lamp is too unlike lamps he has known, it may be rejected just on this basis. If it is unfamiliar, it is wrong. Liking or not liking a lamp may have very little to do with its aesthetic qualities.

For first grade children, the liking or disliking of our lamp may not be based quite so much on the familiarity of the lamp; by now children have had a good deal of lamp experience, and the lamp concept has grown to include a wide range of lamps. Not liking may be more because the bulb is burned out, or the paint is chipped, or the shade is scorched and not because of some aesthetic qualities. One study (Holland, 1955) found a developmental progression in the responses of children to some plates, glasses, wallpaper, and so forth; in

grade one, many responses referred to the self, whereas responses relating to color, design, and shape showed a great increase from grade one to grade eight.

It would probably not be until nine years or so that children would be able to deal with the abstract concepts of lampness: its function, its utilitarian qualities, its ease of cleaning, or its sturdiness. And it probably would not be until eleven or twelve that the aesthetic qualities could be evaluated aside from the concrete qualities of the lamp. And, of course, a question comes to mind: why would anyone want children before the age of twelve to consider the aesthetic quality of anything anyway?

There is a difference between aesthetic preference and aesthetic judgment. Most youngsters can tell which picture they like best if given a choice, but the ability to judge one picture as better than another is a different problem. Some youngsters are able to predict quite well what the teacher wants, but this may be quite different from their own likes and dislikes. Child (1964) asked elementary school pupils from grades one through six to choose which they thought experts would consider best. Youngsters up through the fourth grade disagreed with the expert choice, and had a strong preference for the "poorer" of the pair of pictures. After fourth grade, the disagreement was not as great. It is rather interesting to note that these youngsters not only picked

THE DEVELOPMENT OF AESTHETIC AWARENESS

the poorer picture but thought that the experts would pick the poorer picture too. Child followed this experiment by a training session with fifth and sixth grade youngsters. He found that it was possible to improve their guesses as to what the expert judges would select as the better pictures, but found that the youngsters' own preferences remained unchanged. Although these children had many weekly sessions of seeing slides, including a wide assortment of landscapes, portraits, still-lifes, sculpture, abstract art, and so forth, the study indicated that this exposure had no effect on children's preferences. In fact, the results were completely negative.

Evidently it is a lot easier to change what children say than what they think. This might be expected, since children in school are usually marked on how closely they agree with the textbook or with the teacher, and not on their thinking abilities. An interesting study was done in England by Rump and Southgate (1966) with three groups of children aged seven, eleven, and fifteen. They found that 77 percent of the children agreed with their teacher's stated preference for pictures, if the teacher was present. However, 71 percent disagreed with their teacher's preference when the teacher was not there! Rump and Southgate also found that the children preferred representational pictures, and the younger children preferred simple items or pictures with few elements. The older high school age children had a definite preference for the more complex pictures.

There is no reason to believe that the development of discrimination in paintings should be different from the discrimination of objects or thoughts in other areas of cognitive processes. The child is satisfied with making representations that are symbolic and definite about his environment, and he does not show concern in his drawings for light and shade, differing atmospheric effects, or variations in color relationships until about the age of twelve. Machotka (1966) did a study analyzing the basis on which children evaluated paintings. This study indicated that children like pictures of increasingly clear and realistic representation until about age eleven. Although younger children would establish an emotional relationship to a painting, it was usually in terms of a personal relationship, such as liking a picture of a person because it reminds him of his father; it was not until the age of twelve that an emotional relationship was established with a picture that was outside the youngster himself, that is, with the atmosphere or character of the picture as a whole. Machotka related this change to a decrease in egocentrism which occurs at about the age of eleven when thought loses its dependence on concrete data. Taunton (1980) asked groups of children four, eight, twelve, and sixteen years of age and some college students their preferences for 24 pictures which had been

Figure 51.
Instead of falling into the trap of advocating admiration of a new set of accepted artists—Picasso, Matisse, Modigliani, and so on —to replace the 1930 set of accepted artists, the teacher should broaden the scope of art by exposing students to all forms of art. ("Oeuficiency," by Matta. Collection, Herbert F. Johnson Museum of Art, Cornell University.)

categorized according to subject matter, space, and realism. The results showed that subject matter was most important for all children up to twelve years of age and that realism was an important consideration for all except the four year olds. Another study (Hardiman and Zernich, 1977) also found that realistic paintings were preferred up to eighth grade.

Many factors within his environment probably will influence the elementary school child in his likes and dislikes, his ability to discriminate, and his development of aesthetic awareness. Schools undoubtedly play an important part in this developing aesthetic awareness, but it may not be as important to guide this development as it is to encourage it.

This is a period of developing critical awareness, and although no sudden changes have occurred, the young adolescent has increased in his awareness of himself as a member of society and has left the egocentric stage behind. One would therefore expect that there would be some changes in the ways in which adolescents perceive their environment and possibly an increase in aesthetic growth. However, this does not seem to be the case. Rather, the young adolescent seems to be on a plateau and does not seem particularly committed to art in any form. This does not imply that he is not interested in art, but rather that development cannot be easily measured and there seems to be no observable growth or change in art products during these years from twelve to fourteen. In a study of eighth grade students, Frankston (1963) concluded that whether or not the students took an art course had no effect on the quality of their art performances. He found no differences from one semester to the next in the quality of the work the students produced, whether they took an art course or not. And he also found the same lack of change in quality in their poetry writing. In a later study, Frankston (1966) tried different methods of teaching adolescents and found great inconsistencies in the individual performances but, again, no changes in group performance level.

In another study of the same age group, Brittain (1968a) found that there was general agreement between the adolescents and their teachers as to which drawings were of high quality. Unlike the teachers, these students showed a strong preference for complexity and technical proficiency in drawings. It may be that children at this age are becoming much more aware of their environment generally, though not to the point of being able to sort the variety of experiences into what might be termed acceptable and unacceptable. It is clear that eighth grade youngsters enjoy seeing art that they themselves would like to be able to do. It may be that this is a key to a good deal of aesthetic preference, and that growth in aesthetic preferences is achieved as a youngster grows in his own abilities to portray his environment. Day (1969) found in attempting to teach some art history to eighth graders that those students who had concurrent studio experiences performed better and gained more knowledge of the subject matter in art history than those students who did not have a studio art class. Possibly the introduction of some discussions applicable to the production of art might begin to make sense to this age.

The high school student who takes an art course is in the minority. Although there are occasional classes that are required of all high school students in the humanities, these too are rare. Schools turn their backs upon the importance of aesthetic growth at the time when its development can best be promoted. The high school student enjoys the opportunity to engage in abstract

Figure 52.

Adolescents preferred the upper of these sketches, the landscape and horse; but teachers seemed to like the lower ones, the fruit and bird. A horse seemed more appealing than a bird to this age, and the detail of the landscape was preferred to the simplicity of the fruit.

thinking and he is no longer tied to concrete operations. His coordination and drive is such that great gains can be seen in his art products, but sometimes these skills are misguided and the student may mimic or duplicate works of art that he considers great. His ability to discriminate is probably at its peak, and

THE DEVELOPMENT OF AESTHETIC AWARENESS

although individuals differ considerably, this is probably the best age at which to deal with problems of aesthetics.

Preference and Personality

Aesthetic awareness is not an isolated variable in human behavior, because it relates to one's total personality. It may be possible to have high school students select the pictures that are judged "better," and even have them become quite proficient at selecting the ones that the teacher himself likes, but changing the patterns of likes and dislikes within the individual student is quite another matter. In a study of male graduate students, Barron (1963) found that there was a definite relationship between the paintings that these students preferred and their acceptance or rejection of tradition, religion, and authority. In general he found that those students who preferred portraits, landscapes, and traditional themes in paintings also preferred simple and predictable sketches; this was closely related to their personality, which tended to be conservative, serious, deliberate, responsible, and so forth. Those students who preferred the experimental, sensual, and primitive paintings also preferred sketches that were complex and irregular; the personality of this group of students tended to be more pessimistic, emotional, temperamental, and so forth.

Further work on the relationship between personality and art preferences has been done by a number of investigators (Knapp and Green, 1960; Roubertoux et al., 1971; Kloss and Dreger, 1971; Juhasz and Paxson, 1978). It is difficult to determine why this relationship exists, but it is well documented that people who have different personality characteristics do have different art preferences. A study by Barrett (1970) using college students concluded that "the aesthetic experience is apparently not closely related to objective visual skills such as color matching or form discrimination but may be based on individual personality factors instead."

An individual justifies his judgments of art by identifying certain qualities in the work that support his preferences. Yet these preferences elicited by the art tell us more about the viewer's disposition toward the work than about the work itself (Sharer, 1980). One assumes that his own interpretation of the characteristics of a work of art is embodied there for all to see. Aesthetic judgment is unconsciously filtered through an individual personality. But, in addition, that individual's personality is a result of social forces.

Possibly real changes in aesthetic preference cannot be made unless there is also a change in one's personality. Burgart (1964) found that there was what he termed a creative personality syndrome that was related positively to art experience, and Burkhart (1964) and Hoffa (1964) have also found indications that the creative personality is associated with a greater amount of art experience. Attempting to teach taste or standards in art to a senior high school art class may not produce a sensitive, alert, aware, and discriminating student unless changes in personality happen at the same time. Obviously this is a difficult task to accomplish, but the objective of education toward a more sensitive population—a population that is also willing to make changes—is certainly a goal worth striving for.

A Program for Aesthetic Growth

Children have joy in exploring, investigating, and expressing their feelings about their environment. Possibly the best means of developing aesthetic awareness is through sharpening youngsters' sensibilities and strengthening their power of self-expression. Aesthetics should not be confused with the appreciation of art. Aesthetics can be a basic way of relating oneself to the environment. That is, looking at, responding to, feeling a part of, being aware of textures and forms, reacting to differences and similarities, liking or disliking an object, noticing differences in organization—all are part of the aesthetic response and part of aesthetic growth. Aesthetics may be thought of as the nonfactual, nonobjective reactions of a person to his environment. As such, aesthetics may be an attempt to discover the nature of self. Matters of beliefs and values take precedence over knowledge.

As people, we are constantly reacting to our environment. Young children do this as well as old. What we have experienced in the past makes us respond in given ways to the present. If an event or an object is before us, we respond to this in terms of past experiences rather than in terms of its actual qualities. Contemplation of a work of art evokes many responses; these may be both positive and negative. Subject matter certainly can have a reference within one's past experiences; young child en particularly respond to pictures in terms of such subject matter content. However, colors, forms, and even the atmosphere of a particular work of art can evoke responses in the viewer that the viewer himself cannot immediately understand. The art of the past is a tradition invariably broken whenever new directions in art are taken. The purpose in developing aesthetic growth is not to honor the work of past or present

Figure 53.
*We often accept what is around
us without question. The
common recurrence of such
surroundings as these reflects
society's lack of concern with
aesthetic sensitivity. Yet someone
has attempted to brighten the
scene by painting flowers around
the door.*

artists, nor is it to teach the vocabulary of art, but rather the purpose is to encourage and develop the aesthetic response of an individual to his particular world.

To a great extent, then, the understanding of art and aesthetic awareness should be combined in a program specifically aimed at the developing child, which becomes part of his natural interaction with the environment. Inattention to environment can be overcome, but attention is an achievement requiring effort (Parsons, 1971). Experiences in large and small enclosed spaces, the opportunity to comment on changing colors in a sunset, pointing out and enjoying the variety of textures in clothing or the feeling of expansiveness in open areas, all have the primary purpose of expanding the youngster's awareness of himself and those things around him, giving him the chance to develop

A PROGRAM FOR AESTHETIC GROWTH

his ideas and examine them, and to realize that his own opinions about his environment are important. In discussing the problems of developing a specific curriculum in aesthetics, Broudy (1971) emphasizes these problems: changes in attitude are harder to bring about than changes in belief; there is less consensus on criteria for evaluation than for truth; and we know less about teaching for appreciation than teaching for understanding.

The Preschool

The pleasure in looking at a brightly colored leaf in the fall and listening to the birds in the spring are experiences that can be readily shared. It is relatively easy to encourage the type of growth that we have been discussing at this age. But encouragement need not be passive on the part of the teacher. Children can respond to questions about whether the clay is hot or cold, whether the paint is too thick, whether the color red is their favorite, whether the painting should be hung high or placed low on the bulletin board, or whether they like

THE DEVELOPMENT OF AESTHETIC AWARENESS

the feel of the smooth piece of maple. To be able to look at, recognize, and respond to objects is probably an important step in aesthetic growth. The discriminatory skills are part of the whole cognitive process and therefore we could not expect young children to go beyond their intellectual level in developing ways of looking at their environment. However looking at, feeling, and talking about objects makes the child much more conscious of this activity as worthwhile.

Preschool children are eager to share their treasures, and these treasures may take strange forms. A nursery school teacher would not be surprised to observe children saving buttons, fingering pebbles, liking stubby pencils, or having favorite socks. It is important that a small child have the opportunity to examine and save part of his environment. Explaining why these things are chosen is not as important. A sensitive teacher will provide a place for the child to put his own collection, for it is important for the child that this be honored. Sometimes group experiences can be meaningful, such as looking at unusual fossils, branches with interesting bark or leaf development, or pictures and reproductions that some youngsters have found appealing and worthwhile. A child's mood comes directly to the surface; his sadness or his joy is obvious; his feelings fill his whole mind and body, with no self-conscious awareness. Too often such exhibitions of expression are treated as if they should be repressed. "Stop doing that. Stop acting like a child. Behave yourself." Probably the biggest role a preschool teacher can play is a supportive one to the child in the development of his awareness of himself and in the joy and pleasure he gets from his own environment.

In looking at reproductions of contemporary paintings, children in kindergarten and first grade usually pick out the subject matter that they can recognize and generally seem oblivious to the artistic qualities therein. However, sixth grade children, particularly girls, seem to be much more aware of the mood and atmosphere of a picture, or the feeling that color or forms impart to the viewer. But then, this is to be expected since children in their own drawings follow this developmental pattern. The child in first grade will be drawing objects placed one beside the other, and his concern for color is more to identify the particular object than it is to impart a mood or feeling to the viewer. The sixth grader will be drawing objects that overlap, there may be many base lines or a feeling for space, and the color that is used may be purposefully applied to give a feeling of anger, hatred, joy, or serenity.

Children react to and express their feelings with whatever instruments or words they have mastered. Sometimes children can mimic words without

The Elementary School

Figure 55.
Relating to art and finding aesthetic pleasure in examining and reacting to representations are based on concrete experiences. Gathering autumn leaves brings an appreciation of the variety of their forms, textures, colors, smells, and sounds.

understanding of their meaning and sometimes these words sound quite amusing when they come out in songs, prayers, or in the "pledge of the legions." Recognition of great works of art at an early age may be possible, but the understanding and aesthetic awareness of these pictures would be missing. Abstract concepts of beauty and ugliness cannot be comprehended by young children. A good example of this is a study by Liedes (1975), where first grade children were asked to bring in things they thought were beautiful and ugly to share with their classmates. The things they brought were based on personal feelings: beautiful things were clean, smooth, and shiny, such as figurines and jewelry; ugly things were broken, dark, or rough, such as bones and dirty stones.

Any sculpture, painting, or drawing is the result of an expression of an individual. In works of art, the artist expresses his relationship to his environment in a subjective way. A painting of a tree is not the tree itself, but the expression of the relationship between the artist and that tree. The elementary school child can also paint a tree but his relationship to that tree will be quite different from that of a professional artist. In part, the differences will be present because one picture is by a child and the other by an adult, but there are greater differences because the two painters are individuals. The same thing

THE DEVELOPMENT OF AESTHETIC AWARENESS

holds true for nonobjective paintings. The artist may be painting primarily for his own enjoyment, may be concerned with the relationship of forms in his paintings, may be developing a particular mood; at any rate, it is his reaction to the environment as seen in the finished product that we examine and it is this reaction that we ourselves respond to. The picture is merely a conglomeration of lines and forms and colors that have little meaning unless we can identify with the artist's purpose. In some contemporary art expression, the product itself becomes destroyed, or is practically nonexistent, placing the focus entirely upon the experience.

Simple questions such as "How do you feel about this picture?" or "What part do you like best?" may be enough to get students involved. This comprehension is geared to the individual, and not to an evaluation of a painting itself. "Why do you suppose the artist painted this? Suppose you had painted this picture, what would have been your purpose?" would be one method of focusing upon the process rather than on the product.

It would be a difficult task to plan a detailed curriculum for aesthetic education for the elementary school, especially since the end product of the instruction is not at all clear. However, attempts have been made. One ambitious course of study (Colwell, 1970) was designed for sixth graders with stress placed on what is called connoisseurship and criticism. The student was taught vocabulary and terminology, with specific procedures, questions, and recommended slides. The student was asked to use Fry's four types of vision—practical, curious, aesthetic, and creative—as demonstrated by an example. If one were to find a piece of driftwood while strolling along a beach, practical vision would enable it to be identified, curious vision would lead it to be examined closely, aesthetic vision would be responsible for one's noticing the smooth texture and the patterning of the grain, while creative vision would occur as plans were made for finding additional pieces to use for display.

It seems logical that children can identify and enjoy pictures that they can relate to. We have seen how past generations of teachers have selected the sweet pictures for children to appreciate; but it is a rare adult who still remembers the artist who painted the little girl and her dog that he was supposed to identify when he was in third grade. It makes good sense to stress that viewing a painting should be an enjoyable experience, not merely the source of facts to be learned. There is no reason why students must echo words of the teacher. Children should be able to select pictures to share with each other. Sometimes schools purchase original works of art for the classroom. These originals or reproductions should be picked out by the children who are going to view them. The teacher, too, should be able to have some say in the selection of such works of art. Since we are functioning in a democratic society, the elementary school provides a good opportunity for the development of likes and dislikes and for the increasing awareness of one's own attitude toward the arts, with a full realization that as a child grows, his tastes and ability to respond to his environment will change.

The Secondary School

The young adolescent finds a vicarious expression in popular music. Possibly there should be popular art for these youngsters too. However, some art teachers are much more concerned about propagating their own standards, and the likes and dislikes of the students tend to be ignored. It is adolescents who begin to spend money on jewelry, art objects, and interesting trinkets. They need support in their ability to make choices. Exposure to and awareness of some of the variety of forms available and the suggestion of alternate outlets for this interest in collecting artifacts could well be a starting point in making aesthetics meaningful.

The developing interest in art which can be seen in the junior high school should be encouraged, but not necessarily in the direction of the usual chronological approach to the evolution of modern art. There are many cultures that have expressed themselves in ways which may be closer to the young adolescent than is the sophisticated art of nineteenth and twentieth century Europe and America. Some of the art forms from Africa, early American folk art like scrimshaw and quilts, and Eskimo sculpture can create great interest, because they express some of the feelings and emotions of these youngsters in a direct manner. Since this age is much more verbal, discussions and examples of a variety of art products can be stimulating, particularly if this is a part of a creative art activity. Care should be taken that these examples are seen as a means of stimulating discussion and of broadening possible avenues for action rather than as examples to be emulated.

The senior high school student is in an advantageous position for understanding some of the problems facing our society in its ignorance of aesthetic values. However, the temptation should be resisted to cram aesthetics down the throats of the unsuspecting students. Their own knowledge and interests should be the starting point. As much can be learned about aesthetics from seeing alternate methods of organizing pieces of scrap metal into a sculpture or from cropping photographs for enlargement as can be learned from armchair lectures about balance and repetition in a slide of a Mondrian painting.

From previous studies (Day, 1969) it seems learning in the cultural aspects of the arts can be enhanced by active participation. It makes sense. Someone who paints enjoys looking at paintings; if you have tried to throw pots,

Figure 56.
Direct, bold art from other cultures has an honesty that appeals to junior high school students. (Mask of Wood, Ivory Coast. Collection of Ithaca College; gift of Mr. William Brill.)

THE DEVELOPMENT OF AESTHETIC AWARENESS

Figure 57.
The type of trinkets available in many discount stores may be the major contact many students have had with "art," greatly influencing their taste.

you enjoy a good piece of pottery; the weaver likes to examine interesting textiles. Basically aesthetics, art appreciation, or art history needs to be part of the active creative search for expressive symbols, for solutions to problems in artistic construction, or for pleasing combinations of form and texture. If these areas are treated in isolation, the high school student can quickly relegate this learning to the same category as some of his other subjects: something which needs to be done for school, but not anything sufficiently exciting to be considered outside the school itself.

An illustration might be a student who is trying to express in paint his resentment against an apathetic society, but it just does not seem to take form. How have others painted anger? Some paint with gory details like Goya, some with distorted symbols like Picasso, some with heavy and bold lines like Rouault, and some with only form and color. The student is thus able to expand his frame of reference, and the history of art is put into a meaningful context.

A PROGRAM FOR AESTHETIC GROWTH   125

Figure 58. (Opposite)
Many museums have programs which relate closely to the interests of students. This equestrian statue was constructed of salvaged auto bumpers. (Colleoni II, by Jason Seley, 1969–71; courtesy of the artist)

Problems in sculpture, photography, design, crafts, graphics can all be approached in similar ways, using the past as a reference for the future, but not to be imitated. Too often all the usual student sees in the way of art is the commercial variety—ads for cars, beer, cigarettes; or the pseudo-art that seems to fill every discount store—garish-colored framed reproductions of saccharine subject matter, plastic reproductions of marble figurines, radios camouflaged as model automobiles, or lamps growing out of the backs of ceramic cocker spaniels. If these are his references for his own art, then the discovery of the serious art of the past may be a source of new perceptions. Care must be taken that the teaching of the arts does not ignore the personal history of the student or the cultural background of the society in which he finds himself.

Often museums initiate programs designed to attract students to their facilities, and many offer special programs for children on Saturday morning. Book publishers and film companies now make available instructional materials which can sometimes be of help in organizing a well-rounded study of art. Philanthropic organizations, foundations, and even state and local art councils have been known to assist in the funding of ambitious projects which are aimed at bringing the arts into the community and the lives of school children. Additional funding from outside sources is not necessary when the school administration is committed to fostering aesthetic experiences for its pupils. Moreover, students are usually more ready than the staff for such activities since flexibility, innovation, and interdisciplinary thinking are necessary in order to break with the traditional school programming. Almost every state has some kind of traveling exhibition; a few bring performing artists into the classroom.

The community itself, regardless of its size, offers a vast resource of aesthetic opportunities. Beyond the obvious, such as museums, art exhibits, music and dance concerts, libraries, and theaters, other nearby resources should not be overlooked. Historical societies are active in nearly every community. Local architecture, in the form of churches and new and old homes, is often a good source. Parks provide good means of looking at landscaping, and their monuments give a tie to the past. Bridges can be both structurally and aesthetically interesting. Local photo shops not only offer materials but can also offer some information. Sometimes post offices or other public buildings have murals from the 1930s. The local radio and television studio can be an excellent source of exploring both the technical and aesthetic problems of program production. Everyone has experienced the feeling of awe inside a large church, but a feeling that is somewhat comparable without religious inferences can be had before large machinery, such as in a mill, factory, or utility com-

THE DEVELOPMENT OF AESTHETIC AWARENESS

pany. At the same time, a watch and clock maker, a jeweler, or a cabinetmaker can provide the source of a different kind of appreciation, as can contact with private collectors or performers.

Some may question whether these experiences are really in the area of developing aesthetic awareness. However, developing sensitivity toward painting may not be as important as developing sensitivity toward life. A high school student who enjoys the work of a fine craftsman, who is sympathetic to the problems of the printer, who appreciates the feel of fabric with the local dressmaker, and who is fascinated with construction methods of the local contractor, is also ready to appreciate the fine arts.

Summary

Aesthetic awareness is part of the total growth pattern of children. It is not the imposition of standards or rules from outside the child, but rather the development of his ability to discriminate and make choices. Beauty is something that changes with each culture, and the opportunity for youngsters to express their own feelings and emotions about things around them is more important than the development of taste according to today's standards.

Clive Bell (1914, p. 249) had some rather amusing advice to give about art and children that makes sense even today. "Do not tamper with that direct emotional reaction to things which is the genius of children. Do not destroy their sense of reality by teaching them to manipulate labels. Do not imagine that adults must be the best judges of what is good and what matters. Don't be such an ass as to suppose that what excites uncle is more exciting than what excites Tommy."

Possibly what is necessary in the development of aesthetic awareness is not an appreciation of a particular picture or object nor is it necessarily the teaching of particular adult values or a vocabulary to describe works of art. Aesthetic awareness may be taught through an increase in a child's awareness of himself and a greater sensitivity to his own environment. There are numerous factors involved in aesthetics, and it is not a simple problem to deal with. Certainly the cognitive behavior of individuals, their affective behavior, and the interaction between themselves and their environment all play a part. The background of a student, his socioeconomic level, the cultural factors of the time, his exposure to mass media, his ability to be flexible in his thinking, and his standing in the classroom all influence the development of aesthetic awareness. It should be understood that aesthetic growth does not necessarily refer to art; it also refers to a more intense and greater integration of thinking, feeling, and perceiving. It thus may bring about a greater sensitivity toward living, and therefore it becomes a major goal in education.

RELATED ACTIVITIES

1 Ask a seventh grade class which of a series of quite dissimilar pictures they would like to hang on the walls of their houses. Ask them which one their parents would like. Then ask which one their art teacher would like best. Does this give any indication of how they see the adults' taste as different from their own?

2 In a drug or variety store, select a few inexpensive containers that are well designed. Select several poorly designed items. On what basis did you make your selections?

3 Ask a second grade class to bring to school something that is beautiful and something that is ugly. Compare their concepts of beauty and ugliness with your own.

4 Look around your own community and make a note of those buildings that are of the most modern design. Who owns these buildings or what function goes on inside them? Locate some new buildings that are more traditional in design. What are these buildings used for? Can you draw any inferences?

5 Select examples of paintings that are related to a particular period of art. Explain why these are representative of their time, referring to subject matter, technique, and mode of representation.

6 Select one large reproduction that shows some distortion of everyday objects, such as a painting by Modigliani or Chagall. Ask some first, third, and sixth graders to tell you what they think about the picture. Keep track of their comments and their acceptance or rejection of the distortion.

Art in the Elementary School

5

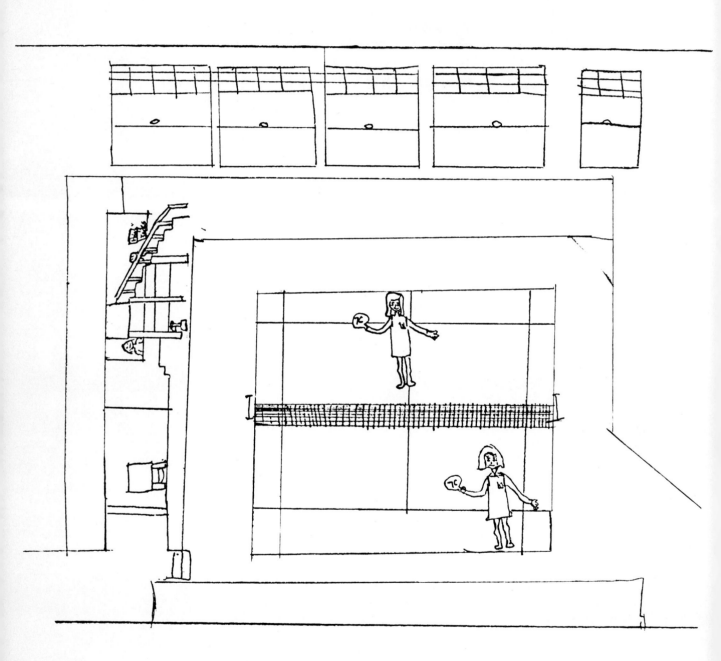

Classroom Procedures

Art is usually considered an important part of the program for the elementary school child. Art activities, however, are scheduled in a variety of ways. Several years ago it was fairly common for an art teacher to push a cart of art materials from one elementary classroom to another. The art teacher worked on a fairly close schedule, and often children would be waiting impatiently for their turn to have art. It is much more common now for a classroom to be set aside for art activities. There are many advantages to this. It seems better to have one room messed up with paper clippings on the floor or clay on the desks, so that the janitor does not have to spend time cleaning several rooms. Also, the art materials are on hand and the activities can be varied, with several different projects going on at the same time. However, Silberman (1971) has decried the fact that art is something separate from ordinary classroom life, and is something you go to another room to study or to do.

Sometimes, in an elementary school with a more flexible program structure, the art room is open for any child who has finished his work or who has the free time to come in and work for fifteen minutes or a couple of hours. In some schools the morning hours are scheduled with the more academic subjects, such as mathematics or reading; the afternoon is free for children to select one or more activities, so that children come and go from the art room at will. Often the elementary classroom teacher himself is expected to provide experiences in art for the children in his classroom. Occasionally there is a schedule where an art consultant will spend several days in one room and then move to another location, to provide for a concentrated art experience.

There are many reasons for these different patterns, most of them economic ones. The most important consideration should be maximizing the value of the art program so as to provide a meaningful experience in the arts, with ample opportunity for the youngsters to express their own relationship to their environment. Classroom procedures are focused upon encouraging each child in his own very personal way. A teacher's function becomes one of developing children's self-discovery and stimulating depth of expression. The atmosphere that is conducive to artistic expression, an environment that will foster inventiveness and exploration, is not the same type of atmosphere that is favorable for memorizing multiplication tables. In the latter activity the student must concentrate on areas outside himself; he is dependent upon the teacher for recognition of his efforts and he must, with the rest of his classmates, deny giving vent to his own feelings. Creative expression is the direct opposite of memorization. Where individual inventiveness, expression, and

Figure 60.
The activities within the classroom must be planned in such a way that social interaction takes place. Exchanging ideas, arguing, and defending one's position are important in the learning process.

independence of thinking are crucial, an entirely different classroom atmosphere needs to be established.

A teacher who wants to foster individual expression in the classroom, who wants to encourage initiative and spontaneity, and who wants to have children motivated to produce freely, will have to accept creative behavior. We wish to encourage the child to be full of curiosity, to poke fun at himself and others, to have original ideas of his own, even to question the teacher's direction, and at the same time we discourage children from feeling withdrawn, quiet, retiring, and dependent upon the teacher for direction and approval. We are trying to encourage every child to look upon learning as a self-initiated activity, for such individuals will become the backbone of our society. Children who are personally involved in an activity may be oblivious to those around them and are not easily distracted. Sometimes a whole class will become so involved in an activity that a classroom will be surprisingly quiet. At other times there may be a great deal of activity and noise as youngsters share ideas and materials. In a summary of Piaget's work, Ginsburg and Opper (1969) conclude that children should talk with one another, argue, converse, and defend their opinions in a classroom atmosphere which supports social interaction.

An art class is often confusing to the outsider anyway, because of the problem of having numerous materials distributed and picked up. A great deal of responsibility can be assumed by the children themselves in handling the art materials. Actually the art experience is more than merely using the art materials in the drawing or painting process; learning takes place in finding how paint is stored, learning how to mix the paint so that it is of proper consistency, and learning how to clean up after the painting is completed. Cleaning and storing the brushes and putting the painting itself away to dry are all part of the experience. Although very young children will have difficulty with paints, even nursery school children can help and there is no reason why the responsibility for paper distribution or putting away crayons cannot be assumed by the youngsters. The teacher who prepares the materials and then assumes the responsibility for cleaning up afterwards puts himself in the position of a housekeeper rather than a teacher. There is some danger in encouraging students to think and do for themselves. But this danger exists only for the teacher who feels insecure within himself.

Older and younger children can engage in many activities together, but usually younger children are oblivious of the ten and eleven year olds. These older children can often be a great deal of help in passing out paints, helping the six year old clean up spilled water, or getting paper off the top shelf. Some elementary schools have the fifth and sixth graders take responsibility for helping with school activities. Some children will work in the library, some in the school office, and some in the art room. The janitor can be of help in knowing sources of materials, salvaging scraps of wood, or helping to hold two pieces of wood together while they are being nailed.

Classroom procedures should be kept flexible enough to allow each child the opportunity to deviate from the group activity. Specific suggestions for motivating children to express their feelings and emotions will be included in later chapters; however, if a particular project does not appeal to some of the children, there is no law that says that all children must be occupied in the same activity at the same time. Working with paper in a variety of ways, such as cutting, tearing, crumbling, or using paper to express some particular feeling by piercing the surface or folding it, might very well lead some children into escaping from the artistic investigation and using the paper for making folded airplanes. This might be a particularly interesting way to upset a teacher, but such use of paper for airplanes can be an exciting project in itself; certainly encouraging these children to make changes in the design of the folded paper—by adding a paper clip to the nose, by using a different type of fold, by trying a variety of weights of paper, and by experimenting with these forms in the hall —can channel the energies and independent thinking of the creative child into a constructive art project. Denying the desire to make such airplanes by treating the child as disruptive and taking disciplinary action against him would not only be frustrating to him, but would also deny the rest of the class the opportunity to deviate in the future from the prescribed procedures that the teacher might arbitrarily assign to the class.

Although undoubtedly every teacher would like to work with small classes, apparently there is no reason to believe that the size of class has much influence over the quality of the drawings of children. Lansing (1956) in working with fifth grade children found that class sizes ranging from 18 to 40 produced no significantly different effects upon the creative drawings of these children. There have been studies done in other fields which indicate that the teacher is the important variable. It is only when a class gets too large, probably over 40, that even the best teacher has difficulty. A poor teacher is boring whether the class size is 5 or 100.

Any procedures used in the classroom should encourage rather than discourage creativity. Children seated in rows with hands folded, waiting for something to happen, waiting for the person in front to pass the paper back, waiting for someone else to use the paint, lining up to wash hands at the sink, or patiently waiting for their turn at the easel may experience long enough delays to make real creative expression difficult when the time finally comes to put a line on paper. In some cases, putting supplies in several locations, grouping youngsters with four or five others who share the same interests, not having everyone working at the same project, and encouraging children to change activities without waiting for teacher approval will provide a means by which greater flexibility is possible.

Those children who have a good deal of energy and who are freer in their responses may need to have these energies channeled into acceptable form; at the same time the passive, quiet child may need real encouragement to overcome a fear of failure; he needs success experiences, so that he may go on to develop independent thinking and to discover the joy of self-expression. Providing encouragement for creative behavior and rewards for independent thinking can go a long way toward developing an atmosphere of creative activity. The classroom procedure can help in this respect, but it is only one factor among many that can provide the background for a meaningful art experience.

Figure 61.
The atmosphere in a classroom
that is engaged in art activities is
quite different from the
atmosphere that is present in the
classroom when usual academic
subject matter is taught.

The Importance of
Materials and Skills

The proper materials and the development of skills play an important part in the expression of art. It is only through the use of the art material that any expression can evolve. Just as words are important in verbal communication, and the structure of sentences and paragraphs are important in written work, in art the artist must develop the skills and techniques necessary to communicate, and he must have an understanding of the materials that he is using in order to be able to utilize their intrinsic qualities.

Figure 62.
The procedures in working with new materials should be explained briefly. Even in working in the woodshop youngsters are much more anxious to do than to learn how to do.

Important as skills and techniques may be, however, they must always remain the means to an end and never become ends in themselves. It is not the skills that are expressed, but the feelings and emotions of the artist. To concentrate only upon the materials that are used in art, or upon developing particular skills to utilize in an art expression, ignores the fundamental issue, which is that art springs from human beings and not from materials. Exercises in penmanship were once popular in our school systems, and children would spend a considerable length of time making neat ovals or copying from moralistic poems so as to perfect their writing abilities. This is no longer true, and a great deal more concern is voiced over the fact that youngsters need to develop a will to express themselves with the written word.

In art the same factors hold true. Merely understanding the differences between art materials and the development of particular skills will avail the

ART IN THE ELEMENTARY SCHOOL

child nothing unless the need and urge for expression is there first. The expression of the self, the urge to put down experiences that are meaningful, the desire to put into artistic form the frustrations or joys of life, must all be present before skills can be developed. Encouraging this expression is the crux of an art education program; the mechanics of art are secondary and can be explained when the demand for this knowledge comes from the youngster. Once the desire for expression is awakened the urge for greater knowledge about the use of materials will follow.

Frequently an artist's work is recognized by the particular technique that he uses. This is often an unconscious approach to the use of materials and is highly individual. With children this can also be true. Some youngsters will paint boldly with a great deal of spontaneity, whereas other children will be more concerned with detail and may concentrate on the outline of the forms they are making. A technique develops according to the individual's own needs. A procedure, on the other hand, consists of the different steps necessary in using a specific material. There are, for example, general procedures in making an etching. These are the preparation of the plate and acid used for etching, the methods of controlling the etching process, the ways in which the ink is applied to the plate, and so forth. These procedures can be explained to older students, and it is often necessary to develop considerable experience before the procedures become so automatic that etching can be used for expression. Needless to say, a procedure such as this would be too complex for children.

Techniques and Procedures

Any material that is used with children must fit their needs for expression. The procedure in using these materials can often be discovered by the children themselves, but occasionally simple explanations or demonstrations of certain procedures may facilitate the use and care of art materials. For example, ten year old children will find pleasure in a discussion of a variety of ways that tempera paint can be used. Colors can be mixed either in a tray or directly on the page, colors will mix on the painting if the undercolor is still wet but not if the undercolor has dried, paint has a different quality depending on whether it is thick or mixed with water; these suggestions may open other possibilities to the youngster. The facts that brushes store better with the handle down and that jar tops must be tight so that the paint will not evaporate are also part of the painting procedures. Much of this is not particularly appropriate to the nursery school child who needs the paint thick so that it does not run down the paper in uncontrolled mistakes; the tightening of his jar lids is probably best done by the teacher. A sensitive teacher can constantly take clues from his children as to when particular procedures would be valuable to discuss or when these children would benefit from finding other ways of using familiar materials.

Art Materials and Developmental Stages

There is an almost unlimited range of materials that can be used for art. Some of these are the traditional materials such as pencils, clay, paint, and so forth. Then there are other materials that are often used for art although their main purpose is for some other function. These include wood, collage materials, and plaster. A third category might include materials that are unrelated to art but which sometimes have a unique contribution to make and can be utilized in various ways in art experiences. These include such things as packing boxes, fish nets, and pieces of discarded water pipe.

Artists, seeing beauty or a message in almost any material, have given the impression that anything can be used for art expression. However, when working with children, materials are not sought out for their unique characteristics or the qualities that make them particularly expressive for the profes-

Figure 63.
The materials should be appropriate for the age of the child and not get in the way of artistic expression.

sional artist. Rather, the youngster sees these materials as being what art is all about, in somewhat the same way as he accepts a pencil to write with and a book to read. Therefore, much harm can be done to a child unless his developmental level is taken into consideration in the selection of the materials he is to use for art expression.

Let us look, for example, at watercolor as one art material. Watercolor is transparent, it has a flowing, merging quality, it mixes easily and can be made into fine gradations. Watercolor also changes easily in its characteristics, and it has a vibrating quality that lends itself to atmospheric effects. This material would be used quite differently by a scribbling child, a child of eight years of age, a youngster of twelve, or a sixteen year old.

A three year old who is scribbling would have real difficulty with watercolor. Because scribbling is primarily a motor activity he would quickly become discouraged and frustrated. If he scribbled with watercolor, the lines he produced with the wet brush would have to be interrupted frequently, as he would need to dip his brush into the water and paint. As he continued to scribble, his paper would fill with brush strokes and the lines would run into one another, merging into a blur, into an indistinguishable mass of colors in which kinesthetic sensation and the child's urge for control would become invisible. For a child who is beginning to name his scribbles this blurred mass would be frustrating.

An eight year old child has developed symbols that he repeats, which signify the concept of order that he has developed within his environment. He paints objects definite colors, such as green for grass and trees and bushes. He knows that these objects are green and continues to paint them this way with satisfaction. Differences in light or shadows do not influence these colors, and the unintentional changes are meaningless and only frustrate him in his desire for mastery. An accident cannot be repeated and an unintentional change is a mistake. What often seems of aesthetic quality to adults would mean a spoiled picture to an eight year old child.

A child of twelve years has found himself as a member of society and a part of the environment in which he lives. He loves to discover new things and to read fantastic stories. He enjoys the opportunity to experiment, and what formerly appeared as an accident in painting might now be considered stimulating. The flowing, merging quality of watercolor is well suited to this age, and the youngster may experiment with the accidents that occur when wet paint runs on the paper and merges with other colors in unexpected beauty. A colorful sky will be made more so by the introduction of reds and greens which can be quite dramatic.

A sixteen year old has become much more critical of himself and the work he produces. Usually he will have definite intentions about what he wants to produce; in some cases the changing effects of distance and atmosphere will be the primary intent, in which case watercolor may be an excellent medium. Another student may not find the same interest in portraying nature, but may want definite concepts expressed in flat tones. Watercolor may be an obstacle to this kind of expression. Not all students will have the desire to use watercolor. For some it may be frustrating, but for others it may be an excellent art material.

The teacher should know the variety of choices available in art materials and introduce them at the appropriate stage. Every material must make its own contribution, and if a task can be done more easily by using something different, then the wrong art material has been used originally. The teacher should know that every child will develop his own method of working with materials and that any help from the teacher can only be valuable if it provides the opportunity for greater awareness and greater flexibility. Often several materials can be used at one time within a classroom, and this provides an opportunity to develop various possible approaches to expression. It is not the material itself that needs emphasis, for art materials must be seen as avenues for expression and not as ends in themselves.

Certain mechanical, routine methods of handling art materials make the art program much more effective. Children at all levels can take a great deal of responsibility for their own art materials. Occasionally a teacher will become so involved with the distribution and cleaning-up processes that he has little time to stimulate the children to depth of expression. Having children take over some of this responsibility not only frees the teacher from the routine of passing out paper, distributing scissors, and cleaning up paintbrushes, but it also provides an opportunity for children to become more aware of an art activity as a total experience that is primarily theirs. A violin virtuoso handles his violin like something sacred not only because it is of material value, but because it is the means by which he can express himself. A true artist develops a kinship to materials, and some of these feelings can certainly be developed within children.

Art Materials in the Classroom

Some materials should be placed where children can obtain them freely. Spontaneous drawing or painting should be encouraged, and the paper, crayons, or paints should be readily accessible not only for the kindergarten child but for all children through secondary school. The older child should be able to gather and put back materials without supervision. Alhough art materials in daily use should be left within easy reach of children, certain materials should be stored out of sight. These are not necessarily the expensive materials but rather those that can have special meaning at special times (styrofoam balls for mobiles, shiny paper for holiday decorations) and those that are potentially dangerous (large glass jars, thin strands of wire, sets of cutting knives).

In no instance should the lack of materials stand in the way of a good art program. This is not to say that such basic materials as clay, tempera paint, and paper can be dispensed with. What is meant is that adding sheets of copper foil, gummed paper, clay glazes, and cans of spray paint do not in themselves insure a good art program. Often children can provide many inexpensive or free materials, such as old newspapers for making papier-mâché, cloth for making collages or banners, boxes for making animals or dragons, and bottle caps and straws for making decorations. The art materials are important to an art program, but they play a secondary role; the materials are not as important as the

Figure 65.
The art program can make use of free or inexpensive materials. Old newspapers are the basic ingredient in this papier-mâché animal being constructed as a cooperative effort.

way in which they are used. Because children at each developmental level have different needs and different capacities for using various media, specific suggestions for art materials will be included in following chapters.

A vital part of any art motivation is the moment before the transition into expression. If this gets lost, we lose an important part of the creative atmosphere. A child who is stimulated by a discussion of shopping in the grocery store, and who is eager to portray his feelings about the canned goods stacked way above his head, the smell of the produce, or the excitement of picking out his favorite cookies, should not have to wait for six children in front of him to pass the paper back before he can get started. The materials should be ready for immediate use once the child is ready for them. Sometimes if the presence of the material would be a distraction, children can be gathered in a circle in a different part of the room for a discussion.

Plate 11.
"Walking Man," drawn by a five year old girl. Inability to control the flowing quality of watercolor made this girl unhappy. The colors may be pleasing to look at, but notice how the color has gone beyond the hair and hands and has also run down the paper, all of which was seen as a mistake by the child.

Plate 12.
"Barns," painted in watercolor by a twelve year old girl. She has been able to control the paint to make a decorative and aesthetically pleasing composition, without concern for arbitrary rules of perspective, proportion, or design.

Plate 13.
"Harbor," painted by an adolescent girl. For some older teenagers the merging, flowing quality of watercolor produces atmospheric effects that can be quite pleasing.

Although children should be given the feeling for the quality and wealth inherent in every material, no undue concern should be shown if the child uses this material in unexpected ways. If a second grader crumples his sheet of paper, do not condemn him to inactivity. A question like "Didn't you like that piece of paper?" may be better than trying to scold him for his actions, and the child himself may not be able to understand why he felt like crumpling paper. A material like clay might be more appropriate, for it can be twisted and crushed without destroying the material itself. Every material should be thought of as meeting the needs of children and not as dictating a particular type of art lesson.

The Teacher of Art

In teaching art to children the most important factor is the teacher himself. If we could imagine a very poor teacher in the elementary school—one who is ineffective, unimaginative and uninspiring—we would undoubtedly feel sorry for the children in his charge. At least we would know that the children could get a great deal from the reading material in the class; the history book and the English reader would be there for them to use; and they would probably be able to develop some competencies in arithmetic. In art, however, there could be some real damage done. The basic ingredient of art comes from the child himself. This is essentially true whether we are talking about an elementary school child or a high school senior. The teacher has the important task of providing an atmosphere conducive to inventiveness, exploration, and production. In art, then, a poor teacher might be worse than no teacher at all.

The Teacher's Behavior Is Important

There are ways that teachers can provide a proper atmosphere for creative activities. There are ways that the environment can be organized to provide optimum conditions for art activities. The teacher of art should be a warm and friendly person. Cogan investigated the relationship between teacher behavior and the amount of required and self-initiated work performed by pupils. Nearly a thousand junior high school pupils were surveyed, and it was found that in almost every classroom positive relationships were found between the extent to which the student described the teacher as warm and friendly and the amount of self-initiated and required work produced. Averaging the amount of work that students did for each teacher clearly showed that the more friendly and warm teachers had pupils who produced more work (Levin et al., 1957). Other teacher characteristics can also be important, but apparently there is no one set of behavioral characteristics that is universally valuable in a school setting, since different teachers affect different children in different ways (Washburne and Heil, 1971).

There is some basis, then, for saying that a warm, friendly attitude toward students does foster productivity. In a study done with eleven year old children, Lippitt and White (1960) tried to find out what effects adult leaders had upon the behavior of children if the leaders behaved in ways called *authoritarian, democratic,* and *laissez-faire.* The authoritarian leader was one who issued orders and directions and gave praise or criticism; the democratic leader gave guiding suggestions, asked for children's opinions and judgments, and joked on a friendly basis; the laissez-faire leader gave out information when he was

Figure 66.
An interested teacher shares the youngsters' thoughts and gives support to their individual creative expression.

asked, but did not take an active part in giving out directions nor in stimulating self-guidance. Leaders changed groups part way through the experiment; the group behavior included a great outburst of horseplay by those children who were released from the authoritarian leader. But one interesting point was the finding that the children under a democratic leader showed the greatest expression of individual differences while at the same time showing less irritability and aggressiveness toward fellow members.

Learning does not take place in a completely relaxed environment any more than it does in a tightly structured setting. There is a middle ground where problems are seen as real, where interaction between teacher and children is open, and where thinking is expected. A study (Belcher, 1975) which examined scores on a creativity test found that students either in a game-like environment or in a stressful situation produced lower scores than did students who had been encouraged to do well as in a normal test situation. In checking the creativity test gains of elementary classroom pupils, Wodtke and Wallen (1965) studied seventy-seven female teachers' methods of classroom control. Some of these teachers preferred a highly ordered and controlled classroom and could not tolerate behavior of youngsters that did not fit into the pattern of order and control. It was found that a high degree of control by the classroom teacher had a detrimental effect on verbal creativity.

A work of art is not the representation of a thing but rather the representation of the experiences we have with that thing. Because experiences will change not only from year to year but from day to day, art expression becomes a dynamic, ever-changing process. The teacher, too, must be a flexible person, able to revise plans and to capitalize upon the enthusiasm and interest of the children. When the teacher is accessible and democratic in nature, youngsters can express themselves freely, both in words and in artistic expression; but it also is vital that the teacher be able to provide the flexible format so that the expression can be formed into an art product. To some extent this becomes a two-way exchange. Not only is the supportive atmosphere necessary, but flexible channeling of the youngster's feelings, ideas, and perceptions must culminate in an artistic form for the process to be meaningful.

Art must be important for the artist. This is obvious at the adult level, but it is also true for children. The youngster must feel that what he is doing is important and that this activity is relevant to his needs. It may be difficult for a teacher to realize and then to face a discrepancy between his own way of thinking and that of his pupils. What can be an exciting experience and a learning situation for an adult might not be appropriate for children's needs. The

Identifying with the Child

Figure 67.

Most nursery school children enjoy scribbling and consider art activities to be one of the good things about going to nursery school.

teacher, therefore, must be able to identify with those students with whom he is working. It is important that art activity be theirs and not the teacher's.

A child who shows signs of inhibitions in art or lacks the self-confidence for his own expression cannot be helped by a teacher who limits himself to instruction in the use of art materials, or in the problems of space relationships or color harmony. For example, a three or four year old who is afraid of becoming involved in scribbling may just put a few lines down in the corner of the page. Telling him to draw larger will not be of much value, even if accompanied by threats such as, "You may flunk nursery school if you do not draw larger." Instead, the teacher needs to identify with this child in such a way that the teacher too can feel the big blank piece of paper as a threat.

The scribbling must become meaningful, and in this case one could ask the child, "Suppose you were in a big empty room. Would you stand in just one corner or would you run all around the room? No one is there and you can do what you like. Wouldn't it be fun to run all the way to one side of the room and then to run back to the other? Now, look, here is a red crayon and suppose this sheet of paper is a great big empty room, how do you suppose the red crayon will act? Do you think the red crayon will just sit quietly in the corner? I don't think so either. Let's see how the red crayon runs around the paper." The tiny motions would thus become enlarged meaningfully because the reason for the large motion would become important. Few children could avoid the temptation of making large strokes all over the paper.

Although this may be an example that is obvious on the scribbling level, identification with the youngster and the problems that he is facing is necessary at any level. A fourth grader who says he cannot draw himself throwing a ball does not need the mechanics of figure drawing or an example that the teacher might make for him to copy, which could even widen the gap between his experience and his ability to express it. He needs an understanding of his own experience: "Show me how you throw a ball. What did you do with your arms, your legs? Let's try it again. Now you threw it up high. What did you do with your hands? Where did you look? Now throw the ball to me again." Such questions, interspersed with a friendly exchange of comments, should develop in the youngster confidence to express these experiences, and the urge for such expression will be strong enough to overcome his lack of confidence.

It is also important for the teacher of art to identify with the youngsters who are successful in their achievement and who can express themselves easily. It is more important to recognize and share this joy of expression and pride in accomplishment than it is to point out that there are some corrections needed in proportion or that the hand has six fingers instead of five. The prod-

148

uct is important for the child while he is drawing. One teacher was observed who told her second grade charges that the drawings would not be saved on this particular day, and that they should throw their papers in the wastebasket on the way out. Obviously this teacher did not identify with these children, and it must be confessed that this observer felt that the attendance sheet she had been working on ought to join the youngsters' drawings in the wastebasket. The self-identification of a youngster with his own work can be a valuable experience, especially when the teacher can identify with his pupils so as to provide the proper motivation and environmental conditions for meaningful expression.

Identifying with the Medium

A teacher who has never experienced the qualities of wood, who has never run his fingers over the grain or sanded a board to a smooth finish, a teacher who has never been frustrated with the splintering of wood or been pleased with a joint well made will never be able to motivate and inspire the youth who has failed to solve a poorly conceived problem in working with wood. To think in terms of the material is an important part of the creative process, especially during the adolescent years. A teacher who has never gone through the process of creating in a specific art material may never understand the particular type of thinking that is necessary to work with clay, paint, or whatever. The teacher must have been truly involved in *creating* with materials, not in dealing with them in an abstract way by reading or mechanically carrying out some project.

This does not imply that the elementary school teacher needs to be an artist. But a teacher of children should have been involved in real creative experiences and competent in some area of expression. In some cases the introduction of new material can be worked through with the teacher himself becoming involved in the activity. However, as the child grows, the final product becomes increasingly important to him, and with the increased emphasis being placed on the product itself, thinking in terms of art materials becomes an integral part of the teaching process. It then becomes impossible for a teacher who has never gone through the experience in a specific material to understand the significance of thinking in terms of that material, whether it is wood, clay, pencil, paint, plastic, or any other medium.

An artist might seem to be the most logical person to teach art. It would be simpler if we said that a painter should teach painting, since art encompasses a great number of vocational areas. Most painters are striving to make some sense out of what they have experienced; that is, they try to put some feelings or emotions into a new configuration or try to place some visual matter in a pleasing, or in some cases a shocking, relationship. Each artist has his own point of reference and because of this we find that each artist paints in quite a different way. It is probably true that some artists are striving for recognition and tend to follow any current fad, even if this means making hamburgers out of an old pair of pants, or taking one's bookshelf and painting it gold. However, the artist is supposedly attempting to make sense out of our strange, diverse, confusing, and contradictory world.

Now this sounds surprisingly like what the child is doing in the elementary school. He too is using himself as a reference point for his artistic creation. He too is trying to make some sense out of his own environment and is putting things into relationships. Essentially, then, the child painter and the adult painter are both striving for the same goals, the main difference being that each has his own reference point, and his own experiences to draw upon.

Since there is no body of factual knowledge in art necessary for the child to learn and retain, a painter's technical knowledge is not needed in the elementary school. At the secondary school level this technical knowledge could be valuable. There may be some point in saying that a competent painter might help throw out some of the tricks and busy work that are often called art. Looking at what galleries are presently exhibiting, the painter would probably cherish and support the spontaneous, free expression of children and look down upon triteness and repetition. However, what might seem spontaneous and free painting by young children might just as easily be random exploration, and as a child grows older he develops a real need for order and repetition, which is reflected in his drawings and paintings. This decrease of spontaneity is actually a step toward the development of abstract thinking, an important factor in creativity. Therefore, a classroom teacher might seem better equipped than an artist to understand the developmental differences. But the education and training of the usual elementary school teacher does not include a real understanding of children's art as a prerequisite to receiving an education degree. In fact, an understanding of the normal development of children's art is often sadly neglected. Instead, a new teacher may have several projects up his sleeve for every occasion: Thanksgiving, Christmas, Easter, Mother's Day, or Friday afternoons when he and the children are both tired— projects that may have no relation to live, thinking, feeling children.

Whether or not a person working with young children calls himself an artist or a teacher may be incidental. An artist may be autocratic, know what is important to teach, and be sure what the paintings of children should look like. An elementary school teacher may be like this too. What is needed instead is an artist or teacher who is warm, friendly, and democratic, someone who wants to help children develop their own concepts, is genuinely interested in what children paint, and has no preconceived notions of what each product should be like. The focus should be on developing the sensitive, aware child. Art can be thought of as a continual process of creativity, because each youngster works at his own level to produce a new form with a unique organization, with countless minor problems of adapting subject matter to two- and three-dimensional surfaces. It is possible to maximize the opportunities for creative thinking in art experiences, and this opportunity should be a planned part of each art activity.

Art has a greater potential in the development of children than is now accorded to it. Until we can shake loose from tradition, until we can stop giving approval to what we, as adults, would like to do, until we can shake ourselves out of the grasp of habit and the status quo, we shall assign a meaningless role to art education in the elementary school.

Figure 68.
Each child should be given the opportunity to paint his own ideas and feelings. It is the child himself who is the basis of art expression.

Motivation in the Classroom

The urge and excitement that children can bring to an art activity is dependent to a great degree upon their motivation. This motivation may come from several sources. A natural drive for expression can be seen in children when they are filled with enthusiasm for a particular topic. At other times it falls upon the shoulders of the classroom teacher to stimulate the interests of the children and to provide such a motivational framework that each child can believe that the art experience was designed especially for him.

It would be quite impossible to say that any one approach to motivation is good for all children. At some times it might be best to have the children divided into interest groups or working on small projects; at another time the children might work with a variety of different materials but on one topic; at another time, children might be working individually on a variety of topics. The method depends upon individual needs, and a sensitive teacher should know when these differences are important. First grade youngsters often have group experiences, such as visiting a fire station, which may excite a whole class so that everyone wants to put down on paper his reactions to such an experience. However, even here some individuals will become involved in particular parts of this experience. Some children may be excited about the big fire truck, others about the size of the wheels, length of the hose, the sleeping arrangement, or the pole that is used to slide down to the waiting truck. Although group motivations can be used effectively, it is still the individual's mode of expression that is important.

Figure 69.

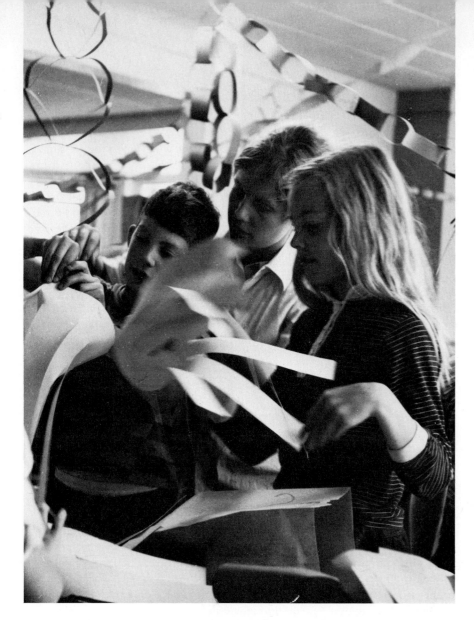

These youngsters have become enthusiastic over the project of decorating the room for a party. Sometimes such art activities can be the most important thing that happens in school.

At times the motivation within the classroom can develop an enthusiasm that becomes contagious. Occasionally fifth grade youngsters can develop such enthusiasm over a group project that it seems like the most important event in the world. Probably a variety of approaches best insures that each youngster is free to use his own mode of expression and at the same time to reject a suggestion if he already is motivated in another direction. The purpose is to translate the motivation into meaningful, purposeful creative activity, not to force a particular topic upon him.

The principle of extending the frame of reference constitutes an important learning device in education. Basically, the principle is to start where the youngster is and extend his thinking, feeling, and perceiving one step farther. This provides the opportunity for an expansion of possible directions in which he can move and which would be a logical extension of his own thinking. If, for instance, a kindergarten boy has drawn a picture of his mother and, as is usual, shown this off with pride, it is possible to extend his thinking into the environment in which the mother might find herself. "Where is your mother? Is she all alone? What is she doing?" Needless to say, such questions are aimed at enlarging the experience that the youngster has with the subject matter and are presented with warmth and interest in what has been accomplished. All relationships with youngsters should be supportive.

At times it seems as if a child becomes inflexible in his drawings, repeating a symbol without much alteration. This symbol may be of something which has particular appeal or is envied. A fourth grade boy might seem to draw just impersonal, generalized trucks. "Stop drawing those silly trucks" will not help; rather, it will show Johnny that the teacher is not interested in what he is drawing, or the skill he has developed, or (by inference) him. Instead, it is better to start where Johnny is and to extend his frame of reference.

"What kind of truck is that? Is it carrying a load? How many axles does it have? Are the tires big? Where is it going?" Sometimes this will be more than enough to stimulate Johnny's thinking, so that the truck symbol takes on the meaning of a particular truck, with a special cargo, driving to a definite destination, on a certain road. However, if this seems to be insufficient, it may be necessary to find other reasons why he draws trucks. The teacher should identify with Johnny. The truck then becomes the important focal point of a discussion. Does his father drive a truck? Or an uncle? Has he seen a truck like that, and would he like to drive one himself? Would he enjoy climbing into the pick-up truck that the vice-principal owns, or sitting behind the wheel of the district's dump truck? Has he counted the lights on the top, or the number of lugs that hold the wheels on? Does he know whether the truck burns diesel fuel, or how much horsepower it has? A genuine interest in trucks may spark a good deal of discussion, and the adult may learn much about trucks.

To some extent every drawing or painting becomes a natural means of the youngster's extending his own frame of reference. The elements in a drawing tend to be additive, that is, they provide an extension of thinking to related objects which are then combined into a new form. The drawing of a person can often extend into the drawing of the ground, trees, houses, roads, and so forth. It is this relatedness that can sometimes lead youngsters to continue their

drawings on the reverse side of the page as though the paper were continuous but folded. It should be mentioned that a child ought to be in a position to reject any adult effort to get him to include a greater number and variety of objects in his drawing or painting. Every child does not have to be totally involved in every drawing, but every child should sometimes be totally involved in some drawings. We will discuss later how to involve the child who seems continually uninterested in art activities, for it may be this child who most needs the motivation of the teacher.

Motivation and Development

A teacher must know the child whom he is trying to motivate. There are certain characteristics of each age that make it different from any other. Not only is it important to realize that what may be an exciting art material for the twelve year old can be a confusing material for the scribbler, but it is also important to realize that at each stage of development the youngster actually has a different relationship to his environment. The interest that a high school

ART IN THE ELEMENTARY SCHOOL

Figure 70. *(opposite)*
This picture of heavy machinery was drawn by a boy who obviously took a great deal of interest in the mechanical details of the equipment.

youngster may have in the structural design of a building will not be shared by a first grade youngster even though this topic is of interest to his teacher. The pleasure that a junior high school youngster derives from making a poster protesting new dress regulations in his school will obviously not be shared by a third grade boy who gets great pleasure from close examination of a caterpillar. To identify with the needs of a particular youngster may not always be easy, but it is important that the teacher subordinate himself and his desires to the needs of the children with whom he is working.

A child who is scribbling at the age of four may begin to name some of the parts of his picture, relating them to objects outside himself. Lines may move up and down across the page and the child may identify this as a dog running. The youngster has made a big discovery: that the motions of running are similar to the up-and-down line that he can see on the page. A sensitive and aware teacher must understand that this can be a satisfying experience, identify

Figure 71.
We cannot expect every child to be thoroughly engrossed in every art activity; however, every child should occasionally be totally involved in some art experience.

himself with the youngster, and share in the discovery. This line is of kines-thetic origin and it would be ridiculous for the teacher to try to motivate the child with visual imagery. To talk about a dog in visual terms, discussing his color and size and the proportion of the head to the body, would be meaning-less. The well-intentioned teacher may seize upon this discovery as a chance to show the child pictures and illustrations of dogs, and may even try to point out the differences between breeds of dogs. But this will all be wasted effort be-cause the teacher has not made himself acquainted with the physical and psy-chological needs of the child.

Not only is it necessary for the teacher to identify with the general needs of a youngster, but he must also be able to discover the specific needs of a par-ticular individual. He may find out that one child lacks freedom in his motions and feels inhibited in his motor activity. Another child may appear particularly timid and fearful of using materials. Still another child may have a very short attention span and never get truly involved in the art process. It is important that the child's general as well as specific needs are understood, for without this background the teacher may never really reach the child with his motivation.

Motivation and the Insecure Child

Most of the children in our classrooms are free and willing to express them-selves in art activities. Occasionally, however, we find a child who is so inse-cure that he has a fear of even putting a line on paper unless it is given prior approval by the teacher. These children often express the feeling that they cannot draw, or that they do not know how to do it; often they want the teacher to show them how or to draw something for them. Obviously, these are the children who need the art experience the most; to ignore this plea for help or simply to say that the youngster really *can* draw is no motivation what-ever. If a child says to the teacher that he cannot bring himself to express his feelings or emotions on paper, it is obvious that this is a statement which should not be contradicted. There may be children who feel at a loss unless they are given clear guidance and direction. This reliance upon adults can in some instances have a very negative influence upon the youngster's thinking; in other cases the child may have been rebuffed in his own attempts at self-direction and may retreat into a world in which his sensitivities and emotions will not be hurt further.

There are instances of children who are overwhelmed by the school situ-ation. One second grade boy was reluctant to draw, and his teacher loudly explained that there was no point in expecting any art work from him. With encouragement, he did produce a timid drawing. Yet later, out of the class-room, this quiet child was extremely verbal and expressed great enthusiasm for his drawing. The school environment was a problem for this youngster, and this seeming inability to draw was reflecting his insecurity.

Sometimes a child will have difficulty in identifying with what he does. Usually such a child laughs nervously and self-consciously about his own products, for he is continually dissatisfied with his achievement. He has to please others. His own experience is less important to him than the product. The final product is only the result of the process, which is a complex learning experience that brings together the thinking, emotional, and perceptual processes resulting from preceding experiences. If the child cannot identify with his own experiences, the final product will show this.

A third grade boy who says, "I can't draw" knows he cannot draw. "What can't you draw?" Perhaps he cannot draw a camel because he has never seen one, which would be quite understandable. But often the problem is deeper than that. "What do you want to draw?" If this third grade youngster says that he does not want to draw anything, then the teacher must find out what experience has been meaningful to him, or in some cases sensitize him to experiences he has had so that these can become meaningful. "What did you do yesterday?" The problem is one of making the youngster more actively aware of himself as a part of the environment, and of stimulating this awareness. Some youngsters actually feel that they have done nothing interesting and can go through life partially sealed off from the outside world.

"What did you do yesterday? Did you just stand up all day? What did you do? Remember, remember exactly where you were yesterday afternoon. Oh, you had to work around the house. What did you do? Oh, you helped wash the car. Was your father with you?" Now here is something definite to talk about. The child has indeed had some experiences that you can discuss and share. Although to the child this may be just another boring day, the washing of the car can be a focal point for a discussion that needs to be carried on with warmth and interest on the part of the teacher. It is important that all of the senses be involved in such a discussion so that the youngster can relive the experience in even more detail than he experienced this originally. "Did you take the car to one of those car wash places? Oh, you washed it at home. Was it very dirty? Did you use a hose? Oh, you used a bucket and a sponge. Was the water cold? Did you get yourself wet? Was the car so dirty that you had to change the water? Did you draw any pictures on the dirt before you washed it? Did your hands get all puffy from the water? Did your back ache when you were through? Did you have to change your clothes after it was finished? Let me see your hands. I can see that your fingernails are clean; you must have gotten them well soaked. Did your father do very much? Did the bucket of water spill? Were your feet cold when they got wet? Did the car look better when you were finished?"

The particular motivation will vary depending upon the age of the child. Sometimes with young children it is a help to have them go through the motions of how they washed the wheel covers. The older child will be able to identify more with the father and share with him the pride of having a clean car. In any case, it is important to make this motivation meaningful to the youngster himself and to stimulate the sensory experiences, what he has seen and felt, as well as stressing his own contributions to the activity.

Although we do not have many very insecure children in our classrooms, it is of vital importance that children who are completely bound up in them-

Figure 72.

The teacher is an important element in children's creative expression, providing motivation and encouragement. Creative expression cannot be dictated in an aloof manner by an uninvolved adult.

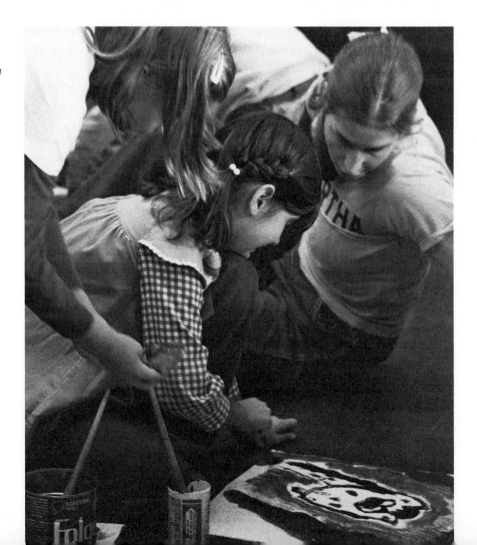

selves and have difficuly interacting in any meaningful way with their environment be given special attention in art. This is one area of the school program that can truly be based upon the youngster's own experiences, and any motivation should be of such a nature that it provides the opportunity for flexible, meaningful growth.

Numerous experiments have been done to assess the effectiveness of various motivational methods upon children's drawings. There is no doubt that the intensity and personal involvement of the motivation plays a most important part in the quality of an art product (McVitty, 1954; Lansing, 1956; Clements, 1964). To a great extent there is a parallel development between the quality of experience that the youngster is trying to portray and the quality of the final product. The higher the quality of the one, the higher the quality of the other. The motivation is a vital element in this process.

Integrated Learning Experiences

Too often within the school learning program, experiences are isolated. At 9:27 the arithmetic books come out, at 10:14 it is time for recess, at 10:33 the music teacher arrives, at 11:05 it is social studies time. This fragmentation of the learning process into isolated segments creates an artificial situation. A child does not grow in single subject matter areas, nor does each area remain isolated in life outside school. This early specialization has isolated some of the subject matter areas from life to such a degree that the subjects have lost contact with society. We can even see this at the upper levels of education, where there is great discrepancy between social and scientific achievement.

Sometimes art is used in an attempt to correct this difficulty, usually with superficial results. Integration in learning means that the single subjects lose their identity and form a new unit within the student. Teachers often think that if history is illustrated, an integration between these two subjects takes place. This is sometimes referred to as correlation, as, for instance, where the students may be studying the American Indian in social studies and drawing wigwams in art. Sometimes this is successful. When third graders draw a picture before they are instructed to write something they produce an increased amount of work (Cecere, 1966). All too often, however, an injustice is done to both areas. After an extensive survey of studies of the relationship between art and reading, Groff (1978) concluded that there is no experimental evidence to support some teachers' enthusiasm for the idea that including art in the program helps children learn to read. Because art is usually looked upon by the child as an attractive experience, and some of the social studies, arithmetic, or writing exercises are less favorably viewed, the correlation of these subject matter areas with art may have a negative value for the art experience. It is a little like mixing medicine with orange juice—both can be rejected.

It is possible that an integrated experience can develop in a school setting, but the separate parts must lose their identity and the individual child must feel that there is a meaningful whole with which he can identify. Integration occurs within the individual. The child is influenced by his emotional responses and perceptual sensory experiences. If the youngster can become totally involved in the learning process, then real integration takes place.

For example, history is often taught only in terms of dates and events. The Pilgrims landed in 1620. Plymouth Rock is somehow important in the event, and a ship called the *Mayflower* was there, too. A request for children to draw this event is a meaningless activity. On the other hand, if children can empathize with the experience itself and focus upon this involvement, the activity may be a meaningful one.

"Have you ever been on a boat? On what kind of a boat? Were you ever in rough water? How did it feel? Do you know how big the *Mayflower* was? That's really pretty small! Did you realize that they had to come all that distance by relying on sails? How many sails were there? Do you know what happens when it is windy? The boat tilts way over and where do you go? Yes, all the people have to go to the other side! Do you get wet? Do you think you would like to stay down below deck? Do you know how long the Pilgrims were on this little sailing ship? That's a long time! Just suppose you had been on that ship all that time! Then you finally see land! Is everyone anxious to get off the ship? Are there any docks built? Oh, you have to get into a little rowboat! How do you go over the side? Hold on, don't slip on the way down! We still have to row to shore! Stay all together! What shall we do when we first land? Build a fire? So we can all keep warm!"

The children must feel the air and the waves, and even taste the salt on their lips. The experience must be *their* experience. The Pilgrims are no longer figures marching across the pages of the history book, but are recreated in the child's own experience. The picture that may result from such an experience can be anything that is of particular interest to the child. It may be the motion of the ship itself, with lines going up and down, or it may be the portrayal of an incident with which the child particularly identifies. Meaningful integration

Figure 73.
The Pilgrims would never recognize this child's interpretation of the Mayflower, complete with engine room, refrigerator, and bathroom.

occurs in the youngster through such a motivation in which an atmosphere is created that is conducive to self-identification and self-involvement. To have the child involved in the learning process and to make these isolated subject matter segments important to him must be an important goal for the teacher. The art experiences that the youngster has had can provide the means of accomplishing this. To some extent, then, art can be the core of the learning environment within the school. Integrated learning does not happen by merely shuffling subject matter around—such integration can take place only within the child himself.

Probably no child has ever failed a grade because of his poor marks in art. One often finds, however, that marks are required in art for report cards at various times. These report cards may take many forms, such as a letter to parents; at

**Grading
the Child's Art**

other times the grade is actually a numerical score, which is supposed to show the percentage of achievement in art. The usual practice is to use some sort of external standard, but this deals only with the product and completely neglects the individual child or the effect that the creative process has had on him. At the high school, each project may be graded and the teacher goes through the process of averaging the grades, which may make it sound somewhat more objective.

This is probably not the place to question the value of giving any grades at all to children, but it is important to state that grading in art has no function. This is particularly true in the elementary school, where the youngster has no conscious awareness of making art in any manner other than that which is natural to him. At this level it would make more sense to grade the teacher, for it is the teacher who has been able to motivate the children to do excellent work, or has not been able to motivate some youngsters, or who may have failed to involve a few youngsters at all in the art activities.

Unfortunately, many teachers do try to grade art, which throws added importance upon the end product. This is harmful to the child because it turns his attention away from creating, to concern for the picture itself. It can be particularly discouraging for a youngster who is beginning to find himself in his creative activity if he fails in the art work that he has been doing.

Often the teacher puts a high mark on the works of art that he himself enjoys, and will grade other works of art lower on the same arbitrary basis. Neatness and fine line control are frequently important in such a grading system, so that the youngster who paints more freely and who is bolder in his drawing tends to be penalized. Sometimes, of course, a teacher who is very aware of trends in contemporary art may reward children who accidentally produce the type of art that is currently in vogue. Both methods are equally meaningless to the child.

The evaluation of an art product can take many forms. Sometimes it is a display of the so-called best pictures; or perhaps each picture or drawing will receive a reward: a letter grade, a gold star, or a written commendation. Whatever the form, these rewards disrupt the learning process. In a survey of studies related to reward and extrinsic incentives, Condry (1977) found ample evidence that offering rewards reduces efficiency and diminishes interest in a project. He concludes that such rewards, even for children as young as five, undermine self-confidence, for in such cases the ". . . activity is of a lower quality, contains more errors, and is more stereotyped and less creative than the work of comparable nonrewarded subjects working on the same problems." Even a group of female college students working under conditions of external evaluation were found to produce less creative art than a comparable group working without such evaluation (Amabile, 1979).

There should be one place in the school system where marks do not count. The art room should be a sanctuary against school regulations, where each youngster is free to be himself and to put down his feelings and emotions without censorship, where he can evaluate his own progress toward his own goals without the imposition of an arbitrary grading system.

There is general agreement that coloring books are detrimental to children's creative expression. These books usually have an outline of some form or other, such as a cow, or a dog, or a complete landscape. The youngster is supposed to color within the lines and some youngsters seem to enjoy this activity. This enjoyment may be because these youngsters do not have to think for themselves. The dependency upon someone else's outline of an object makes the child much less confident in his own means of expression. He obviously cannot draw a cow as good as the one in the coloring book. Parents, however, are becoming much more aware of these problems, and often blank pages can be purchased in tablet form for youngsters to use. The lines that a child makes himself are more meaningful, and children who mark all over a coloring book do not do the same type of marking over their own drawings.

We can decry the use of coloring books for children, but some of the same objections can be raised to the paint-by-the-number kits that adults use. Just as a poem can be copied without understanding the message, the rhythm, or the metaphor, painting a picture with a paint-by-the-number kit is an automatic procedure that merely reinforces one's own inabilities.

It may come as somewhat of a surprise to find that workbooks used in arithmetic often greatly resemble coloring books. One arithmetic book has a child draw 76 repetitions of a stereotyped rabbit, 88 repetitions of a bird, 62 of a kite, 80 of a balloon, and so forth. Such repetition is meaningless. A study by Heilman (1954) indicated how dependent some children can become upon these workbooks, for the data revealed that the general growth pattern through creative work was seriously influenced by these workbooks. However, Daniel (1958) compared drawings by 90 children whose parents said they were frequent users of coloring books, to drawings from 90 children who never or rarely used coloring books; he found that the quality of the drawings seemed more affected by the mental age of the child and by his socioeconomic level than by coloring book usage. Possibly parents who value art experiences are buying coloring books for their children, whereas those parents who do not feel that art is important are not; this can confuse the findings. In some

Workbooks and Coloring Books

Figure 74.
Coloring books affect a child's creative expression. (Courtesy of Dr. Irene Russell, Research Bulletin, The Eastern Arts Association, *Vol. 3, No. 1, 1952.)*
(Top) This bird shows one child's expression before he was exposed to coloring books.
(Center) Then the child had to color a workbook illustration.
(Bottom) After coloring the workbook birds, the child has lost his creative sensitivity and self-reliance.

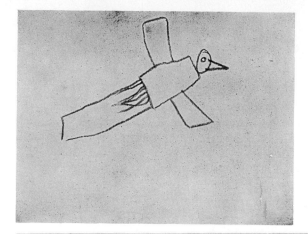

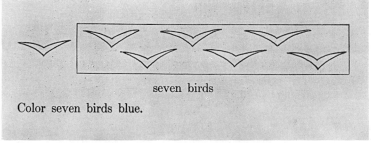

seven birds

Color seven birds blue.

experiments conducted by Russell and Waugaman (1952), 63 percent of all children who had been exposed to coloring book birds lost their original concept of bird and changed their drawings to resemble the workbook stereotype.

Often the excuse is given that these workbook exercises are fundamental to learning arithmetic concepts or to developing recognition of a letter. However, a thesis by Johnson (1963) indicated that tracing over a letter up to ten

ART IN THE ELEMENTARY SCHOOL

times was of no value in recognizing that letter later. There is no evidence that these laboriously colored balloons and kites actually help to develop either number concepts or reading abilities. Although no one will admit it, one of the main reasons for using these workbooks may well be that they give the classroom teacher a chance to have some rest while the youngsters fill in the appropriate number of birds or color the proper kites green.

Surprisingly enough, dittoed sheets are still occasionally handed out for youngsters to color that may have silhouettes of George Washington, a Thanksgiving turkey, a Halloween pumpkin, an Easter rabbit, or a Christmas tree outlined on them for the children to color in. One particular example showed Pilgrims standing in front of their log cabin holding blunderbusses which had not been invented yet; actually Pilgrims lived in huts made of sticks and vines until they built clapboard houses, because "Neither the English nor the Dutch built log cabins at first, and apparently did not even know how to do so. . . ."(Stewart, 1954, p. 152). Sometimes art projects also smack of the same absurdities, as when youngsters are given copper foil to press over some preformed design to mount for Christmas presents. Even May baskets preplanned by the teacher for the first grade youngsters to cut out fall into the category of being detrimental to creative expression.

Art instruction that includes these kinds of activities is worse than no art at all. Such predigested activities force youngsters into imitative behavior and inhibit their own creative expression. These activities make no provision for emotional growth because any variation the child makes can only be a mistake; they do not promote skills, because skills develop from one's own expression. Instead, they condition the child to accept adult concepts as art, art that the child is unable to produce, therefore frustrating his own creative urges.

Exhibits in the classroom are usually held for the children. A youngster enjoys seeing his own work displayed, and for some children this becomes particularly important. The child who is not able to achieve in other ways can see himself as a member of the class in good standing when his art products are displayed with everyone else's. Generally, the work to be displayed should be selected by the child himself and hung at his cyc level. The preparation for an exhibit can often be an exciting occasion, and when properly guided, children can take over most of the work of hanging the pictures. Classroom exhibits should be frequently changed, for a youngster quickly loses the intimate relationship to his own work, and it is senseless to display work that was done weeks or even months earlier.

An exhibit for parents may be a different problem. Here the reason for

**Exhibits
and Competitions**

Figure 75.
The stimulation children receive from one another can contribute to a creative atmosphere. This sharing of thoughts and enthusiasm is quite different from copying from one another.

the exhibit should be clear. Often the purpose is to educate the viewer rather than to display pictures for parents to admire. It is possible to combine these two functions, but such exhibits take a good deal of planning. Often carefully lettered signs help in conveying the message; a carefully labeled exhibit will be able to explain itself. It is better to have a small exhibit stressing one theme such as individual differences, the variety in expression of a particular topic, or a sequence of drawings showing changes in development, than to have an exhibit that is too large to be easily seen and that may be too hastily put together.

Competition in art is of two types. Natural competition is inherent in every classroom situation, where a youngster has a natural desire to improve upon his own achievements. Forced competition is usually imposed upon a class or group of children, and prizes are often given as rewards. Growth is a continuous competition with one's own standards and achievements, and this is a most natural and healthy form of competition. Children in the lower elementary grades are usually unaware of any competition in art, for their drawings and paintings are merely a means of expression. Each child differs from his classmates, and usually there is no feeling that one drawing or painting is better than another. The situation changes somewhat as the child grows older and as the final product becomes more and more important. In the upper grades of the elementary school the stimulation children receive from each other's creative work is a valuable contribution to their own flexibility. The youngster is usually exposed to many different styles and modes of expression. These he can evaluate in terms of his own experiences, and reject or adapt them as he chooses. Such natural competition is not based on standards outside the youngster himself. This sharing of ideas is not to be confused with a copying of forms by the insecure child, where the problem is quite different because the youngster is copying a configuration without any understanding of the process behind it.

Occasionally forced competition is unwittingly brought into the classroom. Sometimes the teacher himself may state that the best pictures will be saved for an exhibit, or the local P.T.A. or Chamber of Commerce will offer a prize in a good-hearted manner to the best picture illustrating how our town can be made more beautiful. Michael (1959) found in an experiment with high school art students that giving a prize for the best painting significantly decreased the aesthetic quality of students' work. A judge of an annual competition of children's art said that each year some children copied the winner of the preceding year in the hope that they would be awarded a prize too. This type of competition is bad for the winner and the loser. The losers know that they do not have the artistic ability to achieve and they therefore lose interest in art expression. The winner has achieved recognition in art and therefore loses the incentive to investigate and explore other means of art expression. Of course, there was the case of the child who could not understand why his picture was entered in the competition, because he did not think it was as good as he wished it were; it was even harder for him to understand why he was awarded a prize. Some schools pride themselves on the number of prizes their students have won in various art exhibits. The results tend to be superficial, with a stress on techniques and an overemphasis on outcome. All this overpowers serious involvement by the child with his own creative experiences. No jury can take into consideration the meaningfulness of an art work to its creator. Even on the adult level the winner of a competition may not be looked upon as a great artist ten years later. Such forced competition has no place in our school system.

Child art is highly individual. No two children express themselves entirely alike. One of the vital aims of art education is to bring out the individual differences that make up each child's personality. To suppress these individual differences, to emphasize the final product, to reward one youngster over another, goes against the basic premises of creative expression.

RELATED ACTIVITIES

1   Collect the drawings from an elementary school class. Ask a classroom teacher, an art teacher, a college student, and a child to grade these drawings, as for a report card. Ask how these judges determined the best and poorest. How do the various ratings compare? Which, if any, seems to be the most valid approach?

2   Plan and display an exhibit of the children's art work with a definite purpose. Organize the exhibit so that it presents a feeling of unity. Identify and label the specific age, grade level, medium, and subject matter or motivation.

3   Observe two separate classrooms of the same grade. Predict on the basis of the teachers' interest and enthusiasm in art activities how the products will differ. Collect drawings from these classrooms on two occasions and compare. Note differences in amount of detail, color use, amount of action indicated, and extent to which the total area of the page is used.

4   Make a survey to determine what competitions are presently being sponsored in a local school in music, art, and so forth. Gather information from teachers and students and discuss the effects of these competitions upon the classroom behavior, the time consumed, and the results of the competitions.

5   Check to find an elementary school that divides its classes according to achievement levels. Compare the drawings of the children in the "fast" classes with those in the "slow" classes. Are there any differences in method of representation? In the number of details used?

6   Pick out one child who does not appear gifted in art. Over a period of several months give special attention to his art performances. Show an interest in his products, encourage him, praise changes in his expression, exhibit his paintings, show him you enjoy what and how he draws, give him confidence to explore new materials, ask him if he would like to be an artist. After the experimental period is over compare his products with those done previously. Do you still consider him not particularly gifted?

The Beginnings of Self-expression

6

The Scribbling Stage
Two–Four Years

The Importance
of Early Childhood

The first few years of life are the most vital in a child's development. During this period, learning patterns, attitudes, and a sense of self begin to be established. Art can contribute a tremendous amount to this development, for it is in the interaction between the child and his environment that learning takes place. Although we usually think of art as starting with the first mark that a child puts down on paper, it actually begins much earlier when the senses first contact the environment and the child reacts to these sensory experiences. Touching, feeling, seeing, manipulating, tasting, listening, in fact any method of perceiving and reacting to the environment is essentially background for the production of art forms, whether it is on a child's level or on that of a professional artist.

Although the child expresses himself vocally very early in life, his first permanent record usually takes the form of a scribble at about the age of eighteen months or so. This first mark is an important step in his development, for it is the beginning of expression which leads not only to drawing and painting but also to the written word. It is unfortunate that the very word "scribble" has negative connotations for adults. The word may suggest a waste of time or at least a lack of content. Actually the very opposite is true, for the way in which these first marks are received and the attention that is paid to them may cause a young child to develop attitudes that will remain with him as he starts formal schooling.

The Development of Scribbling

Scribbles tend to follow a fairly predictable order. They start with random marks on a paper and gradually evolve into drawings that have content recognizable to adults. But between the ages of about eighteen months and about four years, when the first visual image appears, a great deal of development takes place. It is rather surprising, therefore, to find that only recently has much research been done on these early drawing attempts. Generally speaking, scribbles fall into three main categories. These are disordered scribbles, controlled scribbles, and named scribbles.

Figure 77. (*Opposite*)

For a nursery school girl, art is a purposeful activity. She is painting masses of color, with no representational intent.

Disordered Scribbling

The first marks are usually random. They vary in length and direction, although there may be some repetition as the child swings her arm back and forth. Often a child may look away while making these marks, and still continue scribbling. The line quality often varies considerably, with somewhat accidental results. A typical disordered scribble is shown in Figure 78. Various methods are used to hold the crayon or pencil. The crayon may be held upside down or sideways, it may be grasped in the fist or held between clenched fingers. The fingers and wrist are not used to control the drawing instrument. It is important to realize that the size of the motions shown on the paper is relative to the size of the child. If an adult swung his arm back and forth, he would cover an arc of about three feet; a child would tend to draw an arc only about twelve inches long. Because scribblers have not yet developed fine muscle control, usually only the larger sweeps will be repeated. We have to remember that the child scribbles with what are big motions for her, although to an adult the result may appear to be on a small scale.

It is important to mention that scribbles are not attempts at portraying the visual environment. To a great extent the scribbles themselves are based upon the physical and psychological development of the child, not upon some representational intent. Making the haphazard array of lines, however, is extremely enjoyable. A child will be fascinated with this activity. It is very important to have the opportunity to scribble. Sometimes scribbling will be done in the dirt, on the walls, or on furniture if the proper tools and place are not provided.

Parents may try to find something in these early scribbles that they can recognize, or sometimes a well-meaning grandparent will attempt to draw something for the child to copy. The two year old typically cannot copy a circle, although some two year olds are able to copy a line. So while a child is still in the stage of disordered scribbling, drawing a picture of something "real" is inconceivable. Such attempts would be similar to trying to teach a babbling baby to pronounce words correctly or to use them in sentences. A parent would not ask a babbling child to repeat the Gettysburg Address, even though this may become important to a child when he reaches fifth grade. The stick figure or apple drawn by an encouraging parent can be just as ridiculous. Such imposed ideas are far beyond the comprehension of a child at this developmental level and may even be harmful to his future development. However, an interest in what the child is doing is important, because the child has to feel that this avenue of communication is an acceptable one.

The child at this age has little visual control over his scribbling, which parents should regard as an indication that he is not yet ready to perform tasks

Figure 78.
In this disordered scribble, the pen has not been lifted from the paper. The child's repeated motions result in a record of a kinesthetic activity.

that require fine motor control over his movements. He is going to be a sloppy eater; he is going to have trouble with his buttons; and he will not be able to follow directions based on visual cues. As long as the child has not established visual control over his scribbling motions it is senseless to require him to have control over other activities.

A very young child may find a crayon more interesting to look at, feel, or even taste. However, the two year old usually has no such problems, and scrib-

THE BEGINNINGS OF SELF-EXPRESSION

bling activity quickly becomes a real means of expression. All children begin with scribbling, whether they are Chinese or Eskimos, Americans or Europeans. It is quite apparent that scribbling is a natural part of the total development of children which reflects their physiological and psychological growth.

At some time a child will discover that there is a connection between his motions and the marks on the paper. This may occur about six months or so after starting to scribble. This is a very important step, because now the child has discovered visual control over the marks he is making. Although a casual glance may show no difference in the drawings themselves, gaining control over the motion is an important accomplishment for the child.

Most children approach scribbling at this stage with a great deal of enthusiasm. When a child discovers the coordination between visual and motor activity, he is stimulated to vary his motions. Now the lines may be repeated, and sometimes they are drawn with a great deal of vigor. These lines may be drawn horizontally, vertically, or in circles. Occasionally we find dots or small repeated patterns, since the child is now able to take his crayons off the page. Children can become very engrossed in scribbling, as the girl is in Figure 79, sometimes with their noses practically glued to the paper.

The child will now spend about twice as long drawing and occasionally likes to try different colors on his paper. Also he often likes to fill the page, while earlier he even had trouble staying on the paper. He still experiments with a variety of methods of holding his crayon, though by the time he is three he usually comes close to an adult grip. He now understands more about trying to copy a line or a cross, but he will not refer to the model given him and usually strikes off in an unpredictable direction. By the age of three he can copy a circle but not a square. The scribblings now become much more elaborate and often the child will excitedly discover a relationship between what he has drawn and something in his environment. There may still be very little relationship between what he has drawn and a visual representation of the subject to which he refers.

This control over the scribble is also reflected in the child's control over other parts of his environment. The mother who, six months earlier, could not get this child to button his jacket now finds that he insists on doing it for himself. The child understands and enjoys practicing this new ability. The physical growth rate is very fast from one to three, a body image is developing, hand preferences are emerging, and the real integration of visual and motor apparatus is beginning, although this integration is not really complete until early adolescence (Cratty, 1970). Because control of motor abilities is an important

Figure 79.
Scribbling is a serious, meaningful activity for young children. Notice the determination and concentration that have gone into this drawing.

Plates 14 and 15.
"Scribble in Line" and "Scribble in Mass," painted by nursery school children. Enjoyment and exuberance in painting can be seen in the lines that record the child's arm movements over the whole paper; the large areas filled in with paint indicate a child's pleasure with color for its own sake. In neither case is representation attempted.

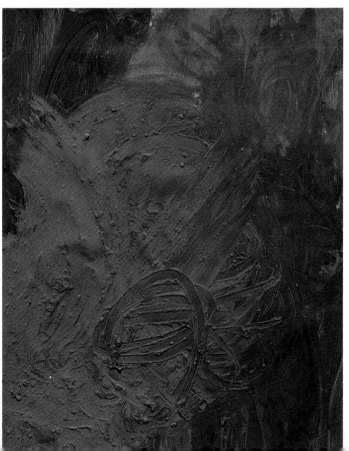

Plate 16.

"Cow," drawn by a four year old girl. A naturalistic representation is not important to the child; rather, this picture shows her concept of a cow. She has drawn the face as she would a human face. Her cow has a large number of legs, what appear to be horns, and a swishing tail.

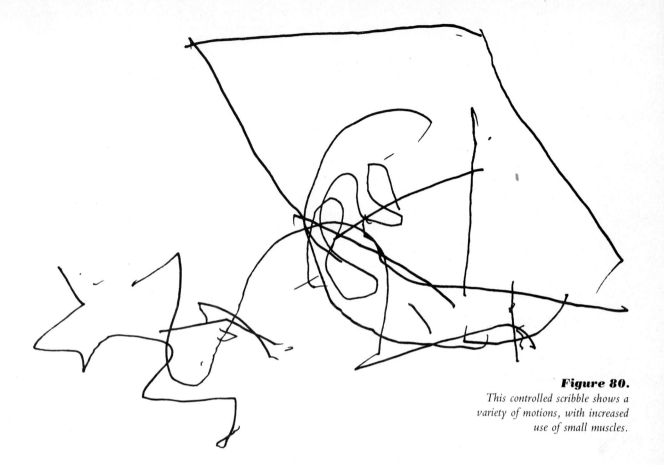

achievement, we can certainly understand that calling attention to some interesting patterns in a child's drawing would not be particularly helpful; at this stage the child's intentions do not go beyond the movement of the crayon, and enjoyment is essentially from the kinesthetic sensation and mastery.

The adult's role is increasingly important now, because children will often run to an adult with these scribbles, eager to share their excitement. It is this sharing of an experience that is important and not the scribble itself.

Naming of Scribbling

This next step is an important one in the development of children. This is the point when the child starts to name his scribbles. He may say, "This is mother," or "I am running," although neither mother nor himself may be recognized. This naming of scribbling is of great significance, for now the child's thinking has changed. Before this stage he was satisfied with marks that resulted from motions, but now he has connected these marks to the world around him, a change from kinesthetic thinking to imaginative thinking.

This next stage usually occurs at about the age of three and a half years. The importance of the change can be simply understood if we realize that, as adults, most of our thinking is in terms of mental pictures. If we try to think back as far as we can, our memory will not likely carry us further than this naming of scribbling stage. It is at this point, then, that the child develops a basis for visual retention.

As children begin to name their scribbles, an important transition takes place. The line becomes more than just the result of a motion, it becomes the

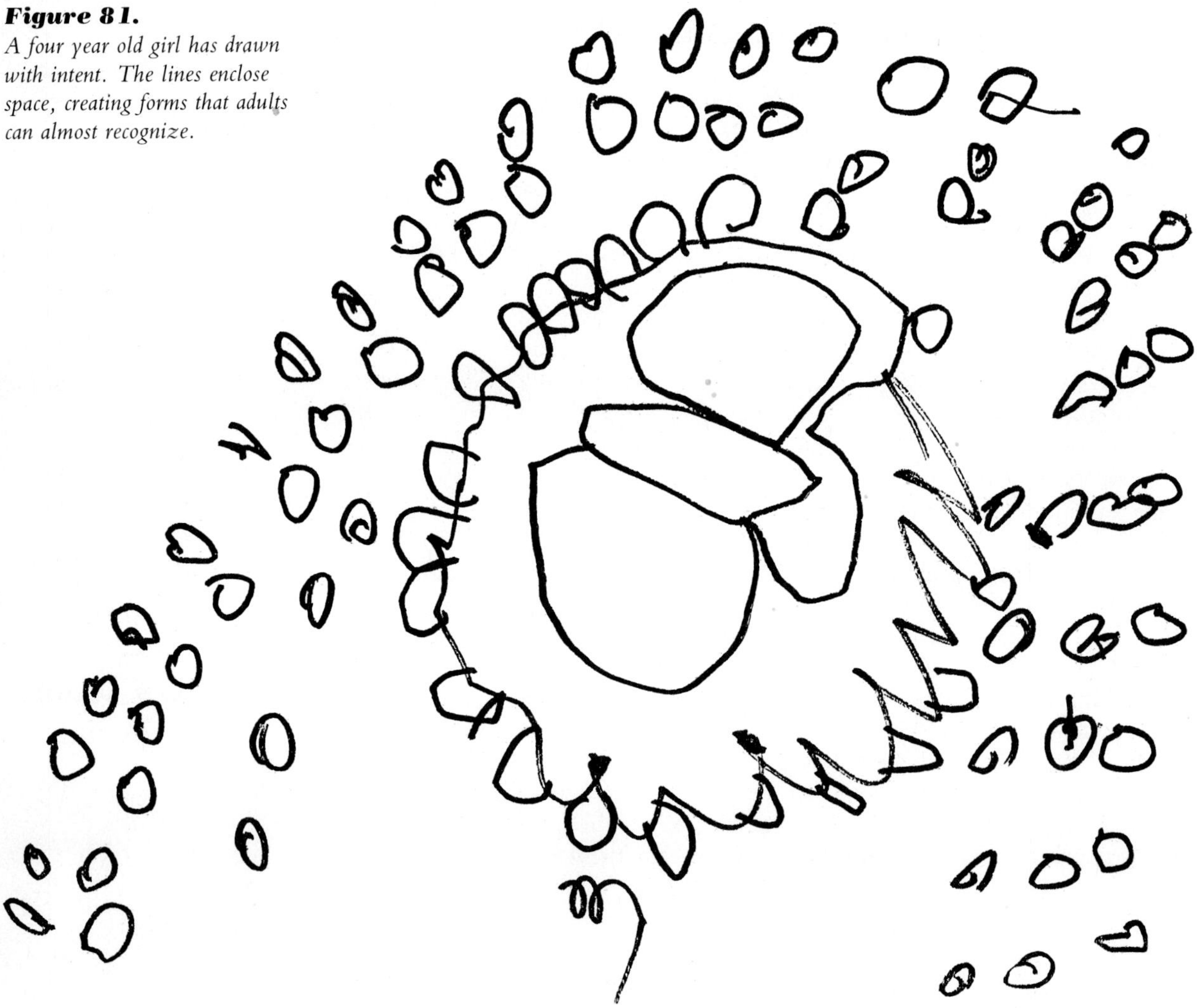

Figure 81.

A four year old girl has drawn with intent. The lines enclose space, creating forms that adults can almost recognize.

edge of a form. This transition is a dramatic one, for as adults we usually draw a line to connote the contour or to symbolize distinguishing features of an object. Up to this point, scribbles have been the result of kinesthetic activity, and children sometimes name these scribbles with reference to a physical activity, such as running or jumping. It is not long before the line has a visible reference, and the space enclosed within lines begins to take on meaning; what has been empty space now can be understood as symbolizing substance.

The drawings themselves have not changed remarkably from early scribbles. Although the child may now start with some idea of what he is going to do, he is also influenced by what he has done. So, as the child makes marks on the page, these marks may have a visual reference for him, which in turn affects the drawings. Whereas earlier he sometimes could see a relationship between what he had drawn and some object, now he draws with intent.

Although the child at three and a half has usually arrived at the stage of naming of scribbling, he will often enjoy the sheer physical motion, and if he is given a new drawing tool, he spends a considerable length of time in trying out his instrument to see how it feels, in much the same way as an adult would do. The amount of time that a youngster spends on drawing will increase even more, and the scribbles become much more differentiated. They may be well distributed over the page, and the marks will sometimes be accompanied by a verbal description of what is going on. This conversation is not directed at any particular adult, but often seems to be a communication with the self. Not all children do this by any means, but it seems apparent that the drawing now becomes a record of how the child feels about parts of his environment, and the method or way in which he draws makes the scribbles an important means of communication.

Sometimes at this stage a child will announce what he is going to draw, or sometimes the drawing will evolve from the first exploratory marks on the paper. It is quite clear that although parts may have some intent as they are being drawn, the child has no preconceived notion as to what his finished scribbling will look like. A line that is drawn at the top of the page may be called a tree but may end up being given a different name before the picture is completed. The wavy line may be a dog running or himself making giant steps. These lines are not always symbols of visual impressions, but can also be representations of a nonvisual nature; roughness or hurry-up lines are just as important. The point is that the scribbles and lines that may appear meaningless to adults do in fact have a real meaning to the child who is making these drawings. Some of the circular motions and longitudinal lines may seem to tie together to make a person in the child's drawing, but adults should not try to find a visual reality there or try to give scribbles their own interpretation. There may be a real danger in parents or teachers pushing the child to find some name or some excuse for what he has drawn. Rather, teachers and parents should give confidence and encouragement in this new kind of thinking.

The Meaning of Color

The experience of scribbling, then, is mainly one of motor activity. At first satisfaction is derived from the experience of kinesthetic motions, next from a visual control of these lines, and finally from the relationship of these lines to the outside world. Color, therefore, plays a decidedly subordinate role in the scribbling stage. This is particularly true when the child is establishing motor coordination. The choice of many colors can sometimes divert the child from scribbling. The child needs to be able to distinguish his marks from the rest of the page. Therefore, it is necessary to select drawing materials that will provide a strong contrast. Black crayon on white paper or white chalk on a blackboard are to be preferred over colors that may not give this contrast.

Most research indicates that discrimination of objects by form comes earlier than differentiation by color. Casey (1979) was able to have one year olds respond to form differences, but color differences aroused little curiosity. One study (Melkman et al., 1976) asked children to match a given colored shape with one which was like it either in color or form; they found that two year olds matched objects on the basis of form, three year olds more often matched on the basis of color, but four year olds again matched on the basis of form. It is interesting to note that four year old children are beginning to make recognizable shapes at a time which coincides with this increased awareness of form.

Some work has been done in attempting to relate color and form to the personality of children of nursery school age. A well-known study by Alschuler and Hattwick (1947, 1969) attempted to relate the paintings of some one hundred and fifty nursery school children to certain of their behavioral characteristics. In a two volume report, support was given to the assumption that in painting, children express their emotional experiences and adjustments. Those children who consistently painted in warm colors manifested free emotional behavior in warm, affectionate relations; children who preferred blue tended to be more controlled in their behavior; and children who used black tended as a group to show a dearth of emotional behavior. More recent research, however, has raised some questions about these conclusions. Corcoran

Figure 82.
*The four year old girl who drew
this picture identified it as her
baby brother in his basket.*

(1954) found evidence that three year old children used colors in sequential order when painting at an easel. That is, the colors were used from left to right or right to left on the easel tray, regardless of what the colors were. Apparently, Alschuler and Hattwick did not control for the placement of colors in their study. Biehler (1953), in a study with nursery school children, found that they tended to apply colors in direct relationship to how these were placed on the easel tray. This might indicate that painting at this age is more a mechanical activity than an emotional one. Scribbling apparently tends to be concerned with a striving for visual control. Color as part of the scribbling process in painting is mainly exploratory, and the use of particular colors may be related more closely to how the containers of colors are arranged than to deep-seated emotional problems of the child.

Changes in color can sometimes be significant in the naming of scribbling stage, for here colors may have some meaning for the child. Colors can also be fun for the child to work with and to explore occasionally. However, it

Figure 83.

Tempera paint must be a thick mixture so that it can be controlled if the youngster will be painting at an easel. Here we see a two-fisted approach to painting.

is of far greater importance in the scribbling stages that the child be given the opportunity to create lines and forms, to develop mastery of his coordination, and to begin his first pictorial relationship to his environment.

Environment and the Developmental Process

With increased attention focused upon early learning and a good deal of concern being shown for the need to develop methods of working with young children, the art experiences of young children are of increased interest. The very young child, before the age of eighteen months, expresses himself with his voice and body. It has been shown that even during the first few months of life children exposed to an enriched visual environment develop faster than children who do not have anything interesting to focus on, such as mobiles hanging over their cribs (White and Castle, 1964). Children raised in an atmosphere of sterility and deprivation apparently fall far behind normal development in all phases of their growth (Bronfenbrenner, 1968). A passive, neutral, sterile environment for young children is not the ideal setting for development. A study of 93 young children (Bradley et al., 1979) found that the competence of children twelve to twenty-four months of age increased when mothers encouraged and challenged their abilities. The interaction between the child and the environment is the crucial element in learning.

Programs for disadvantaged children are often started at a very young age. Some experimental programs have been concerned with mothers; others have started when the child at the age of three or four arrives in the nursery school setting. Some of these programs are called enrichment programs, in which children are exposed to a great number of activities that are expected to provide some of the background that youngsters in nondeprived homes would normally experience. A number of these activities are essentially art activities, with youngsters involved in painting, drawing, manipulating clay, or working with two- and three-dimensional forms. Some programs force the child into learning situations (Bereiter and Engelmann, 1966). The theory behind most of these programs is essentially the same: that the interaction between the child and his environment needs to be increased so that the child actually sees, hears, smells, tastes, and uses all his senses to make this interaction process meaningful. Although there were high expectations for these preschool programs, early

Figure 84.
*It is important for children
to have the opportunity to
manipulate and organize parts of
their environment.*

evidence indicated that such programs did not have any lasting effects. However, a recent study (Darlington et al., 1980) of children in seventh grade shows
evidence that those children who had been in a preschool program fulfilled
school expectations significantly better than a comparable group who did not
have this advantage.

One study on the drawing development in preschool children (Goertz,
1966) found that experience in working with art materials increases the development of a child's drawings. Probably the attitude of the parent toward a
child's drawing behavior is indicative of the attitude of the parent toward the
child himself. An interest in the child's drawings may indicate a real interest in
supporting development in all spheres.

THE BEGINNINGS OF SELF-EXPRESSION

In a study of preschool children's attention Bee (1964) expected that children who were not easily distracted would have parents who would leave them alone to solve problems. However, this was not borne out. What she found, in fact, was that children who were easily distracted had parents who offered children ready-made solutions, whereas the children who were not easily distracted had parents who gave them suggestions only for means of finding their own solution. Apparently it is better to interact with children, to help them find ways to solve problems, rather than to leave them alone or to provide specific answers.

Art in itself is a constant problem-solving situation. This is true at the preschool level as well as at older ages. The parent or teacher who provides the

ENVIRONMENT AND THE DEVELOPMENTAL PROCESS

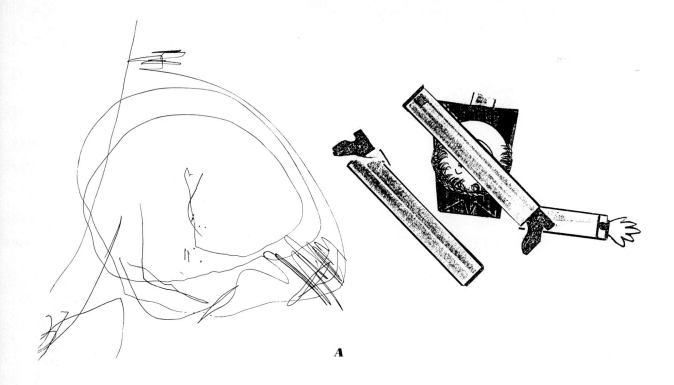

A

task and the solution may be doing as great a disservice to the child as the teacher who stands back and lets the child create on his own. What seems to be needed is a teacher who can provide alternate suggestions, give encouragement, and make the child feel that his end product is worthwhile.

Some teachers feel it important that young children experience success in art. After all, these teachers say, it is difficult for three year olds to manipulate scissors and to control a pen or pencil. Such teachers plan projects which they feel will have a good chance for success: a valentine heart will already be cut out, or grape leaves will be duplicated so children can paste precut purple circles on the paper to represent bunches of grapes. Needless to say, these projects are doomed to failure if the children cannot produce what the teacher wants. Some children fail more than others.

There is also the feeling that some materials are easier for young children to use. If a child is having difficulty drawing a person, he may be given precut

THE BEGINNINGS OF SELF-EXPRESSION

B

Figure 86.
A change in material does not produce a change in the child's concept of a human form. Here are the works of two children; the scribbling child (A) showed a consistent lack of organization, and the child who drew a head-feet representation (B) repeated this concept when pasting paper forms.

body parts to assemble, with the asumption that even very young children should be able to assemble pieces into a recognizable figure. However, when children were asked to draw a man, make a man from clay, and paste pieces together to make a man (Brittain, 1979), there seemed to be no difference in the representation regardless of material. In a follow-up study (Brittain and Chien, 1980), children between two and five years of age were asked to draw a man, were given colored paper circles and rectangles to make a man, and were also given colorful pieces of paper clearly representing body parts to make a man. Again there was little difference. If a child could draw a person, he could paste one together; if he scribbled, he pasted geometric shapes or body parts randomly distributed about the page and showed no concept of man.

These children easily identified body parts, but assembling the shapes into a cohesive whole was beyond their abilities. It is not a problem of eye–hand coordination or physical dexterity, since although the pasting task was easy, the pasted man was no more successful than the drawing. For most children up to the age of four, and for some even later, the task of conceptualizing a total configuration is beyond their cognition. The children were not aware of failing to complete the figure accurately. As far as they were concerned, they had done the task satisfactorily. They seemed content with pasting pieces of paper on the page, regardless of the fact that the results looked little like an adult concept of a person. In the transition from recognition to reconstruction, perceptual awareness is transformed into a concept.

The very young child's perceptual abilities develop earlier than his motor abilities. As the youngster has increased contact with his environment, he moves from manipulative activity in infancy to the development of concepts; he proceeds from motor activity to perceptual to cognitive. His understanding of space develops, and his organization of space follows an orderly sequence.

Even an adult artist uses his senses to acquaint himself with his surroundings and also to translate these reactions to his environment into paintings and constructions. The growth of sense apparatus is a vital necessity for everyone. The opportunity to examine the common materials of our environment provides a source of both kinesthetic and tactile experiences. By encouraging the exploration of a variety of tactile sensations, an adult can stimulate the child who approaches clay through the use of his finger tips only. A child who does not enjoy tactile sensations may avoid contact with different textures. Encouraging children to experience and become aware of a variety of tactile differences can help develop this area of perceptual growth. Noticing the differences between hot and cold, hard and soft, or just enjoying the tactile differences between feathers and glass or between metal and velvet can be an exciting experience.

Scribbling as a Reflection of Growth

The growth process is continuous, but not smooth. This can be seen in the physical growth of children. Although we can say that children of a certain age have an average height of so many inches, we find great differences in individuals; sudden spurts of growth, especially during adolescence, make us realize that growth is extremely uneven. This same holds true for the development of young children. We have said that art is a reflection of man's reactions to his environment; in the scribbling stage this is easily seen, for scribbling can be considered a reflection of the physical and emotional development of children. Just as we find differences in growth, we also find great individual differences in the scribbling of children.

Holladay (1966) documented the drawing abilities of children from two through five years of age. He collected unmotivated, spontaneous drawings, and also had the children attempt to copy numerous forms. A record was kept of the way drawings were made, including type of grip, choice of crayon, drawing time for each child, and so on. He was able to show seven different stages of scribbling, from undifferentiated scribbles to decorative scribbles. Dempsey (1971) examined the drawings by children three to four and a half years of age and recorded their verbalization of the meaning of these scribbles. In both the Holladay and Dempsey studies, it appears that these scribbles have symbolic meaning to the child after three years of age, even though an adult cannot get an understanding of this meaning just by looking. We have to listen, too; but the words that the child uses to describe these scribbles, as Piaget (1955) has pointed out, utilize personal meanings which are not necessarily the same as for adults, and emphasize the difference between the thought processes of the scribbling child and the adult.

Cognitive development and language development are related intimately. In a review, Houssiadas and Brown (1980) document the sociolinguistic research on children's language development from early egocentric speech to later social and communication uses of speech. There are clear indications that language development is far from complete at age five (Palermo and Molfese, 1973). In the early stages of development, motor activity plays a more important role than language in the discovery of reality. To represent this reality, a child between two and four develops the ability to make something—a symbol, a word, or an object—stand for something which is not present (Ginsburg and Opper, 1969).

Early scribbles are a record of kinesthetic activity, in which lines may appear to be random or to be repeated as if to master a particular stroke. Gradually the trained adult can perceive changes as the child begins to make a closed shape or several closed shapes joined together into complex configurations. This does not imply that the child is attempting a visual representation of objects, or that he lacks sufficient motor control to draw a visual representation of objects. Rather, the child's concepts beyond the self have not fully developed nor has he full visual-motor integration. The nursery school child operates within touch space; what he touches and manipulates has more meaning than what he passively views or what is distant and incompletely perceived.

Figure 87.
This girl pays close attention to her scribbles as she develops her motor skills and forms concepts.

SCRIBBLING AS A REFLECTION OF GROWTH

189

Figure 88.

It is not possible to teach children how to copy a square; but, by the age of four, the development of this skill is a proud accomplishment.

Although the circle can be copied by most children at the age of three, it is not until four that a square can be copied successfully. Identifying these shapes seems to be no problem for the preschool child. Cratty (1970) has determined that the perceptual abilities mature in a predictable manner, with very young children understanding the vertical dimension first, followed by recognition of the horizontal, with the diagonal being the last dimension to be understood. The scribbling child will not be able to copy a diagonal since this is a task that most children can accomplish only after five years of age. Even training does not seem to bring any noticeable change in this ability. As mentioned previously, Brittain (1969) attempted to increase young children's ability to copy squares. He found it impossible although he tried all the usual procedures of having children trace around cardboard squares, showing them feltboard squares, helping them to construct squares from straws and clay, making squares from paper strips, and pointing out square shapes in the nursery school. In a further study Brittain (1979) found that if the edges of the 8 ½ by 11 inch paper the children usually used were trimmed to a triangular shape, it

THE BEGINNINGS OF SELF-EXPRESSION

was even more difficult for children to copy a square; but the triangle was easier on the triangular paper, although children normally cannot copy that shape until they are five.

Sometimes nursery school teachers feel it is important to teach children how to copy squares and triangles since these shapes are useful in forming letters. But the evidence indicates that it is frustrating for both children and teachers to spend time trying to develop copying skills, when this ability seems to come naturally at a later date. Even calling these shapes a different name, such as calling a triangle a witch's hat, did not make it easier for children to copy them (Trisdorfer, 1972). The process of drawing is a learning experience in which children devise ways to depict their world on a two-dimensional surface. They will learn to draw circles, squares, and triangles on their own.

To a great extent the differences in levels of scribbling reflect physiological and psychological changes in the child. On the average, we expect children to start scribbling at about the age of two and to continue until they are about four years of age. If there is a marked discrepancy, the child is either above or below average for his age. If we find a child in kindergarten who is still scribbling, we could normally expect that this child is below average for his age. This is not a lack of talent but rather a stage of development that is a reflection of the total child at the time. In some cases a child may regress if he is afraid or unsure of himself. That is, he may scribble for a short period of time even though his normal development has gone beyond this stage. However, if we find a child of seven who has never done anything but scribble, we must assume that this child is not functioning at the level normal for his age.

In our society, intelligence is seen as the quality of a child's performance relative to that of all children of the same age. A child who performs tasks typical of an older child tends to be considered more intelligent. Since scribbling is a reflection of the child's total development, here is an indication of the child's intellectual growth, particularly at a time when the usual group-type intelligence tests are not usable. Therefore, a kindergarten child who is still in the scribbling stage will not be able to perform at the level usually expected of kindergarten children. In first grade the same child could not learn to read. It is obvious that the understanding of scribbling can help us to understand children.

Teachers should look at the scribbles of children as part of the total child. The beauty that we often see in preschool children's art may be because, as adults, we see these markings as a free, uninhibited approach to painting, whereas actually this beauty may have very little to do with the child's intent. Some individuals even go farther in this interpretation and look at children's

Figure 89.
During the scribbling stage, children should have the opportunity to develop a pictorial concept of a person, with drawing instruments they can control.

THE BEGINNINGS OF SELF-EXPRESSION

Figure 90.

Clay is a three-dimensional material which can be pushed, stretched, squeezed, and pounded.

drawings as an indication of inner feelings and inhibitions. When an adult looks at an ink blot, he can often see within this blot figures or forms that remind him of certain aspects of his own life. Adults can also look at scribbles in the same way and see certain forms or shapes, but this has very little to do with the child's meaning.

Art Motivation

Usually in the first stages of scribbling no special motivation is needed except to provide the child with the proper materials and the encouragement to go ahead with the activity. Most children will eagerly cover two or three sheets of paper with scribbles. The very young child will continue at this activity for no more than a few minutes. The child of three may be involved for as long as 15 minutes. The four year old child, if he has arrived at the naming of scribbling stage, or if he has been introduced to a new material, may keep at this activity for 20 to 30 minutes. However, no clock should dictate the length of time a child may spend in expressing himself on paper.

Scribbling should not be interfered with. Sometimes a nursery school teacher will see a child painting a picture that accidentally turns out to look quite like a piece of modern art. It is a great temptation to stop the child at this point and "save the picture." However, the child will not understand this interruption to his scribbling. The child should decide when a picture is completed.

Occasionally one finds a child who seems to be afraid of scribbling. Certainly a parent or teacher should encourage this important developmental activity. There may be several reasons for this hesitancy to engage in a creative activity, from being told "No" by parents when he has started to scribble in the past, to a more deep-seated problem of anxiety or fear in a particular situation. Establishing mutual trust is important, and it is sometimes necessary to make the art experience into a tempting activity. Providing the child with a mound of easily workable clay might be a good start. "Is it cold? Can you squeeze it? How high can you make it? Can you push your finger through it? Can you make it smooth? Can you make it lumpy?" Once a child gets involved in the clay, other means of expression will come more easily as the child develops confidence. Colored chalk or a new felt pen may be enough to make a youngster eager to draw. Most children will scribble quite eagerly after motivation.

A child, by naming his scribbling, gives a definite clue to his thinking. This new direction, the relationship of his scribbles to the environment, should be stimulated. The child's thinking can be motivated in the direction he has already indicated. For example, when the child says, "This is Daddy," it is possible to stimulate a greater awareness of Daddy. "Is your Daddy tall? Does he have big feet? Does he ever lift you up? Do you ever feel his whiskers? Do you like your Daddy?" The purpose here is to encourage imaginative thinking. The motions that are made on the paper are satisfying, although they may not be recognizable to adults; some lines may represent a feeling of lifting or the texture of whiskers, or even be symbolic of being held. The inclusion of many senses is important. If the child says he is going shopping, such things as smells, sounds, and personal involvement, his own part in the shopping experience, his likes and dislikes for this activity, can all be included in the discussion. But the child should also feel free to ignore these comments and be satisfied simply with the relationship between his scribble and his imaginative thinking.

During the very first stages of scribbling, no particular motivation is necessary, whereas any topic the child suggests during the last stage of scribbling is suitable to extend his thinking process. Most important in all stages is the adult's understanding and encouragement. Creative children scribble independently. Children who constantly ask questions, wondering how to use the material, asking the way things should be done, are also the ones who are most easily influenced by the work of others. If one child starts with big, round motions, they will start to imitate him. These children lack confidence in their own creativeness, and they are easy victims of coloring books and patterns.

Ideally, each child should be self-motivated to express himself and to feel satisfaction with the process. Because scribbling is the beginning of creative expression, it is especially important at this time to give him independence and responsibility for his own work. It is sad but true that projects planned for the scribbling child occasionally undercut his confidence—projects that are too difficult for a young child to accomplish by himself, projects that are conceived by and for adults.

Art Materials

Any art material used with children must fit their needs. Since during scribbling a child needs to practice and experience kinesthetic sensations, the materials used should encourage free expression without the intrusion of technical difficulties. Watercolor, for example, is a very poor medium for this age because the colors tend to run and flow easily. The child is unable to gain control over his motions or to follow his motions on the paper and is therefore discouraged by the material. The usual type of pencil is also unsuitable for the scribbling child because sharp points prevent gliding along the paper, and of course the points break easily.

There are numerous art materials that *do* lend themselves to the needs of the child at the scribbling stage. A big, black, unwrapped crayon is excellent and easily obtained. White chalk on a blackboard or a felt- or nylon-tipped pen with black ink are also excellent materials. Any art material should facilitate expression rather than be a stumbling block.

Because of some adults' feeling toward scribbling, we sometimes find that old newspapers, the back of wallpaper samples, or wrapping paper is used for the scribbling child. Although these materials may be used in the art program at a different developmental level, these materials have no place in the nursery school or in the kindergarten. Drawing a dark line over a printed news page is much too confusing, the back of old wallpaper tends to be rough and prevents the easy flow of a crayon, and wrapping paper does not provide good contrast with the drawing medium. A 12 by 18 inch size light-colored or white paper is best for crayon; a larger 18 by 24 inch size is best if paint is going to be used.

Tempera or poster paint can be used to advantage. The paint must be mixed to a fairly thick consistency so that it does not dribble or run down the page. The opportunity to use paint can satisfy some of the emotional needs of the scribbler better than a crayon. The result is obvious joy in exploring a range of colors. A horizontal surface is best for a child to paint on, since the problems of running paint are thus minimized and the child can work from all sides of the paper. However, in situations where space is at a minimum, it is better to use an easel, or even to fasten paper to the wall, than not to give a painting experience at all. Large, fairly absorbent paper, three-quarter-inch bristle brushes with the handles not too long, and some variety of thickly mixed tempera paint provide a wonderful opportunity for an emotional outlet and a truly artistic experience.

Clay is also an excellent material for this age. Handling a three-dimensional material provides the opportunity for the child to use his fingers and muscles in a different way. Beating and pounding the clay without any visible purpose is a parallel stage to disordered scribbling. Forming coils and balls without attempting any specific object is parallel to controlled scribbling. At some point the child may pick up a lump of clay and, perhaps with accompanying noises, call it an airplane or say, "This is a car." Psychologically, this is exactly the same change in the process of thinking as discussed under "Naming of Scribbling." The child has changed his kinesthetic thinking to imaginative thinking. The clay should not be so hard as to be difficult to work with nor so thin that it sticks to the fingers. Clay of proper consistency can be stored in a plastic bag for an indefinite length of time. Since the scribbling child does not have good control over his small muscles, the clay chunk should be large enough to be grasped with both hands. A grapefruit-sized piece of clay is probably adequate. Since the child is exploring and manipulating the material in a kinesthetic way, there is no need to let the clay harden or even to think of firing these products.

Providing an opportunity for children to become aware of color and texture by handling various collage materials is of value. Although it is interesting for the child to select some materials he enjoys and then put them into some sort of assemblage, the continual use of collage materials may stand in the way of the development of motor-visual experiences. However, the occasional use of collage materials is certainly worthwhile for the scribbling child.

In some nursery schools and kindergartens finger paint is a favorite material. There is some real reason to doubt the advantages of using this medium with the scribbling child. Just as we would hesitate to have a very young infant handle and use a crayon, if the prime enjoyment from the crayon was scratching it or chewing on it, we should hesitate to use finger paint with the scribbling child who tends to be concerned with its sticky consistency. If we think of art materials as primarily providing the opportunity for the child's self-expression, then the misuse of materials may interfere with the activity for which the finger paint was originally planned. We also have evidence from experiments and direct observation that the young child may sometimes regress into

Figure 92.
The teacher's purpose in this activity was to make puppets, but it was satisfying enough just to paint the bag green. Art activities need to be carefully geared to the ages of the children.

an earlier stage of behavior. Finger paint, because of its very consistency, may remind children of these former stages and retard development temporarily. You may easily see this effect by watching children. If they are more concerned with the sticky consistency and with smearing the paint all over than with using it for expression, then they are not using finger paint to satisfy the desire to control their kinesthetic movements. However, for tense, timid, or fearful children finger painting may provide an important outlet even when used in such a manner.

Figure 93.
The child's purpose in painting is not picture-making. Experimenting with new materials can be an end in itself.

There is no place in the art program for those activities that have no meaning for the scribbling child. Occasionally a nursery school or kindergarten teacher may plan certain art activities such as pasting, lacing, tracing, folding, or cutting; these are designed for a particular end product, such as May baskets, Pilgrim silhouettes, cute snowmen, or projects for Halloween, Christmas, or Mother's Day. Such activities are worthless and should never be included in a program planned for scribbling children, because they only point out the inability of the child to perform on a level foreign to his understanding and ability. Sometimes teachers have an interest in discovering new and novel activities for children. Any new material should be looked upon with a great deal of care to make sure that it can further the natural development of children. It must not obstruct the opportunity for the child to gain control over his material; rather, it should promote his own creative expression.

Summary

For an understanding of the child, it is of great importance that scribbling be recognized as part of the total growth pattern. During this stage a child's intellectual and emotional development will be reflected in his creative work. He will pursue his scribbling vigorously and yet be flexible enough to change his movement whenever new experiences demand such changing. He will enjoy his kinesthetic development through his scribbles and will gradually gain visual control over these markings. Creatively, he will be independent and free from disturbing influences.

The young child will freely explore his environment through a variety of senses, and some of these experiences will appear in his scribbles when he begins to name them. The drawings themselves will have a healthy variety, beginning before two years of age with a series of random markings, changing to continuous or controlled motions about six months later, and becoming much more complicated when he begins to name what he has drawn. In working with paint, these stages will closely parallel work with crayon, and he will particularly enjoy the use of color when he begins to name his scribbles. He will also enjoy working with a range of three-dimensional materials.

This period of life is extremely important for developing attitudes about oneself and in establishing the feeling that the world is an exciting and interesting place to live in. The roles of the teacher and of the parent become very important in helping the child develop these attitudes. The nursery school teacher is in an excellent position to provide the opportunity for a child to grow by means of his art experiences, to help him develop the confidence and sensitivity important for self-expression, and to provide a range of materials and the environmental setting for creative activities. Most important of all is to provide the stimulation and motivation necessary for developing an increased awareness of the environment and to provide the encouragement and approval for the creative act. All these responsibilities rest squarely upon the shoulders of the parent or teacher.

RELATED ACTIVITIES

1 Collect examples of art work from a nursery school or preschool group of children. Observe the variety of expression. Try to classify the scribbles according to disordered, controlled, or naming of scribbling stage. Compare the drawings for use of space, control of line, boldness or timidity of motion.

2 Collect the scribbles of one child over a period of several months. Date each drawing and note any remarks the child made while drawing. Keep a notebook in which you record observations on length of attention span, materials used, amount of concentration or diversions, type of motions used, and the emotional reactions of the child. Compare these notes with the child's motor coordination when eating, dressing, and so forth. Draw conclusions from the three sources of information (the scribbles, the notes, and the behavior) as to the child's growth during this time.

3 Find out the effectiveness of your motivation during the period of naming of scribbling by comparing one scribble done when the child was left completely alone with another made when you motivated the child in the direction of his thinking.

4 Observe children working with clay. See if those children who make forms or shapes also give these forms names. How does this relate to the scribbles of these same children?

5 Watch children paint at an easel several times. Make a list of the amount of paint used and the order of use. Shift the order of paints in the easel trough and see if there are any changes in the paintings. Experiment with

two or three different consistencies of paint each week. Repeat this for several weeks to see if the children make any comments or if there is any relationship between paint consistency and length of time spent painting.

6   When a child starts to name his scribbling, does he introduce certain lines or motions for certain objects or experiences? Collect scribbles and keep notes on the changes in the scribbles when naming begins. Observe the development of a form for a person.

First Representational Attempts 7

The Preschematic Stage
Four – Seven Years

The Importance
of the Preschematic Stage

A different method of drawing has begun—the conscious creation of form, the beginning of graphic communication. This stage grows directly out of the last stages of scribbling. Although the drawings themselves may not look particularly different to the adult, to the child this stage of development is very important. Now he is consciously making forms that have some relationship to the world around him. The marks and scribbles have lost more and more of their relationship to bodily movement, and these marks are now controlled and related to environment. In scribbling the child was mainly involved in a kinesthetic activity, but now he is involved with the establishment of a relationship with what he intends to represent. This gives him a great feeling of satisfaction.

These new drawings are important not only for the child but also for the parent or teacher, who now has a tangible record of the child's thinking process. This gives the adult a concrete object he can see and discuss with the child, and it also provides clues about what is important in the child's life and how he is beginning to organize his relationship with his environment. Usually by the age of four, children are making recognizable forms, although it may be somewhat difficult to decide just what they are. By the age of five these marks are usually quite distinguishable as people, houses, or trees. By the time the child is six, these shapes and forms have evolved into clearly recognizable pictures with subject matter. However, there is much variation among children, and even the material influences how they draw. Several factors may influence the kind of drawing that is done at any particular moment, and these will be discussed.

Characteristics
of Preschematic Drawings

Usually the first representational symbol attempted by children of this age is a man. Typically, the man is drawn with a circle for a head and two vertical lines for legs. These head–feet representations are common for the five year old child. It is not surprising that the first representations are of people.

Figure 95.

As children grow older, their drawings reflect the development of an ordered thought process.

The importance of people in most children's drawings is quite evident throughout childhood. It is not as clear why the head-feet representation should be the first method that the child uses to portray people, but there is general agreement that a child of this age is not trying to copy an object in front of him. Showing five year old children pictures of people or having them look at people while they draw does not change the way they draw a person. It may be that the child is actually drawing himself; if we were to try to draw what we see of ourselves as we look straight ahead, the representation would probably be a somewhat nebulous circle for the head with legs and arms at-

206   FIRST REPRESENTATIONAL ATTEMPTS

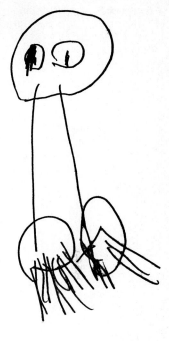

tached. This assumes that the child is involved primarily in the self; his egocentric view of the world is actually a view of himself.

Another point of view is that the head-feet representation is what the child actually knows about himself and is not a visual representation at all. The head is where all eating and talking goes on. Piaget (1960) found that some six year old children thought that the thinking process goes on in the mouth. Certainly the eyes, ears, and nose make the head the center of sensory activity. The addition of legs and arms makes this center movable and may indicate a really functional being. However, children know a great deal more about the body than they portray, for most children can quickly identify body parts.

Another view is that the first representational attempts result neither from visual stimulation nor from a concept, but are a representation of the method by which a child perceives. For example, the sense of touch in actually running the hands over an object may be as important at this stage as visually seeing this object or understanding its function. At any rate, the first drawing of a man should not be looked upon as immature representation, for it is fairly obvious that a drawing is essentially an abstraction or schema from a large array of complex stimuli and demonstrates the beginning of an ordered thought process.

The head-feet representation becomes elaborate with the addition of arms sticking out of the sides of the head, the addition of what seems like a belly button between the legs, and the eventual inclusion of the body. There are many variations in this development, and by the time the child is six he typically has a fairly detailed drawing of a man.

Although it is not clear just how the person symbol originates, the universality of the circle for the head and the two lines representing legs gives support to the notion that this is somehow biological in nature; that is, all children, either through their sight, hand control, or cognitive development, make surprisingly similar configurations for a person. Golomb's studies (1977) of the representational development of the human figure found no differences attributable to socioeconomic or cultural influences.

The drawn symbol is not particularly influenced by the real world. Pointing out to a child the discrepancy between his drawing of a person and how a person really appears does not influence or change the symbol. It is as if the symbol is a shorthand notation for an object, more generic than specific. In examining drawings by five and six year old children, Barrett and Light (1976) had children draw from a model of a house without a door, then told a story about a magical person living in a house without a door and asked the children to draw the house again. They found almost no effect on the drawings of the

Figure 97.

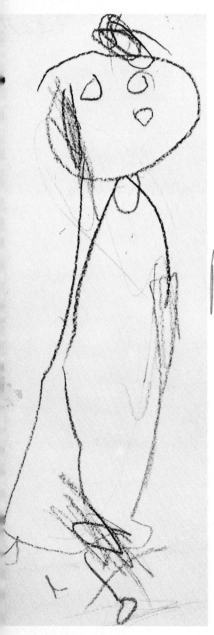

Figure 97.
"A Man," drawn by a four year old child. The first representational attempts develop naturally from the child's scribbles.

youngest children and noted little change in the drawings by the six year olds. The authors felt that the information was entirely ignored by those children who were drawing symbolically. Apparently a house has to have a door.

While the child is forming new concepts, his representational symbols are constantly changing. He will represent a man differently today from the way he will represent a man tomorrow. This is not only true of his drawings of a man but also of his representation of houses and trees. But, by the age of seven, the child will have established a schema; drawings by children in first grade can usually be identified by the way an object is drawn the same again and again.

The Meaning of Color

During the stage of the first representational attempts, more interest and excitement are stimulated through the relationship of the drawing to an object than between color and an object. The child has begun consciously to create forms and it is those forms themselves that become important. This does not mean that children in the preschematic stage are not aware of color, but it indicates that the ability to make forms of their own choosing dominates their thinking.

In drawings and paintings done by children of this age there is often little relationship between the color selected to paint an object and the object represented. A man may be red, blue, green, or yellow, depending upon how the various colors appeal to the child. To an adult these color relationships may seem a little odd. In fact, one study (Marshall, 1954) compared adult schizophrenics with normal five year olds and found the use of color with these two groups quite comparable.

This does not mean that these colors do not have significance to the child who is using them. Lawler and Lawler (1965) found that nursery school children of about the age of four selected yellow crayons to color a happy picture, whereas the same picture was apt to be colored brown if the child was told a sad story about it. It would not seem strange, then, for a child to select a favorite color for painting a picture of his mother, especially if he feels a warm emotional attachment. There are often other reasons for the particular selection of a color for an object. Some of these are simply mechanical in nature. That is, the color selected may be thicker and less likely to run, or perhaps the red has not been used, or maybe the brush used for one of the colors has a longer handle.

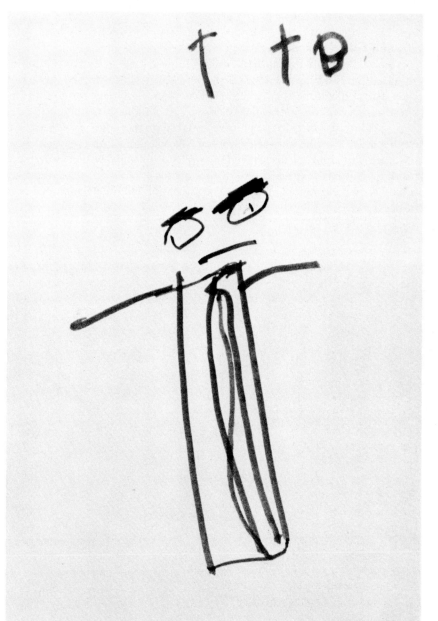

Figure 98.
This child's concept of a person is
unusual. The separate features
are shown, but there is no outline
for the head. Arms and legs are
also indicated.

THE MEANING OF COLOR

Children may have deeper psychological meanings in their color choice, but these meanings tend to be highly individualized, and adults would be put in a difficult position to try to interpret what these colors mean.

For children of this age, the use of color can be an exciting experience. Although the child has no desire for exact color relationship, he can and does enjoy using color for its own sake. This is particularly true when using paint where rich masses of color can be painted quite fluidly. It is obvious that criticizing a child's use of color or pointing out the correct color for objects would interfere with his freedom of expression. Ample opportunity should be provided for the child to discover his own relationships with color, for it is through continued experimentation that a child establishes a relationship between his own emotional involvement with color and the harmonious organization of color on the page.

Figure 99.
Children enjoy painting as they explore and experiment with color.

The Meaning of Space

The representation of space in drawings or paintings by adult artists differs widely, depending not only upon the individual artist but also upon the culture in which he finds himself. Our own society tends to look upon the representation of space as being appropriately shown by the use of perspective, a mechanical perspective with vanishing points and horizon lines. This has not been true for other times or other cultures; for example, an Oriental concept of space shows objects in the distance drawn higher on the page. Many contemporary artists have rejected mechanical perspective of space in favor of placing subject matter honestly on a two-dimensional surface. It can be readily seen, then, that there is no right or wrong way to portray space in a drawing.

A child's drawings in the first representational level show a concept of space quite different from that of an adult. At first glance objects in space tend to be represented somewhat randomly. However, closer inspection will show that the child conceives of space as what is around him. That is, objects will appear above, below, or beside each other in the way the child understands them. He does not see himself standing on the ground with other objects also on the ground beside him. Possibly this could be better understood if we were to quickly look around the room and list the things we have seen. "There is a table, there is a light, here is a chair, and I am in the middle." No spatial relationship has yet been established outside the child's concept of himself. Space, therefore, is conceived of as revolving around the child, with no relationships established between objects. During the stage when the child codes the location of things in relation to his own position, he is not yet able to specify the location of things in relation to adjacent landmarks. According to Harris (1977), only later as the child develops will he be able to determine location by relating it to landmarks as well as by relating it to the self.

Since the child himself is the center of his environment, in what might be called a stage of egocentrism, those experiences that are directly related to himself are the most meaningful. Just as children draw what is around them in an apparently random fashion, their comments tend to be loosejointed and disconnected. If a child of five is asked what he did at a birthday party, his reply does not follow any logical sequence. In fact his remarks may be more closely tied up with their emotional significance to him rather than with any orderly array of events.

The child's inability to relate things to each other in space, in his drawings, is a clear indication that he is not yet ready to cooperate socially and that he does not have the ability to relate letters to each other or to learn to read. There

Figure 100.
*The use of symbols to represent
objects and to represent words
develop simultaneously.*

is no advantage in trying to teach this child how to read (Sibley, 1957), or in
getting him to reason in an abstract way the logical relationships of numbers.
Although children can learn early how to count (Pentz, 1965), or to recognize
words, there is no genuine understanding of content. Right and left confusion
is typical for children. Cratty (1970) indicates that by five years the child
knows there is a right side and a left side, but is unable to identify them accurately. At six, he still has some indecision in identifying them. At seven, he has
accurate right and left judgment, and a judgment of visual space with himself
as a reference point. While right-left confusion persists, he will have difficulty
distinguishing between "b" and "d," some letters will be written backward, or
words will be written from right to left. Expecting such a child to perform
school or art tasks before appropriate maturation, proves discouraging to child
and teacher alike. A kindergarten teacher can readily tell from a child's drawings whether the child is ready to participate in tasks that require spatial coordination. Forcing a child too early into tasks that he is not yet ready for may

lead to undesirable actions and attitudes, and these may last longer and be more important in the end than doing the task at the moment.

A child's conception of his world may be so bound up with himself that he may even confuse his own thoughts and feelings with those things around him. If a chair falls over, he is concerned about the chair's being hurt (Piaget, 1960). It is almost as though he were the chair. We can say, therefore, that the child at this stage is emotionally involved in his spatial relationships. The size of objects and the subject matter he selects from his environment, and the way in which these are placed in this early stage, are to a large degree conditioned by value judgments. The way in which a child portrays space is intimately tied up with his whole thinking process.

Liebermann (1979) asked nursery school children to put a series of photographs into proper order. The photographs, taken at the children's eye level, showed four views of the nursery school, from the entrance to where the children hung their jackets. Although all of the children identified objects in the photographs, it was impossible for those children who were in the early scribbling stages to put the photographs in order, but those children who were drawing recognizable objects had no difficulty in putting these in proper sequence. Apparently understanding of ordering or of sequencing (or what Piaget calls seriation) begins with the manipulation of objects, or in this case photographs, before it becomes evident in drawings by children. Piaget (1976) conducted a series of experiments dealing with seriation, in which children tried to arrange a set of objects according to size. He believed that understanding the relationships between sizes comes during the process of manipulation or follows the successful completion of the task. By age seven, children had acquired an operational scheme to use and could order objects consciously. It is not surprising therefore that children's drawings in the preschematic stage show little relationship of one object to another and a pleasant disregard for size relationships.

When 98 children of this stage were asked to draw a house with a tree behind it (Kalyan–Masih, 1976), they had no success in making their drawings look visually correct. Those children under four tended to make scribbles, those under five ignored the instructions and drew the house and tree alongside each other, and those about six often placed the tree above the house, or drew the house directly over the tree so both could be seen, or put the house on one side of the paper and the tree on the other. None of the children under six solved the problem of how to represent the house with a tree behind it. Even when children are shown how an object can be partially hidden by another, they are incapable of drawing this. Cox (1978) asked 130 five, six, and seven

Figure 101.
*This drawing progresses all
around the page, with what
appear to be two suns and several
people arranged in egocentric
order.*

year olds to look at and draw a red and green ball, one behind the other; the
most common drawing showed one ball above the other. To attempt to teach
children of this age an adult concept of space representation would not only be
confusing, but might actually damage a child's confidence in his own creative
work. There would be no comprehension that the representation was other
than correct. The child's concept of his environment is just as valid as an
adult's.

The Development of the Four to Seven Year Old Child

Some children start school at the age of three or four, in either a community or
church sponsored nursery school; the kindergarten child is usually five or
sometimes six years old; formal schooling for all children has begun by first
grade. The Preschematic Stage, then, tends to fall between the time when some
children enter nursery school and the time when all children begin formal education in the first grade.

Children differ tremendously during this age. Each child is a product of

FIRST REPRESENTATIONAL ATTEMPTS

his background, and just as parents and the environment vary so will the child himself. In a study of kindergarten-aged children in Finland (Liikanen, 1975), it was found that those parents who had more artistic and creative interests had children who scored higher in fluency, flexibility, and originality in a battery of tests. The psychological literature indicates that this is a time of great intellectual growth, and family factors such as the number of siblings, amount of television-watching, or even the diet can influence a child's energy and attitude toward learning. The background that the child comes from, then, cannot be ignored. However, all children of this age tend to be generally curious, full of enthusiasm, eager to try tasks, particularly those that involve manipulation of material, and they are often anxious to express themselves, although not in logical ways. Apparently, the child has developed a logic of his own, and although he may be full of questions, of "Why?," he seems to see the world as

Figure 102.
Drawing is an expressive activity which may be shared, since by now children begin to be curious about each other's work.

Figure 103.
This six year old boy has added a body to his head-feet representation. Body and legs both relate to the head but not to each other.

being how it is without realizing that he himself can make changes in it. The world tends to revolve around him, and his knowledge is obtained through firsthand contact with his environment. The preschooler plays by himself or alongside other children rather than with them, and often his conversation is more a reflection of his own thinking than the development of a social grace.

We can expect that the art of the child will follow the same developmental patterns as other aspects of his growth. In fact, the study of children's drawings can give us great insight into the method and reasoning behind his actions. It may be well to mention that although there are general trends and a clearly predictable developmental path visible in drawings, these do not come automatically. Rather, they evolve slowly in spurts, and at times the children will regress to an earlier stage. Growth is never a smooth process.

Preschematic Drawings as a Reflection of Growth

Drawing is much more than a pleasant exercise for the child. It is a means by which he develops relationships and makes concrete some of the vague thoughts that may be important to him. Drawing becomes in itself a learning experience. Although children can recognize and name numerous objects around them, these objects can be somewhat peripheral to the child's functional thinking. One study attempted to compare how five year olds recognized missing or deformed arms and legs in incomplete pictures of people (McPherson et al., 1966). They found that five year olds drew anatomical parts with much more accuracy than they recognized them. Apparently a picture is not as important to look at as it is to draw. It may be that through the drawing experience the child is beginning to establish some sort of conceptual organization, and this experience is not one that can be imposed. That is, attempting to teach certain artistic skills or techniques to a child of this age will not help him to use drawing and painting as a means to understand himself and his own relationship to his environment.

The development of concepts in art and their relationship to reality can help us understand the thinking processes of these children. Because this is an age where we find great flexibility and change in drawings, it is also an age at which we find rapid changes in the mode of thinking. We are not discussing thinking here as the quiet contemplation of a problem but rather considering

216   FIRST REPRESENTATIONAL ATTEMPTS

total intellectual development, which at this age is nicely infused with fantasy, reality, and biological responses to the environment.

A child who has reached the chronological age of four or five and who still thinks in terms of motions has not advanced intellectually to an average stage of growth. In looking over a series of drawings by a five year old child, we would normally expect some representational attempts. The more differentiated these attempts are, the more highly the intellectual processes have been developed. Generally, the more details included in a drawing, the more aware the child is of those things around him. Our whole concept of intelligence is based primarily upon this assumption. One well known test of intelligence is based upon how completely a child draws a man (Harris, 1963). The more a person knows about his environment, the more he is actively aware of and can utilize the various factors within it, the more intellectually developed he is. It is fairly obvious, then, that the child who has not yet developed concepts of his environment at the age of five is retarded in his intellectual growth.

Figure 104.
The child's concept may be puzzling to an adult, but obviously these forms have significance of a very personal nature.

One of the important attributes of this preschematic stage is the flexibility of the child. This can best be seen in the frequent changes in his concepts. A child whose drawings are merely repetitions of the same symbol without any deviations uses that symbol to hide behind, and will exhibit in his other behavior a tendency to withdraw or to hide behind social stereotypes. A child who reacts toward meaningful experiences in an emotionally sensitive way will show this emotional sensitivity in his art work. In his drawings he will exaggerate those things or parts with which he has become emotionally involved. For example, John walked barefoot in the grass after the rain; the obvious delight of this kinesthetic experience shows in his emphasized toes, almost to the extent that we, too, can feel our toes in the cool grass. A very sensitive child who becomes bound up with one part of his drawing may easily lose contact with the rest of his subject matter. This can sometimes be seen in greatly overexaggerated details.

Drawings reflect a child's development honestly, but sometimes adults can be misled by words children use. Adults may mistake the use of words for an understanding of these words and try to carry on a conversation with a youngster, teaching him according to what an adult would mean by the use of these words. One teenager recalls that a song she learned in nursery school about springtime had a phrase in it that warned her to "watch out for the first crocuses popping up from the ground." The teenager remembers that she was scared stiff for weeks because she was afraid crocuses popping up from the ground might bite. In fact, she still does not like crocuses.

The way things are represented is an indication of the type of experiences

the child has had with them. The image a person has of himself and of the things around him will change as he becomes more aware of the significant characteristics of these objects. *Perception* means more than just the awareness of the visual appearance of objects; it includes the use of all the senses, such as kinesthetic or auditory experiences. Later, when a child establishes more than the mere meaning of an object, visual differentiation begins. For example, look at the drawing in Figure 106, where only geometric forms are used. All such geometric details convey a meaning only in context. The same situation exists in color at this age, for a child uses color for the sake of color itself. It does not relate to the subject matter.

Since growth in perceptual discrimination is very rapid at this age, drawings also change rapidly; some children by the age of six or seven draw parts of objects that interest them in great detail, although not always in proportion. Salome and Reeves (1972) attempted with some success to improve the visual discrimination of some four and a half and five and a half year old children with several training tasks, involving discussion, visual aids, and exercises containing information about contour lines. However, there is a lack of data on the long term effect of such training, that is, in six months or a year. It is usual to find that any special attention given to a group of children has favorable results, particularly if there is enthusiasm and a feeling of significance for the project at hand.

FIRST REPRESENTATIONAL ATTEMPTS

During this stage of first representational attempts the creative child expresses independent concepts and will not ask how to draw a mouth or a nose. The child's own concepts can readily be distinguished from those taken from other sources by their free and flexible use. In a group the creative child remains uninfluenced, although he may show interest in what others are doing. The creative child spontaneously paints or draws or manipulates materials and does not create only when encouraged to do so. The development of creative growth within the context of art education is one of the prime justifications for art experiences for any age group. A creative first grade girl was motivated by the Christmas story to paint the manger scene (Figure 107). Notice how she has shown the top view of the basket so we can look inside, but has shown the side view of the stable. An angel is just arriving on the scene from the left, carrying the star. This is an age when early patterns of behavior are established by which a child can develop into a creative adult or by which he can develop a dependence in thinking.

This age is a time of great growth in many areas, such as the change from scribbling to the development in drawings of readily recognizable subject matter. The child is egocentric; even his speech is concerned with himself. He enjoys talking to others, but is not as concerned that he be understood. The kindergarten child certainly needs to talk, but sometimes a whole class will be forced to listen, which seems such a waste. Communication is important to develop; this can be done in small groups, sharing experiences, bringing something special to talk about, or explaining a drawing, but not to an entire, bored, eager to talk but not eager to listen class. The usual five year old knows what he has drawn and expects it to be obvious to everyone. One study (Korzenic,

Figure 107.

Plan and elevation are combined in this drawing of the manger scene by a six and a half year old girl. The basket with the handles on each side has been tipped up so we can look inside.

1975) found that kindergarten children blamed the viewers if they could not understand what the drawing was about; it was not until second grade that children began to realize that their drawing might not really communicate to others.

The particular skills a child has, whether manipulative or cognitive, seem not very conducive to acceleration. He will not be able to copy a triangle before five years of age or a diamond, which seems even more difficult, until about seven. Although attempts have been made to increase this ability (Brittain, 1969; Rand, 1973), they have not been successful. Probably attempts at increasing particular skills are doomed to failure because they ignore two fundamental considerations. The first is the erroneous assumption that practice on a task, no matter what the task, will improve the skill in accomplishing that task. The prerequisite experiences needed may be missing; until those are developed, the particular task is meaningless. For example, trying to teach a three year old how to draw a cube would be a big waste of time. What would be needed are a lot of pre-cube experiences: a year of scribbling to establish visual-motor control, a year of manipulation of objects to acquaint the youngster with two- and three-dimensionality, a year of two-dimensional drawing to establish drawing abilities, a year of physical expressiveness to perfect the understanding of left and right, up and down, front and back. Now, the youngster is ready to learn how to draw a cube.

The second consideration that may be overlooked is the cognitive one. To accomplish a particular task, a comprehension of the task itself is necessary. Piaget and others have provided evidence that learning is tied to maturation—a physiological, biological functioning that is predetermined in each individual. Within this restriction there can be great differences, but the development of concepts such as that necessary to draw a cube would not come until well beyond our four to seven year age span and not until the child has developed the ability to deal abstractly with the concept of dimensionality.

In spite of the above considerations, many art educators feel it important to try to teach certain artistic skills. Although it is unclear why five year olds should not be allowed to enjoy expression on their own level or why they need to develop some skill at five that will come naturally at seven, some educators try hard to do just that. Castrup et al. (1972) list several skills that four and five year olds could do, such as distinguish some colors, identify some geometric shapes, hold a crayon correctly, and so forth, and some they could not do, such as draw one line thicker than another, use the proper amount of paste, or point to a dull or bright color. The study stated that those skills which were difficult would be given added emphasis in their program. It has been suggested that

Figure 108.
Knowing how much paste to use
must be learned by experience.
This kindergarten girl is
discovering how much paste she
needs for her project.

one reason children lose their spontaneity and pleasure in art is because they go
to school where art is "taught." In some cases there may be good justification
for that statement.

Art Motivation

Any motivation should make the art experience much more than just an activity; it should stimulate a child's awareness of his environment and make him
feel that the art activity is extremely vital and more important than anything
else. To merely follow an adult's instructions for working with materials or to
be handed paper and told, "Draw what you want," or even to have a range of
material and activities to do over a period of time—any one of these can result

222

in busyness yet fail miserably in being a meaningful learning experience. A child cannot be expected to gain in knowledge and confidence and in sensitivity toward his environment if there is a barrier between adult and child. The teacher as well as the child needs to feel that this is an important, meaningful, and stimulating experience.

The atmosphere for art experiences is also important. The way something is said can be more important to the child than what is actually said. In a study of the influence of a nursery school environment upon children's drawings (Reichenberg-Hackett, 1964), it was found that children in what was termed a supportive-permissive atmosphere made drawings that were rated higher than drawings by children in either an authoritarian atmosphere or in a laissez-faire atmosphere. Cratty (1970), in reviewing research on the relationship between child behavior and adult attitude, concluded that strictness on the part of adults brings anxiety and noncooperative behavior on the part of children. Other studies have tended to support these conclusions: that the attitude of the teacher is vital to the learning experience. When the adult shows an interest, provides an atmosphere of support for the activity, and acts as though there were nothing more important in the world than the drawing experience, then the environment is ready for art. The two other extremes, that of standing back and not particularly caring what a child does, or the authoritarian role of dictating what must be done, apparently have a negative influence upon drawing and therefore a negative influence upon children.

The four to seven year age is an important one in the area of perceptual growth. At least one study (Spitz and Borland, 1971) found that children between the ages of four and eight showed remarkable growth in the ability to recognize familiar objects from line drawings that had a portion of the drawing deleted. Although four year olds had difficulty in identifying the objects, the ability of adults was not much greater than that of the eight year olds on this task. In another study of young children, Birch and Lefford (1967) conclude that between five and eight years appeared to be the period of most rapid improvement in perceptual analytic ability. It would seem therefore that these years are the ones in which to develop the ability to look, examine, and take pleasure in a visual awareness of things in the environment. This perceptual growth is not difficult to encourage. Pointing out the bright colors in the fall, sharing an interesting looking stone, looking at footprints in the mud, having youngsters find a smooth barked tree and then a rough one, looking for a prickly weed in the grass, noticing how the sun feels hot on your back, listening to the sound of the wind, or noticing the smell of the garbage truck are all perceptual experiences that can be encouraged.

Figure 109.
The young child does not need to be taught how to draw; this comes as naturally as learning how to walk or speak. Proper motivation should assure the child's involvement, so that art expression is a vital activity.

ART MOTIVATION

223

One of the best means of stimulating the child's relationship to things around him is to start with the function of the various body parts. The results of stimulation of a child's concept of his body parts will show readily in the drawings by children at this age. For example, six year olds who draw only a line for a mouth can be motivated to include teeth and other facial features by stimulating an awareness of teeth in a topic such as "Brushing Your Teeth in the Morning."

"When do you get up in the morning, children? What time do you get up? At seven? How long does it take you to get dressed? Does your mother call you? Do you have an alarm clock? How long does it take you to get dressed then? Does your mother have to help you? Do you have to catch a bus? Where do you have your bedroom? On the second floor? All by yourself? After you are dressed are you ready to catch the bus? No? Oh, you haven't eaten your breakfast yet? But you forgot! You went to breakfast without brushing your teeth! Oh, you brush your teeth after breakfast! Don't you have to hurry? Especially if it's raining? Oh, you brush your teeth anyway! Why? You mean it's bad to leave all that food in between your teeth all day? Do you brush your teeth every morning, Johnny? How do you hold your toothbrush? With just two fingers? Oh, you hold it this way! Do you brush your teeth back and forth? Oh, no; you mean you do it up and down? Why? Did you ever get your toothbrush caught between your teeth? Does it hurt? You have to be a little careful when you brush your teeth, don't you! But, Johnny, did you forget the toothpaste? Some people don't use toothpaste! Do you? Let's think how we brush our teeth. Let's really brush them good and clean! Now are we all set to go to school? Oh, no; not with all that toothpaste still in there!

Now, we are going to draw a picture about how we get up in the morning and go to the bathroom and brush our teeth."

Every child should now have a feeling for brushing his teeth and one may even have a pain where he got his toothbrush caught between his teeth. But every child will be conscious of his teeth, and each drawing will include teeth as an active part of the child's awareness. We can compare former drawings with those drawn after the motivation; if an enrichment of the form concept has taken place, the teacher was successful. In this topic, "Brushing Your Teeth in the Morning," an enrichment of the concept of mouth and a closer coordination between mouth and arm may also be expected.

The motivation for a lesson such as the one above can be achieved by actively engaging the child in an actual experience. One example might be to pass out a bag of crisp apples for the children to munch on. "Is it hard? Do you really have to bite with your teeth?" Activate the child's concept of the en-

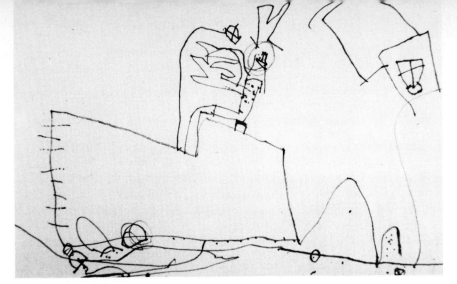

Figure 110.
In this drawing a rural boy imagines himself driving a tractor. Notice the special significance given to the hands and the steering wheel.

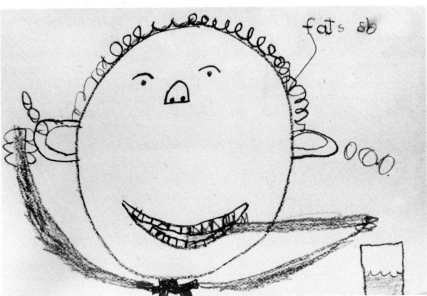

fats sb

Figure 111.
The small body with the elongated arms is dwarfed under the huge head and toothbrush in this drawing by a seven year old boy.

vironment through his own body. Any such motivation should include as many senses and sensory experiences as possible, and should stimulate the child's thinking, feeling, and perceiving.

The length of motivation may depend upon several factors. If the children have just engaged in an actual experience, a short discussion may be quite sufficient. However, in some cases the motivation may take longer than the actual drawing or painting. Discussing how a child feels in the rain, how the rain feels on his face, or the clothes the child has to put on, and stimulating an

ART MOTIVATION

awareness of the sensations of walking with boots on or even how his feet feel if they are wet inside his boots, may take a longer time.

In some cases the motivation may be concerned primarily with the material itself. When first working with clay or collage material, the experience with the actual qualities of the material will be most important. "How does the clay feel? Is it hot or cold? Can you push your finger into it? Does it bend easily?" This type of question may be the only motivation necessary to stimulate a child to a greater awareness of his own senses and to help him to identify directly with what he is doing.

A motivation based primarily upon recall of something in which the children have all been involved should provide the opportunity for each child to express his own feelings and emotions in his own individual way. No attempt should be made to censor the child's creative expression, but rather we should try to stimulate the greatest variety of responses. The atmosphere for the particular topic should be generally established by a discussion, for example, of going to school. "Where do you go to school? What time do you go to school? Do you walk? Do you ride a bus? How do you get on the bus? Do you hold on to the door when you climb in? Is the first step a high one?" Topics for motivation should therefore include the *where* and *when,* the *what,* and the *how.*

Subject Matter

The most important consideration in the selection of topics for children in these first representational attempts should be the meaning of the activity for the children. The more involved the child becomes in the art activity, the more he identifies with what he is doing, the more he is actively using his senses, the more the project is really his own, the more meaning it has for him. At this age it is particularly important that any motivation or any subject matter be related directly to the child himself.

This is an age that shows great gains in awareness. Developing a sensitivity to his own body parts should be one of the prime considerations for subject matter. Just as we have seen that the head-feet representation of a man is usually the first symbol a child makes, his interest in people continues to be central in his drawings; not people living in igloos in the Arctic, not Swiss children in the Alps, but his own family and especially himself. Basic subject matter stresses an awareness of body parts, such as "The Time I Hurt My Knee," "I Have a Cold and My Nose Hurts," "I Have a Stomach Ache," or "I Am

Figure 112.
"I Am Playing in the School Yard," drawn in chalk by a five year old boy. Apparently the teacher only watches while the youngster plays on the slide, for the child has drawn the teacher without arms.

Brushing My Teeth." Several activities include the body and are good topics, such as "I Am Drinking My Milk," "I Went to the Dentist," or "I Am Eating Breakfast." Just presenting a topic is not enough, for the child needs to be involved and become actively aware of the details.

Size relationships can also be stressed. "My Family" is a topic which brings an awareness of the size of each family member, from father to little baby sister, and maybe even the cat. Other subjects might be "My House Is Big" and "I Am Pushing the Shopping Cart." The flexible use of symbols should be encouraged with topics such as "I Am Putting on My Clothes" and "I Am Tying My Shoes." Another type of topic, such as "I Am on The New Swing at School," or "I Am Crawling on My Stomach," or "I Am Standing on the Table" provides for an awareness of the self in relation to space and objects.

Children often have subject matter within themselves, requiring no motivation or further encouragement for it to spill out. Every kindergarten teacher realizes that if Michael's cat has kittens, this news will come out in arithmetic class, during social studies, or maybe when the child bursts into the room first thing in the morning. Ample opportunity should be given children to express on paper their feelings and emotions. Some of these feelings will be quite apparent to any adult. Such topics as "The First Snowfall," "The Storm," "An Approaching Holiday," "A Big Fire" are all subject matter that

SUBJECT MATTER

227

cannot be ignored. Some subject matter will be a great deal more personal to the individual child. Such topics as "My New Baby Sister," "I Got Hit by a Car," "I Got Lost in the Store," "My House Caught on Fire," or "I Have New Shoes" all provide appropriate subject matter for any age. The child who produced Figure 112 eagerly explained that his teacher, represented by an armless figure, watched while he played on the new slide in the kindergarten play yard. When the child is eager for expression, art should certainly not be limited to a specific time of the day or regimented to a particular topic.

Another subject matter is the art material itself. Any art material should play a subordinate role in an art experience, and the child's own expression should be of predominant importance. However, at this age children have been exposed to only a few art materials, and in some cases their experience with these materials may have been limited to a restricted use. The prime reason, then, for using an art material as subject matter is to provide the child with a positive attitude toward material and to insure the greatest amount of exploration and flexibility in its use. Such experimentations should be related directly to the child himself and should not be concerned with any adult consideration of "artistic qualities." The use of an art material as a subject matter should therefore take the form of exploring and experimenting with the various qualities of clay, tempera paint, or other materials.

Art Materials

Because the child at this age is excited by his ability to represent what is meaningful to him, any art experience should provide the opportunity for developing mastery of the material itself. The process of creation is of greater significance than the final product, which means that an art material should be selected that meets the need of the age group for which it was planned. Constantly introducing or changing art materials may actually stand in the way of a child's mastering the material enough to express his own feelings, his own reactions to his sensory process, and his own intellectual concepts of his environment.

Any art material should truly be an art material. Expression itself is not limited to any age group, so any material used with children should be of such a nature that a child may use this material throughout his life. There should be no "cute" art materials for nursery school or kindergarten children to use, because these provide no opportunity for continued growth.

Thickly prepared tempera paints, used with a bristle brush on a somewhat absorbent large, heavy sheet of paper, are excellent material for this age level. Absorbent paper (about 18 by 24 inches) is recommended because it prevents the paint from running. A low, flat table provides the best surface on which to paint; the floor can also be successfully used. If the limitations of space do not allow painting on a horizontal surface, easels or a bulletin board can be used. Here, however, the paint should be of a thick enough consistency so that the child can control his painting without the frustration of dripping accidents.

Good quality colored crayons and smaller sheets of paper (12 by 18 inches) are also excellent materials. The quality of the crayon can be determined by the amount of surplus wax that can easily be scratched off the paper. The more surplus there is, the poorer the quality of the crayon. The crayon should be large and unwrapped. Too often a new set of wrapped, sharply pointed crayons is looked upon as a treasure to keep rather than as material to use. Unwrapped crayons can be used on the sides and ends, unlike pencils.

Pencils may provide the opportunity for some children to draw in detail. The usual kindergarten pencil works quite well. A study comparing crayon and colored pencils used by children in kindergarten (Salome, 1967) indicated that drawings made by crayon tended to be rated higher on several measures, but some youngsters spent more time and were able to include more detail with pencils. It is more important that the child be given the opportunity to draw, even if he has to use a pen or poor pencil, than that he not be given the opportunity at all.

In addition to these basic materials, there are many other materials that are quite suitable for this developmental level. These include colored chalk, fiber tipped pens, colored papers, collage materials, and other materials that truly give the child an opportunity to explore and manipulate his environment and provide for a flexible development of his concepts. Tricky use of materials should be avoided, such as dripping paint, pasting cereals, printing, and using stencils, or using materials in methods that are foreign to the child's own intentions. Purposely, no decorative projects have been suggested, because on this level no child feels the conscious need for decoration. As long as the search for a concept of form and space is predominant, the desire for decoration generally does not develop.

Clay is an excellent three-dimensional material for the preschematic stage. As in drawings we find a search for a definite concept of form; in clay this search is seen in a constant change of modes of representation and in the representations themselves. Pulling out all meaningful parts from the lump of clay and the action of adding parts together to make a form can both be observed. A child who starts with a lump of clay and pulls parts out from the whole usually does not go into as much detail as a child who starts with separate parts and then puts these together. But either method comes naturally

Figure 113.
"Indians," drawn with a felt-tipped pen by a seven year old girl. This material lends itself to a bold, direct presentation of thought. Every art material has its own characteristics and specific values.

from the child and is acceptable. Moist clay can be easily stored in plastic bags, and water can be added as needed to maintain the proper consistency. Plasti-cine, which is essentially clay with an oil base, is much more expensive than clay, may stain, and the consistency cannot be altered.

There is no place at this age level for cutting out paper flying angels or Pilgrim hats. A nursery school or a kindergarten teacher should not be concerned with mass-producing little stereotypes for holidays or seasonal events, because such activities can only make the child feel inadequate and tend to reduce his confidence in his own means of expression.

Summary

The art of children in the stages of first representation can be seen as a direct reflection of the child himself. Not only are the drawings and paintings by a child a record of his concepts, feelings, and perceptions of his environment, but these drawings and paintings also provide the sensitively aware adult with the means for a better understanding of the child. In our discussion the concern has been primarily to see art as one of the essential components in a child's total development.

The art of children provides us not only with understanding of a child but also with an opportunity to promote growth through the area of art education. Here we mean something a great deal more significant than changing the outward appearance of the drawings themselves; we are concerned with the total process of creating. We cannot positively affect a child's behavior by providing him with patterns or procedures to follow in order to achieve a "better-looking" product. The change in the product itself should come about through the changes in a child's thinking, feeling, and perceiving. It is through the *process* that changes in behavior or changes in growth patterns develop. It is also through the process that meaningful changes take place in the product.

The art motivation for this particular age group concentrates upon the experiences the child himself has had, either in his own physical self, or in fantasy, or in vicarious experiences. Art plays a crucial part in our educational system, particularly in the area of perceptual growth, the developing awareness toward those things around us through all our senses; through creative growth, the development of characteristics of flexibility, imaginative thinking, originality, and fluency of thinking; and also through emotional growth, the ability to face new situations, the ability to express feelings both pleasant and

Figure 114.
*Children enjoy using adult tools.
The opportunity to explore,
investigate, and invent new forms
through art activities is an
absorbing experience.*

unpleasant. Art also provides the opportunity for growth in the intellectual, social, and aesthetic areas.

The majority of children who are beginning to attend school will be in the stages of first representational attempts. It is therefore imperative that their introduction to art experiences be a meaningful one. A great deal of what goes on within school is dictated by adult society; however, as we have discovered, the child is not a miniature adult nor does he think in adult terms. Art can provide the opportunity for growth in several vital areas and the opportunity for a child to investigate, invent, explore, make mistakes, have feelings of fear and hate, love and joy. Most essential, he should have all these experiences of living for himself, for himself as an entity—an individual who can, should, and will think for himself.

FIRST REPRESENTATIONAL ATTEMPTS

RELATED ACTIVITIES

1 Collect drawings over a period of time from a child who is still scribbling and trace the evolution of his first representative symbols. Keep in
chronological order, and then see how his symbol for a person develops.

2 Collect drawings that include symbols for the mouth. Stimulate the children by a motivation built around chewing peanuts. Compare the drawings done before and after the motivation to see what changes, if any,
have taken place in the symbol for the mouth.

3 Observe the activity of a group of kindergarten children during their free
play and during organized games. Relate the amount of parallel play to
the discussion of the use of space in drawings. What are the differences or
similarities between these two activities?

4 Compare the development of representational symbols in drawings with
symbols in clay. Photograph the clay products to keep a record of the
development in clay to compare with the drawings.

5 Observe a child who is making his first representational symbols. Keep a
verbatim record of his comments for several different fifteen-minute periods. What relationship is there between his verbal and his graphic expression?

6 From a collection of paintings by five year olds list the objects that are
painted with a visually established color–object relationship. List those
objects that are painted with no visually established color–object relationship. What might cause some of these choices of color?

The Achievement of a Form Concept

8

The Schematic Stage
Seven–Nine Years

The Importance of the Schematic Stage

After much experimentation, the young child arrives at a definite concept of man and his environment. Although any representative drawing could be called a *schema,* or symbol, of a real object, here we refer to schema as the concept which a child has evolved and repeats again and again whenever no intentional experience causes a change in this symbol. These schemata are highly individualized. For some children the schema can be a very rich concept while for others the schema can be a fairly meager symbol. Differences in schemata depend upon many things, but just as no two children are the same, we find that no schemata are identical. Although there is no magical time for the formation of a schema, most children arrive at this stage at about seven years of age. The schema for an object may be determined by how a child sees something, the emotional significance he attaches to it, his kinesthetic experience with or touch impressions of the object, or how the object functions or behaves.

A pure schema in a child's drawing occurs whenever a child's representation confines itself to the object. "This is a tree." "This is a man." However, when intentions are present that alter the forms, we no longer speak of a pure schema. Thus, a pure schema, or schematic representation, is a representation with no intentional experiences included. When there are modifications of the schema, we know that the child has portrayed something of importance to him. Studying the kinds of modification to the schema allows us to understand the child's intention. As Stacey and Ross (1975) point out in their study of six year old children's memory of their own drawings, children of this age can produce alternative schemas for objects and events when asked to do so. This is of special importance to the teacher, who can determine the effects of his teaching by comparing the schema with its deviations.

The mental images a child has of objects in his environment are the result of his thinking process; the drawing we see on the paper is the symbol of that mental image, the symbol standing for the object. His art product, then, is an indication of the way he interprets and comprehends information. The schema refers to space and figures just as to objects. For example, a child may usually draw a house, without including a chimney. But in the winter, when it is cold and there is talk of Santa Claus coming down the chimney, his schema may change to include a chimney. Through this change of the schema the child shows a particular experience. But this development of a schema takes time.

Figure 116.
*By the age of seven, most
children have developed schemas
for elements of their environment.
This boy has an elaborate schema
for a house.*

Although the schematic stage normally starts at age seven, some children will develop a schema earlier than this for certain things, such as people, whereas other children will remain longer in the preschematic stage.

Characteristics
of Schematic Drawings

Human Schema

At about the age of seven, the drawing of a human figure by a child should be a readily recognizable symbol. The child will portray body parts depending on

THE ACHIEVEMENT OF A FORM CONCEPT

his active knowledge of them. Not only will there be a head, body, arms, and legs, but also some of the various features. The eyes should be different from the nose, the symbol for nose should be different from that for the mouth, and there should be hair and sometimes even a neck. Usually, the child includes separate symbols for hands and even fingers and of course a different symbol for feet. Often clothing is drawn instead of the body. The average schema for a seven year old includes most of these items. The opinion that the profile represents a more advanced stage in a child's creative concept is, according to experiments, incorrect (Harris, 1963). Apparently, for some children the symmetry of the body, the two arms, the two legs, the two eyes, the two ears, is of most importance. In some cases the side view, or profile, concept is the first schema. Some schemata can have a mixed profile and front view that includes a representation of two eyes and profile nose.

The schema usually consists of geometric forms, and when separated from the whole these lose their meaning. Sometimes ovals, triangles, squares, circles, rectangles, or irregular shapes are used as schema for the body, though

Figure 117.
Four nearly identical schematic figures represent this girl's family. All are looking straight forward, rather than relating to one another.

all kinds of shapes are used for legs, arms, and clothes. In Figure 117, "My Family," notice how the girl repeats her schema for each member of the family. This child is not attempting to copy a visible form, but rather a concept is arrived at by a combination of many factors: her process of thinking, her awareness of her own feelings, her development of perceptual sensitivities, and her own special interests and priorities. The human schema is therefore highly individualized and is used when the child requires a generic symbol for a person. Even when asked, kindergarten and second grade children do not draw people looking at each other. Ives and Houseworth (1980) asked kindergarten, second, and fourth graders to draw two people, two horses, or two dogs. Generally the two horses and two dogs were drawn side view. But when asked to draw the two people talking to each other, it was only the fourth graders who drew the people facing each other; the younger children repeated their usual schema—two people looking straight forward.

Space Schema

There is now a conscious awareness of a definite order in space relationships. The child no longer thinks, "There is a tree, there is a man, there is a car," without relating them to one another as was typical during the preschematic stage. A child now thinks, "I am on the ground, the car is on the ground, the grass grows on the ground, mud is on the ground, we are all on the ground." This is expressed by a symbol which is called a *base line*. This consciousness, which includes all objects in a common space relationship, is expressed by putting everything on the base line.

The base line is universal and can be considered as much a part of the natural development of children as learning to run or skip. In a study of over five thousand drawings, it was found that only 1 percent of the children included the base line at age three, that by age six more children included the base line than did not, and that by eight years 96 percent of the children included the base line in their drawings (Wall, 1959). The base line appears as an indication of the child's realization of the relationship between himself and his environment; this line can apparently represent not only the ground on which objects stand but can represent a floor, a street, or any base upon which a child is standing. This line might be thought of as a travel line, somewhat like a map, with objects appearing in order along the line. Siegel et al. (1979) had children take trips through a model town and then asked them to construct the layout from memory. Although small scale space can be perceived at a single time, large areas need to be perceived through a number of separate observations. They concluded that the understanding of space is determined by the perceptual and motor mechanisms by which it is explored.

THE ACHIEVEMENT OF A FORM CONCEPT

Plate 20.
"I Am Standing in My Back Yard," painted by a six and a half year old girl. Notice the developing signs of the child's awareness of the relationship between objects and color; the grass is green, the sky is blue, and the girl's hair is yellow. She has painted herself much larger than the tree; the relative sizes show the child's egocentrism at this stage of development. She is holding a doll in the picture, and a doll carriage is on the right.

Plate 21.

"Lightning and Rain," drawn by a seven year old girl. Here the relationship between objects and color is more firmly established: sky is blue and lightning is yellow. Large hands grasp the umbrella, which does an effective job of keeping the child dry.

Plate 22.

"Spring," drawn by an eight and a half year old child. There is a sky line at the top, a base line at the bottom, and a pond in the middle which has been folded up to show the water, cattails, and the turtle who lives there.

Figure 118.
*"Eating Ice Cream."
A typical base line and
skyline frame the action, with
the important sun partly above
the skyline. The legs of the
smaller figure are especially
long, to reach the ground.*

It is quite obvious that in nature neither objects nor persons actually stand upon a line. When questioned, children invariably identify this base line as being the ground. A counterpart to the base line appears in drawings as a sky line. This is drawn at the top of the page, and the space between this and the base line is identified by children as being air. As adults we usually think of the sky in pictures as coming down to ground level; however, this is actually an optical illusion. Not only does the sky never actually meet the ground, but of

CHARACTERISTICS OF SCHEMATIC DRAWINGS   241

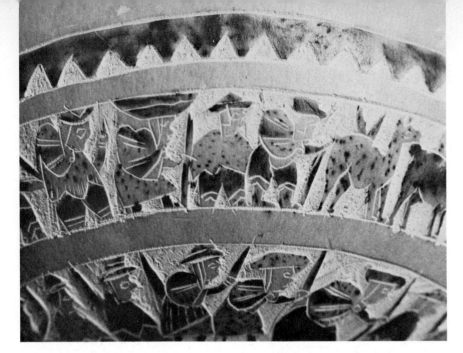

Figure 119.
This detail from a Peruvian bowl with an incised design shows the figures moving along a base line, a practice common in cultures widely separated by distance and time.

course there is no tangible sky, only an accumulation of air over a dark background. The concept of the sky above, ground below, and air between is just as valid as our concept that the sky and ground meet. Both are illusions.

At this stage of development the child has not developed an awareness of how to represent the three-dimensional quality of space. We find, therefore, that the schema is usually a representation of two dimensions. Occasionally some abstract lines are substituted for depth, but the biggest discovery is that there is a definite order in spatial relationships. The space schema is almost entirely abstract and has only an indirect connection with nature as adults see it.

In creative products of primitive cultures the base line was often used as a means of indicating motion. It may be that the origin of the base line is the kinesthetic experience of moving along a path. The use of the base line is also very apparent in the art of some complex cultures, such as in the carvings on the tombs in ancient Egypt, or the vase decorations of ancient Greece, or the cylinder seals of the Hittites, where pictorial matter is arranged on a line for a narrative purpose. When children use their art as communication, it may be natural to think of objects coming one after another on a line.

The Base Line as Part of the Landscape

When a child is drawing or painting an outdoor picture, the base line can be used to symbolize the base on which things stand and at another time to represent the surface of the landscape. In the painting in Figure 120 one base line symbolizes the level ground while another represents the mountain. Apparently, the child wishes to indicate that this second base line is elevated over the plain. It can readily be seen that the mountain is still meant as a base line

THE ACHIEVEMENT OF A FORM CONCEPT

from the fact that the flowers stand perpendicularly to the mountain. Even the figure is bound to its base line. It is as if the base line were a length of straight wire with flowers attached to it. If the wire is bent according to the kinesthetic experience of going up and down, the flowers attached to the wire stand out perpendicularly, just as in this drawing. It is not the mass of the mountain that is of significance but the line itself, which goes up and down. When children in this schematic stage draw a building, the chimney is typically drawn perpendicular to the line of the roof, which serves as a base line, just as the line of the mountain became a base line.

In Figure 121, entitled "Fruit Harvest," two base lines represent an orchard. The child himself is shown on the lower part of the paper picking apples off a tree. Above him is the sky and above that another base line upon which his father appears driving a wagon full of apples. Notice the schema the child has for apple tree. Notice also the size of the apples on the tree as compared to the size of the apples in the basket. The ripe apples have great importance on

Figure 120.
"I Am Climbing a Hill,"
painted by a seven year old boy.
The hill is an upper base line
which is bent, representing the
experience of climbing up and
down.

the tree, but once they are in the basket they become less important. One can get a real feeling for the freshness of children's expression from this, and it is this freshness that many adult artists strive to emulate. The bird in the upper corner becomes important, too, for apples pecked by a bird must be discarded. The showing of two base lines usually is a later development, and is a step toward perspective in drawings. However, this is strictly a two-dimensional representation, as can be seen by the fact that the sky is represented in both halves of the painting. Children rarely draw anything that is not directly related to the base line, even if two or more base lines appear in one picture. A better understanding of "Fruit Harvest" may be had by seeing the top portion as a more distant row of trees in the orchard, beyond the lower or closer trees.

In this picture everything functions and has meaning. The child wants to say, "This is an orchard," therefore he is not satisfied by merely drawing one tree. "The apples on the tree are the most beautiful ones, because I want them, but I have picked some into the basket. I am just now reaching for one. Those in the basket are no longer single apples, they are the dozens of apples I have collected. Daddy is carrying them to town. Birds are pecking on the apples. We don't want the birds." We can see how the child relates himself actively to his environment. He is on the ground, the basket is on the ground, the apples are in the basket, the tree is on the ground; and farther away, the wagon is on the ground, the horse is on the ground, and the bird is in the air with the

THE ACHIEVEMENT OF A FORM CONCEPT

sky above. The picture signifies the child's understanding of himself and his environment.

Although the base line usually represents space in drawings and paintings, occasionally a meaningful experience forces a child to deviate from this type of schema. These are subjective space representations. *Folding over* belongs to this category, expressing a space concept by drawing objects that appear to be upside down. Figure 122 shows the process of folding over; the child has depicted himself waving to the ferry. After the child drew himself waving with his handkerchief, standing on one side of the bay, he decided to draw the boat. He drew it apparently upside down. But it is not really upside down. This child was leaning on the floor and, after drawing himself on one side of the base line, he walked around his paper and drew the other side of the bay and the ferryboat. You can even see where the ferryboat is landing. This concept can best be understood if the paper is folded along a base line on which the boy is standing

Other Means of Space Representation

Figure 122.
"Norfolk Ferry," painted by an eight year old boy. This painting is an imaginative example of representing space by "folding over."

so that the child stands upright and faces the boat. By folding the other side of the bay upright also, we get a model of the scene and suddenly realize the interesting concept of the two skies, one at the bottom and the other at the top of the paper. Actually this is a perfectly valid concept: the child feels that both sides of the bay are important because his experience is that of being in the center of the scene.

This experience shows very clearly that it is an advantage to have children work on the floor or on low tables, so that the drawing or painting can be approached from all directions. In Figure 123, "I Say Hello to My Friend on the Other Side of the Street," drawn by a nine year old partially blind boy, the principle of folding over is used in a different manner. In this drawing the sides would be folded down rather than up to show the opposite sides of the street.

Sometimes children will not use a base line as the ground, but instead put objects or people in a circle, such as around a table. Figure 124 shows a family eating, with each member of the family viewed separately as though from the

Figure 123.
"I Say Hello to My Friend on the Other Side of the Street." These children frequently called to each other at the street crossing. Here the base lines are at the edges of the paper, in contrast with their location in the previous illustration.

THE ACHIEVEMENT OF A FORM CONCEPT

Figure 124.
The child has drawn from several points of view with family members seated around the table, which is tipped up to show the plates.

center of the table. Possibly the edges of the table could be understood as a substitute for a base line, but an important consideration is that the child includes a variety of viewpoints in one drawing. The scene is not to be viewed from outside the picture plane, but rather each person is seated at the table, seen from directly in front of that person, and in each case the person is smiling pleasantly back at us.

Subjective space experiences can result in mixing plan and elevation. The drawing "Eating Out at Joe's" shows the table tipped up on its side so that the plaid tablecloth can be seen. The plates and tableware are perched on the table edge; however, the chairs and diners are drawn side view. This combination of plan and elevation describes the important elements, although little related to a naturalistic representation.

Another drawing that combines plan and elevation is "Amusement Island", (Figure 126). The child visited an island on which were all types of amusements, people playing cards, hot dog stands, and so forth. There were boats for rent, and in such a boat the child took a ride around the island. The

CHARACTERISTICS OF SCHEMATIC DRAWINGS

Figure 125.
The knife, fork, and spoon are ready to be used but are drawn with the table edge as a base line. The light fixture overhead seems to be turned on.

drawing shows a top view of the island, because it is important to show that water surrounds the land. Since the child rode around the island in a boat, it is important that this, too, be portrayed. Each of the events is shown as a separate activity as the child experienced them. It is a listing of events, with each table folded over or boat tipped to explain what went on. Here it seems as if three edges of the paper have become three separate base lines. Similarly, it is not unusual to see all four sides of a house portrayed at one time, nor to see all four wheels drawn on an automobile. What a child includes in his paintings is a direct reflection of subjective experiences. There is obviously nothing wrong with these representations. The sensitive adult can gain insight into a child's relationship to his world by observing his creative expression.

X-ray Pictures

A child may use another interesting, nonvisual way of representation to show different views that could not possibly be seen at the same time. He depicts the inside and outside of a building or other enclosure simultaneously whenever

THE ACHIEVEMENT OF A FORM CONCEPT

Figure 126.
*"Amusement Island," drawn by
an eight year old boy. The boy
had gone around the amusement
island in a rowboat.*

Figure 127.
*This is a picture of a coal mine
painted by a nine year old girl.
She has shown both the inside
and outside features of the mine
in one representation.*

the inside is of greater importance. Apparently unaware of the impossibility of such a visual concept, he mixes up the inside and outside in his drawing. Sometimes the child may become so involved with the inside that he will treat the outside as if it were transparent.

In Figure 127 the illustration "Coal Mine" shows an X-ray representation in which both inside and outside are shown. She realized the significance of the mine shaft and tunnels and became quite absorbed in the interior of the mine and how the coal was produced. Note that the mountain surface is treated like a bent base line, with the house and trees placed perpendicular to it. It is not surprising to find that the child was the daughter of a coal miner living in a company house near the mine a generation ago.

Space and Time Representations

Space and time representations include in one drawing different time sequences or spatially distinct impressions. Just as a child invents a way of showing two- and three-dimensional objects, sometimes by using plan and elevation at the same time, so he also invents a way of showing events that occur in sequence. Apparently, children have different reasons for developing these space and time representations, and an understanding of them is important because they can provide a rich source for motivation.

One purpose of space–time representation is communication. A child likes to listen to and tell stories. This is one reason several episodes are represented in one sequence of drawings. The pictures may be separate, like those in a comic book, although they may not be divided by a line. Journeys, trips, travel episodes, or other events that require a sequence of time belong in this type of representation. The series of separate pictures show a complete event, so the topic is usually the same. Not only children have utilized this method of space–time representation; a classic example is the Bayeux Tapestry, telling the story of the Norman invasion of England in 1066.

Placing the various aspects of a particular experience next to one another in one space is a method of portraying its distinctive qualities. For a typical example, refer to Figure 129, the drawing entitled "Searching for the Lost Pencil." The figure on the left both is looking for and has found the pencil. The child uses the next figure to express putting the pencil into his pocket with one hand, while the other hand shows that it no longer has any function. In other words, by means of two figures he has represented four different time phases. In a sense he could have given one figure four arms, as has been done in medieval manuscripts, but this would have contradicted his concept of a man. He was so involved with his experience—searching for the pencil, finding the pencil, picking it up, and putting it into his pocket—that he drew all these events.

Significance of Variations in the Schema

If the schema is the concept of man and environment that the child has developed, then every deviation has special importance. Rarely does the basic schema itself change, but rather variations can often be noticed in sections or parts. Three principle forms of deviations are: (1) exaggeration of important

THE ACHIEVEMENT OF A FORM CONCEPT

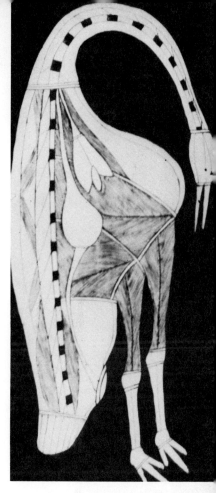

Figure 128.

The x-ray method of representation is not unique to young children. Other cultures, other times, have felt this was an appropriate means of representation. This typical x-ray painting on bark of a Brolga Bird was made by an Australian Aboriginal.

parts; (2) neglect or omission of unimportant or suppressed parts; and (3) change of symbols for significant parts. All these characteristics refer to the way in which adults see them. Children are not conscious of these exaggerations; rather, they create size relationships which are "real" to them. The origin of such deviations lies either in autoplastic experiences (that is, the feelings of the bodily self or muscular sensations), or in the relative significance the particular part has for the child.

Figure 129 displays many types of deviations. First we see a schematic representation of a man that the child drew when simply asked to draw a man. Thus, in this drawing no intentional experiences are represented. In comparing this schema with the drawing "Searching for the Lost Pencil" (Figure 129), note that the arms and the hands express the searching and groping about for the pencil. The enormously lengthened groping arm and changes in the shape of the symbol for hand in the first figure shows how the representation has been modified by the experience of reaching. "With this hand I have just found the pencil." The arms show a double line, indicating their special functional importance. Notice, too, the exaggerated pencil, showing the importance it had for the child when he found it. "With this hand I put it in my pocket," the child says, and points to one of the arms of the second figure which, in fact, represents the same person. The arm putting the pencil into the pocket is now far less emphasized and is represented by a single line only; the second arm of

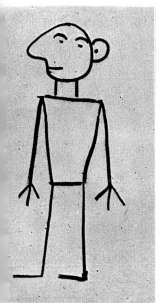

Figure 129.

(left) This is a child's schema for "A Man." No particular experience is portrayed. (right) "Searching for the Lost Pencil." Notice how the schema has been changed to show how the child looked for and found the pencil.

Figure 130.
*"Playing Football." Only the
arms of the figures have been
changed from the boy's usual
schema. The jumping figure is
raised above the base line.*

the figure, no longer having a function, has shriveled to a mere stump. The pencil has been reduced in size now that it has been found. An experience of bodily sensations is also shown. The left figure in the drawing is supposed to be bent forward, and this is expressed by means of shorter legs, a lowered head, and an elongated neck. The figure on the right is standing upright while putting the pencil in his pocket, and since the sensation of bending down is no longer important, the head and the neck diminish in size and the figure looks more like the schema. We may also speculate that the introduction of a base line in the second drawing might be caused because of the awareness that the pencil is on the floor and therefore it is important to show the floor.

In examining variations in schemas, Goodnow (1978) asked 320 children from nursery school age to fifth grade to draw a person picking up a ball. The younger children showed the least change from the usual schema; they placed the ball near the figure, lengthened an arm to touch the ball, or drew the ball raised, but left the body unchanged. Sometimes the first and second graders would have the figure side view, but it was not until third grade that most of the drawings began to show the figure itself bent. In a second study, Goodnow asked children to draw two people, one walking slowly and the other running fast. There was no particular difference between these two figures except for altering the legs.

Disproportions nearly always result from some definite intention or experience, though this does not mean that the experience is necessarily conscious. Therefore there are no "inaccurate proportions," since such a judgment is determined by an adult visual attitude. Because the child is not aware of making these exaggerations or omitting parts, correcting such drawing would only serve to confuse the child. The pictorial representations of children follow laws of their own that have little to do with "naturalistic" laws. An awareness of the variety and an understanding of the meanings of these types of space schema give us a greater insight into the inner thought processes of children. In some cases the subjective space representations may look confusing or incomprehensible. Although a child should never be forced to justify or interpret a painting, most children are more than eager to discuss their involvement in the experience that motivated the picture. A sympathetic and understanding adult can learn a great deal about the meaningfulness of these activities by showing an interest in how and what a child thinks.

The Meaning of Color and Design

The child discovers naturally that there is a relationship between color and object. It is no longer a random choice or emotional relationship that determines which color he selects for objects in his painting. The child draws his environment more objectively, and has developed definite space relationships. In color, too, the child has discovered a similar definite relationship. Just as he will repeat again and again his schema for a man, or for space, he also repeats the same colors for the same objects.

The establishment of a definite color for an object and its constant repetition is part of the continuing development of the child's thinking processes. The child now has the capacity to categorize, to group things into classes and to make generalizations. "What color is the sky?" "The sky is blue." "What color is grass?" "The grass is green." To the visually discriminating adult the answers might vary, depending upon whether it is a hazy day or a stormy sky, or whether the grass is dry and brittle or fresh from a spring rain. To the child, however, just to be able to realize that the color in his painting is the same as the object which he is painting is an important accomplishment and a satisfying experience. He has begun to find some logical order in the world and is establishing concrete relationships with things around him.

Although there are common colors used by most children for particular objects, each child develops his own color relationships. The origin of the individual's color schema is probably to be found in a visual or emotional concept of color. Apparently, the first meaningful relationship that the child has with an object can determine his color schema. If the child's first impressions were of a muddy back yard, and through repetition this concept has become firmly established, then all ground will be brown, regardless of whether there is grass over it or not. This color schema will not change unless the child becomes involved in an experience in which a change in color becomes important.

In looking at Plate 20, "I Am Standing in My Back Yard," facing page 240, the child has established definite color-object relationships. Notice that the eyes, lips, and hair, and also the grass, tree, and sky have been painted in very direct bold colors that seem to indicate that the child "knows" the color of these objects. Plate 21, "Lightning and Rain," is drawn with crayon. Notice that the sky retains its blue color although it is raining. Criticism of the use of color in these two pictures would only be upsetting to the children. Also the

Figure 131.

As children paint, they develop color-object relationships; they now establish schemes for colors as well as for objects.

Figure 132.
While experimenting with colors, this girl has spontaneously repeated the same wavy line, displaying an innate design sense.

happy accident when colors run into one another, which may stimulate an adult, can be very frustrating to a child. Not only is he unable to capitalize on these accidental happenings, but for the child such accidental happenings are just mistakes. The color schema is an indication, therefore, of the developing ability for abstract thought and shows that he can generalize to other situations from his own experiences. This is an important step in the developmental process.

A certain third grade boy had a new classroom teacher, one who felt that her youngsters needed more opportunity to paint. He was amazed to learn that she wanted the children to mix their own colors, because never before had they been allowed to mix poster paints. He spent the entire hour mixing paint and, to his delight, discovered brown, all kinds of brown. So his jars of brown paint were carefully stored for him to use as soon as he could make time for art again. Sometimes children will make such discoveries when mixing paint. Wondering how this happened and trying to do it again can be exciting. When there is no green paint, but plenty of blue and yellow, children may find that color mixing is a challenging experience. This is quite different from telling children to mix a couple of drops of blue into the yellow to get a cool green. At this age there is little awareness of subtle variations in hue.

THE MEANING OF COLOR AND DESIGN

The evidence indicates that a child of this age has no concern for any formal aspects of art; art for him is chiefly a means of self-expression, and he is not aware of the beauty in what he does. However, adults can see many design qualities in what a child of this age paints or draws, often taking a great deal of interest in this native or innate design sense of the child. This was not true a century ago. Today it is obvious that freshness and directness in expression have become important in the adult art world, and this same freshness and directness can be seen in children's drawings during this schematic stage.

One of the important attributes of design is rhythm, and this rhythm is often to be seen in children's paintings in their repetition of form. Looking over drawings or paintings by children of this age will quickly show that the way children deal with space contributes greatly to this "design." This is a natural part of the child's development. He paints spontaneously and the repetition of form or schemata is done unconsciously, whereas an adult artist uses repetition and manipulates forms on a conscious level. The teaching of design fundamentals would be detrimental to the spontaneity and freedom typical of children's drawings.

The Development of the Primary School Child

Drawings reflect the child's total being; the emergence of a definite schema has many implications and can give an understanding adult some valuable insights into the child's development. The child no longer represents objects in relation to himself but now begins to represent objects in some logical relationship to one another. A younger child of five will draw a house or a tree or a toy in juxtaposition without any objective order. Now, however, the child includes himself in his concept in the same way that he includes the tree, the house, or the whole environment. This experience—"I am on the street, the house is on the street, John is on the street"—is a decisive step in the psychological development of the child. His egocentric attitude changes, and this is reflected not only in his drawings but also in his total development. The child seeks to find order in his environment and to develop formulas for proper behavior (Piaget, 1959). These may make no sense to an adult but can often become very important in a child's life. Most of us can remember some of the laws governing our behavior at this age, such as avoiding stepping on the cracks in the sidewalk for

THE ACHIEVEMENT OF A FORM CONCEPT

Figure 133.
"Daddy is Coming Home."
*This child shows great
awareness of his environment,
with the car parked outside,
the father coming through the
door, and the family inside the
house waiting to greet him.*

fear of dire consequences, or performing some private ritual if two children said the same thing at the same time, or touching every desk in the row before sitting down to insure good luck. These laws and rules for behavior make a schema of sorts in another area of the child's development.

The development of the schema also signals a change to a more cooperative attitude (Wall, 1959). The differences between the preschematic and schematic stages can easily be recognized by observing children in a kindergarten and then comparing their behavior with that of children in second grade. Kindergarten children play and work together only when urged to do so. One child will be going in one direction imitating a train, another child will be sitting self-concerned in a chair, whereas a third will be playing in the sand, scarcely noticing the others. Their conversation will also be ego-involved. Although they apparently are talking to one another, they seldom listen to, nor seem to expect a reply from, those near them. Their talk is usually tied up with

THE DEVELOPMENT OF THE PRIMARY SCHOOL CHILD

257

their own play and seems to be more concerned with explaining what is going on to themselves rather than to others. This is clearly indicated, as we have seen, in the spatial concept of children during that age. However, when the schema develops and we detect a definite order in space, the child begins to relate to others and see himself as part of the environment.

Before the development of the schema is not a period for cooperative games. An awareness of others and of others' feelings will not be understood. It may well be that a tremendous amount of time is wasted at the kindergarten level in trying to maintain order and quiet, since true learning apparently takes place whenever a child is expressing himself, whether others are listening or not. At that egocentric age it is most important to converse with oneself and

Figure 134.
The boy who drew this picture of himself has a developing awareness of size relationships and order. The objects on the table are arranged in a line for us to see.

with one's own expression, whereas during the schematic stage the ability to share and understand others' feelings is beginning to develop.

The introduction of the base line in the schema has other important implications for the understanding of children. Since a child can now see logical relationships between objects in his environment, it is possible to begin to think of a meaningful reading program. In reading, for instance, this same correlation is necessary in relating letters to one another in order to form a word symbol. Sibley (1957) gathered reading readiness scores, teacher estimates of reading potential, and several drawings from three kindergarten classes. The following year when these same children were in first grade, reading achievement scores and the first grade teachers' evaluation of their reading skills were obtained. It was found that the reading readiness and reading achievement scores were closely related, which would be expected since the material the children were tested on was similar. However, the drawings gathered from the kindergarten children were a better predictor of how well they would be reading when they got to first grade than were the estimates of the kindergarten teacher! Another study utilized art in a program to develop reading skills. Platt (1971) has developed a method using drawings by children as the basis for teaching reading, in which children put together their own reading books by making drawings with the names of the objects added. Mills (1973) developed an art program for first grade Appalachian children that sought the inclusion of details by activating the children's passive knowledge. Mills concluded that the reading ability of these children was measurably improved.

Others report that art helps in the reading program, but a survey of some studies relating art to reading (Groff, 1978) concludes that concrete experimental supporting evidence is missing. It appears that intellectual ability influences both reading and art ability; art exercises tied to some reading lesson to make it more palatable are not going to result in measurable reading improvement and may have a negative effect on art. Stein (1972) compared the effectiveness of a reading readiness program with another program involving a number of creative art activities for kindergarten children. On a later reading readiness test, there were no significant differences between these groups; rather, a control group of children who helped plan their own activities, and were read to a lot, scored higher on the test.

It was found that trying to teach nursery school children how to make squares and triangles was a frustrating task (Brittain, 1969). However, after waiting a year, most of these same children could do the copying tasks easily. Some of the same factors may be important to consider in this seven to nine year age range. It is usual to teach skills in art or to develop competence in reading or mathematics by merely taking the desired educational outcome and dividing it into small teachable components, but apparently this method does not work. Trying to improve visual discrimination, motor coordination, memory, or understanding of spatial relations seems unrelated to improvement in children's reading ability (Larsen and Hammill, 1975). It might be expected that training in visual discrimination would have a positive effect on children's drawings, but a study of drawings by six to ten year olds (Miller et al., 1977) before and after twelve weeks of perceptual training showed no more differentiated drawings than a control group who had no such training. Some of the visual discrimination tasks demanded that children trace around objects or color in certain shapes; happily, the aesthetic quality of the children's drawings did not seem to be adversely affected. Although we focus upon the process in art, and realize that the product is only a record of that process, sometimes it is easy to forget that reading is also a product, reflecting a child's thinking process. In art as in reading, trying to improve the product without an understanding of children's thinking and the experiences which influence the process, makes teaching toward adult goals meaningless.

Schematic Drawings as a Reflection of Growth

Within any classroom we find a large range of individual differences. It is not unusual in the area of intellectual development to have a third grade class composed of children whose IQ may range from 75 to 125. This means essentially that the mental age of these children will range from the six year level to the ten year level. We will also find a wide range of physical differences. In looking at the drawings by children in this same third grade, we can also expect to find a comparable range of individual differences. A few drawings and paintings, in fact, may be more typical of either a first grader or a fifth grader. We have come to expect the child who is more developed intellectually to be in general more developed physically, and because art is a reflection of a child's total development we can expect his artistic achievements to follow the same general pattern.

One of the indications of the child's growing intellect is his understanding of the world that surrounds him. Objects may be meaningful or meaningless to the child, depending upon his emotional relationship to them and his

THE ACHIEVEMENT OF A FORM CONCEPT

Figure 135.
*"Playing Checkers," painted by
a seven year old boy. The
checkerboard has been tipped up
because it is important to see the
top view when playing.*

intellectual comprehension of them. Piaget and Inhelder (1971) believe the continual assimilation of external factors is necessary for the development and modification of concepts. Learning, growing intellectually, depends upon the ability to take into the system new information, which can be combined and integrated with the concepts we already hold. This new information is gradually internalized and, once assimilated, provides new concepts and an altered schema. Whether or not the world has become meaningful to the child partially depends upon the degree to which he has formulated his concepts. It is to be expected, then, that the child will express in his drawings a definite symbol for the things he repeatedly represents. If we look at the drawing of the children playing checkers in Figure 135, we can see where the child repeated his schema of a man for both figures; however, the sizes as well as the motions of the figures differ. Notice that the nose and the eyes are expressed with the same symbol, just a dot. Yet obviously these parts have different functional characteristics.

The active knowledge of the child reveals his understanding of and interest in the world about him, and this is what is expressed in his drawings. Our checker playing youngster shows little awareness of these details. His eyes have no eyebrows, lids, or any other details, nor are the nose or mouth indicated by more than a mere generalization. The only concept that shows some detail is the concept for hand, which consists of the palm and five fingers. Of course, our checker player may not have been very involved in this particular picture; several drawings would be useful to help us understand him better. However, the field of art can contribute a great deal to a child's growth by stimulating an awareness of the things around him. "Do you have to watch the moves carefully in checkers? Are you hoping your partner will not notice that he can jump you? Do you keep track of how many men you have left?" The clarifications of concepts and the stimulation of an awareness of details can be a big step toward developing a greater awareness of eyes. Children are a product both of their heredity and of their environment, which means that we should strive to make their environment as rich and stimulating as possible. Figure 136 was drawn by a boy after a trip to a firehouse. He not only remembered the rubber boots and pole but became very involved with the fire truck, and was particularly interested in the hose and ladder. Such overlapping is unusual for this age.

The area of emotional growth can often be neglected in a classroom. A child who has hurt his finger usually gets immediate attention from the teacher and often from a nurse or even a physician. A child with hurt feelings, however, usually has no one to whom to turn for help in patching up his wounds. It has been well established, however, that a child's emotions, feelings, and attitudes can affect his learning. The opportunity to express in socially acceptable fashion the feelings of anger, fear, and even hatred not only produces a release of tensions but also allows the child to discover that constructive use can be made of one's emotional involvement. An experiment (Francis, 1973) was done with 143 third grade children which has given support for the assumption that creative activity can provide the atmosphere for reduction of frustration. Here purposely frustrated children were given a chance to make fierce animals out of clay, while a control group colored and cut out dittoed tulips. Although some of the children's teachers were more creative than others, which confused things, the "fierce animal" experience groups did better in a subsequent learning experience.

When a schema is used in a rigid fashion, it may actually be an escape from facing one's own feelings and emotions. On the other hand, the flexible use of the schema is an important requisite for true self-expression. The very nature of the schema, the child's symbol used over and over again whenever he needs it, makes it dangerously likely to be considered a stereotype that is repeated without any personal involvement. Flexibility in thinking should be given special attention during this period. Usually many changes and deviations in the schema can be observed, especially if the child is free to express his own reactions without fear of being censored. When the schema is used too rigidly, a child may hide behind these stereotypes. Variation in the sizes of the represented objects indicate their significance. Exaggerations, neglect, or omissions, which indicate a child's relationship to his environment, are not only typical of this age but indicative of a child's healthy emotional reactions. It is not normal for a child to concentrate on one part of the figure to such an extent

THE ACHIEVEMENT OF A FORM CONCEPT

Figure 136.

"At the Firehouse." The boy felt as if he were a fireman. At the left is the back of the truck with its hose and ladder.

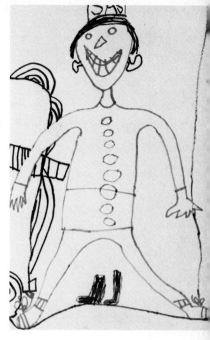

that the body appears only as an appendage. Continued and extremely distorted exaggerations are quite rare; however, ego-involved reaction to the environment continues to be typical at this age.

Art not only provides an opportunity for the release of emotions but it can also provide the child with an opportunity to use these emotions constructively. Schools have to limit the degree of emotional outbursts that can be accepted within the society of a classroom. Outbursts of anger, frustration, envy, and sheer joy are usually not tolerated. Even so, the usual, bland classroom goes far beyond this and strives to make an emotionless environment in which only the intellectual pursuits are worthy of consideration. Art should encourage a greater emotional involvement in a healthy tension-free environment.

The social growth of children can also be seen in their creative productions. The child has become less ego-involved and more aware of himself in an objective way; the use of the base line signifies that he is beginning to view himself in relation to others. The self-identification of a child with his own experiences in his creative work is one of the prerequisites for establishing contacts outside the self. It is necessary to identify one's own actions and to feel responsible for, and to have some control over, these actions before one can develop a greater group consciousness. For example, in Figure 135 our checker playing friend went beyond the immediate self by establishing contact with another person, as well as the rest of his environment. The awareness of things around the self, which have no immediate relationship to the central experience, shows a high level of social growth, although he did not include any particular characteristics of the lamp or the window.

Related here is the child's development in perceptual growth. The mere portrayal of a symbolic form for an object indicates little perceptual awareness. Since perception includes many of the ways in which a child acquaints himself with his environment, the development of perception is of prime importance. The awareness of textures, sounds, smells, tastes, and visual shapes and forms can all be shown in a variety of ways in drawings. Developing a sensitive perceptual awareness becomes crucial when we realize that it is the interaction between a child and his environment that can establish the amount or kind of learning that takes place.

Toward the end of this schematic stage, the child's drawings are increasingly influenced by his visual perception of his environment. Sixty British children, from five through nine years of age, were asked to draw several common objects, including a cup. Then each child was able to hold and manipulate a straight sided mug, with a handle and an applied flower design. Then he was asked to draw the mug; the handle was turned away from him, out of sight,

Figure 137.
"In the Bathroom." Notice the awareness of details in this drawing; even the tiles and water pipes are included. This child has a rich concept of his environment.

and the flower was toward him. The handle, which is characteristic of a mug, was drawn by the five, six, and seven year olds but was dropped by most eight and nine year olds; whereas the flower was drawn by only a few of the younger children and one third of the eight year olds, but by all of the nine year olds (Freeman and Janikoun, 1972). This change in drawings illustrates the children's shift from drawing what they know about an object (their concept) to drawing what they see (their percept). Freeman (1980) reports subsequent experiments, in which a clear, handled glass mug was the object to be drawn. The transparent mug was more difficult for the children to draw than the opaque mug had been. Freeman suggests that it is unwise to merely judge the success of the final drawing products, but instead we should consider the children's systematic efforts to solve tasks, as children try different strategies and change their repertoire of rules. These children did not want their drawings to be ambiguous, and therefore included handles, which are a defining feature of cups and mugs.

THE ACHIEVEMENT OF A FORM CONCEPT

Light and MacIntosh (1980) asked 64 six and seven year old children to draw a small model house placed inside a transparent glass beaker and to draw the same house placed behind the beaker. From where the child sat, the visual image looked virtually identical. However, the drawings differed considerably. All of the children drew a beaker shape or circle surrounding the house when the toy house was placed inside; but when the house was placed behind the glass, most children drew the two separately, with the house above or alongside the glass. Apparently the information about the two conditions was most important to the children, and the visual impression they received of the house and glass played a minor role in its depiction.

To some extent even physical growth can be seen in the productions of children. A child who is physically active is much more likely to give his figures movement and action than a child who lacks physical energy; continuous exaggeration of the same body parts may indicate some defect. The child who drew our friends playing checkers was hard of hearing and typically emphasized the ears, as in Figure 135. Children are now much more able to handle art materials effectively; there should be less concern about paint being spilled, and youngsters will want to use smaller details in their paintings.

Aesthetic growth does not start at any particular age. Whenever objects or forms show an integration of thinking, feeling, and perceiving, the child has developed an aesthetic awareness either purposefully or unconsciously. The lack of aesthetic growth can be seen in pictorial representations that are either disorganized in thought and feeling or lack organization. Rhythm, one of the basic elements of design, consists mainly of repetition, a natural type of expression during this schematic stage. Some children, especially those whose aesthetic growth is more developed, utilize this repetition in an intuitive way for decorative purposes. The bold and direct use of color, so typical of this age, adds to this decorative quality. However, this is a natural outgrowth of the development of a child. No dogma regarding rhythm, balance, or harmony will ever have anything but a negative effect upon a child's natural growth pattern. The child has no use for rules of aesthetics, which change anyway as society's values change. It is the effect of art experiences and processes upon the individual, not the final product, that contributes to aesthetic growth.

If a child casually starts drawing somewhere and either does not have enough space to place everything he wants to draw, or discovers he has nothing to add and too much blank space left, he obviously lacks a sensitive awareness of the relationship between his paper and what he is expressing. To develop aesthetic sensitivity, we need to involve the whole child. "Imagine that your paper is a treasure map of a large island. You will need to have an X

Figure 138.
"Playing Basketball" shows how the youngster throws a ball through the hoop. The path of the ball is portrayed by a series of ball shapes, almost as if we were seeing the scene in slow motion.

marked where the treasure is. What else will you need on this map? Harbor? Boats? Trees? Mountains? Swamps? Lakes? Streams? Graveyard? Stockade?" A motivation should make a child more sensitively aware of his personal relationship with those things around him. It must be stressed, however, that there are no set rules that can be applied to any individual. What is harmoniously right for one child may not be right for another. Just as artists are striving for variation and innovation in design, we should also expect and encourage large differences in children's work.

Art Motivation

The kind and type of motivation a teacher should use at the different age levels grow out of the needs of the children during each particular stage of development. The task of the teacher is to give each child an opportunity to use his concepts, not as rigid symbols, but as meaningful experiences by stimulating the child's consciousness and awareness. A whole class discussion on a particular topic can be exciting, as group contagion may provide a positive force for creative activities. However, sometimes small group or individual motivation is important, depending on the particular subject at hand. Discussion should include consideration of *we* (I and somebody else), *action* (what we are doing), and *where* (actual description of the place, not depth or distance).

Of great importance is the need to create an exciting atmosphere that is flexible and open to any suggestions from the child. Any motivation should make the child more sensitively aware of himself and of his environment, should develop and stimulate an intense desire to paint a meaningful picture, and should encourage the child to be flexible in his approach to both materials and subject matter. Every motivation should have an introduction, culmination, and summary. So, a topic such as "We Are Playing on the School Grounds," would begin with a general introduction. "When do you play? Didn't I just see you playing outside a short time ago? When do you usually play on the school grounds? When? During recess; I see. Where do you play? Do you use the whole playground? What do you play? Do you just stand out there and look at each other? Oh, you play tag! Yes, I have played tag, too. How do you play this game? You have to run! Do you run fast? Do you keep yourself nice and straight and tall? You mean you can't run fast that way? You have to bend forward when you run; why do you bend forward? If you run fast would you fall on your back if you didn't lean forward? Johnny, show me

Figure 139.
Children create from their own experiences. Any motivation will result in a variety of responses from children, depending upon their backgrounds and awareness.

how you run fast! Yes, you really do have to lean forward! If you leaned too far, what would happen? You would fall on your knee! Oh, some of the gravel even got stuck in your knee once—that made it all bloody; yes, I know it hurts. Sometimes your body wants to go faster than your legs can. If you didn't bend forward at all, you would fall backward and hurt your head. . . . I guess it is better to hurt your knee than your head! How about your legs? Do you have both legs in front at the same time? No, that's like a rabbit! You are right, we cannot jump like rabbits and go very fast. Could both legs be on the ground at the same time? What happens when you run? Oh, one leg is in the air. Isn't that funny! One leg is in the air, did you ever think of that?" (In stimulating a child to a greater awareness of his own actions you have developed a flexibility within his schema for a person. Now the child can actually sense his legs and feet on the ground, so he has become personally involved in the motivation.) "Does everyone know how to play tag? We have all played tag! Let's draw how we play on the school grounds."

It is important in any motivation such as this to be sure that each child is personally involved. However, there should be a wide range of topics so that the child has the opportunity to identify with his own particular interests. Each child should feel that the motivation was planned just for him.

Subject Matter

Ideally no subject matter should be needed if every child drew, painted, and constructed that which was important to him, and if he were free of external pressures to perform in certain ways. However, our society is filled with messages from teachers, parents, peers, television, and radio to behave in certain

Figure 140.
Girls and boys may display different interests in their drawings. Here a boy shows an awareness of, but not an understanding of, the mechanical features of this tractor.

THE ACHIEVEMENT OF A FORM CONCEPT

ways; and there is conflict between what a child can do, what he is supposed to do, and what he would like to do. In art, the child is not forced to conform to external standards. The art experience has many tasks: It must truly be the youngster's expression, and it must also be a growing, expanding awareness experience that can help to extend the youngster's frame of reference.

Many topics come to mind in which action plays a major role in encouraging a flexible use of the schema. Starting with the *we,* adding the *action,* and following with the *where* includes the essential aspects of the experience. Many topics come from the children themselves without much effort, such as "Playing on the School Grounds" as mentioned, or "Running To Catch the School Bus." Others might be "We Are Climbing a Tree," "We Go on a Hike," "We Are Jumping Rope," "We Are Playing Hockey," "We Go Sledding," "We Are Planting Bushes Around the School," "I Am Wrestling with My Friend," and so forth. Some topics can provide for the use of profile and front views, such as "A Tug of War," "Playing Games on a Rainy Day," "Watching the Parade," "I Am Eating Pancakes with my Brother," "The Dentist Examines My Teeth," or "I Am Being Taught How To Swim."

Several topics are excellent for a variety of space-time representations. These would include "How We Cleaned Up Around Our Neighborhood," "We Visited the Crowded Shopping Center," "Our Trip to the Bakery," or "We Made Cookies for the Holiday." Discussing various aspects of the experience will encourage some children to include many elements in one drawing, but some children will portray the one part that seemed most important, like eating the cookies after they were baked. X-ray pictures will be produced if both inside and outside are important in some experiences. This would include drawings of "Our Class Visited a Newspaper Office," or "Our Trip to the Dairy"; other topics might be "Shopping in the Hardware Store with My Father," "We Are Staying in a Hotel," "The Time I Was in the Hospital," or "Riding in an Elevator."

Just as it is important to develop a flexible, functional form schema, it is also important to develop a flexible approach to color. Although it is obvious that some of these topic areas overlap, the following may give some suggestions for developing color concepts. It is possible to see how effective a motivation is by comparing the use of color after a particular motivation with the use of color before motivation. Many topics lend themselves to color awareness, such as "The Workmen Are Painting Our House," "I Like Ketchup on My Hamburger," "We Got Our Shoes Covered with Mud," "The New Grass in the Yard Is Beginning To Grow," or "We Are Raking Leaves in the Fall."

Another area of importance to consider for subject matter is the private

world of the child. This includes topics that have emotional significance, such as fantasy and dreams. When a child paints what is of deep concern to him, or reveals certain desires and conflicts, it should be remembered that any subject matter is acceptable. Although the teacher may show interest in the representations, under no conditions should any moral judgment be made about the content of these pictures. Personal involvement would be high for a topic such as "The Time I Was Most Afraid," or "I Had a Horrible Dream." But emotions can also be sublimated in topics such as "I Am Making Believe I Am a Fierce Animal," "If I Were Teacher," or "I Am the Richest Person in the World."

One other area of subject matter that should be considered is the topic of the particular material itself. The principal reason for concentrating on the material is to insure that the child uses materials in a flexible fashion and has an opportunity to investigate their possibilities. Unfortunately, some children will use this nonrepresentational theme as a means of retreating from a creative expressive experience. This lack of involvement can be seen when children too often hide behind the phrase "I am just making a design." However, getting to know how paint runs or how a drawing instrument behaves is important for further expression. Making a collage, using crayons in different ways, making tall things with holes out of clay can be both interesting and fun.

Art Materials

The selection of an art material, its relevance to a particular group of children and their needs at a particular time, and its preparation and handling are all important considerations. Any art material should facilitate the self-expression of children and not be a stumbling block. When children have become eager to create after a meaningful motivation, the art materials should be ready for their use. How frustrating to get all excited about painting "How I Broke My Leg While Sledding" and then have to sit still waiting for paints! Often the material can be prepared and distributed with the help of the children, and then the motivation can take place in another part of the room.

Three things are important in developing methods of working with materials. First, the teacher should know that each child must develop his own techniques, and that every "help" from the teacher in showing the child a "correct" technique will only mean restricting the child's individual approach. There are many ways of working with art materials; and, as mentioned above, time should be taken to explore many procedural possibilities. No child should be stopped in the middle of his expression to show him the "proper" way to hold a brush, use a crayon, or fill his paper. The teacher's job is to introduce the appropriate material at a time when a child is most ready to use it.

Second, every material must make its own contribution. If a task can be done in a different art material with a better effect, the wrong material has been used. Therefore it is important that the teacher know the qualities of the material being used so that the best material will be used for any particular expression.

Third, the teacher should not force too many materials on the children. In some books on art education, many materials are introduced and used from the very beginning of childhood. At a time when the child is eager to create, when he is full of intuitive power, too many different media may not only be wasteful but can often prove distracting as well.

The child at the age level from seven to nine years is not concerned with the representation of distance. What is most characteristic of this level is that the child has found a form, space, and color concept, which through repetition develops into his schema. At times these repetitions develop a designlike quality. The child should be able to repeat the same colors for the same objects whenever he wishes. An art material that does not afford him the opportunity of experiencing mastery or self-assurance is not a good medium for this developmental stage. The consistency and texture of poster paint or tempera serve this purpose best, but crayon or colored chalk can also be used successfully.

There is no reason whatsoever for introducing water color at this time. Water color is transparent, runs, and at times results in happy accidents. The transparency of water color serves best to paint atmosphere and landscape, but does not lend itself to repetition or to painting the designlike qualities so typical of this age. Since the child in his painting is more concerned with expressing his own ideas than with visual stimuli, these happy accidents can turn into sad disappointments. The child is striving for order and attempting to categorize his knowledge into a working form. At older age levels, when the urge for repetition is not important, water color will serve to inspire the child. It is quite apparent, then, that an art material should be selected because it can contribute to the child's development, and should not be introduced merely for the purpose of changing a material.

Larger paper can be used at this age, to give the child more freedom than smaller sheets provide. Since he has developed better coordination, and his arms have grown longer, the larger sheets may fit his needs better. Also, brushes made of hair can now be used along with bristle, because children have developed a greater awareness of detail.

Clay is not just another material. Since it is three-dimensional, it stimulates another kind of thinking. A material is wisely used only if it fulfills the purpose for which it is intended. Thus, nothing should be done in clay if it could better be painted, and nothing should be painted if it could be done better in clay; likewise nothing should be done in clay or paint if it could better be done in wood. It is important that the material selected suit the type of expression.

The unique characteristic of clay is its plasticity. Because of this plasticity, clay can be used most advantageously with children of this age, for the very nature of the material will facilitate the flexible use of concepts. Whereas a drawing demands a simultaneous concept of one event (with the exception of the space–time representations), the process of modeling with clay permits a constant and continual changing of form. Figures can be added or taken away

Figure 142.
*Each art material has
its own characteristics, which
call for different kinds
of expression.*

Figure 143.
*"I Am Rowing the Boat." Clay
can provide the opportunity for
developing spatial concepts and
understandings. It was not
important that this product could
not be fired.*

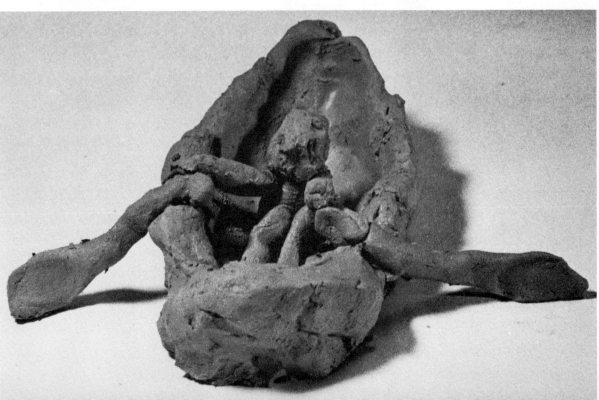

Figure 144.
*In the synthetic method of
modeling (left), single pieces are
put together. In the analytic
method of modeling (right), single
parts are pulled out from the
whole form.*

or changed in their position and shape. Therefore, action can be included in
any motivation and should be related directly to the child' experience. A comparison of the three-dimensional qualities of clay with space in nature could
result in an attempt at small scale model making, which is not a creative activity but simply the development of a technical skill and has no place at this age
level. However, the child may include objects of the immediate environment
spontaneously. An example of this might be a child who models a picnic scene,
making visitors come and sit down, and actually moving an arm up to indicate
eating.

 Two different methods of working with clay can be observed. One is
that of pulling out from the whole and the other is that of putting single parts
together. In Figure 144 are examples showing these two different modes of
expression. Since each method reveals a different kind of thinking, it would be
disturbing to a child to be diverted from his own method of thinking. Pulling
the clay out from the whole means to have a concept of the total, however
vague, from which details will be developed; this method is called the *analytic
method.* The other method of expression described as putting single representa-

tive symbols together into a whole means that the child is building up a synthesis out of partial impressions; this method is called the *synthetic method*. Pulled out or putting together is not merely a superficial means of achieving a form, but grows out of the child's thinking. Some teachers feel that it is wise to discourage modeling by the synthetic method of putting details together, because such modeling cannot be fired in the kiln. It is true that such pieces cannot be fired easily because of the danger of air bubbles and because the parts may separate in the firing process, but it is an adult concept that clay products made by children should be fired.

There are, of course, a number of materials in addition to those mentioned that can meet the needs of this age group. Colored paper, oil crayons, fiber tip pens, collage materials, paste and scissors, many natural materials such as twigs or pebbles, and even a large soft pencil can be used to advantage. Care should be taken to insure that the child has an opportunity for a depth of art experience and that new materials are not introduced just to stimulate the teacher. Ideally, art materials should provide the opportunity for both a variety of experience and a depth of expression.

Summary

To some extent the products of this schematic stage appear more rigid than the drawings and paintings of younger children. However, we realize that the child is structuring his thinking processes in such a way that he can begin to organize and see relationships in his environment. This is not a step backward. The child is also beginning to structure his drawings and paintings to allow himself some basis for change and reorganization. Creative thinking is not disorganized thinking; rather, it is the ability to redefine and reorganize in a flexible manner those forms and elements with which we are familiar. Abstract thinking is based entirely upon symbols, and during this stage we can see the child's first steps toward this development.

It is essential that a child be given constant encouragement to explore and investigate new ways and methods. Occasionally children will try to copy each other, particularly if one child has just received praise and another wishes that he could have this praise too. Putting a positive emphasis upon differences and praising nonconformity and experimentation will encourage creative thinking. A child's *own* creative effort should be accepted regardless of how meager the product appears. Ideally, each child should be eager to create, with the teacher's role being primarily that of encouraging depth of expression and a meaningful experience. The child who clings too closely to stereotypes, or repeats too often a particular schema, or is constantly looking for suggestions is the one who needs the attention and special guidance of the teacher to bolster his own self-confidence and to provide him with positive experiences in self-expression. At this age the opportunity to establish the self as an acceptable being who thinks for himself and is able to express these thoughts, whatever they are, becomes most important. Because the child is searching for a pattern or structure within the environment, his concept of himself as developed at this time may be an important factor in his relationships with learning abilities and with people. To develop a positive image of oneself, to encourage confidence in one's own means of expression, to provide the opportunity for constructive divergent thinking, should certainly be basic aims of the art program.

RELATED ACTIVITIES

1 Collect drawings of a man done by a first grade class. Find how many different symbols are used for nose, mouth, body, arms, and so forth. What percentage of these children are using geometric shapes for their expression? Compare with drawings done by a third grade, to see if the percentages change.

2 Find one child's schema for a person. See how this is repeated over a period of several weeks. After a strong motivation centered upon some physical activity, notice the deviations in his schema. A week later, has he reverted to his usual schema?

3 In observing the behavior of children of this age, outside the classroom, can you detect any social schemata? Are there fixed rules for games? Are there set patterns for certain activities? Are there set songs or chants for such games as jump rope? Is there any evidence of adults' pressure for these patterns, or do they come from the children themselves?

4 How many children in a first grade use the base line in their representations? Compare the percentage with a second grade class.

5 Collect samples of X-ray drawings, folding over, and space–time representations. Why were these subjective representations important to the

child's expression? How would adults portray the same event? Which is the most adequate portrayal?

6 In examining children's drawings and paintings, show how the use of color parallels the establishment of a schema in form. What are some of the differences found in color schemata for common objects?

7 Keep a list of the different reasons for exaggerations, omissions, or neglect of parts as shown in drawings. Illustrate each from examples of children's work.

8 Plan and carry out an experiment similar to that of Freeman and Janikoun (1972). Gather drawings of a common object with distinctive features from a third grade class. Determine how many children have a more visual representation and how many still draw their concepts. How do the differences in their drawings relate to other activities of these children?

The Dawning Realism

9

The Gang Age
Nine–Twelve Years

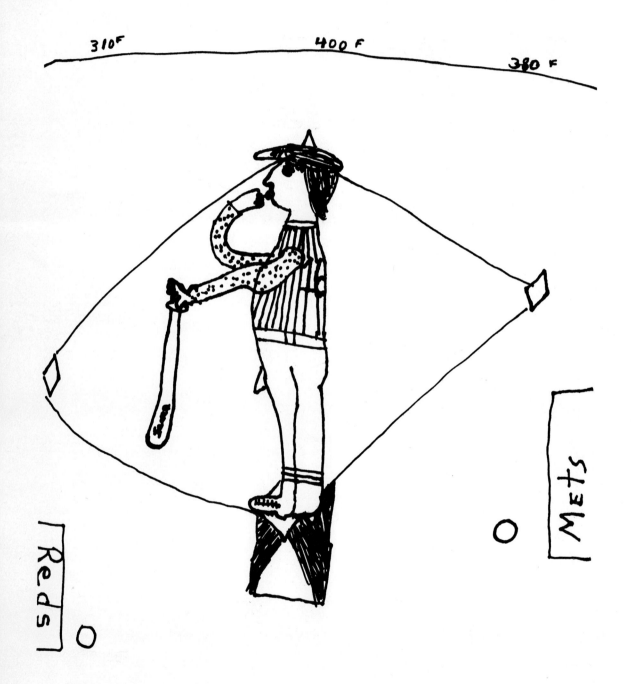

The Importance of the Gang Age

One of the outstanding characteristics of this age of development is the child's discovery that he is a member of society, a society of his peers. It is during this time that children lay the groundwork for the ability to work in groups and to cooperate in adult life. The discoveries of having similar interests, of sharing secrets, of the pleasure of doing things together, are all fundamental. There is a growing awareness that one can do more in a group than alone, and that the group is more powerful than a single person. This age is the time for group friendships and peer groups or gangs. The word *gang* has taken on some negative connotations within today's society, but we as adults may have some very happy memories of the gang of kids we went around with when young. This age shows an increasing development of social independence from adult domination, a learning about social structures in a personal way. This is an essential part of the developmental process and an important step in social interaction.

Groups or gangs are commonly of the same sex. Boys ignore girls, and girls despise boys. It is a time when youngsters go camping, belong to groups that have rules of their own, and take greater interest in group sports. Boys may build elaborate hideouts from boxes or stray pieces of lumber, and not infrequently lead wars against girls. Girls begin to pay attention to clothes, enjoy parties, sit with their own group, listen to a stereo, invent their own secret codes or languages, and not infrequently lead wars against boys of their own age, although often secretly admiring an older junior high school boy.

These important feelings of an awakened social independence are often in direct conflict with the desires of parents or adults who do not want to give up the close supervision and guidance of their children. It is mostly for this reason that adults consider this stage of development as an undesirable one that often interferes with their own lives. Needless to say, teachers who are unaware of the important implications of group activities often find themselves the uncomfortable target of secret groups. Instead of giving support to this awakening feeling for group cooperation and the discovery of social independence, both parents and teachers often counteract it by trying to prolong close dependency through authoritarian means. Instead of showing sympathetic and warm understanding of their children's desire for group life, they often oppose it, not realizing that by such actions they only drive their children into secrecy. Cooperation with adults reaches an apparent low point, and "delinquency usually has its beginnings at this age" (Stone and Church, 1968). The attitudes of adults may be responsible for some of the causes of delinquency.

Children's increase in size, skill, and strength provides opportunities for

Figure 146.
By this age, there is great variety in children's abilities, including art abilities. The boys seem to have grouped themselves together on the right, and the girls are on the left.

them to become more independent. It is not unusual for ten year olds to earn their own spending money by running errands or doing small tasks. Although adults may now find it easier to carry on a discussion with them, children who become dependent upon adults for approval tend to lose status in their group or gang. A fifth grade class may have a wide spread in abilities, with some children reading at third grade and others at seventh grade level. Their art products will also vary. Some girls will have reached puberty, some children will have had tangles with the law, and some will have gained recognition for their skill in dance or music. This is an exciting age.

A youngster of this age is becoming increasingly aware of his real world, a world that is filled with emotions, but emotions that are hidden from adults; a real world with friends, plans, and memories; a real world that belongs only to him. There is sometimes confusion in the use of the term *realism*. Often it is confused with the term *naturalism*. However, these terms can be self-explana-

THE DAWNING REALISM

Figure 147.
*Children of this age continue to
exaggerate certain important
elements in a drawing. An eleven
year old girl here portrays her
experiences in the bowling alley.*

tory so long as it is remembered that naturalism refers directly to nature and realism refers to what is real. Nature can be looked upon by many people. Their backgrounds, reactions, or emotions do not affect what is there. Nature may be snow on the ground, a hot summer day, or any part of the environment—it is this way whether we look at it or not. What is real, however, is firmly rooted within us. One can be inspired by the beauty in nature, be disgusted with the selfishness of man, or be full of hope for the future—and all of these are very real.

THE IMPORTANCE OF THE GANG AGE

A work of art is not the representation of an object itself; rather, it is the representation of the experience with the particular object. A mere photographic imitation of the environment is not expressive of a child's individual relationship to what he perceives. The question is not whether the child should draw in a photographic way or be forced to rely upon his imagination, but whether the art experience provides the opportunity for a child to identify with his own experience and encourages him in his own personal, sensitive, artistic creation.

Characteristics of Drawings During the Gang Age

For the child, this age may be the most dramatic and healthy period of discoveries, as can be clearly seen in his creative work. The schema is no longer adequate to represent the human figure during the gang age. The concept of the human figure as expressed during the earlier schematic stage was a generalized expression of a person. Now the child is eager to express characteristics of sex, to show differences in clothing; the schematic generalization cannot suffice. Greater awareness develops at this age; the modes of expression of the preceding stage are no longer suitable to express this increasing awareness.

In earlier stages of drawing the separate parts of these drawings were not self-explanatory, but were composed of geometric shapes. A part removed from the whole lost its meaning. Now, however, geometric shapes no longer suffice as the child moves to a form of expression more closely related to nature. But the child is still far from a visual representation. For example, children in their drawings do not yet draw their clothes with folds or wrinkles. The hemline is usually drawn straight across. The drawing is not a result of the child's careful visual observation, but rather a characterization of what is seen. The child gains a feeling for details, but often loses a feeling for action; a greater stiffness can be seen in the representations of the human figure. Every body part has its meaning and retains this meaning even when separated from the whole. Drawings have taken on a certain rigidity and formality.

Although at the age of nine most children still exaggerate the size of the human figure, studies have shown that this exaggeration tends to disappear during this stage of development (Lowenfeld, 1952). The child begins to substitute other means of expression to show emphasis, such as an accumulation of details on those parts that are significant. The greater awareness and concern for detail at this stage of development can even extend to making a left hand quite different from the right. This can occasionally make the total look distorted. Sometimes this exaggerated concern will even make a child exclaim that he has "goofed" if he has not drawn the proper number of buttons on his shirt. This growing awareness of the visual appearance of objects has little to do with naturalism, as can be readily seen in these drawings and paintings, where there is no attempt at showing the light or shade, the effect of motion, or atmospheric effects. Rather, the child is characterizing his environment by indicating its distinguishing features.

X-ray drawings, and drawings using folding over, are now criticized by the children themselves as being unnatural. That type of representation is primarily subjective, so children who are becoming more aware of nature no longer consider such a mode of organization appropriate. Girls of this age often focus a great deal of interest upon drawing horses. Now that the anxiety about animals has disappeared, children will project their own feelings into this animal form. For some the horse becomes a symbol of running, dashing freedom that is part of the joy of growing up. Boys identify more with cars, and it is not unusual for boys with questionable mathematical ability to be able to spout statistics about the horsepower and displacement of the latest engine design. Sometimes it even seems as if the boy *becomes* the car, making shifting noises as he draws, just as the girl can seem to *be* the horse. The emotional and psychological concerns of children of this age demand constructive outlets, and at any age the feelings and concerns of an individual are the basis of true art expression.

There is a consistency in the way expression changes. The child moves from a rigid color–object relationship to a realization of the properties of color. Now he distinguishes between a bluish-red sweater and a yellowish-red sweater. This greater understanding of color differences cannot be called a true visual awareness because he does not indicate the changing effects of colors in light and shade, or the effect of atmosphere upon color. Some children will find that the sky has a different blue from the blue of the river or the lake, and some will find that the tree is a different green from the green of the grass. If a child in this stage of development still uses rigid color–object relationships, he has not yet refined his visual sensitivity sufficiently to see the differences that distinguish a green shrub from a green lawn.

The closer a child comes to a visual relationship between color and object, the more teachers are tempted to misuse the dawning sense for naturalistic

Figure 148.
As his big sister steadies him, this ten year old shows how he is learning to ride a bicycle. His awareness of the details of the bicycle, even from the back, would make an adult envious.

The Meaning of Color

colors by teaching how to select and apply color. There is no place in the elementary school for the teaching of color theories by means of color wheels or other such aids. Such teaching would only disturb the child's spontaneity and would make him insecure in his own developing sense of color relationships. A child can be made more color-conscious by emphasizing personal reactions to color and making meaningful the interaction between child and color. The child enjoys colors and is now capable of being much more sensitive toward differences and similarities; his eager explorations through fall leaves, or his sudden realization of the constantly changing sky colors should certainly be encouraged. Any discussion of color, therefore, should focus upon experience and not upon the "proper" use of color in a particular painting.

Figure 149.
Children of this age are gaining control over the expressive media and are more concerned about mixing the proper shade of paint.

During this stage, nine to twelve, the child is gradually moving away from his dependency on the concrete; he is now beginning to deal with abstract concepts. He can now do more in his drawings than place things in a row as we saw in the previous stage of development. Art is not merely the representation of objects, but rather is the reaction to and expression of concepts of those objects. The ability to arrange several images on a piece of paper so that they have relation to one another, means that the child is able to deal with these objects simultaneously, rather than merely to arrange them in a line. The tree no longer stands in isolation beside the house but becomes a shade for the house, although just where the shadow is cast is still not fully understood. And the man no longer stands aloof beside the house, but is now seen in relation to the tree and may be coming out of or going into the house. In a study of English children, Kutnick (1978) found that young children drew their classroom in a static fashion: that is, making symbols or drawings which merely indicated the presence of pupils and teacher. However, a transition took place between the ages of nine and ten, when children moved to an active representation, with drawings portraying the actual roles of pupils and teacher.

Just as greater awareness of the self and the environment leads a child to realize that geometric forms are inadequate to express the human figure, the

The Meaning of Space

Figure 150.
These children playing ball overlap the mountains in the distance, but are on a common base line with the house and tree. The grass in the foreground has become a horizontal surface in which flowers grow. The sky is no longer just a line and includes clouds and a bird as well as the sun.

Figure 151.
The ten year old girl who made this drawing used multiple base lines. The limbs of the elaborate tree overlap the foliage, and the sun is peeking out from behind a cloud.

representation of space reveals a change from the symbolic use of the base line concept to a more naturalistic representation. As a result of this growing visual awareness the child discovers the space between base lines which becomes the plane.

The change from a single base line to the use of the plane is usually a fairly rapid one. The stage of transition can be seen in drawings that include several base lines; we find the space between these base lines being filled in. We can only speculate on how the child physically discovers the plane: perhaps through increased physical activity and developing curiosity. One can picture a first grader walking to school, carefully following a prescribed route. Compare this with a fourth grader who acts as if the sidewalk were there to ignore, who is much more interested in walking on the wrong side of the hedge, kick-

THE DAWNING REALISM

Figure 152.
Here a boy obviously enjoys
driving this interesting car. A
beginning awareness of
overlapping can be seen, as the
car partially covers the large
building, but the small house is
raised so it can be seen.

ing a can in the gutter, or going around in back of some of the houses to see if something interesting is happening. At any rate, the base line begins to disappear, the trees and houses no longer stand only on the edge of this line. Although for some children the base line mode of space representation remains in frequent use, the space below the base line now takes on the meaning of ground.

For the most part, prior to this age children have very little understanding of maps, particularly of geographic maps of foreign countries. This may seem unusual, since nursery school children can make what are essentially maps from blocks, and then drive toy cars around from one location to another (Blaut & Stea, 1974). However, a vertical, two-dimensional configuration covered with cartographic symbols is generally not understood until a youngster is eleven or twelve years old. Gerber (1979) divided children from fourth to ninth grade into four groups based upon their map-reading skills. Drawing ability was one of the significant factors that differentiated between these groups. Possibly one way to improve or develop map comprehension would be to have children make maps of their own spatial experiences. Until a logical map of "the route to school" can be drawn, it would be useless to try to teach map reading.

The sky is no longer drawn as a line across the top of the page. It now extends all the way down to what at the beginning may be a base line but which gradually assumes the significance of the horizon. The child has not yet become aware, however, of the meaning of the horizon. He has not yet developed conscious visual perception of distance, although he has taken the first steps toward such an awareness. With the sky all the way down, the child soon

Figure 153.
*The girl who drew this picnic
struggled with the perspective but
was able to represent the scene
from a single point of view.*

realizes that a tree growing from the ground will partially cover the sky. Hence he becomes conscious of overlapping. A more naturalistic representation has been achieved, as can be seen in the buildings behind the car in Figure 152. It is exciting for children to discover that objects can overlap; this awareness can be utilized by the sensitive teacher. That one object can cover another is important, because it implies a recognition of the interrelationships between objects.

The child of this age is now beginning to think socially, to consider the thoughts and opinions of others, but it is a slow shift away from egocentric thought. His understanding of interrelationships, of causality and interdependence are only starting. Piaget's experiment (Piaget and Inhelder, 1967), in which he asked children to identify pictures of a model of a mountain taken from a viewpoint other than their own, has been carried out in a modified form by Laurendeau and Pinard (1970). They experimented with 700 children and found that, on the average, children are eleven before they can free themselves from their own point of view and successfully select pictures that show how a scene would look if they were in a position other than their own.

It would seem logical then that an eleven year old would portray a scene differently from, for example, an eight year old. An eight year old might show a scene such as "eating" from several points of view, as if looking separately at each person sitting around the table. An eleven year old would more likely

THE DAWNING REALISM

portray the same scene from a single viewpoint, as if observed from another part of the room, and with an attempt at perspective. Hooper (1977) asked second, fourth, and sixth graders to sit at a table which had been arranged with dishes and flatware. It was only in the sixth grade that most of the children could successfully select from several the picture that correctly showed how the table would look from different positions. Hooper also asked the children to draw a table and to draw "eating." There was a significant relationship between drawing development and the ability to identify how another person might see the table from a different position. Children of this age might enjoy drawing tasks that require problem-solving abilities, but are not eager to learn formulas or to assimilate rules for "proper" representation of perspective.

As children now discover the meaningfulness of their environment and begin to relate this to themselves, it becomes most important for education to give them a feeling for what is honest in our environment and what is insincere and imitative. At this age it is vital to stimulate children's thinking and provide them with opportunities for discoveries relating to the natural beauty of materials that are found unspoiled within our environment. This means developing a feeling for differences in rocks, pebbles, shells, barks, moss—all the wealth we can find in nature. Children of this age are normally collecting a variety of objects anyway, from bits of string to toads, as any parent of a nine year old can testify.

The sincerity of beauty as found in nature should be stressed, because this is a natural extension of the child's own direction at this age. Much of our society now has a heightened awareness of ecology, and children need but little encouragement to develop a concern for their environment. Collecting a pile of pebbles can be very exciting. Discussing the different shapes and different colors, noticing how the water has worn down some edges, or seeing how the light tries to shine through some varieties but not others—such discoveries can awaken perceptual sensitivity. These explorations require a relaxed atmosphere, for such learning cannot be rushed. Occasionally children will enjoy putting their collections into some form, such as putting the pebbles into a little sand in a box and pouring plaster over the back of them to make a mosaic, or arranging material in a collage. Becoming sensitive to the qualities of a material is of great importance, and children improvise on their own account combinations of materials that need not necessarily serve a useful purpose. Discovering the beauty of natural materials need not be limited to woods and streams alone. Even scrap material can have beauty hidden in it. Rusty iron, or wrinkled paper, or even mold and mildew can be pleasing to look at if we are

Figure 154.
A fifth grade girl is capable of making aesthetic judgments about her own work, but these are not based on formal instruction in elements and principles of design.

able to redefine our values and not think of them as discarded and rejected parts of our sometimes oversterile environment.

It may seem as if undue emphasis is being placed upon a knowledge and understanding of materials, while the area of design may appear to be by-passed. However, there should be no separation between the material and its function, or between crafts and design. The inspiration for working with materials should come directly from the structure and nature of the material itself. Establishing relationships between a child and materials will be crucial in enabling the child intuitively to create designs that utilize qualities inherent in the materials. In the world's greatest cultures, workmanship and skill have been inseparable from design. Today there are again signs of a closer relationship between the craftsman, the material, and the function or design.

Drawings and paintings by children in this stage of development begin to show decoration. Girls more and more frequently decorate clothing, and boys become more aware of the plaid of their shirts. This developing awareness of

THE DAWNING REALISM

pattern and decoration does not provide an excuse for the formal teaching of design. The formal elements of grammar are not taught to a two year old child who is discovering that he can make his needs known through speech, nor are the formal problems of balance, rhythm, or half-drop repeats taught to a child who is beginning to discover these patterns within his environment. A project such as designing a decorative border for a tea towel has little relevance, and it is entirely unsuitable to plan a design carefully on paper for possible transfer to some other material with which the child is not involved. Learning the nature and behavior of materials is important not only educationally but also ethically, because it will promote a feeling for sincerity and truth in design.

The Development of the Gang Age Child

During this stage a child begins to develop a greater awareness of and sensitivity to his environment. He has come to wonder why things work the way they do, and about his own being. He may now raise questions about areas that not very long ago he felt were unquestionable. The child is becoming increasingly critical of others and of himself, and some children will begin to hide their drawings from an inquisitive adult or else make some disparaging remark about their efforts. Children of this age also develop a sense of justice and may object violently to actions that "aren't fair." There is also an increasing concern with sex differences; although publicly the opposite sex is treated with a great deal of disdain, privately there are awakening feelings of curiosity and affection. A child of ten has gained a fair amount of information about the working of the world, both natural and social, but to a large extent this tends to be isolated, concrete learning. Much of the information that has been drilled into him in the classroom therefore tends to be meaningless. The fact that the Pilgrims landed in 1620 is readily repeated in a test, but whether 1620 was before or after the last Ice Age is not clear. Some of the concepts children develop by this time continue with them through adult life. This is even true of their drawing characteristics. Studies have shown that there is surprising similarity between drawings by children during this stage and the drawings by adults who have had no formal art training.

This is also a period when children are beginning to develop a self-concept, an understanding of themselves as independent individuals. Developing

Figure 155.
Fairness and cooperation now are basic considerations. Two boys confer and decide how their group art work should proceed.

a positive self-concept is essential to establish personal attitudes, and is closely related to the ability to learn. One experiment attempted to change the self-concept of thirty boys who had just completed sixth grade (White and Allen, 1971). During a summer program half of the boys were enrolled in a traditional nondirective counseling group, and half were in an art counseling group, where numerous art activities were carried on that were designed for expression of feelings, and the boys were encouraged to verbalize about their art products. The results were surprising: " . . . the art counseling approach was more effective in bringing about self-concept changes among pre-adolescent boys than was the traditional nondirective counseling program." The authors state that during a follow-up study 14 months later, the growth effect of the program was still evident.

At this age children have not yet developed full control over their emotions, and often a seemingly minor incident will be of extreme importance to a youngster. This intensity of feeling can be utilized within the art program. The emotional relationships a child develops with various segments of his environment can often be expressed either directly or symbolically. Topics centering around religious themes, individual justice, or the expression of love or hate may involve a youngster completely. In such cases exaggeration or overemphasis of particular parts within a composition will be noted. Color in such cases can also be used symbolically, as in painting a face green. Such distortion is very acceptable, and support should be given to the free use of exaggeration and distortion for emotional effect.

Gang Age Drawings as a Reflection of Growth

The ability to break away from the schema and to perceive and be attentive to the variability within the environment is typical of this age. To a great extent, however, these children do not remove themselves from their own observations. That is, their drawings and paintings show quite clearly that they see things through their own experiences, and assume that this "reality" is the way things are. Children can sometimes be critical of the drawings of others and even of their own drawings if these do not live up to their own interpretation of what is real. Naturalism is not the ultimate goal at this age, because there is

294

usually no attempt at showing light and shade, atmospheric effects, or even color reflections or folds in cloth. The child, then, has left behind the schema and laws for behavior; instead he has developed a curiosity about himself and those things around him, but he has not yet achieved an objective, naturalistic viewpoint. It should be emphasized at this point that there is no value judgment implied in discussing the various stages of children's development. Our concern here is simply to understand these differences and to become more sensitive to the great variety of artistic expression. How much he has departed from schematic representation and how much he feels the need to characterize particular objects, figures, and his environment is indicative of intellectual growth. A child of low mentality neither becomes aware of the changing environment nor discovers those characteristics that make it possible to individualize objects or figures.

Plate 24, "Standing in the Rain," facing page 305, was drawn in crayon by an eleven year old girl. The schema has practically disappeared except for some facial features: note the repeated symbol for the nose in the three central figures and the sharp nose form in the rest of the figures. One of the distinctions of this stage is that parts of a drawing can now be subtracted from the total without losing their meaning. No longer do geometric forms suffice. It can be noticed in "Standing in the Rain" that the feet or facial features would remain as recognizable parts even if they were removed from the context of the drawing. It is also very apparent that the child has departed from her base line representation and has a distinct feeling for the plane. The inclusion of such details as puddles, houses with windows, raincoats with buttons and belts, boots of various colors, and umbrellas of various patterns clearly shows that this child is very much aware of her environment.

Notice for comparison the drawing, "Man with Umbrella," in Figure 156, where the awareness of detail is much less. Could intelligence alone cause such differences in representation? In comparing "Standing in the Rain" with "Man with Umbrella," might not lack of motivation be a real consideration? A closer look at these drawings can give us a better understanding and some insight into thinking processes. Lack of motivation may cause great differences in drawings, but this is a matter of functional intelligence, how one actually acts and performs within the environment. In some cases a potentially brilliant person may never be motivated to utilize this potential. One of the important roles of the teachers is to motivate and excite children to utilize their potential to its fullest capacity. It might be a little more exact to say that these two children have differences in their functional intelligence that may be caused by several unknowns. For the teacher, however, it is clear that promoting a greater

sensitivity to a child's changing environment and awareness of his own thinking, feeling, and perceiving will help him to develop to his fullest potential.

To some teachers, intellectual growth connotes only improved mathematical and reading skills. But in some cases it shows up in an art-related activity. Fourth grade children were given a multiple seriation task which required them to arrange colored circles in a rectangular array according to increasing size in one direction and color differences in the other (Watson, 1979); thus it was necessary to keep in mind two dimensions simultaneously. Those children who had a strong mental grasp of the whole did not need to check visually where each circle should go. Poor readers tended to rely on trial and error, and some children never could see the relationships. Success in such tasks is strongly related to reading comprehension and is not achieved through instruction.

Art experiences provide the opportunity for the development of emotional growth. Within our society, all too often, children's emotions and feelings are squelched. This is particularly true of boys, who at an early age are told not to be sissies. Even within a group of age-mates a boy usually has to conceal his true feelings in order to remain "manly." To be able to express sensitivity and to develop in emotional growth, children need to identify with their own experiences in their art. Children who constantly depend upon stereotypes are not able to express their true feelings.

Schools themselves can often produce a great deal of anxiety. The smaller boy may be ridiculed, or the tallest girl may feel embarrassed to find that she is now taller than any of the boys and sometimes even her teacher. It is a rare classroom that does not contain some periods of boredom, listening to explanations repeated for the slower learners or reading what seems like irrelevant information, some periods of frustration when important questions go unanswered, or periods of fear when the homework is left undone, or periods of terror at test time. There is no evidence that tests motivate children of this age. An Australian study (Campbell, 1975), using a large sample of sixth graders under test and non-test conditions, found that these children had little motivation to learn spelling lists when tests were to be given; instead, tests tended to reinforce a fear of failure in girls and to increase impulsive risk-taking in boys. These emotions can sometimes be expressed in drawings and paintings, although these may be hidden in notebooks or appear as highly embellished doodles. An indication of emotional interest in a particular part of a drawing or a painting is the attention to details in this particular part. The child naturally uses more affection and spends more time on a part that is of emotional significance.

Social growth, during this period, is one of the outstanding facets of development, yet when something interferes with this new feeling of social belonging the child may withdraw and remain an outsider. Whether or not the child identifies with a group can be recognized by two indications from creative work: the content of the work, and participation in group work. The child who drew "Standing in the Rain" (Plate 24), is aware of people and has made the children different sizes. However, every figure is looking straight ahead and seems to have but little relationship with the others. The figures appear more like a group of individuals who happen to be standing next to each other. To some extent, however, the topic may have been responsible for this lack of a common feeling of participation. The illustration indicates that the child has identified strongly with the scene and with the people involved, but has not shown much interaction within the group. This child is obviously socially conscious of the environment, however. Not only is a particular setting portrayed, but there are differences in clothes, an awareness of everyone's being in the rain, and in turn the rain, boots, and puddles indicate an awareness of the child's own relationship to her environment.

The ability of children to participate in group activities can readily be seen when children work together on murals. Children of this age usually have the urge to work in group activities, but it may be the child who withdraws from such activities who needs this social experience most. To a great extent democracy is based upon social action. A child who avoids the group and who is unable to relate to his own experiences in his drawings may need some support from the teacher in order to develop greater social awareness. Experiences such as being in charge of a section of a mural may be of value. Certainly the individual's contribution to the group should be recognized, and a sensitive teacher can insure that each child is able to participate.

It is readily apparent that changes in drawing and painting will come about naturally when a child has experienced greater interaction in group activities. Pointing out that his figures do not relate one to another would only make the child unsure of his own creative abilities, and would in any case be contrary to the basic premises of art education. It is only through the child himself and his interaction with the environment and with people that significant changes will take place in creative productions.

Figure 157.
These children are working on a mural; such a group activity requires social interaction and cooperation.

Figure 158.
In this drawing a sixth grade boy is listening to his stereo in his bedroom. He includes bunkbeds, posters, and dresser in his refuge from the adult world. Art should be based on the child's experiences and environment.

The child who drew Plate 24 ranks high in perceptual growth. The child's growing visual awareness and her awakening feelings for nature are part of her perceptual growth. One of the first indications of a child's visual awareness is the inclusion of the horizon line and the painting of the sky to meet this line. The child has become very much aware of distance, even though no sky is indicated. Another aspect of visual perception is the child's awareness of overlappings, and here there is not only overlapping of people but overlapping of objects. There is also a visual awareness of differences in color, although, as expected during this age, there is no particular awareness of light and shade. The hemline continues to remain straight, at least in this particular illustration. The child has an advanced awareness of detail, which can be observed in the raincoats and in the background buildings. Certainly the encouragement of perceptual sensitivity is a vital part of any art experience.

There are also indications of aesthetic growth in this picture. Notice the conscious awareness of design in the umbrellas. Aesthetic growth can also be seen in the way children relate the material to the subject matter; that is, how sensitive they are to the qualities of the material with which they are working, and to what extent their treatment of the subject matter reflects this awareness. Children of this age are now much more aware of the nature of the clay, paint, or crayon with which they are working. Using a material to its fullest extent and utilizing its intrinsic qualities is a characteristic of aesthetic sensitivity.

Children who work with clay as if it were a flat drawing material are not aware of its distinctive qualities. Apparently, our artist who drew "Standing in the Rain" was very much aware of the possibilities crayon could afford.

One of the most important areas of growth to which art can contribute is that of creative growth. During this stage of development there is a great deal of pressure put upon children to conform not only to the wishes of adults, but also to the demands of the group. To function creatively, however, one must first be able to function as an individual. The encouragement of the individual child's own approach to working out problems is vital, which means that imitation and conformity to patterns must be discouraged. A child's creativity at this age can be seen in the desire for experimentation, exploration, and invention. A child who is rigid or does not utilize material in new ways needs to be encouraged to be flexible. Encouraging new and different ways to use materials and rewarding the interesting stipple or the effect of one color being placed over another will be positive steps in the direction of supporting creative growth.

Art Motivation

Adults often have pleasant memories of childhood; however, most of these memories are of happenings and situations outside school. Probably each of us has memories of this particular time. One adult remembering this stage had the following to say:

> If I remember back at my childhood—now, you see, if I remember back at this stage, it must have made a very distinct impression on me, but I remember very distinctly how we converted a small, little, oh, island into something, into a wonderland. When I was a child we were in a gang—a wonderful gang—and we would sit on a footbridge over a small stream, I am quite sure it was not larger than a few feet, but when we went over this bridge it appeared to us like, oh, miles long, you know, going over the bridge and entering our land which no one knew. This was fascinating. We made a building there at the highest point—there was a little hill, and we made our own money, of course, we collected the money, you know, for entrance into this island. I can still remember that we had pockets full of paper money which we ourselves printed. And we had there, we found bones of a dead animal and made a little sign saying, "These are the bones discovered of an animal two thousand years ago," and we really looked at it as we put it there in a certain order, and you know, this was something magic to us. And an-

other place was the Snake Point where we had spread out a dead snake which we found, and when we went there we really got goose pimples. This was the Snake Point, let's go to the Snake Point, and then, you know we collected gravel and built little paths, and these were then real paths, you know. We had a hideout when it rained, so this island was really something magic.

Imagine if we could promote in school these same intense experiences. All too often school is considered a place to "behave," a place to endure. But school should be a stimulating, exciting place, where natural drives of children

Figure 159.

A cooperative venture in building construction, including plumbers, riveters, and crane operators, is drawn in great detail by a fifth grade boy, with many erasures and corrections.

are not only accepted but utilized to develop stimulating education that is meaningful for the students.

Motivation now should capitalize upon youngsters' greater independence in order to give support to their self-esteem. An art experience must provide an opportunity to express a growing awareness of sex, to develop a greater awareness of self, and to satisfy a new curiosity about the environment. It must also inspire the child to use cooperation with others to achieve results. To inspire cooperation, two methods can be used. The first or *subjective* method of cooperation deals with representations of individual experiences of cooperation, or the representations of scenes in which cooperation is important. Much depends upon the way such motivation is presented to the group and the atmosphere the teacher develops during the motivation. Such topics as "Helping the Flood Victims" or "Cleaning Up After the Storm" can be presented very dramatically. Whenever a child can identify with a large undertaking in which he feels himself part of the group effort, a topic will inspire cooperation. "Whose house is under water? Suppose you were living there and we could watch how the water rises and rises! How would we feel?" The youngsters need to identify with the flood victims. They should also identify with those people who are responsible for social welfare. Such activities as drawing the firemen during the big fire or the policeman during the evening rush hour can also effectively stimulate greater social cooperation.

The second or *objective* method of cooperation deals more directly with group work itself; a whole group works on one project. Here also the type of motivation will determine its success. Group work can be quite simple in its planning, such as having each child make a fierce animal of clay and then assembling these animals into a large zoo. Straws or sticks can serve as bars, and the children will enjoy making signs for the various parts of the zoo. Group work can become quite elaborate, with a class dividing up into several working units. An example might be making a mural of a city. "What makes a city? Yes, houses and stores and factories. But we cannot have them all mixed up together! How would you like to live right next to a factory? Yes, we need to have some zoning laws. We will certainly need the residential district. How many children would like to work on the residential section of our city? There are so many different kinds of buildings that people live in! Now we have the industrial area for our factories. How many would like to work on this section? And, yes, the shopping area, too. But there are more than just stores in the commercial district! What other districts do we have? Oh, yes, playground and recreation area, fine! Does everyone know what section he is going to be working on? You had better pick a leader to help your group decide what kind

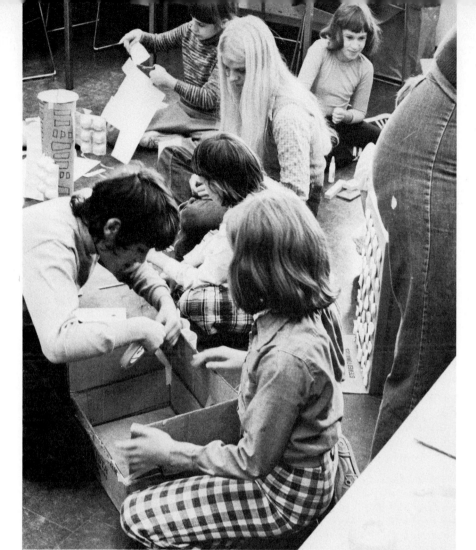

Figure 160.
Here a group of youngsters are involved in constructing a three-dimensional city. Much planning and discussion goes into this activity, but the finished project is much larger than one child could do alone.

of buildings you are going to need. You say we still need a school district? Oh, I think the residential area committee should worry about that. Why, Ed and Maria, you are not on any committee! Would you like to plan the background for our city? Should we have a stream or river near the city? Do you think we should have some mountains, fields, or forest land around?" Probably a material such as colored paper would be quite suitable for this topic. A large background paper or board would be needed. It should not be expected that a cooperative enterprise like this will be a smooth, quiet operation. Democratic action may not be easily learned, but it is an essential part of our way of life.

When the various committees of the city have completed their districts, the city can be assembled. A lack of trees may be apparent, or some small houses may be needed, and maybe nobody has remembered to make cars and trucks for the streets. In such a way all the children can become involved in the activities. It is probably best to staple or tack the various buildings in place so that these buildings can be readily moved from one spot to another. There may be a sudden cry of dismay as Hannah finds that someone has placed a church right over her house. This provides a fine opportunity for some explanation of overlapping, now that overlapping can be understood. "Did you ever go to a movie and find a nice seat where you could see the screen, and right in front of you a lady with a big hat sits down and now you can see nothing? Is that good? Would it be all right if a little boy sat in front of you? It wouldn't matter if a little boy sat in front because you could still see and people could still see you. Overlapping is fine, but one should not completely cover the other. Maybe the small house can go in front of the church since the church could still be seen. And look, a tree can go in front of the house." The child has developed a fair amount of understanding when he can accept a minor role for one of his buildings, but maybe he can feel better when his tree goes in front of someone else's building. Every individual, every child in the class, should think, "I could not have accomplished by myself what the whole group has done." This is the heart of cooperation.

The teacher's role is a subordinate one in this activity; he is a catalyst. It is a far harder task to stimulate and encourage children to learn, produce, and explore on their own. An easier method of producing products would be to authoritatively assign projects and have the "best" method for achieving results already worked out beforehand. But to provide a rich, meaningful experience for children, such authoritarian methods must be discarded. It is much more important to increase children's interest in the materials of expression, it is much more important to give a sense of discovery, it is much more important to provide an opportunity to determine personal relationships with the world than to worry about how "artistic" particular products look. Any art motivation must insure that children have ample opportunity to develop their own method of expression. There is a need for group activities, but these group activities should never press for conformity nor submerge individual interests.

Both boys and girls at this age can develop an interest in particular, individualistic subject matter. A few years ago it was possible to say that girls would spend a considerable length of time drawing flowers, fanciful figures, and particularly horses and that boys would spend an equal amount of time drawing airplanes, guns, and particularly cars. However, as society changes, so will the products of that society. If boys are not pushed into a male stereotype, it may be that more of them will develop an interest in flowers, and, con-

Plate 23.

"We Are Exploring the Surface of Venus," a four by eight foot mural painted by a group of ten year old boys. In a project such as this, where imaginative subject matter is used, diverse ideas are welcomed by the group and cooperation is encouraged. No one boy could have done the mural by himself.

Plate 24.

"Standing in the Rain," drawn by an eleven year old girl. Color, use of space, and wealth of detail combine to give an aesthetically pleasing whole. Here a growing visual awareness is coupled with a child's directness and freshness.

versely, that girls may become more interested in the mechanical aspects of their environment. But, it seems that sex differences exist in drawings. Majewski (1978) found that, while girls did not draw more delicately than boys, they did draw more scenes of the environment, more smiling people, but fewer sports pictures. Freedman (1979) found that in non-Western cultures the interests of boys and girls, as seen in their drawings, were not the same as in Western societies. Brown (1979) asked 366 children from five to eleven years old to draw a person. A few of the five year old boys drew females; but from eight years on, boys drew only males. As might be expected, most young girls drew females. By nine years, 28 percent of the girls were drawing males, and 100 percent of the boys were drawing males. One could speculate why, when asked to draw a person, girls begin to draw males at nine and ten, but it is important to realize that this seems to be normal. Whatever the particular interest of these youngsters, this interest can be capitalized upon in the art program by expanding the frame of reference.

Figure 161.
A ten year old girl's drawing of herself displays the traditionally assumed feminine interests in hair style, pattern in clothing, and flowers.

Subject Matter

Subject matter is the subjective relationship of man to his environment; as the child changes, so does art expression. The following suggestions are based upon the particular characteristics of this developmental level. These topics are meant to be only suggestions; it is assumed that they will always be adjusted to the particular classroom and to the particular group of children involved. Topics, then, are not to be considered as assignments, but as areas of interest which can be pursued with enthusiasm by both teacher and children.

To stimulate subjective cooperation, to develop the feelings of being a part of a group, and to identify with group activities, several suggestions are appropriate, such as "Picking Up After the Storm," "Gathering Wood for Our Campfire," "Decorating for a Party," or "Building a Clubhouse with My Friends." It is also important to stimulate cooperation through the identification of the child with the forces of social preservation and maintenance. This identification comes through an understanding of the duties and responsibilities of the person and an emphasis on how it would feel to be the telephone repairman, the policeman in five o'clock traffic, the nurse on the night shift in the hospital, or a member of the crew repairing a broken water main.

There are of course many ways in which a group can work objectively together for group cooperation. There should be opportunity for small groups

of children to work together on such a project, and the final product should be large enough and complex enough so that each child can contribute in his own way and so that no one child could possibly do the whole project alone. Some suggestions for group projects might be, "Making a Circus," "Sale Days at the Shopping Plaza," "Making a Dairy Farm," "Picking Berries and Making Ice Cream for a Festival," and "Exploring the Surface of Venus."

With the disappearance of the base line, ample opportunity should be given children to explore the possibilities of using the plane. Since there is an increasing awareness of differences in sex and a greater attention to detail, the children should be allowed to express these. It should be stressed that all sub-

THE DAWNING REALISM

Figure 162. (*Opposite*)
When students occasionally draw from a posing classmate, the teacher should encourage the students to imagine the feelings and emotions of a specific situation as well as the visual aspects.

ject matter should have meaning for the child and should relate to his own experiences. Suitable topics might include "Sitting Around a Table for Supper," "Planting a Garden in the Spring," "Watching the Parade Come Down the Street," "Skating on the Pond in the Woods," "Playing Baseball on the School Grounds," and "Keeping Cool at the Fire Hydrant."

With the beginning awareness of overlapping, discussions will arise normally during the painting procedures. Specific topics might include "Looking Out the Window of the Crowded School Bus," "Sitting in the Stadium," "Looking at Clothes in the Store Window," and "Performing in the School Assembly."

There is another large area of subject matter in art that is related more to the development of skills and the increased familiarity with the nature of materials. These experiences with different materials may not have a specific subject or topic to represent, but the purpose and reason behind each of the activities should be made quite clear to the youngsters. Because children of this age are becoming more outspoken about themselves and about adults, these children should have a knowledge and understanding of the purposes of any project. A number of craft activities can be included under this heading, although care should be taken to insure that the direction and planning of them rest with the children involved. This means that activities such as those that are preplanned by the teacher or those that are cute or tricky are inappropriate. Some suggestions for projects in this general area are making a collage for fingers to feel, making a funny animal from papier mâché, making some prints for a card, putting together an object from wood, making a mosaic from pebbles and plaster, making imaginative animals in clay, experimenting with macrame, using shiny paper for decorations, and weaving with grasses.

There is one very important subject matter area in art that should never be overlooked, and this is the subject matter that is within each child. In some cases this subject matter may be very apparent, such as a child's love for working with tools; sometimes, however, it can be hidden beneath the surface, as in quiet feelings of rejection. There should be ample opportunity for these extremes to be expressed. Not only should the joy and pleasure of creating be given free rein, but deeper emotional feelings and subconscious drives should also be given a chance to be faced. Some materials lend themselves to such expression of the inner self better than others. Finger paint provides a direct release for such feelings; working in clay can provide the opportunity for frustrations to be eased. Ideally, every child should express himself freely, but in some cases the understanding support of a sensitive teacher is necessary to guide strong feelings and emotions into artistically constructive channels.

Art Materials

The child has advanced beyond the use of geometric forms and base line representations. With the discovery of the plane he feels the need of filling in spaces, as, for example, in the representation of the sky, which is now usually painted down to the horizon. Although crayons can be used on their sides to fill large areas, a better material for this purpose is poster or tempera paint. Since the child now has greater control over the paint, it is no longer as necessary to have the paint mixed to a thick consistency. In fact, the child himself can add water to the paints to make them the consistency that he himself likes, and he can also be responsible for refilling his own paint container.

Because they are more concerned with detail than formerly, some children will want to use a hair brush in addition to the bristle brush. Although children of this age differentiate their color-object relationships, using different greens for grass and trees, it is not necessary to increase the number of colors available. Actually, having a limited number of paints encourages children to creatively mix colors. Good crayons also mix, but this is more true with poster paint. If children are given a limited scale of colors they are encouraged to invent their own colors if they feel the desire; if they do not feel the desire for greater color differentiation, it is useless to give them a larger color scale anyway. Actively engaging in mixing colors for a particular reason is much more desirable than having a variety of hues that are passively accepted.

A material is good only if it conributes to children's needs and helps to express their intentions. Although there are unlimited materials available for the use of children, care should be taken that those chosen lend themselves to expression and do not restrict children's originality. If a material is by its very nature restrictive or inhibiting it should be discarded. Some strange creations have resulted from some misguided "arty" programs. Such things as marshmallows on toothpicks, wilted phonograph records, decorated light bulbs, lamps made from old ginger ale bottles, or egg cartons decorated with macaroni and gilded can make a mockery of an art program.

Colored paper is a basic material for this age. It provides a natural means of overlapping and is an appropriate material for the early stages of cooperation through projects. Another essential material is pottery clay, which can be used for many three-dimensional projects. This clay can easily be stored in plastic bags and, of course, it can be used again and again. There are certain advantages to using materials that are considered adult art materials, and clay is certainly one of these. However, sometimes clay is used as a craft material to make such things as plaques and ash trays. Unless these objects meet a real

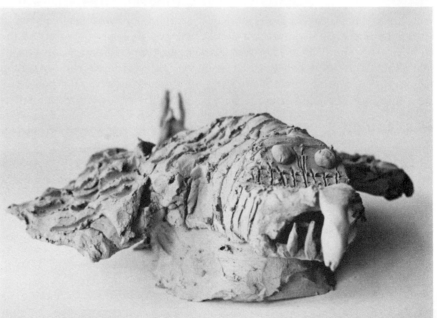

need in the life of children—and not very many children between nine and twelve smoke cigarettes—these projects will be merely busy-work. Pressing various textures into clay, or exploring the possibility of space and form, such as holes in clay, or repeating a pattern of lines in a clay batt may have some utilitarian value if the clay pieces are fired. However, the teacher must not put the emphasis upon the preservation of the final product. If the child can participate in the total process—from seeing the clay in its natural state to watching it come fired from the kiln—this can be a very worthwhile experience. Occasionally, however, teachers take the clay pieces away and have them fired. Then the finished product has no relationship to the child who made it; the color, texture, and consistency have been so altered that he can no longer identify his product. Under such conditions it is better to leave the clay piece unfired. Clay that has been modeled or made to represent some object, person, or animal is usually not fired anyway. This is merely because the experience has been expressed in the process itself, and the procedure of firing can often cause these pieces to break apart. Most of the synthetically modeled pieces (those put together from single details) would not be able to stand firing. It is not worthwhile to sacrifice the child's individual thinking to conform to mere procedure.

Finger paint is a material that has not been considered to any degree before this stage. Now, however, it can be used for expression without the concern that children will be too involved with its textural consistencies. Needless to say, there should also be a good supply of other basic art materials. These include scissors, a stapler, paste, masking tape, and some woodworking tools. For craft work many materials can be used, such as wood, papier mâché, wire, cloth, and a scrap container with a wide range of straws, buttons, boxes, colored cellophane, and anything else that looks interesting. Children themselves will collect barks, rocks, pieces of wood, feathers, or whatever happens to attract them. Although some care should be taken to insure the safety of the children from such things as broken glass or sharp points, undue concern for sanitation and cleanliness may stand in the way of a child's developing skill in hammering or cutting, or of his digging up a particularly pleasing pebble.

It is quite possible to stimulate a greater sensitivity toward common materials within the usual classroom setting. For example, a common material like paper has many possibilities. "What can paper do? How does it feel? Is it smooth or rough? Can you fold it or crease it? How does it look when it is crumpled? Notice how it tears. Can you make it turn or bend so that it looks happy? Can you make it feel sad?" Other materials can be treated in somewhat the same way, with the emphasis being upon the process of manipulation and exploring the material and not upon achieving a nice-looking finished product.

Figure 165.
*Gang age children are eager to
construct, build, and carve
projects of their own devising.
They have no need to follow
someone else's plan.*

There is no reason why all children should be equally occupied and interested
in the same materials. Children at this age often develop great enthusiasm for
working with wood. If simple tools are available a great deal of interest can be
generated in discovering the qualities of wood, and the physical exertion of
hammering and sawing and nailing often gives positive release to bottled-up
energies.

A word should be said here about exposing insincerity in the use of art
materials. We constantly see around us examples of sham and falsehood in the
use of materials. There is so much in the way of natural beauty for children to
discover, that exposing the artificial flowers, the imitation stone floors, and the
false chimneys for what they are should be a part of these children's education.
To a great extent children accept the things around them as appropriate, and

ART MATERIALS

311

unconsciously may go on living in an insincere environment. To promote a more truthful society, it is not too soon to stress the sincerity of design.

Now that children have developed an interest in the possibilities of working with a variety of materials, they can be "pushovers" for a range of noncreative craft projects to be found on the market. Such items as precut leather tooling kits, easy-to-glue-together plastic objects, or mosaic kits that "anybody can put together" can be a real menace to normal curiosity and development. The teacher should point out that making a boat from scrap wood can be a much more enjoyable activity than trying to fit together some adult's preconceived plastic model. If children could learn to get satisfaction from working with a range of common materials, and if misguided parents would stop praising products instead of children, the precut, already-thought-out "easy projects" companies would be out of business.

Summary

Art contributes much to total development. One of the greatest needs of children during this period is to find themselves, to realize their own power, and to develop their own relationships within their own group. Each child needs to discover his own sincere relationship to his environment and to the objects and materials that make up this environment. There are no short cuts to the development of perceptual abilities or creative growth. Although the range of individual differences can be very great, the end product should be viewed only as an indication of individual development. Standards of value should never come from the teacher, nor should group influences be so strong as to dictate a particular kind or type of product. Growth affects the products and also affects the aesthetic awareness of children; any standards outside the child himself are false.

During the earlier Schematic Stage children had a need to repeat the same symbol again and again. Now, however, the repetition of form should gradually disappear, and there should be a development of new forms or shapes that are not constantly repeated. Working in unfamiliar materials can often have a positive effect upon drawings and paintings. Children who have worked in collage materials may become much more aware of a variety of textures and forms and be able to transfer this awareness into a painting medium. Art should certainly give support for individual expression and creative thinking.

Having gained a greater understanding of this peer-group age, one can readily see how the teaching of particular techniques in art may stand in the way of children's exploring and experimenting for themselves. Adults help a great deal in the physical development of children by providing them with the proper nutrients and the place and encouragement for the development of the necessary physical skills; in the same way adults should provide the essential ingredients for children's artistic development—but cannot do this developing for them.

RELATED ACTIVITIES

1   Collect the drawings of a fourth grade class and tabulate how many children use base line concept. How many use more than one base line? Have any children begun to use the space below the base line as a plane?

2   Save the drawings of a third grade child over a period of several months. Trace the development of the symbols used in representing forms. Compare with drawings from a fifth grade child during the same period.

3   Observe several group activities within a school setting at several grade levels. Which activities were the most productive? Which were most satisfactory from the child's point of view? Analyze the reasons why some activities were more successful than others.

4   Make a list of materials used in a fourth grade art program. Revise this list according to the appropriateness of these art materials for expression at this age level. Compare this list with what is appropriate at the kindergarten level.

5   Make a list of examples of children's growing awareness of design and textural pattern in their drawings. Pay particular attention to clothing and objects important to the artist. Are any differences observable between the sexes? How does the extent of awareness compare with academic ability?

6   Keep a record of which children begin to make the sky come down to the base line. What is the first realization of overlapping beyond this initial step? Are these the same children who are also more socially developed?

Art
in the
Secondary
School

10

The Role of Art

Art ought to play a very important role in the lives of students in the secondary school. Within the framework of our public school system, however, art usually plays a subordinate role, whereas within our society it is taking on greater importance. Art is more than pictures on a museum wall, more than the making of paintings or sculpture, more than the creation of our environment by building structures or planning and landscaping open spaces. These are the tangible evidences of art within our society, and those people who call themselves artists are the ones who design, build, paint, and cast. But art can also mean an attitude toward living, a means of formulating feelings and emotions and giving them tangible expression. It is a means by which sensitivities to experiences are heightened and refined. In a broad sense, art is both external and internal. The responsiveness to the things around us develops through a system of attitudes and experiences into new forms.

Even with such a broad point of view, it is quickly apparent that most school experiences are unrelated to art. The art classes currently offered in most public schools tend to emphasize the production of art rather than the development of artistic attitudes. This is not to say that the production of art is bad in itself, but an undue emphasis upon producing paintings or pieces of sculpture may be detrimental to the process of thinking, feeling, and perceiving in an artistic manner. It is the *process* of art that is important, not the products themselves.

There is an increasing awareness of the need for developing not only sensitivities to our environment but sensitivities to the needs and feelings of others. This whole area is one which in the past has been ignored by our public school system. The usual secondary school curriculum is divided into small segments of subject matter, and these segments are usually justified on the basis of vocational or educational preparation. However, in our rapidly changing society, there are emerging professions and specific job opportunities that were not dreamed of thirty years ago, and youngsters in our junior and senior high schools may be preparing for jobs that have not yet been defined. There is a common attitude that "science has all the answers," placing great emphasis and reliance on technology. But there is also an increasing awareness of the fact that the study of science alone cannot provide the means to deal with values and attitudes. In a changing society those values and attitudes established by older generations are not values and attitudes that can be easily assumed by youngsters in the junior and senior high schools. The means of expression that are socially acceptable and at the same time available for youngsters of this age to use, are strictly limited. Art may be the only field within the framework of the school system where the development of feelings and emotions is given proper recognition.

Mills and Thomson (1981) report that, in 30 states, 50 percent or more of the high schools offer art sequences. Only a small fraction of students take art beyond ninth grade, even if available. But this dismal picture may be changing somewhat; it is reported that enrollment in arts electives is increasing in high schools, as much as 10 percent within one year in some localities. Neville (1973) attributes much of this increased interest to the greatly expanded offerings of mini-courses that capitalize upon the interests of students, for short courses of ten weeks or less. Schools frequently provide credit for art-related out-of-school work at community centers, alternative schools, multi-cultural schools, schools without walls, learning centers, and comparable special interest centers (Carnegie Council, 1980). Occasionally there is a required course in the humanities for all high school students, which attempts to combine art with other subjects to make a supposedly meaningful whole for these students. Intellectually, this may have some value, for the student needs to understand art as a reflection of the culture of the times and recognize its relationships with the changes in our society; but the establishment of values and attitudes cannot be imposed from without. Personal involvement is essential to a feeling for art. On the other hand, some schools have changed very little in their attitudes toward art. It almost seems as if they feel it is the responsibility of the schools to indoctrinate students in conventional "good taste." A century ago, Quackenbos (1871, p. 182) advised that "Taste, being in a great degree the result of assiduous study and cultivation, requires long and careful training to attain perfection."

The Psychological Change from Elementary to Secondary School

Children in the elementary school paint and draw without inhibition. This can be seen especially at the nursery school and kindergarten levels. However, by the time they arrive at fourth, fifth, and especially sixth grade, children become increasingly aware of their own products. Spontaneous and uninhibited expression disappears, and by seventh grade a critical awareness has developed. This critical awareness is not limited to art products, for the youngster is now agonizingly conscious of himself and his own limitations within the society of his peers. At this age a youngster begins to realize the unhappy position in which he finds himself: he is now an aware, thinking individual but is not yet in a position to take any particular action to change his circumstances. These youngsters are hostile toward their parents, disillusioned with school, and at times discouraged with themselves. It is not surprising, therefore, to find that they are also critical of their own art products.

Now that the child has lost his uninhibited approach to drawing and painting, he has become very conscious of his actions. This is indeed a critical period in his development. He has not developed a conscious objective approach to his actions, yet he is at the same time insecure with his childish approach to art. This is one reason so many individuals stop their creative work when they are through with the required courses of art in the junior high school. It is only for those students who have developed a profound interest in the subject, or have found in it a mechanism by which they can satisfy some of their needs, that art can take on greater meaning. There are, of course, earlier indications of this change coming about. The sixth grade child usually covers up his drawings when an adult comes by. The seventh grader is quite reluctant to show anything or have any sort of outside evaluation made of his product. By comparison, the kindergarten child will eagerly show and explain his products to any and all interested adults. One of the important tasks of art education during the secondary school, and particularly during the junior high school, is to provide confidence in his own means of expression so that the child will continue in his use of art.

For the purpose of investigating the change in imaginative concepts in the school years, the topic "Playing Tag on the School Grounds" was assigned to three different groups: to a number of elementary school children of the first three grades; to boys and girls of the upper elementary school; and to students in the secondary school. There were approximately 300 subjects in each group. The topic was presented to the youngsters with no requirement that they draw it, and they were allowed to select other topics they preferred if they so desired. Ninety-five percent of the lower elementary school children made some attempt to represent this experience, whereas only 35 percent of the secondary school students tried to depict this game. The drawings were analyzed on two variables: the ways of expressing the experience of catching and being caught, and the spatial relationships representing the schoolground.

The elementary school children of the first three grades generally made no attempt at naturalistic representation. This was true both in the representation of the human figure and in the representation of the schoolground. The

Figure 167.

At this crucial age of increased self awareness, students are critical of their own art products. Although some secondary schools do not offer art, there is a real need for an art program where students' sensibilities and sensitivities can be expressed openly, and learning in artistic media can take place.

environment was almost entirely missing in the youngest group tested. Figure 168, done by a boy aged six and a half, is a typical representation. Here the boy has used an oval for the body and a circle for the head. Arms and legs are expressed differently in the two figures; whereas the arms of the captive are entirely missing, that of the captor is greatly overemphasized. Notice particularly the exaggeration of the grasping hand. Apparently only one hand is needed for tag. The legs of the captor are longer than those of his playmate, which may give some indication of the faster running ability of one child. Notice also that the schoolground is indicated only by a base line. The child's method of perceiving space is determined primarily from his own being and not from a visual experience. The child's world of images is bound up with the self, with personal experiences and emotions, and is not involved with a naturalistic representation.

The second drawing, Figure 169, is a more elaborate drawing by a nine year old girl from the upper elementary school. This, too, is typical and shows quite clearly that the girl is aware of naturalistic details and her own relationship to her environment. The girls are wearing dresses; there is even an attempt to show the hair blowing in the breeze; the schoolground is clearly indicated, surrounded by trees and a fence. The upper section of the picture serves as a base line for the school and swings. The lower section has a base line with the girls and what appears to be a slide resting on it. Also, additional playground equipment has been placed between the two base lines. The addition of some "ground lines" has transformed this empty space into the school yard. One arm of the chasing girl is exaggerated, but otherwise the figures are quite stiff. There is a beginning awareness of overlapping, but for the most part each object stands separately, and the girls are looking at us rather than paying attention to where they are running. Although there is a greater awareness of nature, the drawing itself is not an attempt at visual accuracy.

The majority of the drawings of the secondary school students make an attempt at naturalistic representation. In a typical drawing, Figure 170, the student has endeavored to make the running boys as naturalistic as possible; they are fairly well proportioned, with arms and legs bent, and parts of the environment are drawn in a sketchy fashion with good size relationships.

The above study was based upon children's utilizing their past experiences, their familiarity with their school playground and its environs, the kinesthetic experience of actually playing tag, and the visual impressions that they recalled. The outcome was less an attempt at photographic imitation of a scene than a drawing of a concept. That is, the drawing showed the child's understanding of what was important about playing tag, and this was organized in a

ART IN THE SECONDARY SCHOOL

Figure 169.
*"Playing Tag on the School
Grounds," painted by a nine year
old girl. Here we see exaggeration
of important parts. There
are two base lines on
which the children and school are
placed.*

Figure 170.
*"Playing Tag on the School
Grounds," drawn by an
adolescent. This picture is an
attempt at naturalistic
representation. Space is shown
through the use of visual
perspective.*

way that reflected a particular developmental level. It could be argued that these differences would not be present if children were to draw from objects directly in front of them. However, Willats (1977) had children from five to seventeen years of age draw a table with a radio, box, and saucepan on it. All children drew from the same point of view. Willats found comparable developmental stages; little overlapping was shown below the age of nine, various attempts at depicting depth and increasing use of overlapping occurred from nine to twelve, but the use of some kind of perspective was still only used by half of the fifteen to seventeen year olds.

This is not to suggest that children draw objects the same way whether these objects are visible or not. Hooper (1977) found that second graders drew a table in somewhat the same manner when they drew the topic "eating" as when they drew a table by itself. However, when sixth graders drew the table as part of an eating scene, they distorted the table, sometimes drawing it from overhead; whereas, when shown one, they more often drew the table with an attempt at perspective. It would be expected that most seventeen year olds would be consistent in their manner of representing the table, whether just drawing a table or illustrating "eating." The important point is that there is not a gradual awareness of a correct system of photographic representation. Rather, there seems to be a process, distinct from perception, which is responsible for a variety of methods of representation.

The Importance of Self-identification

To some extent, the period of development covered by the secondary school could be considered a time when a youngster finds himself. The child just out of sixth grade has left behind him close attachments to his parents. Up to now, however, the child has been controlled, guided, and commanded by the older generation. At the other end of the secondary school system the adult emerges, ready to take his place in society. The six years or so between these two stages can be characterized by a search for the self. "Who am I? What am I going to do with my life? What do I believe in?" These are all problems to be worked out during this period. Yet the school curriculum is usually planned so as to provide little opportunity for contemplation, and little time for the youngster to face himself. Somehow, this time for thinking is considered dangerous; the old axiom of a busy person being a happy one is forcibly applied to most of the secondary school population.

The art program in the secondary school ought to provide the means for this important self-identification. The adolescent is constantly bombarded by a world of advertisements stressing the importance of the proper hairspray, toothpaste, or deodorant, all of which can lead to success as measured by gaiety, activity, and attention from the opposite sex. By age fifteen, the average American child has spent about 20,000 hours watching television, more time than in school (Swerdlow, 1981). His value system is greatly shaped by the world of television, which can be confused with reality. Rigid conformity to peer-group standards is a must; being seen in the "right" places, having the proper style of hair, or brand of jeans shows quite clearly that the individual is under tremendous pressure to belong. In fact, the adolescent can be quite ruthless in his criticism of his peers who are unwilling or unable to conform to the latest fads. His scorn, of course, is often leveled at parents and teachers.

Unfortunately, art in the secondary school is usually aimed chiefly at producing technically acceptable products. Little attention is focused upon the needs and desires of the secondary school student himself. This is somewhat preposterous when one considers that most students who elect art in the secondary school are not going to become artists. In fact, the limited learning that takes place within these elective art courses usually needs to be unlearned if the student does continue on to a professional art school (Brittain, 1961). Most elective art courses ignore the problems of the students as people; yet it is from the needs, desires, and frustrations of adult artists that great art is made. The focus of these school programs should clearly be on the process of making art and not on the art product.

To identify with oneself, to identify with others, to identify with a product and be able to say "This is mine," to be able to set problems and goals for oneself and to be responsible for the direction and method of expression—all these are important considerations in developing an art program for the secondary schools. The life of the junior or senior high school student is not to be ignored. It is the resource upon which the program should be built.

A variety of art activities can take place that provide this important means for self-identification. Certainly painting, sculpturing, making prints, pots, and murals can all be executed with the youngster's own means of expression and own subject matter. However, it is also possible to identify with the work and art products of others. Here it is important not to analyze and look at the art work itself in abstract or objective terms, but rather to identify with the creator and with the problems and emotional relationships that he has

Figure 171.
Secondary school students often catch the bus by 7:30 in the morning and do not return home until 4:00 or later in the afternoon. The day is spent with their own age-mates and usually within the confines of the school grounds.

had in completing his work of art. Each person as an individual reacts and responds to objects on different levels. To ignore the responses and concerns of the individual students could cause a frustrating experience. The important consideration is to make the individual sensitive to the values, attitudes, and judgments in an appreciative experience. To impose set standards or to teach rules for discussing art may be irrelevant to the student. Certainly political or social history may be a factor in the development of a particular work of art, but this is secondary to whether it is enjoyed or rejected by the individual. Personal preferences should be expected to develop and to change with increased exposure and understanding.

To be more specific, the study of a mobile should not be limited to an appreciation of the work of Alexander Calder. Rather, nature itself can provide the understanding for this type of art in observing how a paper flutters when the breeze strikes it, or how the leaves of a tree create constant new patterns as the light changes, or how maple seeds or thistles glide as the wind carries them. An understanding of the mobile in this context becomes much more meaningful than looking at the mobile only as an abstract art form. Identifying with the artist as he views his environment and tries to translate an aesthetic experience into a tangible product makes the appreciation of art part of the experience of the viewer.

The importance of identifying with oneself at a particular moment should not be minimized. Painting or drawing is usually the most expressive type of art, but posters and montage provide an opportunity to deal with the social problems of our time. Where they are going and the problems of getting there are very real issues to senior high school students. For both girls and boys, the problems of sex and marriage are frighteningly close, and the prospect of finding and holding a job is of increasing concern. For both, the voting age is getting closer, and the will to do something constructive about the present condition of our country is a powerful driving force. Art has not limited itself to the portrayal of the beautiful in the past, and the art of youngsters in the secondary school does not have to be beautiful today. It is much more important to provide an environment in which serious expression can be encouraged than to be concerned about the development of good taste in these students.

It is interesting and rather surprising to note that youngsters who have run into problems with the law and been put into institutions under the label of "delinquents" have apparently not been able to express themselves creatively. In a study by Burgart (1968) it was found that a group of delinquent boys ranked lowest on a creativity test, compared with other groups of school children and some nonschool groups. Another study comparing creative thinking between delinquent boys and nondelinquent boys (Kuo, 1967) found that sixteen and seventeen year old boys reading at the fourth grade level tended to be nondelinquent if they scored high in measures of creative thinking compared with delinquent boys who scored low on the same measures. Although there were no differences in intelligence, another study (Anderson and Stoffer, 1979) found that nondelinquent boys scored significantly higher on tests of verbal creativity than did delinquent boys. Apparently having the opportunity to express oneself in creative fashion provides some means of reacting to the social environment in ways that are acceptable to that society. Possibly those who find they cannot create, who have found no satisfaction in building or producing, may react in negative ways. Unable to contribute in a positive manner,

Figure 172.
Art can take many forms, but the youngster's own expression should be considered the most important element of any product. Solving the problems of joining wood is a learning experience.

they destroy or deface what others have built. There may be more danger in having a passive view of life than in being aggressive about one's role. Gibbens (1968) reported that submissive, helpless, and unrealistic boys having an inadequate response to life were more apt to be reconvicted to jail sentence than those boys who rated as being aggressive, extroverted, and dynamic. It is clear that the problem is not one limited to delinquent boys. Everyone, particularly those who are confined to our school institutions, needs to have a means of self-expression, and this should be especially encouraged for those who seem disinterested and submissive. Art can play many roles, but the channeling of energies into productive outlets and the opportunity for self-identification should certainly be stressed at the secondary school level.

The Development of Two Creative Types

At about the age of twelve or so it is possible to see examples of two types of expression. One is called the *visual* type, and the other is usually referred to as *haptic* (from the Greek word *haptos,* meaning "to lay hold of"). Theoretically at opposite ends of a continuum, these types refer to the mode of perceptual organization and the conceptual categorization of the external environment. The visually minded person is one who acquaints himself with his environment primarily through the eyes and feels like a spectator. The person with haptic tendencies, on the other hand, is concerned primarily with his own body sensations and subjective experiences, which he feels emotionally. Most people fall between the two extremes. The very visually minded individual would be disturbed and inhibited if he were to be limited to haptic impressions, that is, if he were asked not to use sight but to orient himself only by the means of touch, bodily feelings, muscular sensations, and kinesthetic functions. An extremely haptic individual, although normally sighted, uses his eyes only when compelled to do so; otherwise, he relies upon his sense of touch and body self as his main means of becoming acquainted with and reacting to his environment.

The initial work in discovering these two separate means of acquainting oneself with the environment was done by Lowenfeld (1939), while working with the partially blind. He found that some partially blind individuals would use the limited sight they had to examine objects, or when they expressed themselves in clay modeling. At the same time, other partially blind individuals would not use their eyes, but preferred to use the sense of touch. This led to his study of normal people, and here he found similar tendencies. Further work was done in measuring these qualities (Lowenfeld, 1945, 1966). Using 1,128 subjects, Lowenfeld found that 47 percent had clear visual tendencies, whereas 23 percent could be scored haptic, and 30 percent received a score somewhere in between. In other words, approximately half of the individuals tested reacted visually, whereas not quite a fourth reacted haptically.

Further evidence that some normally sighted individuals may relate themselves to the environment through the sense of touch was indicated in a study comparing blind and normally sighted blindfolded college students (Kennedy and Fox, 1977). When asked to identify common objects imprinted in outline, some of the normally sighted students did not mention visual imagery, but instead relied on shape and form; identification was obtained through the sense of touch and the object's function. In England, Millar (1975) studied figure drawings by sighted children under visual and blindfold conditions, and compared these with drawings by blind children, to try to determine the roles of visual and haptic feedback in drawing. By age ten the blind children used the same two-dimensional representations of body parts as did sighted children. She concluded that success in figure drawing does not depend only on visual experiences but comes also as a result of haptic perceptions.

Using an electroencephalogram, Walter (1963), in a study of alpha rhythms—the brain waves or electrical pulsations that are recorded with the mind at rest—discovered that in one group of persons these rhythms persist even when the mind is active and alert. He administered a test to 600 individuals that enabled him to distinguish between a visualizer (the M type), the nonvisualizer with a persistent alpha activity (the P type), and a mixed type (the R type). Individuals with persistent alpha rhythms that were hard to block with mental effort tended to have kinesthetic and tactile perceptions rather than to have visual imagery. This group of persons had continuing alpha rhythms even when the eyes were open and the mind active. However, the visual type retains mental pictures of his environment and, according to Walter, thinks primarily in terms of visual images.

In a study by Drewes (1958) using a variety of testing devices, Rorschach responses from a group that he called visualizers tended to be whole and three-dimensional forms, while the nonvisualizers in his population produced more kinesthetic movements and shading responses. Some work by Flick (1960) indicated that haptic expression can be found not only in the fields of art, but also in literature and other areas.

Figure 173.

"Pain," sculpture by a sixteen year old blind girl who is visually minded. (A) The general outline is made. (B) The cavity of the mouth is formed. (C) The nose is added. (D) Eye sockets are hollowed out. (E) Eyeballs are put in. (F) Lids are pulled over. (G) Wrinkles are formed. (H) Ears are added. (I) Hair is added. (J) In the finished product, all features are incorporated into a unified surface.

THE DEVELOPMENT OF TWO CREATIVE TYPES 329

Figure 174.

"Pain," sculpture by a sixteen year old blind boy who is haptically minded. (A) The chin is constructed. (B) The teeth and tongue are put in. (C) The mouth is closed, hiding inside features. (D) The nose is added, eye sockets are made. (E) Eyeballs are put in from inside, head is closed. (F) Ears, muscles, and hair are added. (G) The head is finished. (H) All features remain isolated as partial impressions on final product.

ART IN THE SECONDARY SCHOOL

H

THE DEVELOPMENT OF TWO CREATIVE TYPES

A thorough discussion of the haptic system was set forth by Gibson (1966). He documented the numerous means of perception that people have open to them in addition to the eyes. The skin feels, the touching of hairs carries a message, heat and pressure can be understood, and the size and shape of objects can be realized. Gibson's work indicated that objects can be identified and selected without their even being seen. Boffoly (1978) gave to 103 eighth graders a series of tests measuring 23 variables to determine how they responded to a variety of perceptual information. Using factor analysis, he found that three factors accounted for differences in how these junior high school students responded: 20 percent responded haptically or kinesthetically, 26 percent visually, and the rest responded in ways he termed cognitively.

There may be some relationship between the haptic-visual theory and a theory dealing with different modes of perception: Field-Independence versus Field-Dependence (Witkin, 1962). However, a study of paintings by some sixth and eighth graders conducted by Rouse (1965) found no correlation between these theories. In an experiment with children's reading ability, Templeman (1962) found that there was a relationship between a first grader's creative type and the ease with which he learns; those children who were considered haptic had more difficulty in learning to read. Kagan, Moss, and Sigel (1963), reporting upon several studies on cognitive style, found results similar to aspects of haptic-visual types in what they termed the analytic and nonanalytic responses of children. Although the ability to discriminate between different shapes seems to be fully developed by six years of age, Gliner, et al. (1969), in an investigation of the development of haptic and visual preferences of kindergarten and third grade children, found that more younger children, when feeling hardboard forms, distinguished between them by their texture, whereas more older children distinguished forms by their shape. Further studies of haptic attitudes have been undertaken (Concannon, 1970; Heller, 1980; Simmons and Locher, 1979) but these have dealt primarily with tactile experiences of children rather than with haptic expression.

This documentation of the haptic-visual theory is less important than its implications for art in the secondary school. Realizing that extremes of either type are rare, it is important to understand that some children may be inhibited by references solely to visual stimulation. This is particularly important to keep in mind for those teachers who themselves may be strongly visually minded. If one thinks of an immediate response to the word "lifting," is the response a visual one such as "box" or "books," or is the response a haptic one such as "heavy" or "straining?" Suppose you were asked how many floors there are in a building that you have been in; would you answer by visualizing it and counting the floors, or by recalling the number of flights of stairs you had to climb? Or if you go quickly down a flight of steps, do you have to watch your feet so you won't fall, or do you get confused if you watch your feet?

The visual type is the observer, who usually approaches things from their appearance. One important factor in visual observation is the ability initially to see the whole without an awareness of the details. Apparently, the visual type first sees a general shape of a tree, then the single leaves, the twigs, the branches, the trunk, and finally everything incorporated into the whole tree. Starting with the general outline, partial visual impressions are integrated into a whole image. The visually minded individual can analyze the characteristics of shape and structure of an object and be concerned with the changing effects of these shapes as they are influenced by light, shadow, color, atmosphere, and distance. How something looks is of prime importance, and even tactile sensations are translated into visual form. For him, the complex and ever-changing appearances of shapes and form are exciting and pleasurable experiences.

The haptic type utilizes muscular sensations, kinesthetic experiences, impressions of touch, taste, smells, weights, temperatures, and all the experiences of the self to establish relationships to the outside world. The sizes and shapes are determined by their importance to the individual. Thinking relates to the details that are of emotional significance (Zawacki, 1956). The haptic person enjoys textures and feels objects pleasurably with the hands. There is no attempt at trying to translate these textures into a visual image. The art of the haptic is more subjective. The artist becomes a part of the picture, and subjective values determine the color and form of objects.

It is important to remember that teaching should encourage the expression of students, regardless of their mode of representation. There is no need to reward one type of representation over another, because our culture provides the opportunity for honest expression of all types. Unfortunately, the teaching of art is usually in visual terms. However, even color is impossible to teach as a purely visual phenomenon. Although color can be described in terms of hue, lightness or darkness, and strength or intensity, there may also be many variations within an object itself, as reflected light or changes in contour affect the color. Color can also be described as bright, cheerful, and warm, or cold, forbidding, and hostile. Even the representation of concrete objects will differ depending upon the way in which an object is viewed and the response of the individual to these objects. Both haptic and visual stimulation should be provided and both kinds of art should be rewarded.

An example of one type of expression is Figure 175. There is a concern

Figure 175.

"A Scene at the Police Station,"
drawn by a visually minded
adolescent. Correct proportions,
lights and shadows, and
three-dimensional quality are
important to the artist.

for correct proportions and measurements, and the changing effects of light and shadows are necessarily a part of the visual image. These are qualities of representation that can be discovered with the eyes. Figure 176 is a more haptic type of representation. Here the human figure is used as a means of expressing emotions and feelings. Because different parts of the body have various functions and importance, the proportion given these parts assumes emotional significance.

The history of art is filled with examples of art of both the haptic and visual types. Michelangelo's "David" is a type of expression very different

Figure 176.
"A Scene at the Police Station,"
drawn by a haptically minded
adolescent. The elements of this
composition are determined
subjectively; proportions, lights
and darks, and space are of
emotional significance.

from a piece of sculpture from the South Pacific islands. Both, however, are true art expression and sincere forms of art. In the past classic Greek sculpture was highly admired. The beauty of the visible form was considered a high achievement and the religious art expression of the medieval period was thought quite crude in comparison. However, the forces that determined the religious expression were symbolic of deeply personal experiences; viewed with this in mind the distortions and exaggerations of the medieval art take on an intriguing beauty quite different from the classic purity.

The experiences of the adolescent youngster can often provide intense motivation for visual awareness. The blazing flames of the sky at sunset, or the reflections of a shimmering image in a puddle, or dark silhouettes in the evening can be inspiring. At the same time, these youngsters can be deeply touched by the human qualities of life and become involved in the struggle of mankind; the sky becomes only a reflection of this struggle, while the puddle reflects merely poverty, and the shadows are symbolic of man's false façade. It is important to provide the range of stimulation that will make those individuals who are at either end of the haptic-visual continuum acutely aware of the problems of artistic expression; and this type of motivation will be equally meaningful to the individuals who are able to produce from both haptic and visual experiences. Yet a visual type may dislike and reject such haptic works as unskilled and worthless, whereas a haptic type could interpret visual representation as superficial and unfeeling. Tolerance and acceptance of other modes of expression need to be learned by students as well as teachers.

The visual-haptic theory is important to understand, for it explains much development in art. Young children's art can be generally classified as haptic in nature, for the experiences portrayed are those that originate primarily with the self, and include what might be considered touch-space. The increasing visual awareness of children can be seen in their drawings and paintings, as discussed earlier. For some the emphasis on visual representation can become a burden with which they are not able to deal, so art for the haptically minded individual may in some cases be a frustrating experience. The rewards in the elementary school may have gone to those children who were the most visually aware of their environment. The teacher in the secondary school may be confronted with children who have rejected the world of visual art and decided, therefore, that they cannot draw or paint. The haptic art that can be elicited from such children whose expression has previously been thwarted is often emotionally charged. Between the two extreme modes of expression are the indefinites, who are also of concern. Gutteter (1976) studied 200 adolescents, identifying those with haptic and visual attributes, but found evidence that students who fell between these groups lacked self-direction and were constricted in thought and action.

Methods of Working in Art

Just as no two students are the same, their ways of working in art will also be different. This may greatly complicate the teacher's role, because he is dealing with the many diverse ways in which youngsters approach an art experience. This can readily be seen in the way some youngsters tackle projects with enthusiasm, while others will begin the same project with hesitation. In some cases these attitudes toward materials or toward certain art activities may be a reflection of how a youngster feels that day; in others, these may be the manifestation of a long term attitude.

In studies by Beittel (1966) and by Beittel and Burkhart (1963) two methods or strategies of learning in art were differentiated. These were called the *spontaneous* and the *divergent*. The spontaneous students began with a big whole that was devoid of detail, experimented with form, and took advantage of accidents. Their products looked quite free and tended to be nonvisual in nature. The divergent students usually began with fine drawings of details and added single elements together developing an organization as they did so. Although this study was done with college students, these types can also be seen in the secondary school. There may be some relationship here to the visual-

Plates 25 and 26.

"Trees," watercolor paintings done by adolescent girls, illustrating two different methods of approach to the same subject. The artist of Plate 25 has utilized the flowing qualities of the material with no concern for photographic representation. On the other hand, Plate 26 is built up out of carefully drawn details: leaves, branches, and flowers. Although an individual may identify more with either the subjective or naturalistic approach, it may be valuable to encourage experimentation with both methods.

Plate 27.

"The Forest," painted by an eighth grade girl. At this stage of development, aesthetic considerations can become important, so that the child may no longer be interested in a literal representation but instead seek to convey a mood and emphasize design qualities.

Figure 177.
*Secondary school students show
great diversity in the attitudes,
the abilities, and the degree of
interest in art that they bring to
art activities.*

haptic theory, but Beittel has been more concerned with analyzing the way students draw than with the development of their modes of thinking. However, it is obvious that these are related.

In studying these two different strategies of working in art, Beittel provided a situation where students could see photographs that were made of their work in progress. The opportunity for students to look at these and clarify their own thinking in turn provided an opportunity for self-motivation. The goals of the student were an important part of this learning situation. The study indicated that self-discovered criteria were more effective and motivating to these students than were some external criteria. But the researcher also played an important part in these studies: the student had someone to talk to. Apparently, it was important to have some means by which the thoughts and

METHODS OF WORKING IN ART

directions that students saw for themselves could be clarified; and the role of the teacher, or in this case the researcher, was merely to listen. Beittel (1972) emphasizes the powerful potential for learning that the "hindsight" method brings to the artist; he urges that everyone engaged in art try to communicate to another person just what he was trying to do, so that he himself may understand it.

Although these two methods of working in art are quite opposite from one another, they also appear to be flexible (Beittel, 1966). At least some students could assume the methods or strategy of the opposite type, for when told to paint with the opposite strategy their work changed. Surprisingly, this shift in method did not mean that their paintings dropped in quality. There may even be an advantage, then, in pointing out to students other methods or ways of working once they have clarified some thoughts and directions on their own.

Teachers need to be aware of their own methods of painting or working with art materials. There is no reason to believe that the spontaneous method of working is any more appropriate than is the divergent method. But there might be some danger in a teacher's imposing his own method of working in art upon his students. Drawing in one method continually could put the student in somewhat of a rut, however, so that he might indeed benefit from the realization that there are other approaches. As an example consider a student who is working diligently and with good control over his drawings. He may have excellent detail and add parts to his composition to make a whole. When drawing buildings he may draw large and small buildings, with fine detailing around the windows, add smokestacks and sidewalks, and be mostly concerned with line quality. A discussion of where he is going and what he is trying to do can probably clarify some of his thoughts. However, if he becomes dissatisfied with this method of drawing, the suggestion that he draw something large and forceful, with rough edges, with a great deal of freedom and movement, using many ways of smudging and shading, may provide him with other approaches to art which he can incorporate into his own method. Of course, the opposite procedure may work well with a spontaneous student. The concern of the teacher, then, is to expand the student's awareness of the possibilities in art and to provide him the opportunity to evaluate and reevaluate his own direction.

Several theories have been advanced to explain how learning takes place in art. The Perception-Delineation theory (McFee, 1970) identifies six points which are felt to be crucial for learning. The first is readiness, including among others perceptual and conceptual development; the second is the psychocul-

Figure 178.
*Depth of personal experience is
of prime importance in art
activity. The meaningfulness of
an art program can be measured
only in terms of the individual.*

tural transaction with the classroom; the third is the visual-physical environment introduced by the teacher; the fourth is information handling, as the child
integrates new information into what he already knows; the fifth is creative
delineation of his response to his own work or the work of others; the sixth is
the evaluation of feedback and the transfer of learning to the next task. Arnheim (1954) feels that artistic production is not based upon intellectual abstraction but upon a broader cognition, and that the form that is represented can not

METHODS OF WORKING IN ART

be derived only from the object perceived. Ehrenzweig (1967) feels that the artist and scientist share similar methods of approaching their work; both have to make sense out of apparent chaos by scanning a multitude of possible links and projecting order into reality. The syncretic mode of vision, focusing upon the total view, is thought to be more flexible and efficient for scanning than is the analytic mode of vision. Hence, Ehrenzweig feels that a child needs to be supported in his aesthetic standards on the syncretistic level, so that the later awakening of his analytic self-criticism will be less harmful.

There are other theories of how learning takes place in the arts (Dewey, 1958; Eng, 1931; Munro, 1956; Read, 1958). How these theories differ is less important than the fact that differences in theory exist. For the teacher in the secondary school it becomes imperative that each student be considered unique and that his way of learning be encouraged. Environmental conditions or situations can be altered so that the student feels his art is respected. In a true art experience the artist displays his inner self; how he sees, thinks, and feels is laid bare. One of the goals of any secondary school art teacher should be to provide an environment where these thoughts and this expression, however it is produced, can be treated with sensitivity and respect.

Creativity in the Secondary School Art Program

In recent years there has been an increase in the interest and concern that educators have shown in the field of creativity. Many innovations have been made in the teaching of the usual academic subjects to provide for the creative responses of students. One method has been to provide problems that students must work through in order to arrive at axioms or postulates in mathematics, rather than having this information memorized in advance. In history, questions such as "What might have happened if the battle had been lost?" or "What would you have done if you were president?" are becoming more and more common. In art, there has always been the feeling that creativity is an essential part of the experience, but unless care is taken to insure that students develop a creative attitude, and that the environmental conditions are such that they will foster creative growth, there is no assurance that art experiences in themselves will develop creativity.

The change from a natural, spontaneous manner of working with art materials, seen in young children, to one of a critical awareness of one's own actions calls for a well-developed plan for encouraging creativity. With younger children, it was a simple matter to encourage and foster the enthusiasm and freedom that seem to be part of life. In the secondary school, however, the development of creative thinking must be an essential ingredient of the art program. Flexibility, fluency, originality, and the ability to think independently and imaginatively must not be left to chance.

The art teacher must therefore plan for experiences that develop creative thinking abilities. It is not enough just to have students produce, even if these productions can be called art. It is important to develop the ability to think creatively, to learn how to create. For some students this may be a difficult experience, because many of them have achieved success by following the formulas or patterns of others. This may be true even of the highly intelligent youngster (Getzels and Jackson, 1962). There is a certain amount of risk involved in setting out on new and uncharted paths. This risk is not limited to the students; the art teacher too takes many risks in encouraging students to think for themselves. It is certainly a great deal simpler for the art teacher in the secondary school to follow a set syllabus and to develop an art program around easily graded projects. However, the excitement of discovery and the growth of the student in the process of exploration can be most stimulating.

Creativity is not fostered in an unstructured, chaotic atmosphere. However, a certain degree of ambiguity and diversity, or what might appear to be lack of organization, may be a better environment within which the individual can develop his own structure than an environment that is already predetermined and made neat and orderly by someone else's standards. The creative person has a greater tolerance of ambiguity (Barron, 1963); and a sterile working environment, both psychological and physical, lacks stimulation.

The usual classroom, and this often includes art classes, has a well defined course of study outlined. The youngster is quite aware of this fact and his usual comment is "What am I supposed to do?" Obviously he does not expect to be included in the planning of the activity. Any opportunity that comes up which provides the chance for him to escape or deviate from this predestined path is welcomed. The problem goes even farther, because the next logical question is "How am I supposed to do it?" This question is customarily followed by "Is this the way you wanted it?" For some students it may be somewhat uncomfortable to shoulder the burden of helping making decisions rather than relying solely on the teacher. This may be particularly true at the junior high school level, where there is an indication that creativity hits a low point (Kincaid, 1964).

Figure 179.

Rather than imposing subject matter, the secondary art program should capitalize upon the interests of students, even if the prime interest is food.

The usual concern voiced on the part of teachers is the tremendous pressure that peer groups have upon the individual in the secondary school. There is good reason for this concern. Studies have shown that individuals are very susceptible to pressures from their peers to conform. Some college students, when asked to pick out the longest line from a series of lines of different lengths, went against what their senses told them and agreed with the group that had already selected one of the shorter lines (Asch, 1952). Apparently, most people are seriously affected and influenced by the decisions and judgments of others. Testing this in other ways, Crutchfield (1963) found similar results. It only takes a minute when observing youngsters in the junior high school to note the conformity and rules of dress and behavior that they impose upon themselves. Similar pressures will be found in the art room and will have an influence on what is produced.

On the other hand, the group can provide a great deal of stimulation and support for innovative thinking. The brainstorming technique perfected by Parnes (1964) has as its objective the goal of freeing the thinking of individuals, with the support of the group. Each individual within a working group is asked to express as many ideas as possible spontaneously, and no negative or critical evaluation is allowed. A different system, which is called synectics, involves a group in trying to join together different and apparently irrelevant elements (Gordon, 1961). In these instances the group is used as a means for furthering creative thinking. The pressures of the group can be used positively if the atmosphere is such that creativity is rewarded, and the new, novel, or unusual response is recognized. An important element in this is the deferment of action, which gives the opportunity to play around with divergent thoughts before evaluating the best method or most appropriate subject matter or the obvious material to use.

Although there are numerous tests for creativity, these have little value in an art room. How a student performs, the way in which he feels free to express himself, the flexible way in which he uses materials, the amount and number of things he can produce, his unusual approaches to drawing or painting, and the number of original or unique solutions that he provides to artistic problems offer an excellent indication of creativity, which can only be approximated by standardized tests.

It would probably be more valuable to know who is the least creative person in the art room, for this is the individual who needs the most support in his creative endeavors. In some cases this may be the highly intelligent youngster who has set overly high standards for himself. In some cases it may be an extremely sensitive individual who is afraid of the unknown, who needs the support of an encouraging adult.

The negative effect of grades, rewards, or other evaluation upon the creative thinking of young children has already been discussed. However, it is not only young children who are adversely influenced. The pressures to conform are particularly strong during early adolescence, but also continue through young adulthood. Any reward or external evaluation apparently changes the focus of an activity from exploring interesting possibilities and satisfying oneself, to trying to conform to others' wishes and to satisfying external demands, even if those demands are not understood. Pearlman (1979) told sixth graders that they could have an extra three points on their next mathematics examination score if they solved a problem correctly. Given the choice of a difficult or an easy problem, most children chose the easy problem. When other sixth graders who were not offered the extra points were asked to solve a problem, most of them picked the hard one. The same negative effects occur with older students. In examining the consequences of external evaluation on artistic creativity, Amabile (1979) told some college women that their work would be judged on creativity, others were told they would be judged on the technical aspects, and others were told they would be judged but with no particular focus. An additional group was told their work would not be judged. Fifteen

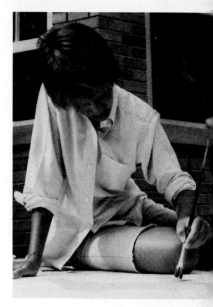

Figure 180.
Sometimes it is important to support the individual who wants to paint or draw alone. Art expression should be free of pressures for conformity.

artists rated the products and determined that the quality of the artwork of the non-evaluation group was significantly higher than that of the others. The negative aspect of evaluation on creative thinking is clear.

It must be emphasized that the art teacher should never forget that the development of creativity is one of the basic reasons for art's existence in the secondary school. Creativity can be improved at any level; the most effective method starts with the unreserved acceptance of a student as a worthy individual with thoughts and ideas of his own. The teacher must deal with the student simultaneously from an intellectual and an emotional point of view by providing a stimulating environment for him within the classroom.

Creative Expression and Brain Specialization

As scientific understanding of the biological functioning of the brain has increased there have been corresponding attempts by psychologists and educators to apply the new evidence to their own areas of expertise. This has not escaped the notice of art educators. Of particular interest has been the discovery that mental activity is not a generalized process, but that certain localized areas of the brain specialize in specific tasks. "Maps" of the brain have been produced showing which areas of the cerebral cortex are responsible for receiving sensation from and initiating movement in specific parts of the body.

Evidence for the location of sensory and motor specializations in various areas of the brain is relatively direct, through the study of stroke and accident victims. It has become apparent that the manipulation of language is located in the left half, or hemisphere, of the brain. Many other functions, such as the ability to recognize faces, to name objects, to perceive spatial relationships, and to perform mathematical operations, are similarly localized; whenever a specific type of task is performed or problem is solved, the area of the brain that specializes in tasks or problems of this type will habitually become active.

On a very broad level the cerebrum may be subdivided into two major areas. The two halves of the brain are the right and left hemispheres, almost completely separated except for a bundle of nerve fibers running between the two halves. For a time surgical separation of the two hemispheres was used as a method of controlling severe epilepsy. Studies of these "split-brain" patients and more recent studies of the electrical activity of the brain (EEG) measured by the use of electrodes placed outside of the skull have allowed researchers to determine which hemisphere is involved in different kinds of thinking. In split-brained individuals this may be accomplished by presenting problems to only one side of the brain at a time, by such devices as putting an object into one hand and hiding it from the other side of the body, or by placing a visual signal where only one half of the brain will be able to perceive it. It is then a fairly simple matter to measure the performance of each side of the brain individually and compare them to see which has done better.

The left hemisphere specializes in monitoring and controlling the right side of the body, processing words in writing and speaking, manipulating numbers, attending to details, and logical thinking. The right hemisphere specializes in monitoring and controlling the left side of the body, producing appropriate emotional states and recognizing and interpreting emotion in others, recognizing and humming tunes, and understanding spatial relationships (Goleman, 1977; Foster, 1977).

Figure 181.
Drawing and painting are thought to be related to the intuitive and the right brain. However, the arts demand as much from the intellect as from the emotions.

Since the left hemisphere has control of the right side of the body, and most people (about 90 percent) are right-handed, and since the left hemisphere contains the areas controlling speech, the right hemisphere being unable to communicate verbally in split-brain subjects, the left hemisphere is spoken of as being "dominant." To many people this apparently suggests a logical, verbal left hemisphere lording it over a sensitive and artistic right hemisphere. These well-meaning people then propose to rescue the right hemisphere from its subjugation by giving it a greater share of the attention lavished on the left hemisphere by our traditional educational system. Artistic pursuits such as drawing, music and dance, and an emphasis on "creative" thinking are supposed to somehow strengthen the right hemisphere through exercise and allow it to take its place as part of a "whole" brain.

In reality, of course, the dichotomy drawn between the left and right hemispheres of the brain is at the same time an oversimplification and an exaggeration. Neither studies of split-brain individuals nor EEG measurements are capable of sufficient discrimination to locate areas of expertise in the brain more precisely than by hemisphere. Judging by the strange deficiencies and inabilities of the victims of minor strokes, other specific skills may be just as highly localized as language has been shown to be. Further, the performance of most daily tasks requires a variety of skills, drawing upon the specialties of many areas. For example, the ability to correctly reproduce the sound of words is useless without the further ability to comprehend their meanings. Researchers studying split-brain individuals were hard pressed to find tasks that one half of the brain, but not the other, could perform (Gazzaniga, 1973), and

EEG studies show only relatively higher amounts of activity in one half of the brain, not activity in one half and inactivity in the other (McCallum and Glynn, 1979). The fact that people can recover from strokes demonstrates that much more of the brain may learn a task or function than may habitually participate in its performance, although this learning may remain passive until called forth (Geschwind, 1979). The cells affected by stroke die and cannot regenerate themselves. Any recovery a patient makes is through surviving areas of the brain taking up new tasks.

Creativity is apparently not one of the specialized areas of the brain. The notion that creativity is exclusively the function of the right hemisphere comes from making a false dichotomy between logic and creativity, or equating creativity with emotion. Creativity is a way of thinking, not a specific skill. Far from being localized in the right hemisphere, it appears that creative thought, like any other kind of problem solving, is a product of the cooperation of both hemispheres of the brain (McCallum and Glynn, 1979). A group of 175 community college students from Illinois, of both sexes and ranging between seventeen and forty-eight years of age, showed no significant relationship between cerebral dominance as measured by conjugate lateral eye movement, a test which discovers hemispheric dominance by observing which direction the eyes move after a subject is asked a neutral question, and creativity, as measured by the figural section of the Torrance Tests of Creative Thinking (Doerr, 1980). In a study comparing the electrical activity of the hemispheres of the brain and the handedness of a sample of students at a large midwestern university, Dorethy and Reeves (1979) found that art majors, contrary to expectation, were even more likely to be left-brain dominant than either art education majors or non-art majors.

Our school systems certainly do appear to be geared primarily towards the acquisition and use of verbal and logical skills, left hemisphere functions, but this may be more a reflection of our innate abilities as humans than anything else. The area of the brain associated with the acquisition and correct use of language has been shown to be larger than the corresponding area in the right hemisphere even in the fetal stages of development (Geschwind, 1979). Each hemisphere of the brain appears to operate almost independently until age two (McCallum and Glynn, 1979), and the final arrangement of hemispherical specializations, at least for language, is not fixed until about age eight (Geschwind, 1979). There is even some evidence for a larger left hemisphere in the great apes and Neanderthal man. Far from being an evil of modern society, an emphasis on verbalization has been an integral part of our evolution and survival as a species.

The Art Teacher in the Secondary School

Unquestionably the art teacher has a favorable position in the schools. In part it may be because art has an aura of being somehow different from other subjects, which permits the art teacher more license. So teachers of art are often able to run a different type of classroom without the wrath of the administration falling upon their heads. In part this may be because it is difficult to evaluate progress in the arts, and in part because art teachers are intrinsically more creative individuals anyway. That is, art has a fascination for people who are willing and eager to express their thoughts and feelings in an imaginative way. It could also be argued that art provides the training for creativity in itself. Either way, the art teacher is usually looked upon as somehow different, and may therefore be in a more enviable position than the usual academic teacher.

The art teacher has other advantages. Youngsters *like* art. There is a delight in teaching a subject which has a natural attraction for youngsters. Although the art teacher must spend hours in preparation and planning, there are no dull hours of correcting essays or papers that plague other teachers at the secondary level. One would expect therefore that the art teacher's job should be a delightful one.

Although the art teacher may view himself as fortunate, the youngsters in his classes view him in a rather different perspective. In an investigation into the character of early adolescent art, Brittain (1968a) found that the teacher is seen by the junior high school student as a potential threat. Most art teachers would like to consider themselves closer to youngsters than the average academic instructor, so this may come as quite a surprise. However, Brittain's study showed that the student clearly rejected the teacher as a fit person to evaluate his work or to set standards for his performance. Apparently, the youngster himself decided whether he was successful on the basis of his own feelings about what he had done rather than on the teacher's evaluation. This study also indicated that the junior high school youngster rejected the teacher not only as an evaluator, but as a source of ideas on what is important to do in art. When placed in the situation of having to perform art tasks assigned by the teacher, the student's own expression was thwarted. The only positive role that students saw for the teacher was that of providing new materials!

This is rather humiliating. Perhaps the traditional-style art teacher these youngsters must have known was concerned primarily with the handing out of materials. Obviously this method is still used in some elementary schools,

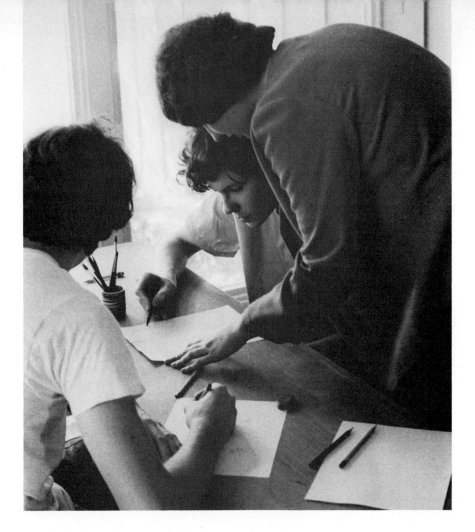

Figure 182.
The art teacher can have closer rapport with students than do teachers of the academic subjects. This role should be one of concern, listening as well as talking, for art is not merely the teaching of factual material.

and frequently one can find programs even in the junior high school that seem to be oriented primarily toward using one material after another. There may be good reasons, in fact, why the youngsters should treat such a teacher as a guardian of materials, rather than as a person able to help them with their aesthetic development and expressive needs.

These findings are borne out in other studies. A group of high school students was asked whose disapproval would be hardest to take: that of their parents, their teachers, or their friends. Although there were slight differences between boys and girls, high school youngsters seemed chiefly concerned about parents and friends disapproving of their actions, for only 3 percent of these teen-agers thought that the teacher's approval was important (Coleman, 1961). Part of the problem may be that adults do not attribute the same values to behavior and performance that youngsters do. A study by Cunningham

(1951) indicated that eighth grade youngsters had different values for certain experiences than did their parents. Whereas the parents thought it important for youngsters to work at home without pay, these eighth graders thought working for pay was much more important. However, the eighth graders thought that talking with adults who were engaged in various types of work was quite important, although parents did not value this highly for their youngsters. High on the list of values for these eighth graders was the opportunity to work or play in a group of four or five people, while the adults ranked this close to the bottom of the list. This finding gives support for the organization of the classroom into small workable units.

Although the teacher may be viewed as a threat and his values may be different from those of the secondary school student, the teacher's perception of students is very important. It has been clearly shown that individuals who are expected to perform creatively, and who are aware of this expectation, do much better than a group of people not so prepared (Hyman, 1964). The teacher's attitude becomes a crucial one in the classroom. A study by Rosenthal and Jacobson (1968) indicated that the teacher can also be influenced by how he expects the student to behave. Some 20 percent of the children from a certain elementary school were randomly selected and the names of these youngsters were reported to their teachers as showing unusual potential. Eight months later these "unusual" children showed great gains in intellectual performance on standard tests compared to the rest of the youngsters. The fact that the teacher expected the best may have paved the way for this to happen. Perhaps the most exciting and creative art class happens because the art teacher expects it to happen.

The usual teacher has many responsibilities before him in an art room full of students. These include a concern for classroom structure, the dissemination of materials, the need to save time for proper clean-up, and the presentation of some new material or method; so it becomes somewhat surprising to find that he also has time to talk to students. However, students may rarely have time to talk to him. A study by Clements (1964) found that teachers rarely paused for student answers to their questions. In an average fifty minute art class in which fifty-nine questions were asked, a total of only five seconds of pausing occurred. Clements looked upon the shortness of pupils' answers and the lack of time allowed for them to answer as casting real doubt on the value that art teachers attached to their students' opinions. Closely related to this is a study by Jones (1964), which showed that art students who replied to the teacher's questions in long statements had definite gains in the aesthetic quality of their products. It may be important in the teaching role to listen as well as to talk.

In addition to all his other responsibilities, the art teacher is expected to be a creative producer of art. Schwartz (1970) reports on a survey he did of 139 art teachers who almost unanimously agreed that art teachers should have personal creative experiences in order to be better able to provide these experiences for children. But, after all, one would expect art teachers to respond that way, just as a science teacher would expect a person who teaches science to have some experience in the field. However, the implications go further than that. Some schools have an artist in residence as an example of what a creative person does or is supposed to do. Financial assistance from governmental and philanthropic sources has supported this program. There is apparently great enthusiasm for the project in those schools that have received funds. However, at the same time, there is little evaluation of the program. Would an electrician or telephone repairman bring as much excitement into the classroom? What is unique about the artist-performer? Are there any positive values that can be documented from the program? Is the art teacher supposed to be the artist-performer in schools that are not so fortunate as to have an artist in residence? To the last question there can be a definite "no." The classroom at the secondary level has plenty of creative potential in it without the teacher adding another element. Within the classroom setting the teacher is a teacher, and many problems of both human and environmental nature take precedence. Also, the particular approach a teacher has to working with materials might be construed as being *the* way of working, and this in itself could be inhibiting. But, away from the class, the teacher can be himself, free to paint or construct art forms and experience first hand the rewards of creative activity.

Summary

Art has now become a means of purposeful expression for the secondary school student. No longer is a picture drawn without inhibition, no longer does self-expression flow freely; rather, a critical awareness of oneself as a member of society has taken over. For some students the development of artistic skills can be a challenge, but the youngster who is haptically inclined may need support for his more personal expression.

The art teacher in the secondary school has an extremely important position. It is through him that the direction and atmosphere for learning takes place. He must have a genuine faith in students and be willing to accept their values as well as his own. He must provide an atmosphere where creativity can be fostered and where external evaluation is absent. He cannot be a threat to students. Certainly the freedom of the individual student in the classroom must in some cases be limited by the physical environment and by the limits of behavior that society imposes. However, the symbolic expression of these feelings need not be limited; the opportunity to put concerns, real or imagined, into constructive art forms should never be minimized.

At the time when there is an increasing concern for individual freedom and a discontent with existing social conditions, we must find ways to use the power of the mind creatively and to unlock the potential of every secondary school youngster. Theories differ as to why students paint and draw as they do, but art must play a major role in the school setting: to provide a means for the constructive outlet of emotions, for the development of creative thinking, and for the enrichment and cultivation of aesthetic awareness.

RELATED ACTIVITIES

1 Compare the drawings of an eighth grade with those done by a fifth grade class. Point out the changes that show the development of a critical awareness toward creative expression.

2 Make a list of the characteristics of the child who tends to be haptic. What would be his preference for subject matter, his manner of representation, his use of color, his use of proportion? Plan a lesson that would emphasize nonvisual responses.

3 Make a list of the characteristics of a child who has a preference for visual stimuli and plan a lesson, as above, emphasizing the visual elements.

4 Discuss the changing relationship between the child and his environment as seen in his representations of space. Point out how the use of space changes and how these changes reflect changes in development as the child grows.

5 In a free and open group discussion among school art students, observe to what extent the group gives support to novel and creative suggestions, and to what extent the group rejects original ideas. Would this vary with different groups?

6 Observe an eighth grade class working on an art project. Keep a record of the number and type of questions or comments made by the students. Keep a record of the teacher's comments and questions. Can you draw any inferences?

The Age of Reasoning

11

The Pseudo-Naturalistic Stage
Twelve — Fourteen Years

The Importance
of the Pseudo-Naturalistic Stage

This stage of development marks the end of art as a spontaneous activity and the beginning of a period of reasoning when children become increasingly critical of their own products. For some this means a change from unconsciously drawing what is known, to consciously relying upon what is seen. These attempts at naturalism indicate the shift to adult modes of expression.

This period is one of the most exciting and yet one of the most trying in one's entire life. It is an age of turmoil and excitement for the child, although the term "child" now no longer truly applies. This is a time when girls start to develop mature sex characteristics and boys are wondering if they will ever grow hair on their chins. This age, sometimes referred to as the period of pubescence or preadolescence, is a time when the youngster finds that he is not a child, but is also sure he is not an adult. It is a period of great individual differences; this is most noticeable in physical changes, but it is also true in the mental, emotional, and social areas as well. In the intellectual sphere, there is a developing capacity for abstract thinking. Social expectations change, bringing a new perspective of the world. The final push toward independence now begins. According to Harlow et al. (1971), there now is a crisis, a choice: either to venture out into the anxiety-arousing world of peers and achieve some mastery, or to withdraw into fantasy.

The organization of schools for this age youngster varies. Often it is the junior high school—grades seven, eight, and nine—that stands as an entity. But sometimes grades five, six, seven, and eight, are put together into a middle school. Teachers of young children often enjoy working in art with them because young children are so uninhibited in their work and are receptive to art ideas. Teachers of older children are apt to consider this the age when teaching a subject becomes meaningful, where concepts can be grasped, and art is elective. The best thing that can be said about the in-between ages is that they are a challenge.

Sometimes school systems will establish alternative methods of education. These methods are largely aimed at the eleven to fourteen year old. Instead of the usual periods following one another for each subject, including art, children are allowed to select the areas in which they wish to concentrate. If art is one of these areas, the person responsible for art activities has a great challenge

Figure 185.
Although unlikely to talk about his concerns with adults, the young adolescent can put a lot of himself into his creative activities.

but there is also an excellent opportunity to put together an exciting learning experience, with the awareness of the history of art, the procurement of materials, contacts with practicing artists, and the creation of art, leading youngsters into every facet of learning. Regardless of the organization of the school, for most children this will be the last public school art they receive. This fact is very important, because we must realize that the attitudes and skills that are developed at this age will influence their reactions and feelings toward art in adult life.

The child from the elementary school has become much more critical and aware of himself as a junior high school student. This developing self-awareness is expressed through a self-conscious approach to his environment. He is concerned about how he looks, how he dresses, what he says, and particularly he is concerned about how he appears to others. The adolescent is reluctant to reveal his real thoughts or to openly discuss issues closely related to the self. A study of fourth to twelfth graders (Elkind and Bowen, 1979) used a questionnaire, including such items as "Would you get up in front of the class if you found a split in the seam of your jeans if it meant extra credit?" or "Do you worry if people like you?" A major finding was that young adolescents were significantly less willing than either younger or older students to reveal themselves to an audience. This is a period of heightened self-consciousness.

The significance of this stage might be better understood if it is considered a transition from a period when the adult world was all-powerful to a world in which the young adolescent is beginning to assume an important role. After the child has gone through the Gang Age, he enters a stage in which he develops intellectually to the point where he can tackle almost any problem, yet in his reactions he is still a child. The difference between children and adults can be seen in the diversity of their imaginative activity. The young child may play hide-and-seek with abandon; he will pick up a pencil and move it up and down while imitating the noises of an airplane, he will laugh or cry when he is amused or hurt, without inhibitions. Such unawareness is characteristic of children. If an adult were to do the same things he would be considered insane. For an adult a pencil is a pencil, and a pencil is for writing. He has no time for games, and emotions must be kept under control. This change in the imaginative activity from unconscious to critical awareness can create conflicts in the child and concern on the part of the adult. This becomes particularly apparent when we realize that at this age some girls are as tall as they will ever be, and therefore are considered big enough to behave as adults.

One parent recalled this stage of develoment with his own child in the following words:

THE AGE OF REASONING

Figure 186.
This carved wooden figure from New Guinea is valued for its honesty of concept and directness of execution.

When Tommy, my son, was in this stage, of course he was a member of a gang, he had his fun, he had his group of children. He was always tall and a little bit out of proportion to the other children, but he didn't even recognize that, he didn't see it. He associated with younger children who were not as tall. He had his wooden gun, or his wooden stick—and enjoyed playing. But there came a time when I came home from my office—when I saw that when I approached the house he sort of tried to hide the gun, and I said, "Why don't you play with the children?" and he said, "Oh, I think—isn't it silly?" I said, "No, not silly at all, why don't you play with them? It is fun, isn't it?" And when I went into the house, of course he went on engaging in his pretend-to-be-games. He felt again as though he were no longer being watched, and since the smaller children accepted him in the group—in the gang—well, he continued the game. But these interruptions became more frequent as he grew older, and I could see him with his wooden gun, sitting there and watching them playing pretend-to-be-games, now and then participating or giving orders, but already standing outside. Until one day he put the wooden gun he had so carefully whittled into the basement, but still he could not part with it. Sometimes he went downstairs trying to improve it, but he no longer associated with the group, just watched them.

Just as the youngster has become more critically aware of his own actions, he has become more critically aware of his art products. During the Gang Age some children were quite reluctant to show their products to adults. Now they focus on the end product itself; a picture has value or is good, not because of the effort, interest, or involvement that went into it, but because of the visual appearance of the product. The recognition of the growing significance to the student of the final product must be accepted by educators. A questionnaire given to seventh and eighth graders asked on what basis these students liked what they had painted (Brittain, 1968a). Seventy percent indicated they liked their art product when it turned out as they hoped it would or if they felt it was better than they had done before, whereas peer approval was important to only 18 percent, and teacher praise or professional appearance mattered to only a few. The role of art in this stage of development should give support to the youngster's individuality, should provide a socially acceptable release for his emotions and tensions, and should ease the transition from the expression of a child to the type of expression typical of an adult. An untrained artist—untrained in the sense of Western traditions of line, color, form, and perspective—from a primitive society develops highly sophisticated images; but young adolescents have the same potential if they are motivated and their products are treated with respect. Untrained does not mean unartistic.

THE IMPORTANCE OF THE PSEUDO-NATURALISTIC STAGE

The Representation of the Human Figure

As expected, changes in the representation of the human figure follow the increased awareness and concern for changes that are beginning to take place in the bodies of preadolescents. Since girls tend to develop earlier than boys, there is usually a greater interest in drawing the human figure among girls. As biological changes occur, there is more interest in drawing in notebooks, on scraps of paper, or on book covers. Usually the sexual characteristics of these drawings are greatly overexaggerated, reflecting the concern of these children over their physical development, for these sexual changes can no longer be experienced in a passive way. There is no reason to look upon these exaggerations as anything but normal. In fact, the very opposite may be true; that is, a child who is beginning to develop sexually and who does not include these changes within drawings may be showing a fear of these changes. Often these drawings are concealed from adults, and in some cases a sense of guilt or shame accompanies the drawings. These should not be censored.

Children will strive for greater naturalism and include joints in their drawings of the human figure. Before this age, youngsters usually employed clothes only for identification. Now, however, there is an increased awareness of changing appearances when clothes fold or wrinkle, when lights and shadows change with the sitting body, when color changes under different atmospheric conditions. The mere statement that a dress is red does not imply a visual analysis but merely factual recognition. A visual experience means that the changes of red are observed according to light and shadow and the influences of distance and reflected light are noticed, that pants change appearance while a boy is running, or that folds and worn spots are observed. This increased visual awareness of the human figure is limited primarily to those who derive pleasure from the changing appearances of objects around them. For those not so visually aware, and at times for all youngsters, great pleasure is taken in cartooning and representing the human figure through satirical drawings. Boys seem particularly interested in developing this ability and sometimes will enjoy making cartoons of teachers, parents, and those of their classmates who hold enviable positions.

Probably one of the most difficult assignments a youngster can have at this pseudo-naturalistic stage is that of drawing himself. The difficulty of coming to terms with one's own identity can clearly be recognized, not only in the drawings, but the self-conscious and reluctant manner in which youngsters ap-

Figure 187.
The representation of the human figure has changed dramatically from the earliest head-feet symbols. These sketches were made by a visually aware fourteen year old girl.

proach such a task. Although an examination of drawings done by preadolescent youngsters will look surprisingly like drawings done during earlier stages, there will be an increased awareness of detail with special attention to clothing, hair style, and facial features. The suggestion that individuals project their own personality into drawings has been given support in psychological literature. If a youngster is concerned about his nose he may exaggerate this or leave it out

Figure 188.
It is sometimes difficult for youngsters of this age to draw themselves. An honest appraisal is often forsaken in favor of an idealistic representation.

entirely, although in drawing other people the nose may become a focal point for ridicule. The drawing of the self becomes, then, a reflection of one's own ability to face oneself; the youngster who has developed or learned certain formulas for drawing a figure will produce a human figure drawing that is less expressive of the self and at the same time less artistically meaningful.

In a study of self-drawings by youngsters from twelve to fifteen years of age, it was found that they treated their drawings in derogatory terms (Brittain, 1968b). These students were asked to put comments on the back of their drawings, indicating the parts they liked best or the parts with which they had the most difficulty. The drawings themselves ranged from what might be more typical of a fifth grade youngster to a quite sophisticated sketch in fair proportion. However, the comments on the back of these drawings were invariably negative, such as "It's terrible," "What a lousy drawing," "It looks nutty," "The head is stupid," and "What a gooney-looking nut." The arms and legs particularly were described in negative terms. It is interesting to note that there seemed to be little relationship between the comments and an objective appraisal of the drawing itself. This might raise the question of whether the development of certain skills in figure drawing is what is important or whether the self is looked upon in negative terms, regardless of how it is drawn.

The Representation of Space

One of the important discoveries for the visually minded youngster is the apparent reduction in size of distant objects. The three-dimensional qualities of space are now understood by some youngsters, who discover the possibility of making drawings with this illusion of distance; consequently many art teachers seize upon this as an indication that all children are ready to learn the mechanical rules of drawing in perspective. In fact, one can often find programs designed for seventh grade students that concentrate upon teaching perspective, starting with one-point perspective, then two-point perspective, three-point perspective, with slanting roofs and stairs going off in a number of directions, with railroads disappearing into the distance and telephone lines marching across the page. Of course, for some youngsters at this age the rules to follow become merely mechanical and have no relationship to the world that they experience. Most children will be able to deal with the problems of representing space in depth, but the question remains whether time is best spent in trying to develop this competency.

Some attempts have been made to teach perspective by other than the usual method of one- and two-point perspective, with vanishing points and horizon lines. Prentiss (1972) devised what he termed an "observational" method, and compared it with the usual academic method and with a control group which was not taught any formal method. For two weeks, 400 fifth, seventh, and ninth grade children were given a concentrated course. A drawing utilizing perspective was collected from these children before, after, and six weeks later. The judging of these drawings by experts and by other children indicated that neither method was supported; the control groups with no formal instruction showed the greatest growth. Prentiss suggests that perspective as it was taught here may serve to confuse and even to deter growth, or that students reject or are apathetic toward teacher directed activities.

The means to represent distance must be discovered by the student. To take this discovery from him by "explaining" perspective deprives him of an important experience. The teacher must capitalize on the child's own findings and start on the child's own level. "What makes the tree more distant in your drawing?" Let him become aware of his own discoveries: that he had drawn

Figure 189.
*The rules of perspective are
mechanically followed and
vanishing points are used in this
typical school exercise.*

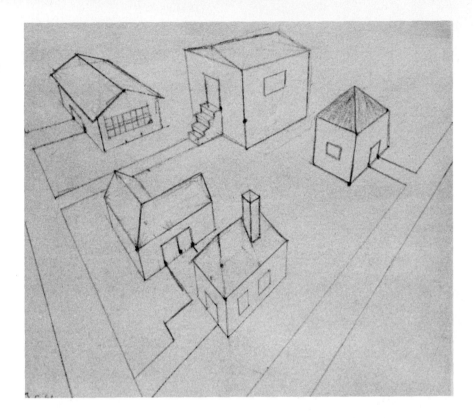

the tree smaller, because distant objects appear to be smaller; that he had included less detail, because one does not see as many details in distant objects;
that he has given it a less intense color, because the air in between makes the
color appear less bright. All this should be used as a frame of reference for later
experiences that may be less simple. One remark a teacher might hear is "I
want the road going to the house in the background, but it looks funny."
Using a previous experience for new discoveries, a good starting point would
be "Let's see whether the road is doing the same as the tree." The child will
soon find out for himself that the road as it goes into the distance would grow
smaller or narrower in his drawing just as the tree does. It may also be less
intense in color. Such discoveries should originate with real experiences. Instead of depriving the child of the excitement of his own discoveries, the
teacher should provide stimulus whenever the need for it arises.

Trying to determine the developmental stages at which children can
draw geometric solids, Mitchelmore (1978) had first, third, fifth, seventh, and
ninth grade children copy a variety of forms. With these forms directly in front
of them, children were asked to copy them with no time limit. It was found, as
expected, that the youngest children merely drew a square to represent the

cube. Some third and fifth graders carefully drew several sides, as if viewing each side separately, but it was not until seventh grade that most children attempted to draw several sides from one point of view. Even the ninth graders had difficulty with the task; only a third of them were able to draw a cube in perspective. Children who had difficulty with this task also had difficulty with some other spatial tasks. This indicates that drawing in perspective is not an isolated skill which can be easily understood, but is closely related to individual behavior and cognitive structures.

Certainly for the child who is more inclined toward haptic responses, the experience of being taught perspective can be a frustrating one. For him, and perhaps to a lesser extent for others, too, art may be more emotionally important. The illusion of distance as achieved through mechanical perspective is unique to our own culture. Possibly culture is not a good word to use here, for perspective seems to be more tied in with the teaching of art in public schools

Figure 190.
This boy's drawing has not correctly followed the rules of perspective. But, as a work of art, it has a vitality that is missing in Figure 189.

than with the field of professional art. At least some art today ignores perspective as it is usually taught; the professional artist may be much more concerned with the representation of his relationship to his social world than he is with attempting photographic likeness. And then there is Escher (1971) whose spoofs of perspective drawings seem to obey all the mechanical rules and yet confuse and confound the viewer. For some youngsters the discovery of methods of portraying three-dimensional space on paper, guided by a sensitive teacher, can be an exciting experience; to other youngsters, possibly in the same class, perspective is irrelevant.

The Importance of Color and Design

It is easy to see that the young teenager has become very aware of design qualities within his sphere of influence. Although the teacher or worried parent may question the aesthetic taste of this youngster, there is no doubt that he has definite likes and dislikes in the selection of clothing, in the colors he wears, and in the jewelry or other accessories that he chooses. This increased awareness of design is sometimes used as an excuse to teach the formal elements of design, and one still hears of art classes spending time making plans for never-to-be-used wallpaper with half-drop repeats. The increasing awareness of color is sometimes used as an excuse to expend considerable effort in making color wheels or color charts. Both of these practices are gradually disappearing. The young teenager has an intuitive sense of color and design, and the formal teaching of these factors seems unrelated to his interests.

Much has been written about the psychology of color and its emotional effects on individuals. Such emotional reactions to color are to a large extent determined by past experiences. To one person, horror might mean red and he might associate it with blood; to another it might be green, and he might associate it with mold or decay. No generalizations should be applied to teaching that deny the individual's right to creative approaches to color. Emotional reactions to color are highly personal, and the nonvisually minded child may use color in contradiction to nature. Color can be highly subjective in its meaning (Corcoran, 1953).

The notebooks of these youngsters may be filled with rather interesting and intricate designs. These are often related to lettering, such as designing

one's name with fancy letters and seeing how these letters can fit into other patterns or can become quite elaborate in a manner echoing the medieval manuscript calligraphy. Sometimes these doodles are of body parts that can look quite grotesque or resemble preliminary sketches for a gargoyle. Sometimes they look more like psychedelic forms that might impress adult artists.

These youngsters also develop a great sympathy and understanding for design in nature. The design on a turtle's back, the scales on a fish, or the pattern of moss as it is growing out of a crack in the pavement can be exciting discoveries. These elements of design are constantly around youngsters and make excellent raw materials from which a genuine understanding of the function of design can spring. In younger children there was an urge to collect many, sometimes unrelated objects. This urge for collecting objects is not limited to the elementary school; the young adolescent, too, can find a great deal of color and design in objects around him. These can be jars and bottles from the drugstore, which may be enjoyed because of their shape or tactile appeal; they can be parts of nature such as worn wood, pebbles, or feathers; or they may be something that has been discarded by society, in the form of a piece of junk mellowed by rust. Putting some of these objects into a setting designed for a work of fine art seems to transform them into things of beauty.

Because most youngsters of this age will not be exposed to further art experiences, attention can and should be paid to industrial products. Although the question of aesthetics is raised once we begin to consider the merits of a variety of designs for everyday objects, the tastes of the teacher should not be forced upon the students. Subtle discriminations in aesthetic judgments can be made by young adolescents (DePorter and Kavanaugh, 1978). A great deal more understanding can be achieved through discussion than by merely having the students guess which kitchen knife the art teacher likes best. The functional reason for good design can be understood. Discussions may have to start with the merits of the best designed sports car, but the concern for and interest in design is much more important than indoctrinating students with what an adult might call good taste.

The problems of color and design can take on new meaning when critically examined by young adolescents. These same art students will be paying taxes, voting, and starting families within the next ten years. Many selections of an artistic nature will be before them: the choice of a dining room set from the local furniture store, a television secured through a time payment plan, and a vote on the proposed new municipal building. It is not too early to raise questions about the aesthetics of our environment. Much harm may be done in our society by citizens who are unaware of the possibility of action. Active

THE IMPORTANCE OF COLOR AND DESIGN

participation in group discussions helps prepare them to assume responsibility for their environment as alert, perceptive adults.

Growth As Reflected in the Art of the Young Adolescent

It is easy to see that the work of young children is closely related to their developmental level. Their feelings and emotions and understandings of the world around them are clearly reflected in their art products. In the same way the products of young adolescents reflect their reaction to the world, although maybe not as clearly. Just as there is great diversity in intellectual ability, physical development, and obvious differences in sex, there are also differences just as great in the art products of these youngsters. The range and variety of art work increases with each grade level. This can easily be seen in the junior high school. The dainty drawing of a popular celebrity that is perfected by a timid girl is just as valid a means of expression as the elaborately decorated bicycle is for a boy.

Between the ages of twelve and fourteen we find many new problems arising for youngsters and many changes occurring, both in themselves and in their relationships to their peers and adults. Boys and girls alike are beginning to break numerous childhood ties to the family and are questioning adults' authority. In addition to their concern about personal appearance and their idealism and romantic feelings about becoming adult members of society, there is also fear and insecurity about the beginning stages of leaving childhood. Girls are no longer making war on boys, but may have a musical recording star for an idol. Boys are attracted to the opposite sex, but are not ready to admit this. Instead they are busy collecting baseball statistics, developing their muscular powers, and seeking out boys who have comparable interests in such things as motorcycles, BB guns, or electronic equipment. Experimentation with drugs sometimes begins at this age. When children were asked (Berndt, 1979) whether they would cheat, steal, or trespass if urged to do so by their friends, it was found that conformity to peers' antisocial behavior peaked at adolescence.

In some schools students are segregated by so-called ability levels. This may mean that some art classes consist of those who have achieved academic success while others may be composed primarily of those who are lowest on

Plate 28.
"My Barber," painted by a
fourteen year old boy. This child
has used flat areas of color and
has not attempted to show light
and shade. Notice the awareness
of detail: the floor at an angle,
the scissors and comb, the barber
pole, and the Barber sign painted
on the back of the window.

Plate 29.

"The Circus," block-printed by junior high school girls. Printing presents a challenge for the young adolescent who is capable of mastering complex procedures. Here a variety of levels of conceptual development are united into a colorful whole, an expression of group cooperation. Overlapping is tolerated and space is not rigidly organized, contributing to the feeling of excitement of the circus.

the academic ladder. A study by Madeja (1967), using secondary school students, found that academic achievement correlated highly with grades in art. At the same time he found that nonverbal tests of creativity of the same students showed no relationship to their grades in art.

Apparently, art teachers are looking for some of the same attributes that teachers in math and science are seeking. The implications of this are somewhat frightening. Those students who have achieved respectability and are able to cope with the system are those who are rewarded in art too. At the same time, those who are not able to adapt to the school setting and are having problems achieving the type of success usually rewarded in schools, are also failing in art expression. Perhaps the art program in the secondary schools needs a thorough overhaul, for it is essential that *somewhere* in the system students should be able to express feelings and emotions that are important to them without the fear of failure. The creative child may not be easily identified. In Japan, Inagaki (1979) found that teachers mis-identified their creative children, being more influenced by verbal recall than by verbal originality. Creative students may not be well liked, and some teachers do not value creativity very highly (Torrance, 1962); this may be so even in the art room.

One college student was asked to write her recollections of her own experience in the junior high school she attended. This particular girl was not only a success in that she was able to go on to college; she was also considered well liked and well adjusted by her teachers. Included are only those parts which seem most pertinent to our discussion of the relationship of art to youngsters of this age.

JUNIOR HIGH/One Girl's View

Junior High is a period of my life I would definitely not want to live over again. It was sort of a changing point, the point where I stopped playing with dolls, started noticing boys, decided I want to be a writer, passed through puberty, first really became aware of such things as "popularity."

I wasn't too fond of life but it never occurred to me that life could be changed so it was any different; I accepted things as they came. Adulthood was a magic, privileged life, to be looked forward to, but for now I was stuck being an early adolescent, forced to accept life. I was usually optimistic about things getting better, but I didn't think anything I did could change them. Perhaps I would have been happier if I had felt at one with a crowd all of whom shared a common misery of being in junior high, but I couldn't verbalize my discontent. Discontent wasn't something you talked about. And if something was wrong, it was *me* that was wrong, not the environment. At the time, I did not think myself unhappy.

Social relations were a very important part of junior high. This did not mean

Figure 193.
This drawing by a ninth grade girl becomes a social commentary on the junior high school population, reflecting her emotions and impressions about her peers.

boys so much as the other girls. Boys were something seen from afar, rarely contacted. Girls, however, were all around. Boys were extremely terrifying objects. I could scarcely stand up when I was in the presence of one I liked. When I was in eighth grade, a boy named George said "Hi" to me in the hall. I had never particularly noticed him before, but I was overcome. I instantly developed a deep binding crush on him. I don't think I could have stood it if he had started carrying on a conversation with me; I would have been completely overcome by it all, but much of my energy was spent in contemplating those "Hi"'s.

Sex had very little to do with boys. It was a subject of its own, fascinating, secret, and frightening. I first heard dirty jokes at a slumber party in seventh grade. A slumber party was a Good Thing because being invited to one indicated being In. From dirty jokes, the way was open for bigger and better things. Any passing reference to sex in a book was hugely shocking and hugely thrilling. I used to lie in bed at night and make up dirty stories of my own. At the same time, I was terrified at the whole thought. Starting to menstruate, feeling that I was suddenly a woman, was a very strange feeling. I was embarrassed by it.

School had very little relevance to anything. It was there and I had to go, and so I went. Homework was something to be avoided, done quickly, gotten out of the way as quickly as possible so I could do something more interesting. If I wasn't doing well, I didn't work harder. To be caught with homework undone was a stomach-tightening feeling, and so I did it. The only saving grace in most of my classes was that Mary sat next to me and we could pass notes. To have fun in school was an inconceivable concept.

If someone had sat down with me and said, "Talk to me about some of the things that are really important to you," I wouldn't have understood. It was one of the facts of life that nobody but yourself really cared about what you really thought, especially grown-ups. Parents might be nice to you, but if you told them your inner thoughts, they would either laugh or beat you up. If you had problems and worries, you didn't broadcast them, didn't even write them in a diary, because they couldn't be admitted, even to yourself. You knew what you were supposed to say and do, and you did it, and you tried to feel what you were supposed to.

I didn't draw as much as I had in grade school. I spent most of my spare time either reading (which I did a great deal) or writing. However, I doodled a tremendous amount, all over my notes, usually overdeveloped girls wearing short skirts.

A lot of the time they carried knives; they were full of self-confidence and off to fight and win in the name of some unspecified desperate-but-worthy cause. Sometimes, in ninth grade, I would draw boys and girls walking together, but girls generally outnumbered boys in my doodles about 100 to 1. If I drew a regular picture, it generally had some sort of sexual overtones or else was drawn in some style of some subject which I thought would meet parental approval. Art class in school was sort of fun; it was the class period you could goof around and get A's without trying. Wallpaper design, three-point perspective, and lettering had no significance for me, but they helped break up the boredom of math and science.

I guess I was really pretty miserable in junior high. The school itself was pretty bad: fierce teachers who'd never try to understand a kid's thoughts; strictly enforced rules about needing a pass in the halls; stairway monitors who grabbed me; boys who called me "bitch" and hit me with their books; waiting in line for ages in the cafeteria for an unappetizing plate of food; looking at trees outside the window and wishing I could go out; having to stand up on the school bus; having to run up three flights of stairs from gym to science after a four-minute compulsory shower; having to stand in line for a toilet at lunchtime. I was trying to figure out who I was and where I was going and not having much luck, perhaps in part because I didn't realize that that was what I was doing. I certainly lacked self-confidence; I used to get all upset and cry if I was criticized and couldn't stand being laughed at. I haven't thought about junior high in a long time, this is the first time I've brought out my memories in quite a while. I'd be just as happy to forget it.

Art Motivation

One of the central themes of the adolescent is the striving for an identity. He needs to come to terms with himself and be able to express intense feelings that need a constructive outlet. He is very aware of being alive and is developing an awareness of himself as one who can build, construct, and create objects. This is no time for prescribed busy-work. The junior high school student is full of thoughts and directions. He resents having to perform art tasks set up by the teacher and denying his own expression. The prime role of the teacher during this period is to provide guidance and encouragement so that this expression can take on a meaningful form.

As previously mentioned, the art teacher is considered somewhat irrelevant to the production of art. It is important that the art teacher quickly establish a role different from that of the customary teacher. If the atmosphere is going to be such that mutual trust and exchange of ideas with junior high school youngsters is possible, then the usual classroom procedures may not be

adequate. Youngsters of this age enjoy and need the opportunity to share and exchange thoughts with a few of their peers (Brittain, 1968a). Possibly the best physical arrangement for an art room would be to have tables arranged for several small groups of students so that activities could be discussed and evaluated by peers as well as by teachers. In addition, the opportunity for isolated work may be important for some students or for all students at some times. An occasional mural project that requires cooperative effort provides a chance for a group to solve artistic problems.

Often an ineffective art program is planned around the use of one material after another. The first three weeks may be devoted to pencil sketching, the following two weeks may be spent doing copper etchings, the next three weeks may be spent working in colored chalk, and so forth. Such a program

THE AGE OF REASONING

ignores the basic principle that it is more important to have something to say in art than to worry about the development of skills in case something might someday be expressed. Yet the need for materials must grow out of the need for expression. The teacher who hides behind the material approach may be afraid of facing the real expressive needs of the adolescent.

Any art motivation should stress the individual's own contribution. At this stage of development it is important to reinforce individualistic thinking. An art program that is primarily concerned with productions may entirely miss one of the basic reasons for the existence of art in the school program, which is the personal involvement of the individual and the opportunity for developing a depth of meaningful self-expression. It is vital that every youngster feel that his activities in art are his own expression. To a great extent the teacher's motivation is responsible not so much for the production of art but for the desire to produce. If the youngster is not involved, excited, and completely swept up in the art activity, then the drawing or painting becomes a mere exercise for the school system.

Probably one of the most powerful features of any motivation is its relevance to the students. To some extent boys have less of an interest in the usual art program than girls have. A practical problem, such as making a three-dimensional working structure, can often challenge boys particularly if there is some doubt implied that they can really do this. Sometimes such a project can become so engrossing that it serves as the basis for expanding into many of the more recognized art areas.

The development of a critical attitude toward the world that surrounds him has made the young adolescent much more concerned about naturalism. The schema seen earlier in drawings has now disappeared. However, the youngster may feel reluctant to become involved in art experiences. In part this may be because his past performances in art have been ignored or even ridiculed. In part it is because of his developing critical awareness. In part it may be a reflection of the feeling that art is not an important activity.

At this age children have not yet developed full control over their emotions and we often find that a seemingly minor incident will be of extreme importance to a youngster. This intensity of feeling can often be utilized within the art program. The emotional relationships a child develops with various segments of his environment can often be expressed either directly or symbolically. Topics centering on religious themes, individual justice, or the expression of love or hate can often involve a youngster quite completely. In such cases exaggeration or overemphasis of particular parts within a composition can be seen. Such distortions should be given support, and the flexible use of

color and the exaggeration of form can develop an emotional impact in the art product.

It is not diplomatic to say, "Put your innermost feelings down on paper about some adult whom you feel has treated you unjustly." Many children have been taught that it is not nice to have unpleasant thoughts about people and in some cases these feelings may very well be directed at parents and teachers. It is usually best to let such feelings of aggression, and in some cases love, be expressed more unconsciously. Such subjects as "The Ugliest Person in the World" would provide the opportunity for the release of such feelings. "What would the ugliest person in the world look like? Would he have smooth or rough skin? Would he have a long or a short nose? How about his ears? Would his teeth stick out? And his hair? What color would go well with him? Could the ugliest person in the world be a woman?"

As already discussed, this stage of development is characterized, among other things, by a tendency toward two different types of expression. The extremely visually minded person and the extreme haptic are relatively rare; often both tendencies can be seen. The awareness of wrinkles and folds when clothes are in motion is usually an indication of visual awareness, whereas the use of distortion, the lack of visual depth in drawings, and the continued use of flat color may indicate a more haptic approach to one's environment. Any motivation should include the opportunity to allow for all types of expression. Limiting opportunities for art expression to the individuals who are primarily visually minded, as is the usual case, may restrict or definitely hamper the expression of those youngsters who are not capable or not ready to portray their world in a method they do not understand.

Once again, it should be emphasized that the drawing or painting or other art product is not the objective or goal of any art motivation. Rather, the goal is the opportunity to develop within the youngster a greater awareness of himself and those things around him. Therefore it becomes evident that changes imposed on the art product may have no effect upon the youngster himself. For example, an increased awareness of textural differences and tactile sensations cannot be achieved by telling a youngster to include more tactile properties in his painting. Time is needed in which to develop an awareness of a variety of textures and to experience these on an intimate basis. To merely "correct" the painting itself does not provide the experience of textures; it might be much more effective to allow the picture to be completed in the way that is important to the youngster himself. Once this is done, the broadening of the youngster's experience in the changes and qualities of tactile impressions can be undertaken.

Involving children in art experiences may take many different directions. The motivation itself should vary considerably, depending upon the conditions of the classroom, the interest of the students, and the objectives of the teachers, but it should also vary just for variation's sake. If the class is concerned with the expression of emotion, quite a different motivation would be necessary than if a problem in design or aesthetics were to be considered.

Youngsters of this age are becoming more aware of beauty, although this must be interpreted in their terms and not the teacher's. Time for thought and contemplation is required if children are to become more aware of and more sensitive to the design qualities of various art forms. Turning a picture 180 degrees and looking at it as if it were an abstraction, relieved of its content, can

Figure 196. (Opposite)

A junior high school youngster's world provides excellent subject matter for art expression. A boy shows himself at home watching television; he has attempted to represent the room and furniture three-dimensionally.

call attention to the distribution of the various forms and colors. Obviously a drawing of loneliness would be quite different in design quality from a drawing portraying excitement. The design of an object as simple as a spoon can arouse critical discussion by means of searching questions. "Why isn't a spoon made out of cloth, or paper, or glass?" "Would the addition of holes in the handle of a spoon, or bumpy roses embossed upon the spoon bowl help or hinder its function?" "Would the spoon work better if its bowl were turned sideways?" The purpose of these questions would be to stimulate thinking about the relationship between material and expression and to sensitize youngsters to the design elements in their environment. This is not a time for listing or memorizing rules to follow; rather, it should be an opportunity for developing an awareness of art as an aspect of life.

A word needs to be said about motivating the youngster who has lost his self-confidence in art expression. He is the "I can't do it" child. It is relatively easy to motivate youngsters who are eager to draw and paint, but the child who refuses to budge may be the person who needs the experience the most. Often the problem can be easily solved by using a material that is not "sissy" or "arty." Clay, wood, or other three-dimensional materials are often a good way to start. A second approach is to start where the youngster himself is. This may be simply having him cut out racing cars and put these into a mobile or collage, or, if the problem is deeper than this, having him put some of his thoughts on a large cardboard, even cut out headlines from the newspaper so as to make his resentment an issue which can be dealt with openly. To try to coax a child, or to tell a youngster that he really can draw, or to make something for the teacher just this once, may do nothing but make this young adolescent even more sure that art is not for him. The motivation, however it is given, or however it is developed, should provide the youngster with a desire to create and not be aimed at getting projects done, or putting marks in a book, or keeping youngsters busy.

Subject Matter

Subject matter itself is much less important than the way it is integrated into the lives of the students. Junior high school youngsters have little opportunity in the usual classroom to have any voice in the subject matter covered. Mathematics follows a pattern that is difficult to break; history, science, and English are outlined in advance of the students' involvement in the class itself. In art,

however, there is ample opportunity for the art teacher to make the content truly a matter over which students have some control.

With the developing awareness of themselves as individuals with opinions, tastes, and voices of their own, it is important that students be involved in the planning in such a way that the projects become essentially theirs. In one study (Brittain, 1968a) the junior high school students clearly saw themselves as the source of ideas for art. In fact, the students involved in this particular study voiced amazement that adults would actually be interested in what junior high school students thought. One of the important roles that the teacher can play is that of an earnest listener who can make these youngsters feel that their thoughts and ideas are worthy of consideration, and that they are not necessarily limited by having to look to the teacher for inspiration.

Occasionally topics are pushed upon the person responsible for an art program, topics that may actually be detrimental to the development of a meaningful art education program. A poster for the local women's club bake sale, mass producing table decorations for the annual teachers' meeting, or making a monogram for the gym team may all be worthwhile, so possibly the art teacher could handle a few of these tasks some Saturday morning; but the art program has a much greater role than to fill its time with busy-work and service activities.

Ideally no subject matter should be necessary. The purpose in any subject suggestions is to extend the frame of reference of the student, to enable him to see many possible avenues of expression, to encourage him to be self-motivated, and to use the arts for pleasurable, meaningful expression.

Feelings and Emotions

The expression of feelings and emotions should play an important part in the school art program. There is little opportunity for youngsters of this age to give vent to their feelings; sometimes they bubble to the surface and are expressed strongly outside school, and sometimes in school. The following suggestions should be used flexibly, and any motivation should open up many possible ways of expression rather than converging on a particular method.

Putting emotions and frustrations into art requires a great degree of sensitivity. A topic such as "Being Alone" would recall in every student a time when he had to walk home in the dark, or was left alone one Saturday, or his feelings of not knowing anyone in a crowd. Other topics could relate to feelings of joy or sadness, of love or hate, of contentment or anger, or to uncomfortable misgivings in a social situation. Sometimes the adolescent has special heroes or secret infatuations with a person far removed. Students might portray "My Favorite Person," or "The Sinister Thief."Sometimes these feelings will come out in abstract paintings, sometimes in three-dimensional constructions, sometimes in direct representation.

The Self and Others

The youngster now has an increased awareness of his own physical development and has developed a curiosity about the opposite sex. It is at this age that drawing from posed models may make an impact such as no other subject matter can. Munro (1956) even went so far as to suggest that the adolescent be given the opportunity to observe and draw from the nude model. Certainly hiding the body seems more the concern of adults than of youngsters; there is no doubt that pictures of nude females are readily available to most junior high school boys, although this is usually in the boys' lavatory and not the art room. However, the best time to introduce the drawing of the nude might be in the

Figure 197.
*Young adolescents are not isolated
from the real world and its
troubles. They are continuously
exposed to all the elements of life
within our society.*

elementary school so that the junior high school youngster would treat the
body in a matter-of-fact manner. Modeling in clay from the posed figure provides another means of expression. A plastic three-dimensional form can be
readily altered and allows for the expression of kinesthetic experience. The
pose should be short for any type of presentation, and the model should be
used only as a stimulus.

During drawing or modeling, care should be taken to provide ample opportunity for the expression of haptic representations, and the pose should be
treated in such a way that the student can identify with the model through personal experience. That is, the drawing of the model should not be a lesson on
proportion, balance, anatomy, or a study in light and shade. Rather, it should
be an opportunity to see the model as someone involved in life, with problems,
with faults, and with whom the student can feel some empathy.

SUBJECT MATTER

With man as a subject, the number of suitable topics seems endless. Man has always been a fascinating subject (and here man is used in the generic sense) for artists everywhere, and the twelve to fourteen year old is no exception. Sometimes this subject is difficult for the timid student, who may feel uneasy looking at himself. Large cutouts or silhouettes, or detailed drawings of a hand or eye, make a good start. Making self-portraits—without the use of a mirror, with a mirror; in small scale, in large; drawn, sculpted in clay, or carved full size out of styrofoam—is even somewhat frightening. Drawing others, sometimes lots of others, can be exciting if many of these are combined with drawings by others into groups or crowds. Rock festivals, crowded buses, or street scenes can be created. People are everywhere and may be used as models even though they may not know it. Youngsters themselves can be their own models, feeling the muscles stretch as they move, or noting the change in sensation as they put their heads down on their knees.

School Life

There are certain activities within the junior high school itself that provide ample opportunity for expression. These can range all the way from annoyance at some seemingly arbitrary rule to participation in a forthcoming fair or dance. In democratic society the opportunity should exist for constructive participation at all ages. This cannot be learned easily, but the opportunity to suggest changes in established procedures or to have a voice in meaningful decisions should always be encouraged. The prospect of making protest posters can be exciting in itself, and the concern for clarity of message and impact on the viewer can develop a real understanding of the problems that some of the artists in our society have to face. A serious school election, or events outside school such as a community action program, can provide the impetus for expression; however, nothing will turn youngsters away from art so fast as the suggestion that everyone make a poster to help raise funds for the local women's club benefit. A rule about dress regulations in the school, objections to passing in the hall, or reactions to shortening the lunch hour, would all make excellent topics.

Since many students feel that school is something to put up with, art activities can play a dual role of helping students express their feelings and helping them become involved in school in a meaningful way. Any subject can be transformed into an art form: drawing or painting a dull, dull textbook, or feelings in the stomach when you are unprepared for a test can be put into abstract form. Making your favorite teachers from boxes, sketching the band or the basketball team, or cartooning the cafeteria staff are all suitable. Of course there are "established" activities that should not be ignored if they lend them-

Figure 198.
Concern for themselves, resentment at rules, and awareness of the problems in society are all becoming important to junior high school students. Clarity, good lettering, and neatness in posters will come later.

selves to the expression of this age group: the daily bulletin, the PTA newsletter, the memos to staff, and even the bulletin boards can be exciting if the students are responsible for layout, distribution, and keeping them current. Halls can be decorated or the basement repainted.

The area of design is unlimited in its applications, and at this age an awareness of beauty and concern for ornamentation are developing. Many shapes, patterns, and forms in shells, wood, moss, or other objects in nature can provide the stimulation for design experiences. Since the laws of symmetry are related to dogmatic periods of history, including periods of symbolism, they seem to be more and more out of place when individualism, emotions, and social changes dominate our lives. No imposed lessons in design can hope to match the design qualities that the youngster is led to discover for himself.

Adapting forms from nature can be quite interesting. The discovery of a

Design and Nature

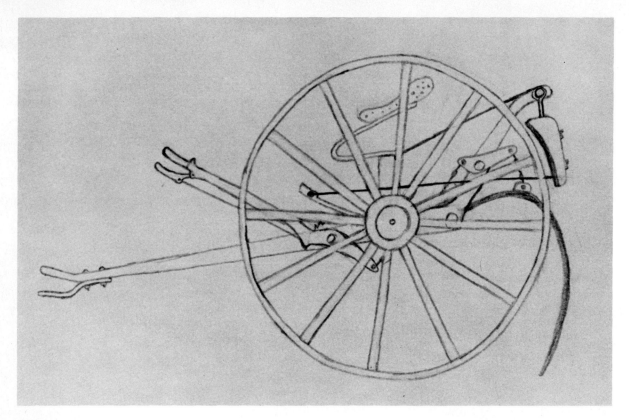

Figure 199.
Although the art teacher provides objects to be sketched, children may find more appealing things to draw, either from the object itself or from memory, as is the case with this old hay rake.

logical order in an orange or an apple core can sometimes come as a surprise. Leaves or bark of trees, dripping water or ripples on a puddle, a skeleton of a fish, or a frog's back can all be transformed. The camera makes an excellent means of studying such forms, but drawing them directly in greatly enlarged dimensions can provide insight into amazing dynamic design qualities of our natural environment.

Found objects, inventions made from industrial scraps, collections of discarded materials such as broken glass or bottles, are all possible ingredients to include in collages, or to mount in frames for exhibit, or to surround with plaster. A personal insignia, such as a name on a jacket or a made-up coat of arms on a banner, not only provides some identification of the student in a tangible way but also is historically one means of identifying a region or a warring faction. Nature constantly provides a source for inspiration, either directly as with tree branches to assemble, mount, or modify, or indirectly as clouds make constantly changing patterns and moods. For the visually aware student, shade and shadow are worth investigating; for the more haptically inclined, there is the desire to convey impressions of movement and mood. For all, the discovery of positive and negative space can be the starting point for creative experimentation.

Art Materials

At any age art materials should play a secondary role in the art program. The material should be geared to the expressive needs of students. Now youngsters have become physically capable of dealing with almost any material, although plaster will still be spilled and paint will still drip, but the experience of working with these materials provides the best means of understanding them.

Care must be taken to insure that art is something special. The usual 12 by 18 inch size sheet of paper may no longer be the ideal size, and crayons may not be the best material to use for color. Both large materials and small materials can be intriguing at this age. The large materials provide the opportunity for real physical involvement and the problem of doing a painting that is three feet wide and five feet high can be a challenge in itself. At the same time, small muscle control provides the opportunity for detail in ink drawings.

Because of the increased ability to work with complex materials, craft projects are often introduced now. These provide excellent opportunities for a variety of artistic experiences and expression of a utilitarian nature. However, the continued use of craftlike material may encourage a narrowing of interests and a concealment of true expression rather than an opening up of new avenues to explore. This is not to say that youngsters should not have the opportunity to concentrate on one art material. However, if a student constantly uses one material mechanically, producing without new discoveries, this may become a substitute for expression.

Depth of expression can be achieved in many ways. One way would be to concentrate on one material, using it for a variety of subject matter; another approach in depth would be to concentrate on a particular subject matter and utilize a great number of materials in its development. For example, the human figure can be sketched, painted, modeled in clay, abstracted, dismembered, drawn in detail, and so forth. At the same time, tempera painting can be used as a means of expressing feelings about love or hate, of studying bold colors, or composing abstract forms, or communicating ideas, or illustrating a theme or mood.

New materials are now available for use in art classes, many of which were not readily available a few years ago. Although tempera paint is most

commonly used, there is an increasing number of other paint materials that are suitable. Polymer, vinyl, and other water soluble paints are available. Plastics of a great variety are usable, as are new drawing instruments and inks. Some of these new materials, and some old ones too, are potential hazards in the classroom; the possibility of strong odors, fire hazards, and danger to the skin are important considerations. A review of these problems and hazards of art materials was carefully documented by Siedlecki (1968, 1972). Mortality studies of artists and others (Franklin, 1981) show the risks of prolonged exposure to solvents and chemicals in paint.

Probably the oldest three-dimensional material is clay. By now the potter's wheel can be mastered. As with many other projects, no preplanning is necessary. When working on a potter's wheel it is almost impossible for the beginning student to start with a preconceived notion of the finished product, for much depends upon the consistency of the clay, the speed of the wheel, and the positioning of the hands and the body. But clay can also be used as an excellent modeling material, and the casting of plaster from original models made from clay can be an exciting experience. Mixing cement with expanded mica, or plaster with sawdust, provides a material that can be both built up and carved down.

Many of the art materials that have been discussed in earlier stages are also appropriate at this level. However, it is important to make sure that any materials used are also used by professional artists. That is, the child should be able to identify with those people who consider art a vocation, rather than thinking of art as a childhood activity. Experimenting with the qualities of charcoal and india ink with brush can stimulate an interest in the potential use of these materials. Exploring other possibilities, such as making papier mâché moon-men, paper-bag puppets, or plaster-and-wire space sculptures should involve the most reluctant youngster in art materials. When the child is encouraged to invent or imagine unusual forms, such as strange machines, environments, and animals, his imagination can definitely be boosted (Kincaid, 1964). It should once more be emphasized that the main function of art materials is to provide a means for increased knowledge, understanding, and expression in the arts and not to be an end in themselves.

Summary

This stage of development is one of very rapid changes. Girls discover that the mass media think they should be pretty and alluring. Boys' voices begin to change and most of them try to become very masculine; they are exposed to a diverse range of models to emulate, so that the outstanding athlete, or the numbers runner, or the television private eye seems more real than does the grocer down the street. The young adolescent not only wants to be well liked by his peers but also wants and needs the respect and attention of adults. The development of a critical attitude has made him aware of the world that surrounds him, sometimes painfully aware. His growing concern for naturalism is reflected in the drawings of objects and figures. Usually the schema that we have seen in earlier stages disappears; for some children the discrepancy between feeling themselves to be adults and seeing their art product as childish brings a shock.

Creative growth must be an integral part of the art program. This is especially true between the ages of twelve and fourteen. Here the child becomes much more critical of his own work; the pressure to conform to adult standards of behavior or to the standards of the crowd may work to stifle the creative urge. The art teacher plays a vital role in developing individuality in expression, in providing the opportunity to delve deeply into an area of interest, and in showing that the thoughts and ideas of youngsters of this age are welcome. The art room should have an atmosphere that is emotionally free and flexible, and provide an experimental and supportive attitude. It is important to stress that every project in which the child becomes

Figure 201.

Education has to counteract the negative effects of the mass media. The expressive arts can provide the means to capture the imagination and stimulate the creativity of young adolescents.

involved should be accepted without any outside criterion or evaluation. That is, the child who produces pleasing looking products and the youngster who is not doing the type of work that suits the teacher's aesthetic taste should be treated with equal respect. This in no way means that a laissez-faire attitude should prevail. The very opposite is true. The half-hearted attempt, the stereotype, and the presence of copying should all be clear indications to the teacher that the program is not a meaningful one. To stimulate the child's thinking, to have him come to grips with a problem, and to encourage a depth of expression are all much more important than making pretty end products. Art is not merely a subject matter area; it is the expression of the total youngster. As children grow into adults the art program should constantly change to meet their needs.

This particular age of development assumes greater importance when we realize that many youngsters have no further art experiences in the public schools after this time. It is unfortunate that school systems are arranged in such a way that at the onset of adolescence a program designed to provide an opportunity for the expression of feelings, emotions, and sensitivities should be dropped for the majority of the secondary school population. Attitudes that young adolescents develop from their art program in school will determine their future interest and participation in the arts. It is therefore vital that teachers of this age group show a high degree of involvement and enthusiasm in the art experience.

RELATED ACTIVITIES

1 Compare a twelve year old girl's representation of females over several months. Are there any changes in drawings that reflect maturation? Compare these drawings with representations by girls a year younger.

2 Collect the drawings of a seventh grade. What proportion of the class are displaying visual tendencies by drawing distant objects smaller? What proportion apparently are showing a nonvisual type of space representation?

3 Observe the working process while students are using clay. Which youngsters give a subjective interpretation of the topic rather than a visual? How does this compare with their approach to painting?

4 Record examples of behavior that show the change from an unconscious approach to that of a critical awareness of the child's own actions. Are there any indications of the child's becoming critically aware of his own drawings?

5 Have children of this age become aware of joints when drawing figures? Are differences in size and age indicated? Collect examples of such drawings. Are there differences in the age at which these changes occur?

6 Observe a class for several sessions. Can you pick out some students who seem to be less involved in their art activities? How does their work show this lack of involvement? Analyze some of the possible reasons for hesitancy or fear of expression. Plan definite steps to take to improve the meaningfulness of the art experience.

The Period of Decision

12

Adolescent Art
in the High School
Fourteen — Seventeen Years

The Importance
of High School Art

Art has by this stage of development become the product of conscious effort. For the student in high school, art has become something he can do, or leave alone. With young children art is primarily an expression of the self, done unconsciously. An eight year old will draw like an eight year old even if he has not had much opportunity to use art materials. The sixteen year old, on the other hand, will draw in the same way that he has been drawing for the past three or four years, unless he has had the opportunity and the desire to improve his artistic skills. This period is important, then, because it marks the beginning of purposeful learning in art. Art in the high school takes on a different atmosphere. It is now geared more toward the teaching of skills and the development of positive attitudes which the student may freely accept or reject. For some, art is looked upon as something unrelated to the drive toward vocational goals; for others, art becomes that goal.

For most teenagers, art is no longer a part of their lives. At least on the conscious level most sixteen and seventeen year old youngsters will not feel that art is essential to their needs. Art is constantly around them, it is dictating the clothes they wear, the buildings they live in, the packaging that induces them to buy, and the automobile they are saving for, but this is not part of what these youngsters consider art. For most high schoolers, art is something that was fun, but that belonged to the elementary school. Only about one out of seven high school students elects art when it is available, although half the schools do not offer art at all. The larger secondary schools are most likely to offer art courses, but even here students are often advised not to take art courses because of the fear that the more capable students will not be able to get into college unless their program is filled with the usual academic subjects. The fact that colleges do accept credits taken in high school in art is either not known or ignored. At any rate, art as an elective in high school is taken by a very small percentage of students.

There is the possibility that art may no longer be considered an important part of learning; society seems to have accorded art courses a very minor place in the curriculum. There may be good reason for this. Often the program of art is geared toward grooming students for an art career and giving some sort of recognition to those who are supposedly talented. For those teenagers who feel they do not have the talent (and this obviously includes most of them), the possibility of flunking or getting a poor mark in art is not appealing.

Even so, not all art classes are filled with talented youngsters, because there are always a few students whom the guidance counselor feels must take a few courses so as to graduate. For the most part, however, art has not been in the mainstream of interests for students in the high school. This is really sad when we consider that both for an individual's needs and for society's needs art can fulfill a real purpose.

There is a great need to bring art closer to the conscious awareness of students in the high school. These are the people who will be making decisions in the future about our society, and the necessity for making art a part of their thinking is vital. Many philosophers and artists have lamented the visible condition of our world, but efforts to change the elements that comprise it will have little success unless the need for this change is made apparent to the citizens of tomorrow. In today's society there is very little opportunity for self-identification, very little opportunity to feel responsible for what one is doing, very little opportunity to master a portion of one's life. Increasingly, demands are coming from sources outside the self: the hours one keeps are decided by the job requirement, the clothes one wears are decided by designers and fashion magazines or peer group pressure, the house one lives in has been built by someone else, the car that is driven was made miles away and is serviced by others, the food one eats is grown elsewhere and purchased in impersonal stores; and to build a fire outdoors or add on a room to one's house requires special permits from an unknown official. As yet society has not fettered art expression. There is a great need to provide a touch of saneness and a contact with one's own thinking, and the high school art program is a valid place for this to happen.

The High School Student

For the past ten, eleven, or twelve years of his life, the high school student has spent a considerable length of time in classrooms. Although there has been some experimentation in organization, he has typically spent six or more hours each day in classes with others his own age and with a teacher in charge. For some, the age of compulsory education cannot be over soon enough. With others, the end of high school means that they now have a choice in deciding their own futures. However, graduation from high school does not necessarily mean the end of society's restrictions for the student. If he has a license to drive, he must pay an additional premium for his car insurance; in some states he cannot legally drink or buy alcoholic beverages; his credit is no good; and generally the teenager receives the message that even after high school he is not fully trusted in adult society.

Like the young adolescent, the older adolescent is concerned about his crowd and with independence from adult domination; he is still seeking to establish his identity. But he has become a great deal more aware of the adult world of responsibility. He is also beginning to be aware of the fact that he must soon be on his own and must fit into society in order to make a living. Love is no longer associated with fantasy and T.V. personalities, but begins to be more closely tied to the nearest members of the opposite sex and the prospects of marriage. Adult responsibilities may be only a year or two away, and it sometimes comes as a shock for girls to see a friend, just a year ahead of them, becoming a wife and mother. This is a time for many decisions, and a great number of these decisions depend upon the teenager himself. Art can play a special role with young people, if the art program is responsive to their needs.

Figure 204.
This elaborate doodle is an art form in itself. Not all art is done by students in art class.

Sex has begun to play an important role. There is no doubt that the awakening of sexual urges gives rise to some of the greatest concerns of this age. Girls are bombarded with advertisements about how to make themselves more femininely alluring by the use of hair rinses, deodorants, cosmetics, by squeezing or padding the body, or by various dress styles. For boys greater attention is often focused upon muscle building and attaining masculinity. This is a real problem for the youngster who develops later than his classmates. Added to all of this, of course, is the general feeling that somehow discussing sex with adults is taboo. The rise in venereal disease among the high school age population indicates increasing experimentation. Forty percent of the births to fifteen to nineteen year olds are illegitimate (Carnegie Council, 1980). It has been shown that in other cultures this uncomfortable period between puberty and marriage may be considerably shorter. Although some girls leave high school for marriage, especially in the lower socioeconomic levels, marriage for others can sometimes be delayed well beyond college. The high school student has not outgrown his concern about himself. The adolescent is concerned about his hair, the pimple on his nose, and the proper clothes to wear. He practices before a mirror to perfect the image he hopes to project. The older and closer to graduation the student gets, the more he decides that he will have to live with himself as he is. The crowd is still important, especially as a reinforcement of one's own feelings.

As Weinstock (1973) has reported, the modern adolescent is a new breed. He sees more, knows more, does more, avoids inactivity at all costs. He drives cars, trucks, and motorcycles; travels here and abroad; has considerable buying power for the artifacts of culture; initiates trends in food, music, dance, and life styles; at eighteen he can vote, and in some states he can also drink at bars, marry, and enter into binding contracts. He has more autonomy than any past generation of adolescents, and yet he is subjected to authoritarian control in school.

Everyone knows of the five year old who is anxious to be a fireman when he grows up, but rarely do we find a sixteen year old who is this definite about his vocational goals. The possibility of making a real choice of a lifetime career is a frightening thought for the graduating senior. Often the choice is accidental. For the youngster whose family is less financially solvent, the part-time job may become a full-time occupation. For the more academically successful student dear old Dad's college may be the easiest route into the insurance business. Few youngsters are able to maintain their idealism beyond eleventh grade, and earlier romantic interests in art are soon put aside. At twelve or fourteen, the possibility of becoming an artist may have sounded

THE PERIOD OF DECISION

Figure 205.
Society places a high value on education, but the students find themselves taking mandatory courses within the confines of the school grounds, and they may consider high school something to survive rather than enjoy.

very nice, particularly for boys who imagined themselves painting delightful nudes in some attic. The idea of sending a high school student on to college as an art major may sound like the beginning of a fulfilling, interesting career, but this may not be at all true. In a survey comparing art, English, and psychology graduate students, Whitesel (1980) found that 82 percent of the art students lacked career counseling, and half of them were uncertain about their career goals. One should not consider education in art as being wasted if a position is not waiting for graduates. Most college students who major in art never get an art-related position, but more often find employment as purchasing agents, insurance representatives, travel agents, and the like. The free-lance artist, painting in a private north-lighted studio and selling paintings to wealthy connoisseurs is a myth. In following 31 former art students' careers, Getzels and Csikszentmihalyi (1976) found that, after five years, 15 former students had left the field of art or were unknown, 7 had stopped painting and were in art only peripherally, and 9 still continued in the field of art, with one outstanding achiever.

Puberty is generally recognized as being the end of childhood. Girls usually begin a period of rapid growth at about eleven years, and by menarche at about thirteen they will have developed the usual feminine bodily characteristics. Girls do not reach their full mature height until about seventeen. Boys start to shoot up about two years later than girls; they do not start slowing down until

The Adolescent and Society

Figure 206.
One function of creative expression is as an outlet for resentment against society at large or even the school environment. A seventeen year old boy clearly shows his opinion of food in the school cafeteria.

School food

fifteen or sixteen, and they reach adult height at about nineteen. Their voices may begin to change, the Adam's apple grows, and a trace of fuzz appears on their faces at about fifteen. With both sexes there are skin changes, and it is not unusual for body parts to grow at different rates. All these changes are of concern to these youngsters and obviously have an effect upon how they view themselves in relation to the rest of society.

When adults say they do not know what the younger generation is coming to, they are speaking about the fifteen to seventeen year old. It is rather strange to consider the fact that this is the one member of society who seems to be constantly getting into trouble. He is the one who is caught speeding, he is the one who experiments with drugs, he is the one who puts on the protest demonstration. Twenty five percent of the reported crimes are committed by this age group (Carnegie Council, 1980). The adolescent is becoming more and more concerned with social problems and cannot accept the values of an older generation without testing them. Parents come in for their share of resentment, and the generation gap may be more a gap in understanding than in age. With changes in the family structure, there are more working mothers and more single parent families. The sixteen year old has little oportunity for rebelling in a socially acceptable manner, and too often parents are seen as rule makers. There are rather strict laws about child labor which give the older adolescent little opportunity to find a place for himself within the larger society. Society itself is responsible for some of this conflict, because it does not provide the means by which a sixteen year old can feel that he has a contribution to make or that this contribution will be accepted by the world of adults.

Some educators and psychologists now feel that high school is an affront to the adolescent—an insult. A few go so far as to suggest that it is no longer appropriate (or, possibly, legal) to require attendance, insisting that compulsory attendance violates individual rights (Weinstock, 1973). With earlier maturity, greater responsibility and accountability, and guaranteed rights as private citizens, the high school population is more truly composed of young adults, although most school administrations or criticizing parents are reluctant to admit it.

Yet the mechanics of education are changing. The open school is less a novelty than it was. Some programs allow students credit for work in the community. In some places capable seniors move on to junior college for some of their credits or else omit the senior year entirely. The schools are participating in the life of the community, utilizing valuable resources of people and institutions. Schools can become part of a larger human resources center, serving a broader population—the entire community. In small towns the school has traditionally been a social center, anyway, along with the church.

Adults have the opportunity in our free society to make decisions about where they will work, the kind of people they want to be with, or if they want to be a part of society at all. The economically disadvantaged adult male has less opportunity for this freedom, but even he has a right to speak up, and this right is protected by law. For the youngster there is no comparable freedom. In fact, the law is usually quite definite in requiring him to attend school for a specific number of years and to take certain courses in high school; even the number of days of attendance is usually clearly specified, and if he is not there everybody gets excited. Society looks upon the public schools as an extremely important part of the training of individuals to perpetuate society. Youngsters are admonished to graduate from high school, and if they reject the school system their chances for economic success are severely limited.

Although society may place a high value on an education, the youngster in the secondary school may view this in quite a different light. Often the high school is looked upon as something to survive rather than as something to enjoy. The successful student is one who has learned to cope with the system, but he may not be the one who is getting the most out of the learning situation. It is fairly common for students not to study anything but that which will appear on examinations; usually the main thing learned in a classroom is what the teacher expects rather than an understanding of the subject. It is a question of survival with the least amount of effort, and it is the rare teacher who is able to instill the classroom with an atmosphere of excitement for learning.

The typical high school program is made up of many isolated subjects that have a tradition from the past as solid academic requirements. Learning is fragmented, and the student has no choice but to attend one class after another according to the bell, which in itself may interrupt learning. Girls seem to get more satisfaction from school than boys, but for both, school tends to be a dull place where interest is found in the unexpected happening rather than in learning. Jackson (1968), in his report on life in classrooms, mentioned studies that have examined student attitudes toward school, their feelings in the classroom, and the amount of attention students pay to the subject under discussion. Jackson feels that all students probably develop psychological buffers to insulate themselves from the wear and tear of the school. This detachment means that feelings of joy or distress are minimized, so the students' greatest complaint is boredom.

Students consider education primarily as the imposition of already established truths, with little or no concern paid to their personal needs or desires. There is no course aimed at providing the high school student with knowledge about himself, his own struggle in society, or even about the dreams and wishes he may have for the future. The usual academic program for those who will attempt to go on to college has no real relationship to objects, people, or jobs. The alternate choice that students have is the vocational program, which is concerned primarily with providing job skills.

Figure 207.
*In the art room, the student
should be able to find a sanctuary
from the usual school pressures, a
place where one has control over
one's activities and products.*

To some extent the secondary school system may be caught in its own web. If the goal of education is not mastery of information—and many educators have come to this point of view—then the emphasis is on gaining knowledge about where information is to be found and on the development of positive attitudes toward learning. The usual routine of keeping track of the students as they come and go, worrying more about attendance than about ideas, and being concerned with grades rather than achievement may be a real stumbling block to change. There seems to be no doubt that the high school student does build up a resentment to society through his experience in the public schools. It may be that if change is going to be made it has to be made by the segment of the high school program that is most flexible and ready to change. Art seems well suited to lead in this respect.

Figure 208.

For the intellectually capable student the school situation usually provides little opportunity for expressing feelings or emotions. Working directly with art materials is a welcome change, where creative involvement is possible.

The Basis for Art in the High School

Art in the high school has tended to reflect society's opinions of the adolescent. To a great extent, school art is too often removed from the real world, and it is concerned with issues that are often removed from controversy, social issues, idealism and the desire for change, and even from the youngsters themselves. Educators should be able to develop an art program that is distinct in its nature and that helps to satisfy the needs of this age and to unfold possibilities for continued growth. The program must provide the opportunity for the adolescent to express his thoughts, emotions, and reactions to his environment. It should be basically a program in which the individual can become totally involved, in which the methods and materials are as far removed from the environmental and psychological restraints of the high school as possible, and which also involves the student directly in the fundamental process of creating a product with real utilitarian value, not only for him but for society at large.

Too often, controversial subjects are considered dangerous; a teacher who encourages students to think about politics, sex, or marriage, who raises questions about the process of law, or who gets his class involved in local issues may very well find himself looking for a new position the following year. Schools tend to isolate youngsters from the real world, at a time when their energies and idealism can best be incorporated into society.

There are, of course, exceptions to this dismal picture. Sometimes programs are attempted that utilize the energies of the adolescent in constructive ways, either through sports or community activities. Too often these school sponsored projects are considered in the same light as other school activities and thus are doomed to failure. Occasional attempts are made at bringing the arts into the curriculum of all students, either under the heading of courses in humanities or by requiring at least one semester in the arts for each student. However, just because a course has a name implying the area of art does not mean that this course provides opportunities for the high school student to get involved in a meaningful way with his society, nor does it mean that he is now able to express his feelings and emotions about himself or the world around him. All too often, the art courses offered in the high school are planned well in advance by some committee in the state capitol, and courses have a step-by-step progression that is clearly stated in the syllabus. Sadly left out of the planning is the student, who differs in interests, concerns, and motivation from

Plates 30 and 31.
Plate 30, "Monster," and Plate 31, "Mask," were constructed of papier mâché. Adolescents are often very critical of their own art and can become easily discouraged if it does not look like their concept of professional art. However, using uncommon materials such as papier mâché can reduce comparison with slick products. As work progresses, this material requires imaginative planning and flexibility; it also lends itself well to expressing emotions through strong form and color.

Plate 32.
"Flowers," painted by a high school girl. The painting shows a sensitivity toward her subject that might not be shared by all students; for some students, a flower may be quickly rejected as inappropriate subject matter.

Plate 33.
"Mallards," painted by a high school boy. Sometimes the interests of students are great enough to become a continuing theme in their art. Here a student's interest in birds has grown to such an extent that his work has developed a high degree of proficiency.

every other student, and from last year to next. The high school art program should be based upon young adults who are involved in and concerned about today's world, not a program that is oriented toward making artists.

The still life set-up, the picture made with water colors, the linoleum blockprint, or the small clay sculpture may not be large enough in impact to involve today's youth. There is a sense of urgency, a sense of social involvement, and a desire to make change that cannot be satisfied with typical high school projects which are aimed at self-improvement. Living is a challenge, and art should reflect this challenge.

There is no correct art. Art has traditionally been a reflection of the culture in which it was found. There are no rules for artistic success, as the rules are made by people, and these are constantly changing. For art to be important it must be a reflection of the individual making it. This is as true at the high school level as it is for the professional artist. Those students who take art as an elective, as a relaxing activity, as a subject to use later as a hobby, as something to relieve the strain of daily living, and as a means of contact with oneself obviously have a variety of ways of utilizing art and a variety of ways of dealing with the world through artistic materials. But so do students who are considered "serious." Holtzman, et al., (1971) gave a great many perceptual, personality, and cognitive tests to eighty-five advanced college students who were judged by their professors to be successful and to have potential. These students had as their major field either abstract art, architecture, or engineering drawing. Highly significant differences were found between these three groups, which led to the conclusions that these three groups had contrasting modes of visual experiences. It seems that there are as many different kinds of art expression as there are students; it would not seem wise to value one kind of expression above another.

Constantly around us are problems concerned with art. Artists and teachers alike lament the fact that we live in a world that ignores aesthetics. Design seems to play a minor role in society as compared with money, and the arts invariably take a back seat when considerations for change are voiced. The art program at the high school level should be an active one. The subject matter should be based upon more than the teacher's files, more than just the school environment; it should become a vital part of the community.

Working directly with a material provides a tremendous satisfaction and a release from the pressures of intellectualizing. Most of the mental activity that goes on within the high school environment is limited to prescribed topics. Little opportunity is provided to think or act creatively as that may be upsetting to the semitranquillity of the classroom. Feelings, such as love, the expression of beauty, and feelings about social issues are equally legitimate concerns of art.

The basis for an art program in the senior high school should therefore be the same as that for the individual in his society. Its purpose should be to involve the student more fully in the culture in which he finds himself, it should provide him with a means of making tangible changes, and it should provide the opportunity for him to face himself and his own needs.

The Structure of an Art Program

The students who will be in the art program of a senior high school must be the first consideration in any planning. Very few of these students in an art course will actually do anything beyond school with art. Rather, they will become plumbers, clerks, scientists, used car dealers, homemakers, policemen, and so forth. A course of art should not be for the talented students, but for all students, so that they discover that art is a valuable means of focusing energies into creative problem solving, not only in school but also after graduation.

Probably one of the most important elements is the attitude that prevails. If an art course is looked upon as just another academic course with quizzes, examinations, and projects to be marked, art will lose its significance and impact upon students. Much time and effort can be spent by the students and by the teacher in what is sincerely considered a good art program. Such projects may include embossing metal plaques, designing stained-glass windows, making safety posters, designing monogrammed napkins, carving book ends, copying various lettering styles, or carving a football player out of soap. The list of such school-type projects is unlimited. These parallel the May baskets and sewing cards at the elementary level. This approach to art education tends to make a sham and a frill out of what should be a vital and dynamic part of the school curriculum.

There is a serious question whether high school students actually learn or retain much from art classes as they are presently taught. A National Assessment of Art (1977) asked nine, thirteen, and seventeen year olds to do some drawing tasks, including drawing a table with four people sitting at it. The drawings were rated on such things as skill in foreshortening and overlapping. Needless to say, the seventeen year olds had more overlapping. However, with one year of art beyond elementary school, only 50 percent of the seventeen year olds drew "acceptable" pictures. With four to six years of art beyond ele-

Figure 209.
This lively scene in a busy school cafeteria shows a girl's awareness of her surroundings, and is a successful drawing in spite of the inaccuracies of perspective.

mentary school, 56 percent of the seventeen year olds drew "acceptable" pictures, a minimal improvement at best. It seems that the artistic skills these students acquired with their additional years of classes did not show. The criteria for judging may be at fault; the representation of a table in perspective is not a drawing task that may be automatically equated with good art, and the more haptic student might be concerned with portraying relationships rather than a photographic likeness. But the fact that a national assessment can rule certain drawings as unacceptable puts pressure on teachers of art to conform and to teach specific formulas for success. Such standards, whether from a local administrator or from a national body, may set a direction exactly opposite to that of a meaningful art program.

It is possible to deal with art in such a way as to make a meaningful and exciting program. Probably the first element would be to treat the adolescents as adults. The implications of this are great. Nowhere else in the school system can a youngster be looked upon as an important being, one who has a contribution to make, one who is the core of the program. Adults would not be interested in grades or other types of evaluation. Treating the high school student as an adult implies that we respect his opinions and realize he has had experiences that may go beyond ours in certain areas, and that he has turned to art as a free choice.

Art Activities

One of the most important activities in an art class is the opportunity to paint. Painting has long been considered the most expressive form of art. With painting, much can be expressed that is important to the high school student. There is no reason to plan exercises that lead up to painting, exercises that may be important to the teacher, but not to the student. Painting from warm to cool, cutting shapes in order to visualize pictorial design, and exercises dealing with positive and negative space are all important at some point, but not necessarily for all students, and certainly not as an introduction to painting. Painting can be done with a range of materials, and there is no reason to expect that students should be in a lockstep procedure. Some students may enjoy polymers and oils, others tempera, and still others water color. To come face to face with an empty painting surface is a challenge, and the experience should be just as fundamental as that faced by the professional painter. The adolescent is critically aware of the immaturity of his product. He can easily become discouraged by the primitiveness and naïveté of his drawings and often seems afraid to project his thinking directly upon the paper. The adolescent is disturbed by the discrepancy between what he produces and what he feels is appropriate for an adult to draw or paint.

A very direct approach to this problem would be to enlarge his concept of adult art. Certainly the fresh and in some cases the blunt painting of some contemporary artists may awaken the adolescent to new possibilities. Even older masters such as Chagall and Klee painted in a very unsophisticated manner. Teachers sometimes overestimate the sophistication of their students, and may not understand what students are striving for. The aesthetic preferences of fifteen year olds were compared to what their teachers thought they would like (Rump and Southgate, 1978); secondary teachers had no significant recognition of the types of pictures liked by students. Another fruitful direction is to

Figure 210.
*The opportunity to paint is often
one reason that students elect an
art course at the high school.
Students should be encouraged to
set their own goals and to feel
free to discuss their satisfactions
or displeasures with the
instructor.*

involve the student with materials and techniques in which the end product is not as readily comparable to professional products. The adolescent has developed the ability to work with more intricate procedures, and in some cases these can be a challenge.

The art program should involve the student in his own school experiences. Although one sometimes hears of a program in which music, dance, and drama become thoroughly combined with art, these programs are very few. Frequently the art teacher feels that the rest of the school activities are irrelevant to the art program and for good reason. However, a real involvement of the student in school activities can work for the total benefit of the school itself. Most high schools have an abundance of empty halls. These provide excellent painting surfaces and there is no reason why art students cannot take advantage of these large blank areas to paint murals. It should be pointed out that a mural is quite different from a painting; since the mural will be part of the architectural surface, the shape available becomes a challenge in which the architecture and the mural must be closely interwoven. Exhibits of paintings can also be displayed in the halls, but these must be ever-changing and carefully labeled. The exhibits become more than merely displaying a student's work for his own pleasure and self-esteem; they become also a means to make all students in the school aware of some of the excitement and variety available in the art area. Painting flats for the school play or designing the backdrops can be important if students are involved in planning and take an active part in

Figure 211.
Seeing the despoiling of the landscape by seemingly endless parking lots can challenge the imaginative thinking of a high school art class to seek more ecologically acceptable solutions.

experimentation. Effects such as the use of film, smoke, flashing lights, and so forth can make this an exciting art experience.

Outside the immediate school is probably the most fruitful area for exploration. In the broad field of art, very few artists are actually painters. Many more people who are considered artists are involved in a wide range of occupations, including architecture, landscape design, interior decoration, industrial design, and so forth. It is not the intent to provide training in these areas to high school students, but rather to involve them in some of these areas and to provide them with some of these skills, so that art does not stop at the closing of the classroom door. There are many areas outside of the classroom in which the planning and designing functions of students can operate. Landscaping a part of the school grounds, making an abandoned piece of property into a small park or playground, developing a series of benches for a bus stop, all make appropriate art projects. It would be a blow to the high school student if these were left in the planning stage; there is no reason why bricks cannot be laid, trees planted, benches cast out of concrete, and playground equipment constructed. It is this type of involvement in a project that can capitalize upon the youngster's intense desire to make a meaningful impression upon his society.

There is little opportunity in our society for teenagers to get involved in apprenticeship training or to gain an understanding of the type of work that adults are involved in. Often a youngster will graduate from high school without having done any more manual labor than babysitting or shoveling snow from a sidewalk. Part of the art program can be incorporated into the community functions in a way that no other part of the high school can. Such involvement could include the planning and designing of a section of a house, such as the kitchen, garage, or bathroom. Most building today is done by a builder without the benefit of an architect. Builders often offer a variety of services, and sometimes the involvement of high school youngsters in such a program can be considered an advertising asset by the builders. This means that the art classes will actually be criticizing and evaluating different plans, checking the building codes, seeing the structure under way, and making recommendations as to the type of flooring or location and arrangement of storage space. Often the art program doodles in house plans, but rarely does the student become committed to a project to the extent that he is able to see changes being made or is able to voice his approval or criticism over an actual structure.

The area of art is almost unlimited in its possibilities. Photography can be important if some culmination, such as a publication, is the ultimate goal. Working with sculpture, if the sculptural forms become part of the community, can also be a powerful force. Printing can be worthwhile if it is related to actual printing and publication, such as a school paper and the high school yearbook, which are usually removed from the students' hands and put into those of a commercial printing house. Excellent journals and books, such as the Foxfire series (Wigginton, 1972–1980), contain material collected and articles written by high school students. Almost any art-oriented project can take on meaning if it is one that combines the needs of the adolescent youngster with opportunities to work on the problems that he is facing.

The Importance of Design

The art program should also provide the basis for cultural directness and honesty. The negative implications and effects upon our thinking processes of accepting falsehoods and imitation as normal should certainly be decried. Pointing out dishonesty and sham when it occurs in architectural planning, in the purchasing of accessories, or in political life should make for a greater realization of such discrepancies.

The secondary school is an excellent place to begin to re-educate toward

Figure 212.
Sensitivity to the patterns within natural objects provides a basis for understanding the relationship between design and function.

a feeling for design as an integral part of the function and use of an object or of a material. Functional design refers to three equally important relationships: the relationship between design and material, the relationship of design to tools or machinery used in its creation, and the relationship between design and purpose. For example, a piece of pottery made on a potter's wheel should look as if it were indeed made on the potter's wheel. If the effects of the working methods are hidden, the truth of functional design is lost. The purpose of a vase may be purely decorative, in which case it needs to be able to stand, or be hung, or be heavy enough so that it will not be easily knocked over. If the purpose of the pot is to hold flowers, however, its glaze must not compete with the flowers, nor should the pot be too wide or narrow for such a purpose. The natural qualities of the materials should always be utilized and preserved as much as possible. Wood, glass, textile, metal, each should be used honestly. Simplicity of line is an important principle of modern functional furniture, with variation introduced by the use of different materials. Fine workmanship is an integral part of the design itself, and joints and braces need not be hidden under a decorative cover.

It is quite apparent that few people would purchase a toothbrush with a Victorian handle or one with an embossed design of flowers. The bristles of a toothbrush are not arranged in little scalloped designs, nor do they attempt to look like something other than bristles. However, we often find tableware with roses on the handle, lamps with scallops on the shade, and chairs with lion's paws for legs. The average American is fairly up to date when it comes to finding a better kind of transportation, range, or refrigerator. In his living room, however, he apparently wants to retreat from today's world and is content with the furniture styled for his ancestors, electing flowers for his living room rug and a colonial weather vane for his garage. The question goes deeper than just introducing the best type of modern furniture or contemporary homes to the public. Students must be made aware of the discrepancy between the demand for truth and the quest for scientific knowledge on the one hand and the acceptance of imitations of eighteenth century styles and wood-grained plastic foam ceiling beams on the other. Learning to recognize the honest use of materials develops through first-hand experience, for there is no formula of "right" answers.

The Organization of the Art Class

Art in the high school should not be a program, which has connotations of a set curriculum; art in the high school should be a concept. Ideally there should be no end to what the students are doing. And ideally there should be no beginning either. In an active program students should be able to enter at any time and participate, to become immersed in an art activity, to explore in depth certain avenues of expression, without concern for previous credits earned in introductory art programs or without concern for proper prerequisites. There seems to be no evidence that segregating art students into ability levels has any particular value except to teachers who have a regimented curriculum to follow. Actually, students seeing a variety of activities, exploring many different media, and participating in large constructions, can lend an excitement to an art program that cannot be achieved through a step-by-step sequence.

The usual time set aside for art in the curriculum at the high school level is not best suited to art experiences. Sometimes double periods are allowed, but the typical pattern is for the art class to fit in between an English lesson and a gym class. It is obvious that the type of program suggested here cannot fit nicely into a predetermined time schedule, because the involvement of youngsters cannot be automatically switched off after forty-five minutes. There may

Figure 213.
The self provides an endless source of subject matter for art, drawing body parts in detail and noting changes in position. Here a boy humorously deals with his own fingers and mouth.

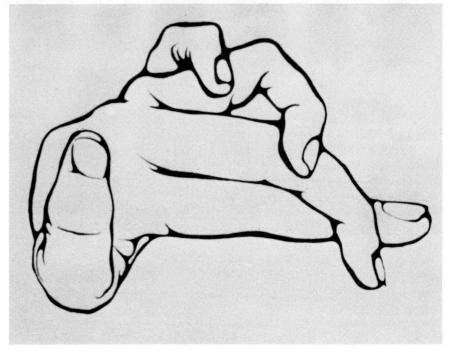

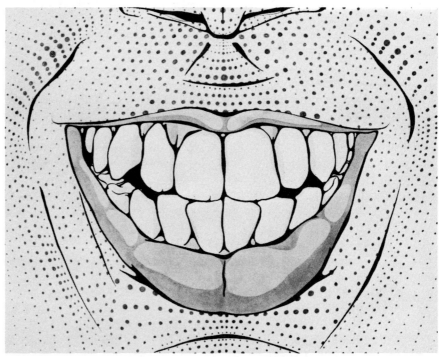

be reason to believe that art classes should not follow the usual academic class pattern. Possibly the usual pattern is not best for academic subjects either, but certainly art might better be offered on a Saturday morning when three hours at a time would be available for pursuing activities. Assuming that such restrictions as may be imposed by the high school administrators are inflexible, it is possible to live within the confines of daily scheduled periods, but even here other arrangements can often be worked out. The important thing is to remove the art program from the tightly scheduled list of activities, and have it more in tune with the youngster's interests and drives than with the clock.

Although the classroom can be the center of a number of planning and discussion sessions, the real activity of the art class could take place elsewhere. As much as possible, the class should be centered in the community and in the youngster's own life. If some students are involved in architectural planning and building, it does not make sense to put together little models from toothpicks and styrofoam when actual building is going on continually outside school. If some students are involved in landscaping a park, building benches for the area, and ordering trees or discussing planting with the community's building and grounds department, it does not make sense for them to be making sketches or layout designs to be filed in a drawer. If students are involved in painting, the subject matter for these paintings can rarely be found in the art room itself, and there is no reason why pictures or photographs need to substitute for the main street in town. Sketches can be made elsewhere and the final painting can be completed in the classroom itself, but the involvement in the subject matter should not be vicarious.

For those students who develop an interest in sculptural form, the industrial arts room may be a better place to do some planning; but the hammering together of parts and pieces, or the welding of steel could probably best be done at those commercial establishments that the youngsters will be able to use once they leave school. Even the firing of clay should probably be in the hands of the youngsters themselves so that they develop an understanding of the firing process and the design and operation of the kiln. Essentially, then, the organization of the art activities should be centered in those parts of the community that can give support and facilities to students once they leave school. The art room should be primarily a central meeting and discussion location, and not a closed, isolated studio.

Some questions will undoubtedly be raised about the possibility of students running wild with such a type of organization. This obviously will put a great deal of responsibility upon students. At the same time, it places additional responsibility upon the teacher, for he is no longer able to control the

Figure 214.
One of the purposes of an art program should be to provide the students with some of the abilities and interests that will keep art important to them once they leave high school. These girls are learning some of the procedures in weaving.

thinking processes of those youngsters who become self-motivated. It is easier to play the role of prison guard, to have students lined up in neat rows in the classroom, to have all students doing the same project at the same time, to have goals set by the teacher, and to give tests to insure that students are developing those skills that the teacher has decided are important. But this is not art. Art is the quality of being human, a quality that is involved in experiences that provide the opportunity for growth and understanding of oneself and others. The production of some form or shape in which one is not personally involved does not constitute art. The most important task of an art teacher is undoubtedly that of making art important and meaningful to high school students. Art activities are too often planned in a way that insures success. Art is not all sweetness and light, and many failures and frustrations are part of the learning process. The threat of grades or marks is poor motivation; threats are hardly the basis for developing a positive relationship with either art, the art teacher, or oneself. In one year or two, the high school student will no longer be in a position to be told what to do and when to do it. If the student can be involved in art activities so that he feels that these are truly his, he will be able to turn to the art teacher and others for guidance, but the drive essentially will originate in the youngster himself.

There are some procedures in art that need to be understood, such as making a plaster mold for a clay form. But these procedures should not be confused with artistic progress, since an activity such as that can be learned at the tenth grade level or twelfth grade level or not learned at all. Art cannot be preplanned in an arbitrary way. Stringing courses together on a continuum such as is necessary in certain areas of mathematics is not applicable to art. But some state instructional syllabuses view art as a sequence with Art I, followed by Art II, followed by Art III, like the beads that a nursery school child would string together.

Organizing the art room so that it is possible for many art activities to go on at the same time allows a great flexibility in the use of space. Unfortunately, when everyone is trying to do the same thing at the same time, there are bottles of ink all over the place, there are not enough pens, all the flat table space is being used; but the sink that was so crowded the week before when a project in tie and dying was underway is now left vacant. However, it does not have to be that way. Instead the bored student from the study hall can find some excitement in the art room and get a taste of what goes on. The twelfth grader who is welding some junk together out in the yard can attract some tenth grade boys; the weaving goes on close to the potter; and, in the corner of the room, kitchen plans are being pored over to present to the local contractor next week. The art room can be exciting, confusing, sometimes organized, but never stagnant.

Youngsters of varying abilities and interests cannot be expected to show equal enthusiasm for all types of projects. The particular projects that these youngsters select are not important. The will to learn, with active involvement in a project, is of prime importance. The art teacher should not feel that he has to be present continually. In fact, his very presence may reduce the amount of self-learning that takes place. He should, however, be available for listening and for broadening the possible avenues of action that students take. It is not just his technical ability that becomes important, for he should be more a model of possible ways to explore and to investigate, not one who provides the answers when called upon. It is probably more useful to say "I don't know, but let's find out" than to always have a ready answer available. There must be opportunities for exchanging thoughts at intervals and opportunities for group discussion. Some basic problems may be encountered; an occasional lecture

which provides specific information about artistic skill, the problems of architectural design, various methods that have been historically used in printing, or a survey of painting methods may be extremely valuable when the need arises.

Integrating Art

The study of art history is too often isolated from the practice of art. Sometimes at the college level, art history is taught with other histories in a college of Arts and Sciences or Social Sciences; the practice of art, the actual painting or sculpturing, is located in a different college entirely, such as in a college of Fine Arts or Performing Arts. And even the area of design may be located in a third college, along with weaving and pottery. There are some historical reasons for this. Art history has had a separate existence from art, often being more attached to museums, archaeology, and social history, and considered an intellectual study. Art, as typified by painting, has been considered more intuitive, more the province of the talented, supported by patrons and free to reflect on society. Design has traditionally been associated with industry, with a vocation, and with the economics of producing and merchandising.

Although some high school programs still cling to these divisions, there is actually no reason why all of these areas cannot be pursued simultaneously, singly, or not at all. Just as there is a history of art, there is a history of music, a history of science, a history of philosophy, and a history of medicine. Possibly the history of medicine would be considered the most important by at least part of society, yet it is not offered in secondary schools. The only reason to include art history is to provide a background for understanding oneself and one's society. To deal with art history as a separate topic, to put this important and potentially exciting area into the framework of another isolated subject to be tested and studied-for-a-mark denies the personal human messages that art has for youth.

It is important that history, criticism, and the analysis of art begin with the tangible, a reference point that can actually be touched or is a natural outgrowth of a problem of the student's own making. Many of these catalysts are already in the school or the community: the painting that the student is working on, the repainting of the school interior, or the designation of a building as a national landmark. The frame of reference for a painting can be expanded by seeing how artists from other cultures dealt with the same subject matter, how painters from a different time and place tried to communicate a similar theme, or how various artists conveyed a feeling for atmosphere or mood. The re-painting of the school opens up many problems and solutions with color: re-flectivity, warmth and coolness, preferences, durability, variability, and cost. And the possible designation of an historic building means research into county records, interviews with past and present owners, examination of the construction, drawing of floor plans, photographing various façades, writing up recommendations, and comparing with other buildings of the same era. Each of the above examples involves the arts fully. An important issue which has life and meaning for a student may lead to a greater involvement and depth in the arts; it is also an important learning experience with a tangible personal meaning.

It is the potter who is attracted to an exhibit of pots, the painter who is anxious to see the coming museum exhibit, and the photographer who appre-ciates the latest foreign films. It is personal involvement in the activity that stimulates the appreciation and the desire to see how others have dealt with problems similar to those faced by oneself. Art should not be separated into its various components; art history, design, criticism, crafts are all part of art. Each should be part of a learning framework to be utilized as needed to help the student understand the importance and meaning of art.

Art Materials

The material from which an art object is made does not have any artistic qual-ity in its natural form. It is only through expression in art that the form as-sumes meaning and the material becomes an art material. The more opportu-nity there is for the high school student to manipulate, change, and build in diverse ways from a material, the better the material is. There are many ma-terials that possess a high degree of structure that can stand in the way of ex-pression. Such materials as colored tissue paper, leather scraps, copper foil, and enameling kits have limited variability and are usually not suited to high school art programs.

It would probably be best if no art materials at all were available for the high school student to use. This would mean that every material would have to be purchased or obtained through the student's own efforts. The clay would have to be purchased locally or dug from a clay bank. Lumber would have to be obtained from the local building supply house, paper from a stationery store, and sculptural supplies from the local junkyard. The advantage in this

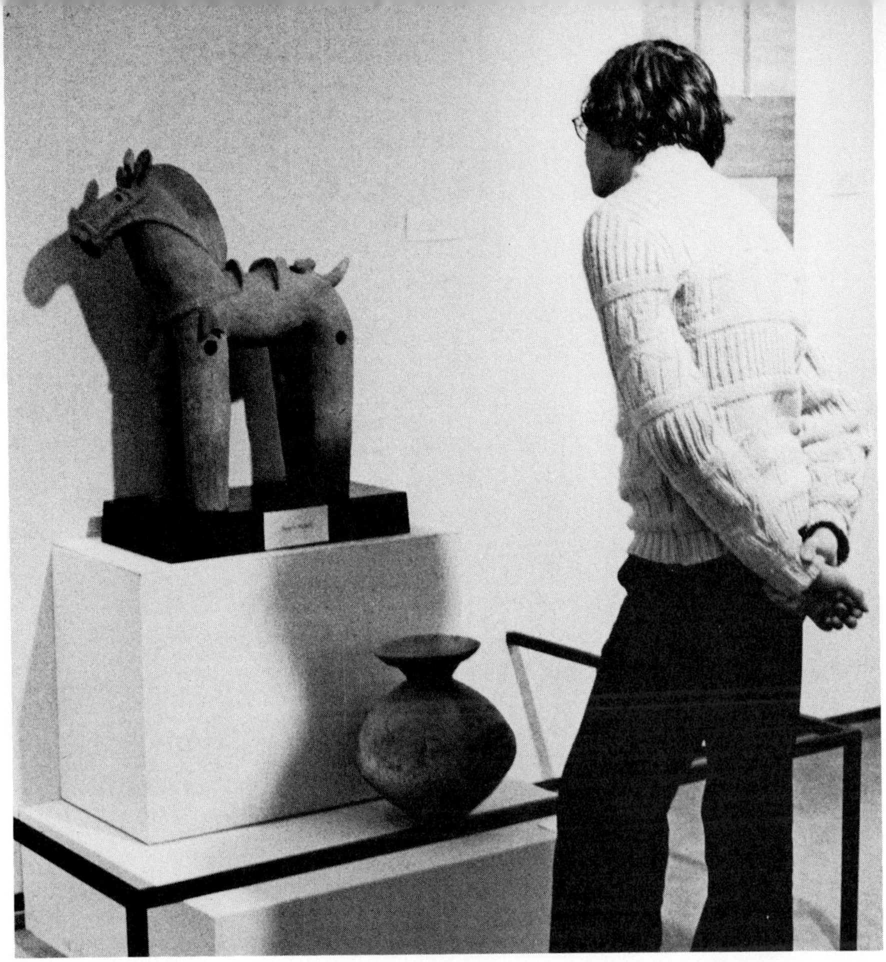

Figure 216.
Sensing the aesthetic appeal of
objects in a museum exhibit, and
seeing the way other cultures
have dealt with artistic problems
which the student himself has
faced, can bring an appreciation
of the history of art.

type of arrangement is that the student will no longer feel that the art material is the prime responsibility of the art teacher. Also it means that the art student must put forth some effort in obtaining these materials, and therefore he will be able to continue using these sources after graduation. The interest in art may die because of the unavailability of materials. Knowing where to get them, how much they cost, and their care and proper handling is an important element in learning about the production of art. This is not to suggest that all students must purchase all their art materials, since this would obviously work to the disadvantage of the poorer youngster. However, the budget for art supplies is customarily an exercise for the art teacher rather than a learning situation for the student. Rather than the art teacher requisitioning the materials and then passing them out when the time arrives, the student should be personally involved in knowing the sources, costs, and availability of the supplies he is using, especially if these are considered part of his education.

ART MATERIALS

417

Figure 217.
Learning how to use clay, getting to know its qualities, and feeling comfortable with the material so that it becomes a normal and natural means of expression were all necessary parts of modeling these heads.

Materials influence the design and final shape of an art form. It would be a mistake to consider a material only the means to an end, because thinking with the material itself and developing a feeling for the function and use of materials may well result in changes in design, revisions in original plans, and a greater flexibility of approach. The high school student needs to know a good deal about a material before it can be utilized. Just how that material is to be used needs to be considered before an abstract lesson on materials can be presented. A material that is going to be used outside in a structure or art form that needs to be sturdy may be quite different from a material used for an object that is going to be suspended and protected from the weather. A good deal of the student's knowledge can be acquired through experimentation. How permanent is a material? How heavy is it? Can it be colored? Does it burn? Can it be cast or carved? How much weight will it support? Is it waterproof? These are all questions that need to be answered about a material before it can be used appropriately in a given environment. Of course, new materials are constantly available, or new ways of using old materials need investigation. This is one way of involving students in art procedures. Certain students can be quickly involved in some problems in art if they need to discover how to join aluminum sheets, and have to decide if the best way is through stapling, riveting, using adhesives, soldering, or by clamping or screwing to a second material.

Students will develop the need for acquiring certain skills, for these will be necessary to gain satisfaction and a sense of accomplishment and self-confidence. Procedures can be explained. These are the steps in preparing materials, in maintaining their working consistency, and in cleaning and preserving the results. Techniques, on the other hand, are highly individual and develop according to personal needs. Each person has a technique which evolves, in part unconsciously, as a result of his experiences in the world that surrounds him. The working through a problem, the development of several possible solutions, the encouragement toward flexibility, and the final achievement of at least partial success will lead to a development of technique. Each individual will therefore develop what for him is the best technique, one that permits him to express himself more easily and with greater depth. Since art education in the secondary school does not prepare for a profession but rather serves to develop the mental, aesthetic, and creative growth of the individual, the teaching of skills must be focused upon the problem of finding adequate means of expression for the student.

The number of materials that could be considered appropriate for art expression seems infinite. For younger children it is sometimes important to restrict materials to ones that can be controlled, so that expression is not frustrated before it even takes form. However, for the high school student, a new or difficult material can be an exciting challenge. Possibly because the elementary school uses drawing and painting extensively and the high school student wishes to display his active adulthood, there is a move away from easel painting as the prime means of art expression. Photography has a respectable place in the art repertoire with the processing and enlarging of negatives or the editing of films being activities that embody much of the same decision making that goes into painting. Videotape presents a different set of problems with the advantage of immediate playback. But some of these activities can be expensive. Light itself can be used as a medium of expression; bright, dull, soft, fluctuating, colored, or moving lights can create interesting effects, but light combined with sound can be exciting. Plastics come in a variety of forms that can be poured, molded, glued, or carved.

A word should be said about the use of tools. The usual tools for an art class are brushes, pans for mixing paint, rollers, palette knives, scissors, and staplers. But there may also be need for a collection of hand tools such as screw drivers, saws, chisels, hammers, pliers, and a few power tools, including a drill and a sander. These tools should be considered the property of the class, and their main purpose is to be used. Sometimes tools can be made for a special purpose, such as mixing plaster, troweling concrete, or mixing up certain adhesives. These are expendable. Durable and inexpensive cameras should also be considered part of the available tools, as should a tape recorder, record player, slide projector, and some equipment more often considered basic to the study of science, such as scales and a microscope. The materials and tools should be of good quality, because in no way should the expression of the high school student be valued less than the expression of the adult artist. It is probably better to limit the materials and tools available if budget problems are a consideration, than to purchase those which cannot be fully used because they are not substantial enough to withstand the active use that teenagers will give them.

Summary

The fourteen to seventeen year old is self-critical, introspective, idealistic, and has a growing concern about his relationship to society. No two teenagers are alike, but they have concerns that are common. For the most part high school students do not have the opportunity or do not elect to take art courses; the art courses that are offered are often unrelated to the youngsters in these classes.

THE PERIOD OF DECISION

Art should provide the opportunity for the high school student to express his feelings and emotions and feel that his art is important to himself and to others.

The art program is in an enviable position to break away from the academic pattern of giving grades and testing for the knowledge that the teacher thinks important. The students and the environment provide excellent sources for art projects that can be meaningful to students and can also have an impact on the school society.

Much of the art that is done by individuals after leaving the secondary schools is of practical value, such as furniture making, rug weaving, photography, pottery making, or even furniture repair and refinishing. However, much misdirected time and effort is presently channeled into nonworthwhile activities by the "easy-to-make, just-follow-the-pattern" type of project. Considerable time within the framework of the curriculum should be set aside to make art meaningful as a continuing activity. People need to have control over, and identify with, a project of their own choosing. From the first conception of the idea, through the problem solving and technical mastery, to the final very personal result—this entire process must be grasped by the individual. Thus, any such creative activity should be an honest representation of its creator and of the material and be designed for its true purpose or function. Art education is ideally suited to maintain this self-identification with the whole span of production, usually unattainable to any one person in our modern, technically oriented age.

RELATED ACTIVITIES

1   Survey the art classes in a local high school to determine who actually takes elective art courses. What major sequence of courses are these students following? How do their academic abilities relate to the total high school population? What are the vocational interests of these youngsters?

2   List the materials presently being used by students in a senior high school. What type of use is made of these? Which of these art materials are used by adults who enjoy and actively engage in art, other than professional artists? On what basis can the use of the rest of the art materials be justified?

3   Observe an adolescent group outside school. Record the way in which these youngsters express themselves, both verbally and socially. Pay

close attention to dress, hair styles, cars, verbal expressions. How much of this expression is controlled through pressure to conform to group standards? How do you see this expression relating to the high school art program?

4 Compile a list of occupations that could be considered as those of practicing artists. What are the specific differences between these occupations? What are some of the skills or training necessary for each of these occupations? What are some of the common backgrounds needed for all fields?

5 Interview several people who are recognized artists in business, in industry, or free-lance. What influenced their choice of career? At what age did they decide to enter the art field? To what extent was the public school art program helpful or influential in their vocational choice?

6 Examine several state syllabuscs for art in the high school. To what extent are these programs designed as preparation for an art career? What activities are included that would be valuable for the usual high school student who does not intend to follow an art career?

Summary 13

Almost every child enjoys the opportunity for creative activity. The pre-school youngster, the sixth grader, and the young adult in high school all look upon art as something which is enjoyable. It is rather sad that our educational system is organized in such a way that most students are gradually deprived of the opportunity to paint, draw, or construct, the farther they progress in the school system. The need for art is not outgrown.

Children's drawings are always a pleasure to observe. They contain a freshness of outlook that is the essence of childhood. Young children particularly, express their ideas, thoughts, and emotions with an honesty that can almost be upsetting to adults. Sometimes professional artists are envious of the youngsters' spontaneous approach to painting; for their directness, frankness, and intuitive feeling for design may be what the artist himself is striving for.

Within itself, the act of drawing or painting is a learning experience. The problem of what to paint, how to paint it, the relationships of form and color, the use of heavy or fine line, the problems of light and dark are all part of the art experience. However, the organization of the elements in the picture or in the construction is only one segment of the experience, because the expression is a concrete configuration of the emotional and perceptual experiences that an individual has had in his interaction with the environment. This is true at all levels of art. It is the expression of the self, the subjective reactions to the environment that make art expressive, not only to the producer but also to the viewer.

Within each work of art a youngster portrays his feelings, his intellectual abilities, his physical development, his perceptual sensitivities, his creative involvement, his social development, and his aesthetic awareness. Although individual children vary considerably, there are general growth characteristics that are typical of any age, and the art products of these youngsters also change in predictable ways.

The very young child enjoys scribbling, but by the age of four, he is usually making scribbles that begin to look like the typical head-feet representation of a person. Most children when they reach kindergarten can draw a great number of objects, although these are only vaguely naturalistic. Soon a base line appears, and children place the objects they are drawing on this line across the bottom of the page. These early stages of children's development are marked by the direct and bold use of color, and it is at this age that children show a great deal of confidence in their own means of expression.

At about nine years of age or so, overlapping appears in drawings, and the youngster draws in much more detail and becomes more critical of his own products. Usually by the age of twelve, youngsters are quite reluctant to show their drawings. For most children the changes in artistic development have come to a halt. Some youngsters may show an interest in portraying the environment naturalistically, and be concerned with the problems of perspective and atmospheric effects; for others, these naturalistic aspects are difficult to understand, and they may get more enjoyment from painting nonobjectively.

The changes that take place in the art product are a direct reflection of the changing child; all of the variables that cause them to be different individuals with different personalities and different interests are also influencing their art products. It should be obvious that we cannot understand a work of art unless we understand the culture in which it was made, the artist's intentions, and the society and environmental conditions that surrounded its making. The same holds true for children's drawings. The school environment, the intent of the child, the intellectual and emotional factors involved, all must be understood if we are to appreciate the importance of art for children.

Teachers play an extremely important role in the development, not only of art, but of children themselves. Because art is essentially an expression of the self, because there are no answers in the teacher's stack of books, because art cannot be produced by the usual threat of failure or rewards, the teacher of art becomes a crucial person in art production. It is only through a strongly supportive teacher who encourages and interacts with youngsters that an increased sensitivity to the environment can grow. The development of positive attitudes toward the self and toward art is something that does not happen automatically. The creative spirit needs reinforcement, and the teacher is one who can provide the environmental conditions that will make the art experience an exciting and rewarding one. It is through identifying with the child, with his needs and interests, that the teacher can best understand the needs and desires of each child. This is particularly true for the child who may not turn naturally to art as a form of expression, for this may be the child who most needs the art experience.

Too often art programs are planned around materials, with emphasis being placed upon learning how to use each material, in the hope that a breadth of experience will somehow be valuable. It is not unusual to see an elementary classroom using crayons one week, finger paints the next, clay the following, and so forth. This constant changing of materials can be frustrating to a child, who is more interested in expressing his thinking, feeling, and perceiving in a meaningful way than he is in doodling in different materials. It may only be the teacher who thinks that it is important to vary the activities for the mere sake of change. In doing so, it is forgotten that the opportunity to become thoroughly familiar with a material so that it becomes a natural mode of expression is an essential part of developing competence and confidence in one's own art.

Within the framework of the usual school system, little opportunity is given for youngsters to express feelings and emotions that are anti-school. By the time youngsters are in the junior high school, many have succeeded in developing methods of coping with this system, so that it is not unusual for youngsters to be more concerned with what will appear on a test than with the material to be learned. Art should not fall into the trap of competing with academic subjects, but should have the integrity to remain basically human. It should be the one area in the secondary school that youngsters can turn to without the concern for being evaluated or without the feeling that they must perform according to someone else's standards. Art can be a vital force in the lives of students if it is relevant to their thinking and becomes the avenue by which they can express the feelings about their society that they are not encouraged to express either in or outside school. For the secondary school student, the potential of art is tremendous, and the energies and enthusiasm of older children can make learning and art exciting and rewarding.

A major emphasis in this book has been that art is entwined with a child's creative and mental growth. There is no pretext that the function of art in the school is to make artists out of children. Rather, the emphasis has been that art can provide the opportunity for growth in ways that other subject matter areas cannot. Growth is not achieved by the development of intellectual capacities alone. The confident, creative child who is eager to express his thoughts, who is sensitive to people and things around him, who is a responsive, productive individual, is much more the concern of an art program. We cannot do this developing for him. Every individual has a potential that is greater than what is realized. Art should provide the impetus for constructive action and the opportunity for each individual to see himself as an acceptable being, searching for new and more harmonious organizations, developing confidence in his own means of expression. The most essential ingredient in an art program is the child, and art education has a vital role to play in his growth.

Summary Charts

This summary cannot do justice to the developmental stages and their significance as they influence the art products of children. This volume has attempted to show the interrelationship between a child and his art, and to emphasize the importance of an adult, aware of the child's feelings and sensitive to the creative process. It is the teacher who is responsible for the learning environment, and a summary of developmental stages ignores the crucial interaction that is central to learning. However, the authors realize that for research purposes, it is sometimes important to have a brief explanation of the differences, changes, and similarities that exist, particularly in drawings, as children grow older. Some of our colleagues have attempted to make their own versions of a drawing scale, using the information presented in earlier editions. It was this fact that gave impetus to the following charts. No attempt has been made to deal with the variations and subtleties of motivation for each of the stages, nor the differences in materials that are suitable for each age. The way color is used and understood by children is a fascinating subject in itself, as is the formation of an intuitive sense of design; however, these topics are better understood by looking at the color plates than by reading a verbal description. The summary of each stage will be limited to a brief description and examples of drawings typical of each stage of development.

It should be emphasized that there is no one way that pictures will be drawn at any age. The stages melt into one another and children progress at different paces, depending upon numerous factors, so that one can even find a seventeen year old making scribbles around the edges of a calculus book, but it would be strange indeed to see a three year old making a detailed drawing of a person. The examples, then, should be considered as mid-points, and the stages themselves as convenient labels for a study of children's art and not as invariant categories.

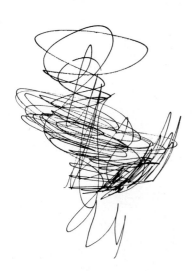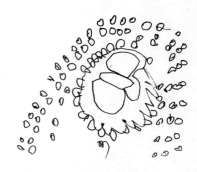

The Scribbling Stage, Two–Four Years: The Beginnings of Self-Expression

Drawing Characteristics	*Space Representation*	*Human Figure Representation*
	Disordered Scribbling:	
Motor activity utilizing large muscles with movement from shoulder	Utilizes drawing surface	No attempts made
Kinesthetic pleasure	Sometimes scribbles beyond paper	
Grasps tool with whole hand	Ignores previous marks placed on a page	
Swing of arm makes line		
Looks away while scribbling		
	Controlled Scribbling:	
Smaller marks	Stays within drawing area	Circles, lines, loops and swirls made, which are prefigural
Repeated motions	Draws around previous marks on the page	
Watches scribbles while drawing	May concentrate on certain parts of drawings	
Uses wrist motion		
Can copy a circle		
	Named Scribbling:	
Relates marks to things known	Scribbles placed purposely	A scribble may be pointed out by the child as being a person
Greater variety of line	Previous marks on the page are utilized	Action may be named, such as running, jumping, swinging
Holds tool between fingers	Empty space may take on meaning	
Identification of subject may change in the process of drawing	Lines become edges of shapes	
Longer attention span		

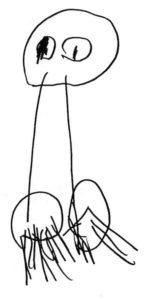

The Preschematic Stage, Four–Seven Years: First Representational Attempts

Drawing Characteristics

Shapes for things are geometric and lose their meaning when removed from the whole

Placement and size of objects are determined subjectively

Objects drawn are not related to one another

Art becomes communication with the self

Known objects seem to be catalogued or listed pictorially

Can copy a square at four, a triangle at five

Space Representation

Objects seem to float around page

Paper sometimes turned or rotated while drawing

Size of objects not in proportion to one another

Objects are distorted to fit space available

Space seems to surround child

Human Figure Representation

Head-feet symbol grows out of scribble

Flexible symbol, constantly changing

People are looking at viewer, usually smiling

Gradual inclusion of arms (often from head), body, fingers, toes

Distortion and omission of parts is to be expected

Clothes, hair and other details expected by end of this stage

The Schematic Stage, Seven–Nine Years: The Achievement of a Form Concept

Drawing Characteristics

Development of a form concept which is repeated again and again

Schema is altered only when special meaning is conveyed

Drawing shows concept, not percept

Bold, direct, flat representation

Drawings reflect a child's active knowledge of the environment

Space Representation

Establishment of a base line on which objects are placed and often a sky line, with the space between representing the air

Two dimensional organization of objects

No or little overlapping

Subjective space representation common

   a. simultaneous representation of plan and elevation

   b. X-ray drawings

   c. fusion of time and space

Multi-base lines

Environment symbolized

Human Figure Representation

Repeated schema for a person

Body usually made up of geometric shapes

Arms and legs show volume and are usually correctly placed

Exaggeration, omission, a change of schema shows effect of experience

Proportions depend on emotional value

The Gang Age, Nine–Twelve Years: The Dawning Realism

Drawing Characteristics

Greater awareness of details

Self conscious of own drawings

Greater awareness of physical environment

Events are characterized rather than drawn naturalistically

No understanding of shade and shadow

Space Representation

Disappearance of base line and emergence of the plane

Overlapping of objects

Beginning of interrelationships between objects

Sky now comes down to horizon

Attempts at showing depth through size of objects

Human Figure Representation

Rigid schema no longer prevails

Greater awareness of clothing details

Less exaggeration, distortion, and omission of body parts to show emphasis

Body parts retain their meaning when separated

Greater stiffness of figures

The Pseudo-Naturalistic Stage, Twelve–Fourteen Years: The Age of Reasoning

Drawing Characteristics

Critically aware of own shortcomings in art

Drawings can become shorthand notations

Ability to focus upon selected parts of environment

End of spontaneous art activity

Details such as wrinkles and folds become important for some

Projection of non-literal, personal meaning into objects and events

Space Representation

For visually minded, an awareness of depth; child draws as a spectator; attempt at perspective

Greater awareness of environment, but only important elements drawn in detail

For haptically minded, space determined subjectively; child draws as a participant

Action goes on within picture plane

Human Figure Representation

Closer to correct proportions

Greater awareness of joints and body actions

Facial expressions vary for meaning

Cartooning popular

Person can be represented by less than total figure

Sexual characteristics over-emphasized

Adolescent Art, Fourteen–Seventeen Years: The Period of Decision

Drawing Characteristics

Drawings tend to resemble 12 year level, without further instruction

Conscious development of artistic skills

Haptic drawings show subjective interpretation

Visually minded students may get pleasure from visual details, light and shade

Extended attention span

Mastery of any material

Control of purposeful expression

Space Representation

Perspective can be learned and utilized by visually minded; awareness of atmosphere

Attention to non-naturalistic representation for haptically minded; portrayal of mood, shifting of space or distortion for purposeful emphasis

Human Figure Representation

Naturalistic attempts by some. Awareness of proportions, actions and visible details

Exaggeration of detail for emphasis by some

Imaginative use of figure for satire

434   SUMMARY

BIBLIOGRAPHY

ALSCHULER, R. H. and HATTWICK, L. W. *Painting and Personality*. Chicago: University of Chicago Press, 1947 (reprinted, 1969).

AMABILE, T. M. The effects of external evaluation on artistic creativity. *Journal of Personality and Social Psychology*, 1979, **37** (2), 221–233.

ANASTASIOW, N. J. Success in school and boys' sex-role patterns. *Child Development*, 1965, **36** (4), 1053.

ANDERSON, C. M. and STOFFER, G. R. Creative thinking and juvenile delinquency. *Adolescence*, 1979, **14** (53).

APPLEGATE, M. Relationships of characteristics of children's drawings to chronological and mental age. Unpublished doctoral dissertation, University of California at Berkeley, 1967.

ARNHEIM, R. *Art and Visual Perception*. Berkeley, Calif.: University of California Press, 1954.

ASCH, S. E. *Social Psychology*. Englewood Cliffs, N.J.: Prentice-Hall, 1952.

BARRETT, M. D. and LIGHT, P. H. Symbolism and intellectual realism in children's drawings. *British Journal of Educational Psychology*, 1976, **46,** 198–202.

BARRETT, S. B. A study of the interrelationship and influences of scholastic aptitude and perception upon aesthetic sensitivity in college students. *Dissertation Abstracts International*, 1971, **31,** 5835.

BARRON, F. *Artists in the Making*. New York: Seminar Press, 1972.

BARRON, F. *Creativity and Psychological Health*. Princeton, N.J.: Van Nostrand, 1963.

BEE, H. The relationship between parent-child interaction and distractibility in fourth grade children. Unpublished doctoral dissertation, Stanford University, 1964.

BEITTEL, K. R. *Mind and Context in the Art of Drawing*. New York: Holt, Rinehart & Winston, 1972.

BEITTEL, K. R. Selected psychological concepts as applied to the teaching of drawing. Unpublished report, Cooperative Research Project No. 3149, Office of Education, U.S. Department of Health, Education, and Welfare, December 1966, 187 pp.

BEITTEL, K. R. and BURKHART, R. C. Strategies of spontaneous, divergent, and academic art students. *Studies in Art Education*, 1963, **5** (1), 20–41.

BEITTEL, K. R., MATTIL, E., et al. The effect of a "depth" vs. a "breadth" method of art instruction at the ninth grade level. *Studies in Art Education*, 1961, **3** (1), 75–87.

BELCHER, T. L. Effect of different test situations on creativity scores. *Psychological Reports*, 1975, 36.

BELL, C. *Art*. London: Chatto & Windus, 1914 (Republished: London; Arrow Books Ltd., 1961).

BEREITER, C. and ENGELMANN, S. *Teaching Disadvantaged Children in the Preschool*. Englewood Cliffs, N.J.: Prentice-Hall, 1966.

BERNDT, T. J. Developmental changes in conformity to peers and parents. *Developmental Psychology*, 1979, **15** (6), 608–616.

BIEHLER, R. F. An analysis of free painting procedures as used with preschool children. Unpublished doctoral dissertation, University of Minnesota, 1953.

BIRCH, H. and LEFFORD, A. Visual differentiation, intersensory integration, and voluntary motor control. *Monographs of the Society for Research in Child Development*, 1967, **32** (2).

BLAKESLEE, T. R. *The Right Brain*. Garden City, New York: Anchor Press/Doubleday, 1980.

BLAUNER, R. *Alienation and Freedom*.

Chicago: The University of Chicago Press, 1964.

BLAUT, J. M. and STEA, D. Mapping at the age of three. *The Journal of Geography,* 1974, **23** (7), 5–9.

BLUM, K. S. A comparative analysis of normal and disturbed children's drawings. Unpublished master's thesis, Cornell University, 1979.

BOERICKE, A. and SHAPIRO, B. *Handmade Houses: A Guide to the Woodbutcher's Art.* San Francisco: Scrimshaw Press, 1973.

BOFFOLY, R. L. A factor analysis of visual, kinesthetic and cognitive modes of information handling. *Review of Research in Visual Arts Education,* 1978, **8,** 17–27.

BRADLEY, R. H., CALDWELL, B. M., and ELARDO, R. Home environment and cognitive development in the first 2 years. *Developmental Psychology,* 1979, **15** (3), 246–250.

BRADLEY, W. R. A preliminary study of the effect of verbalization and personality orientation on art quality. *Studies in Art Education,* 1968, **9** (2), 31.

BRISSONI, A. Creative experiences of young children. *Art Education,* 1975, **28,** (1), 19–23.

BRITTAIN, W. L. *Creativity, Art, and the Young Child.* New York: Macmillan Publishing Co., Inc., 1979.

BRITTAIN, W. L. Some exploratory studies of the art of preschool children. *Studies in Art Education,* 1969, **10** (3), 14–24.

BRITTAIN, W. L. An investigation into the character and expressive qualities of early adolescent art. Unpublished report, Cooperative Research Project No. 6-8416, Office of Education, U.S. Department of Health, Education, and Welfare, October, 1968, 55 pp. (a)

BRITTAIN, W. L. An exploratory investigation of early adolescent expression in art. *Studies in Art Education,* 1968, **9** (2), 5–12. (b)

BRITTAIN, W. L. (Ed.) *Creativity and Art Education.* Washington, D.C.: The National Art Education Association, 1964.

BRITTAIN, W. L. Creative art. In Fliegler, L. (Ed.), *Curriculum Planning for the Gifted.* Englewood Cliffs, N.J.: Prentice-Hall, 1961. Chap. 10.

BRITTAIN, W. L. and CHIEN, Y-C. Effect of materials on preschool children's ability to represent a man. *Perceptual and Motor Skills,* 1980, **51,** 995–1000.

BRONFENBRENNER, U. Early deprivation in mammals and man. In Newton, G. (Ed.), *Early Experience and Behavior.* Springfield, Ill.: Charles C Thomas, 1968.

BROOKOVER, W. B. et al. Self concept of ability and school achievement. In Miller, H. L. (Ed.), *Education for the Disadvantaged.* New York: The Free Press, 1967. Pp. 64–68.

BROUDY, H. S. Enlightened preference and justification. In Smith, R. A. (Ed.), *Aesthetics and Problems of Education.* Urbana: University of Illinois Press, 1971.

BROWN, E. V. Sexual self-identification as reflected in children's drawings when asked to "draw-a-person." *Child Development,* 1979, **49,** 35–38.

BRUNER, J. S., GREENFIELD, P. M., and OLIVER, R. R. *Studies in Cognitive Growth.* New York: Wiley, 1966.

BURGART, H. J. The development of a visual-verbal measure of general creativity: The symbol test of originality. Unpublished report, Cooperative Research Project No. 7-8168, Office of Education, U.S. Department of Health, Education, and Welfare, February, 1968, 71 pp.

BURGART, H. J. Art in higher education: The relationship of art experience to personality, general creativity, and aesthetic performance. In Brittain, W. L. (Ed.), *Creativity and Art Education.* Washington, D.C.: The National Art Education Association, 1964.

BURKHART, R. C. The interrelationship of separate criteria for creativity in art and student teaching to four personality factors. In Brittain, W. L. (Ed.), *Creativity and Art Education.* Washington, D.C.: The National Art Education Association, 1964.

BURKHART, R. C. *Spontaneous and Deliberate Ways of Learning.* Scranton, Pa.: International Textbook Co., 1962.

BURKHART, R. C. The relation of intelligence to art ability. In Mooney, R. and Razik, T. (Eds.), *Explorations in Creativity.* New York: Harper & Row, 1967. Pp. 246–258.

CAMPBELL, E. M. Do tests really motivate pupils? *The Australian Journal of Education,* 1975, **19** (1), 15–25.

Carnegie Council on Policy Studies in Higher Education. *Giving Youth a Better Chance.* San Francisco: Jossey-Bass, 1980.

CAROTHERS, T. and GARDNER, H. When children's drawings become art: the emergence of aesthetic production and perception. *Developmental Psychology,* 1979, **15** (5), 570–580.

CASEY, M. B. Color versus form discrimination learning in 1-year-old infants. *Developmental Psychology,* 1979, **15** (3), 341–343.

CASSIDY, H. G. *The Sciences and the Arts.* New York: Harper & Row, 1962.

CASTRUP, J., AIN, E., and SCOTT, R. Art skills of preschool children. *Studies in Art Education,* 1972, **13** (3), 62–69.

CECERE, J. G. The effect of verbal stimuli and artistic self-expression on children's motivation for writing. Unpublished doctoral dissertation, The Pennsylvania State University, 1966.

CHILD, I. L. Development of sensitivity to esthetic values. Unpublished report, Cooperative Research Project No. 1748, Office of Education, U.S. Department of Health, Education, and Welfare, 1964.

CLEMENTS, R. D. Art student-teacher questioning. *Studies in Art Education,* 1964, **6** (1), 14.

COIE, J. D., COSTANZO, P. R., and FARNILL, D. Specific transitions in the development of spatial perspective-taking ability. *Developmental Psychology,* 1973, **9** (2), 167–177.

COLEMAN, J. S. *The Adolescent Society.* New York: The Free Press, 1961.

COLWELL, R. *An Approach to Aesthetic Education; Final Report.* Bethesda, Md.: ERIC Reports, ED 048, 315 and ED 048, 316, 1970.

CONCANNON, J. A review of research on haptic perception. *Journal of Educational Research,* 1970, **63** (6), 250–252.

CONDRY, J. Enemies of exploration: self-initiated versus other-initiated learning. *Journal of Personality and Social Psychology,* 1977, **35** (7), 459–477.

CORCORAN, A. L. Color usage in nursery school painting. *Child Development,* 1954, **25** (2), 107 ff.

CORCORAN, A. L. The variability of children's responses to color stimuli. Unpublished doctoral dissertation, The Pennsylvania State University, 1953.

COVINGTON, M. V. Teaching for creativity: Some implications for art education. *Studies in Art Education,* 1967, **9** (1), 18.

COVINGTON, M., CRUTCHFIELD, R., DAVIES, L., and OLTON, R. *The Productive Learning Program.* Columbus, Ohio: Charles E. Merrill, 1972.

COX, M. V. Spatial depth relationships in young children's drawings. *Journal of Experimental Child Psychology,* 1978, **26**, 551–554.

CRATTY, B. J. *Perceptual and Motor Development in Infants and Children.* New York: Macmillan, 1970.

CRUTCHFIELD, R. S. Independent thought in a conformist world. In Farber, S. M. and Wilson, R. H. L. (Eds.), *Conflict and Creativity: Part Two of Control of the Mind.* New York: McGraw-Hill, 1963. Pp. 208–228.

CSIKSZENTMIHALYI, M. G. and GETZELS, J. W. Discovery-oriented behavior and the originality of creative products. *Journal of Personality and Social Psychology,* 1971, **19** (1), 47–52.

CUNNINGHAM, R., et al. *Understanding Group Behavior of Boys and Girls.* New York: Teachers College, Columbia University, 1951.

DANIEL, R. A. The effect of frequency of coloring book usage upon the creative drawings of third grade children. Unpublished doctoral dissertation, The Pennsylvania State University, 1958.

DARLINGTON, R. B., ROYCE, J. M., SNIPPER, A. S., MURRAY, H. W., and LAZAR, I. Preschool programs and later school competence of children from low-income families. *Science,* 1980, **208,** 202–204.

DAVIS, D. J. *Teaching Methodologies in Art: An Experiment in Depth and Breadth Approaches to Instruction.* Lubbock: The Texas Tech Press, 1969.

DAVIS, D. J. and TORRANCE, E. P. How favorable are the values of art educators to the creative person? *Studies in Art Education,* 1965, **6** (2), 42.

DAVIS, G. A. Instruments useful in studying creative behavior and creative talent, Part 2. *The Journal of Creative Behavior,* 1971, **5** (3), 162–165.

DAY, M. D. The compatibility of art history and studio art activity in the junior high school art program. *Studies in Art Education,* 1969, **10** (2), 57–65.

DEMPSEY, A., JR. A descriptive study of ideational patterns and the evaluation of graphic form in drawings by preschool children. Unpublished doctoral dissertation, The Pennsylvania State University, 1971.

DENNIS, W. *Group Values through Children's Drawings.* New York: Wiley, 1966.

DePORTER, D. A. and KAVANAUGH, R. D. Parameters of children's sensitivity to painting styles. *Studies in Art Education,* 1978, **20** (1), 43–48.

DEWEY, J. *Art as Experience.* New York: Capricorn Books, 1958.

DISSANAYAKE, E. Art as a human behavior: toward an ethological view of art. *The Journal of Aesthetics and Art Criticism,* 1980, **38** (4).

DOERR, S. L. Conjugate lateral eye movement, cerebral dominance, and the figural creativity factors of fluency, flexibility, or originality, and elaboration. *Studies in Art Education,* 1980, **21** (3), 5–11.

DORETHY, R. and REEVES, D. Mental functioning, perceptual differentiation, personality, and achievement among art and non-art majors. *Studies in Art Education,* 1979, **20** (2), 52–63.

DREWES, H. An experimental study of the relationship between electroencephalographic imagery variables and perceptual-cognitive processes. Unpublished doctoral dissertation, Cornell University, 1958.

DREYER, A. S. and WELLS, M. B. Parental values, parental control, and creativity in young children. *Journal of Marriage and the Family,* 1966, **28** (1), 83.

EHRENZWEIG, A. *The Hidden Order of Art.* Berkeley and Los Angeles: University of California Press, 1967.

EISNER, E. W. The development of information and attitude toward art at the secondary and college levels. *Studies in Art Education,* 1966, **8** (1), 43–58.

EISNER, E. W. Stanford's Kettering Project: A radical alternative in art education. In Hurwitz, A. (Ed.), *Programs of Promise, Art in the Schools.* New York: Harcourt Brace Jovanovich, 1972. Pp. 5–14.

ELKIND, D. and BOWEN, R. Imaginary audience behavior in children and adolescents. *Developmental Psychology,* 1979, **15** (1), 38–44.

ENG, H. *The Psychology of Children's Drawings.* London: Routledge and Kegan Paul, 1931.

ESCHER, M. C. *The Graphic Work of M. C. Escher.* New York: Ballantine Books, 1971.

FLICK, P. An intercorrelative study of two creative types: The visual type and the haptic type. Unpublished doctoral dissertation, The Pennsylvania State University, 1960.

FORMAN, S. G. and McKINNEY, J. D. Creativity and achievement of second graders in open and traditional classrooms. *Journal of Educational Psychology,* 1978, **70** (1), 101–107.

FOSTER, S. Hemisphere dominance and the art process. *Art Education,* 1977, **30** (2), 28–29.

FRANCIS, A. S. Creativity as an outlet for frustration and an aid to learning. Unpublished master's thesis, Cornell University, 1973.

FRANKLIN, B. A. Paint use is linked to artists' cancer. *The New York Times,* May 17, 1981, p. 17.

FRANKSTON, L. Effects of two programs and two methods of teaching upon the quality of art products of adolescents. *Studies in Art Education,* 1966, **7** (2), 23.

FRANKSTON, L. Some explorations of the effect of creative visual art experiences upon the poetry writing quality of eighth grade students. *Studies in Art Education,* 1963, **5** (1), 42–59.

FREEDMAN, D. G. Infancy, biology, and culture. Chapter 2 in Lipsitt, L. P. (Ed.), *Developmental Psychobiology.* New York: Wiley, 1976.

FREEMAN, N. H. *Strategies of Representation in Young Children.* New York: Academic Press, 1980.

FREEMAN, N. H. and JANIKOUN, R. Intellectual realism in children's drawings of a familiar object with distinctive features. *Child Development,* 1972, **43,** 1116–1121.

GARDNER, H. Children's sensitivity to painting styles. *Child Development,* 1970, **41,** 813–821.

GARDNER, H. and GARDNER, J. Developmental trends in sensitivity to form and subject matter in paintings. *Studies in Art Education,* 1973, **14** (2), 52–56.

GARRETT, S. V. Putting our whole brain to use: a fresh look at the creative process. *The Journal of Creative Behavior,* 1976, **10** (4), 239–249.

GAZZANIGA, M. S. The split brain in man. In Ornstein, R. E. (Ed.), *The Nature of Human Consciousness.* San Francisco: W. H. Freeman and Company, 1973.

GETZELS, J. W. and CSIKSZENTMIHALYI, M. *The Creative Vision.* New York: Wiley, 1976.

GETZELS, J. W. and JACKSON, P. W. *Creativity and Intelligence.* New York: Wiley, 1962.

GERBER, R. V. Development of competence and performance in cartographic language by children at the cognitive level of map-reasoning. Unpublished doctoral dissertation, University of Queensland, 1979.

GESCHWIND, N. Specializations of the human brain. *Scientific American,* 1979, **241** (3), 180–199.

GIBBENS, T. C. N. Drugs and the young law breaker. *Mental Health,* 1966, **25** (3), 36–37.

GIBSON, J. J. *The Senses Considered as Perceptual Systems*. Boston: Houghton Mifflin, 1966.

GINSBURG, H. and OPPER, S. *Piaget's Theory of Intellectual Development*. Englewood Cliffs, N. J.: Prentice Hall, 1969.

GLINER, C. R., PICK, A. D., PICK, H. L., and HALES, J. A developmental investigation of visual and haptic preferences for shape and texture. *Monographs of the Society for Research in Child Development*, 1969, **34** (6).

GOERTZ, E. C. Graphomotor development in preschool children. Unpublished master's thesis, Cornell University, 1966.

GOLEMAN, D. Split-brain psychology: fad of the year. *Psychology Today*, October, 1977.

GOLOMB, C. Representational development of the human figure. *The Journal of Genetic Psychology*, 1977, **131**, 207–222.

GOMBRICH, E. H. *The Story of Art*. Oxford: Phaidon Press Limited, 1978.

GOODNOW, J. J. Visible thinking: cognitive aspects of change in drawings. *Child Development*, 1978, **49**, 637–641.

GOOR, A. and RAPOPORT, T. Enhancing creativity in an informal educational framework. *The Journal of Educational Psychology*, 1977, **69** (5), 636–643.

GORDON, W. J. J. *Synectics: The Development of Creative Capacity*. New York: Harper & Row, 1961.

GOTTESMAN, M. A comparative study of Piaget's development schema of sighted children with that of a group of blind children. *Child Development*, 1971, **42**, 573–580.

GOWLER, D. and LEGGE, K. "Locked-in" employees and organizational design. In Legge, K. and Mumford, E. (Eds.), *Designing Organisations for Satisfaction and Efficiency*. Westmead, England: Gower Press, Teakfield Limited, 1978.

GROFF, P. Art and reading: is there a relationship? *Reading World*, May, 1978, 345–351.

GUILFORD, J. P. *Intelligence, Creativity and their Educational Implications*. San Diego, Calif.: Robert R. Knapp, 1968.

GUILFORD, J. P. Progress in the discovery of intellectual factors. In Taylor, C. W. (Ed.), *Widening Horizons in Creativity*. New York: Wiley, 1964.

GUTTETER, L. J. The psychological functioning of early adolescents who have failed to develop a precise drawing style. *Studies in Art Education*, 1976, **18** (1), 50–60.

HAMMILL, L. C. and LARSEN, S. C. The effectiveness of psycho-linguistic training. *Exceptional Children*, 1974, **41,** 5–14.

HARDIMAN, G. W. and ZERNICH, T. Influence of style and subject matter on the development of children's art preferences. *Studies in Art Education*, 1977, **19** (1), 29–35.

HARLOW, H. F. Mice, monkeys, men and motives. In Fowler, H. (Ed.), *Curiosity and Exploratory Behavior*. New York: Macmillan, 1965.

HARLOW, H. F., McGAUGH, J. L., and THOMPSON, R. F. *Psychology*. San Francisco: Albion, 1971.

HARRIS, D. B. *Children's Drawings as Measures of Intellectual Maturity*. New York: Harcourt Brace Jovanovich, 1963.

HARRIS, P. The child's representation of space. In Butterworth, G. (Ed.), *The Child's Representation of the World*. New York: Plenum Press, 1977.

HATTIE, J. A. Conditions for administering creativity tests. *Psychological Bulletin*, 1977, **84** (6), 1249–1260.

HAZEN, N. L., LOCKMAN, J. J., and PICK, H. L. JR. The development of children's representations of large-scale environments. *Child Development*, 1978, **49,** 623–636.

HEILMAN, H. An experimental study of

the effects of workbooks on the creative drawing of second grade children. Unpublished doctoral dissertation, The Pennsylvania State University, 1954.

HEISLER, W. J. Worker alienation: 1900–1975. In Heisler, W. J. and Houck, J. W. (Eds.), *A Matter of Dignity*. Notre Dame, Indiana: University of Notre Dame Press, 1977.

HELLER, M. Reproduction of tactually perceived forms. *Perceptual and Motor Skills,* 1980, **50,** 943–946.

HOFFA, H. E. The relationship of art experience to conformity. In Brittain, W. L. (Ed.), *Creativity and Art Education*. Washington, D.C.: The National Art Education Association, 1964.

HOGG, J. C. and McWHINNIE, H. J. A pilot research in aesthetic education. *Studies in Art Education,* 1968, **9** (2), 52.

HOLBROOK, S. H. The log cabin myth. *The American Mercury,* 1945, **61** (263), 614–619.

HOLLADAY, H. H. An experimental and descriptive study of children's pre-representational drawings. Unpublished doctoral dissertation, Cornell University, 1966.

HOLLAND, J. D. Children's responses to objects in daily living, a developmental analysis. Unpublished doctoral dissertation, the Pennsylvania State University, 1958.

HOLTZMAN, W. H., SWARTZ, J. P., and THORPE, J. S. Artists, architects and engineers—three contrasting modes of visual experience and their psychological correlates. *Journal of Personality,* 1971, **39,** 432–449.

HOOPER, J. Children's drawings of a table and an adaptation of a Piagetian coordination of perspectives task. Unpublished master's thesis, Cornell University, 1977.

HOUSSIADAS, L. and BROWN, L. B. Egocentrism in language and space perception. *Genetic Psychology Monographs,* 1980, **101,** 183–214.

HUBER, J., TREFFINGER, D., TRACY, D., and RAND, D. Self-instructional use of programmed creativity-training materials with gifted and regular students. *Journal of Educational Psychology,* 1979, **71** (3), 303–309.

HURWITZ, A. (Ed.) *Programs of Promise, Art in the Schools*. New York: Harcourt Brace Jovanovich, 1972.

HUSTON-STEIN, A., FRIEDRICH-COFER, L., and SUSMAN, E. J. The relation of classroom structure to social behavior, imaginative play, and self-regulation of economically disadvantaged children. *Child Development,* 1977, **48,** 908–916.

HYMAN, R. Creativity and the prepared mind: The role of information and induced attitudes. In Taylor, C. (Ed.), *Widening Horizons in Creativity*. New York: Wiley, 1964.

INAGAKI, K. Relationships of curiosity to perceptual and verbal fluency in young children. *Perceptual and Motor Skills,* 1979, **48,** 789–790.

IVES, W. and HOUSEWORTH, M. The role of standard orientations in children's drawing of interpersonal relationships: aspects of graphic feature marking. *Child Development,* 1980, **51,** 591–593.

JACKSON, P. W. *Life in Classrooms*. New York: Holt, Rinehart & Winston, 1968.

JENKINS, I. Aesthetic education and moral refinement. In Smith, R. A. (Ed.), *Aesthetics and Problems of Education*. Urbana: University of Illinois Press, 1971. Pp. 178–199.

JOHNSON, L. J. The effect of interpolated writing on paired-associate learning. Unpublished master's thesis, Cornell University, 1963.

JONES, L. H. Student and teacher interaction during evaluative dialogues in art. Cooperative Research Project No. S-050, Office of Education, U.S. Department of Health, Education, and Welfare, 1964.

JUHASZ, J. B. and PAXSON, L. Personality and preference for painting style. *Perceptual and Motor Skills,* 1978, **46,** 347–349.

KAGAN, J., MOSS, H. A., and SIGEL, I. E. Psychological significance of styles of conceptualization. In Wright, J. and Kagan, J. (Eds.), Basic cognitive processes in children. *Child Development Monographs,* 1963, **28** (2).

KALTSOUNIS, B. Instruments useful in studying creative behavior and creative talent, Part 1. *Journal of Creative Behavior,* 1971, **5** (2), 117–126.

KALTSOUNIS, B. Additional instruments useful in studying creative behavior and creative talent. *Journal of Creative Behavior,* 1972, **6** (4), 268–274.

KALYAN-MASIH, V. Graphic representation: from intellectual realism to visual realism in draw-a-house-tree task. *Child Development,* 1976, **47,** 1026–1031.

KELLOGG, R. *Analyzing Children's Art.* Palo Alto, Calif.: National Press Books, 1969.

KENDRICK, D. A dilemma concerning the compatibility between creative and arithmetical measurements. *Studies in Art Education,* 1967, **8** (2), 37.

KENNEDY, J. M. and FOX, N. Pictures to see and pictures to touch. In Perkins, D. and Leondar, B. (Eds.), *The Arts and Cognition.* Baltimore: Johns Hopkins University Press, 1977.

KERN, E. J. The study of art. *Studies in Art Education,* 1978, **19** (3), 50–53.

KINCAID, C. The determination and description of various creative attributes of children. In Brittain, W. L. (Ed.), *Creativity and Art Education.* Washington, D.C.: National Art Education Association, 1964. Pp. 108–115.

KIRST, W. and DIEKMEYER, V. *Creativity Training.* New York: Peter H. Wyden, 1973.

KLEINMAN, J. M. Developmental changes in haptic exploration and matching accuracy. *Developmental Psychology,* 1979, **15** (4), 480–481.

KLOSS, M. G. and DREGER, R. M. Abstract art preferences and temperamental traits. *Journal of Personality Assessment,* 1971, **35,** 375–378.

KNAPP, R. H. and GREEN, S. Preferences for styles of abstract art and their personality correlates. *Journal of Projective Techniques,* 1960, **24,** 396–402.

KOGAN, N. and PANKOVE, E. Creativity ability over a five year span. *Child Development,* 1972, **43,** 427–442.

KORZENIC, D. Changes in representation between the ages of five and seven. *Psychiatry and Art,* 1975, **4** 95–104.

KUO, Y. Y. A comparative study of creative thinking between delinquent boys and non-delinquent boys. Unpublished doctoral dissertation, University of Maryland, 1967.

KUTNICK, P. Children's drawings of their classrooms: development and social maturity. *Child Study Journal,* 1978, **8** (3), 175–186.

LANSING, K. M. The effect of class size and room size upon the creative drawings of fifth grade children. Unpublished doctoral dissertation, The Pennsylvania State University, 1956.

LARK-HOROVITZ, B. and NORTON, J. Children's art abilities: The interrelations and factorial structure of ten characteristics. *Child Development,* 1960, **31** (3), 453–462.

LARK-HOROVITZ, B. and NORTON, J. Children's art abilities: Developmental trends of art characteristics. *Child Development,* 1959, **30** (4), 433–450.

LARSEN, S. C. and HAMMILL, D. D. The relationship of selected visual perceptual abilities to school learning.

Journal of Special Education, 1975, **9,** 281–291.

LAURENDEAU, M. and PINARD, A. *The Development of the Concept of Space in the Child.* New York: International Universities Press, 1970.

LAWLER, C. O. and LAWLER, E. E., III. Color–mood associations in young children. *Journal of Genetic Psychology,* 1965, **107,** 29–33.

LEE, L. C. The concomitant development of cognitive and moral modes of thought: A test of selected deductions from Piaget's theory. Unpublished doctoral dissertation, The Ohio State University, 1968.

LEVIN, H., HILTON, T., and LEIDERMAN, G. Studies of teacher behavior. *Journal of Experimental Education,* 1957, **26,** 81–91.

LEVY, J. Lateral dominance and aesthetic preference. *Neuropsychologia,* 1976, **14,** 431–445.

LEWIS, H. P. Spatial representation in drawing as a correlate of development and a basis for picture preference. *The Journal of Genetic Psychology,* 1963, No. 102, 95–107.

LEWIS, H. P. and LIVSON, N. Cognitive development, personality, and drawing: their interrelationships in a longitudinal study. *Studies in Art Education,* 1980, **22** (1), 8–11.

LIEBERMANN, A. L. Exploratory studies of children's pre-representational drawings. Unpublished master's thesis, Cornell University, 1979.

LIEDES, L. A. Disclosures of beauty and ugliness by selected six-year-old children. Unpublished doctoral dissertation, The Pennsylvania State University, 1975.

LIGHT, P. H. and MacINTOSH, E. Depth relationships in young children's drawings. *Journal of Experimental Child Psychology,* 1980, **30,** 79–87.

LIIKANEN, P. Increasing creativity through art education among pre-school children. *Jyvaskyla Studies in Education, Psychology and Social Research,* 1975, **29.** (Finland)

LIPPITT, R. and WHITE, R. K. An experimental study of leadership and group life. In Haimowitz, M. L. and Haimowitz, N. R. (Eds.), *Human Development.* New York: Thomas Y. Crowell, 1960. Pp. 312–326.

LIVINGSTON, H. F. What the reading test doesn't test—reading. *Journal of Reading,* 1972, **15,** 402–410.

LLINAS, R. R. The cortex of the cerebellum. *Scientific American,* 1975, **232,** (1), 56–71.

LOWENFELD, V. *Creative and Mental Growth* (3rd. ed.). New York: Macmillan, 1957.

LOWENFELD, V. Tests for visual and haptical aptitudes. *American Journal of Psychology,* 1945, **58** (1), 100–111. (Reprinted: In Eisner, E. and Ecker, D. (Eds.), *Readings in Art Education.* Waltham, Mass.: Blaisdell, 1966. Pp. 97–104.)

LOWENFELD, V. *The Nature of Creative Activity* (Rev. ed.). New York: Harcourt Brace Jovanovich, 1952.

LOWENFELD, V. *The Nature of Creative Activity.* London: Kegan Paul, Trench, Trubner, 1939.

LYNCH, D. J. An investigation of left and right hemisphere processing specialization and the implications for the Satz maturational lag model of specific reading disability. *Dissertation Abstracts International,* 1980, **40** (11).

McCALLUM, R. S. and GLYNN, S. M. The hemispheric specialization construct: developmental and instructional considerations for creative behavior. Proceedings, National Association of School Psychologists, San Diego, 1979.

McFEE, J. K., *Preparation for Art.* (2nd ed.) Belmont, Calif.: Wadsworth, 1970.

MacGregor, R. N. Imposed controls in subject matter and art media choice. *Alberta Journal of Educational Research,* 1967, **13** (2), 103.

McKinney, J. D. and Forman, S. G. Factor structure of the Wallach-Kogan tests of creativity and measures of intelligence and achievement. *Psychology in the Schools,* 1977, **14** (1).

McPherson, M. W., Popplestone, J. A., and Evans, K. A. Perceptual carelessness, drawing precision, and oral activity among normal six year olds. *Perceptual and Motor Skills,* 1966, No. 22, 327–330.

McVitty, L. F. An experimental study on various methods in art motivations at the fifth grade level. Unpublished doctoral dissertation, The Pennsylvania State University, 1954.

Machotka, P. Aesthetic criteria in childhood: Justifications of preference. *Child Development,* 1966, **37** (4), 877.

Madeja, S. S. A systems approach to teaching the arts. In Hurwitz, A. (Ed.), *Programs of Promise, Art in the Schools.* New York: Harcourt Brace Jovanovich, 1972.

Madeja, S. S. The effects of divergent and convergent emphasis in art instruction on students of high and low ability. *Studies in Art Education,* 1967, **8** (2), 10.

Majewski, S. M. The relationship between the drawing characteristics of children and their sex. Unpublished doctoral dissertation, Illinois State University, 1978.

Malone, C. Safety first: Comments on the influence of external danger in the lives of children of disorganized families. In Miller, H. L. (Ed.), *Education for the Disadvantaged.* New York: The Free Press, 1967. Pp. 53–64.

Marshall, M. L. A comparison of schizophrenics, children, and normal adults on their use of color. Unpub-

lished doctoral dissertation, Vanderbilt University, 1954.

Maslow, A. H. *Toward a Psychology of Being.* New York: Van Nostrand, 1962.

Maxwell, J. W., Croake, J. W., and Biddle, A. P. Sex differences in the comprehension of spatial orientation. *The Journal of Psychology,* 1975, **91,** 127–131.

Mednick, S. and Mednick, M. T. An associative interpretation of the creative process. In Taylor, C. W. (Ed.), *Widening Horizons in Creativity.* New York: Wiley, 1964.

Melkman, R., Koriat, A., and Pardo, K. Preference for color and form in preschoolers as related to color and form differentiation. *Child Development,* 1976, **47,** 1045–1050.

Michael, J. A. *A Handbook for Art Instructors and Students Based upon Concepts and Behaviors.* New York: Vantage Press, 1970.

Michael, J. A. The effect of award, adult standard, and peer standard upon creativeness in art of high school pupils. *Research in Art Education,* Ninth Yearbook, National Art Education Association, 1959. Pp. 98–104.

Millar, S. Visual experience or translation rules? Drawing the human figure by blind and sighted children. *Perception,* 1975, **4,** 363–371.

Millar, S. Visual and haptic cue utilization by preschool children. *Journal of Experimental Child Psychology,* 1971, **12,** 88–94.

Miller, S. R., Sabatino, D. A., and Miller, T. L. Influence of training in visual perceptual discrimination on drawings by children. *Perceptual and Motor Skills,* 1977, **44,** 479–487.

Mills, E. A. and Thomson, D. R. State of the arts in the states. *Art Education,* 1981, **34** (1), 40–44.

Mills, J. C. The effect of art instruction

upon a reading developmental test: An experimental study with rural Appalachian children. *Studies in Art Education,* 1973, **14** (3), 4–8.

MITCHELMORE, M. C. Developmental stages in children's representation of regular solid figures. *Journal of Genetic Psychology,* 1978, **133,** 229–239.

MITTON, S. (Ed.), *The Cambridge Encyclopaedia of Astronomy.* New York: Crown Publishers, Inc., 1977.

MOHOLY-NAGY, S. *Native Genius in Anonymous Architecture.* New York: Schocken Books, 1976.

MORRIS, D. *The Human Zoo.* New York: McGraw-Hill, 1969.

MUNRO, T. *Art Education.* New York: The Liberal Arts Press, 1956.

National Assessment of Art. *Design and Drawing Skills.* Washington, D.C.: U.S. Government Printing Office, 1977.

NEPERUD, R. W. An experimental study of visual elements, selected art instruction methods, and drawing development at the fifth grade level. *Studies in Art Education,* 1966, **7** (2), 3.

NEVILLE, R. E. (Ed.), *Inside Education.* Albany, N.Y.: State Education Department, December, 1973. P. 6.

NICHOLS, G. W. *Art Education Applied to Industry.* New York: Harper & Row, 1877.

NICKI, R. M. and GALE, A. EEG, measures of complexity, and preference for nonrepresentational works of art. *Perception,* 1977, **6,** 281–286.

NORDSTROM, C., FRIEDENBERG, E. Z., and GOLD, H. *Society's Children: A Study of Ressentiment in the Secondary School.* New York: Random House, 1967.

ORNSTEIN, R. E. *The Psychology of Consciousness.* New York: Harcourt Brace Jovanovich, 1977.

PALERMO, D. S. and MOLFESE, D. L. Language acquisition from age five on-ward. In Rebelsky and Dorman (Eds.), *Child Development and Behavior.* New York: Alfred A. Knopf, 1973. Pp. 401–424.

PARNES, S. J. *Creative Behavior Workbook.* New York: Scribners, 1967.

PARNES, S. J. Research on developing creative behavior. In Taylor, C. (Ed.), *Widening Horizons in Creativity.* New York: Wiley, 1964.

PARSONS, M. J. Herbert Read on education. In Smith, R. A. (Ed.), *Aesthetics and Problems of Education.* Urbana: University of Illinois Press, 1971, pp. 42–63.

PAYNE, P. A., HALPIN, W. G., ELLETT, C. D., and DALE, J. B. General personality correlates of creative personality in academically and artistically gifted youth. *Journal of Special Education,* 1975, **9** (1), 105–108.

PEARLMAN, C. The relationship of effectance motivation to creativity and the effects of a penalty/reward versus no penalty/reward situation on the demonstration of effectance motivation. Unpublished doctoral dissertation, State University of New York at Buffalo, 1979.

PENTZ, M. R. A study of kindergarten children's concept of five. Unpublished master's thesis, Cornell University, February, 1965.

PHILLIPS, V. K. Creativity: performance, profiles, and perceptions. *The Journal of Psychology,* 1973, **83,** 25–30.

PHILLIPS, W. A., HOBBS, S. B., and PRATT, F. R. Intellectual realism in children's drawings of cubes. *Cognition,* 1978, **6,** 15–33.

PIAGET, J. *Judgment and Reasoning in the Child.* Paterson, N.J.: Littlefield, Adams, 1959.

PIAGET, J. *The Child's Conception of the World.* (Trans. by Tomlinson, J. and Tomlinson, A.) Paterson, N.J.: Littlefield, Adams, 1960.

PIAGET, J. *The Grasp of Consciousness.* (Trans. by Wedgewood, S.) Cambridge, Mass.: Harvard University Press, 1976.

PIAGET, J. *The Language and Thought of the Child.* New York: Meridian, 1955.

PIAGET, J. and INHELDER, B. *Mental Imagery in the Child.* New York: Basic Books, 1971.

PIAGET, J. and INHELDER, B. *The Child's Conception of Space.* New York: Norton, 1967.

PLATT, P. *Big Boy* (also teachers manual, *Early Reading Program*). Menlo Park, Calif.: Addison-Wesley, 1971.

PRENTISS, B. V. A study of the effect of the teaching of perspective on the drawing quality of children in the 5th, 7th and 9th grades. Unpublished master's thesis, Cornell University, 1972.

PRINCE, G. M. *The Practice of Creativity.* New York: Harper & Row, 1970.

QUACKENBOS, G. P. *Composition and Rhetoric.* New York: D. Appleton and Co., 1871.

RAND, C. W. Copying in drawing: The importance of adequate visual analysis versus the ability to utilize drawing rules. *Child Development,* 1973, **44,** 47–53.

READ, H. *Education through Art.* New York: Pantheon Books, 1958.

READ, H. *The Redemption of the Robot; My Encounter With Education Through Art.* New York: Simon and Schuster, 1966.

REESE, H. W., PARNES, S. J., TREFFINGER, D. J., and KALTSOUNIS, G. Effects of a creative studies program on structure-of-intellect factors. *Journal of Educational Psychology,* 1976, **68** (4), 401–410.

REICHENBERG-HACKETT, W. Influence of nursery group experience on children's drawings. *Psychological Reports,* 1964, No. 14, 433–434.

ROSENTHAL, R. and JACOBSON, L. *Pygmalion in the Classroom.* New York: Holt, Rinehart & Winston, 1968.

ROUBERTOUX, P., CARLIER, M., and CHAGUIBOFF, J. Preference for non-objective art: Personal and psychosocial determiners. *British Journal of Psychology,* 1971, **62** (1), 105–110.

ROUSE, M. J. A new look at an old theory: A comparison of Lowenfeld's "haptic-visual" theory with Witkin's perceptual theory. *Studies in Art Education,* 1965, **7** (1), 42.

ROUSSEAU, D. M. Technological differences in job characteristics, employee satisfaction, and motivation: a synthesis of job design research and sociotechnical systems theory. *Organizational Behavior and Human Performance,* 1977, **19,** 18–42.

RUMP, E. E. and SOUTHGATE, V. S. Teachers' understanding of pupils' aesthetic preferences. *Review of Research in Visual Arts Education,* 1978, **8,** 37–42.

RUMP, E. E. and SOUTHGATE, V. S. Variables affecting aesthetic appreciation, in relation to age. *British Journal of Educational Psychology,* 1966–1967, **36–37,** 58–71.

RUSSELL, I. and WAUGAMAN, B. A study of the effect of workbook copy experiences on the creative concepts of children. *Research Bulletin,* The Eastern Arts Association, 1952, **3** (1).

SALOME, R. A. A comparative analysis of kindergarten children's drawings in crayon and colored pencil. *Studies in Art Education,* 1967, **8** (2), 21–36.

SALOME, R. A. The effects of perceptual training upon the two-dimensional drawings of children. *Studies in Art Education,* 1965, **7** (1), 18.

SALOME, R. A. and REEVES, D. Two pilot investigations of perceptual training of four- and five-year-old kindergarten children. *Studies in Art Education,* 1972, **13** (2), 2–10.

SCHWARTZ, F. R. *Structure and Potential in Art Education.* Waltham, Mass.: Ginn-Blaisdell, 1970.

SHARER, J. W. Distinguishing justifications and explanations in judgments of art. *Studies in Art Education,* 1980, **21** (2), 38–42.

SIBLEY, A. G. Drawings of kindergarten children as a measure of reading readiness. Unpublished master's thesis, Cornell University, 1957.

SIEDLECKI, J. T. Potential hazards of plastics used in sculpture. *Art Education,* 1972, **25** (2), 21–26.

SIEDLECKI, J. T. Potential health hazards of materials used by artists and sculptors. *Art Education,* 1968, **21** (9), 3–6.

SIEGEL, A. W., HERMAN, J. F., ALLEN, G. L., and KIRASIC, K. C. The development of cognitive maps of large and small scale spaces. *Child Development,* 1979, **50,** 582–585.

SILBERMAN, C. E. *Crisis in the Classroom.* New York: Vintage Books, 1971.

SIMMONS, R. and LOCHER, P. Haptic perception of nonrepresentational shapes. *Perceptual and Motor Skills,* 1979, **48,** 987.

SINGER, J. L. *The Child's World of Make-believe.* New York: Academic Press, 1973.

SNOW, C. P. *The Two Cultures and the Scientific Revolution.* New York: Cambridge University Press, 1961.

SPELLER, K. G. and SCHUMACHER, G. M. Age and set in creative test performance. *Psychological Reports,* 1975, **36,** 447–450.

SPITZ, H. and BORLAND, M. Redundancy in line drawings of familiar objects: effects of age and intelligence. *Cognitive Psychology,* April 1971, No. 2, 196–205.

STACEY, J. T. and ROSS, B. M. Scheme and schema in children's memory of their own drawings. *Developmental Psychology,* 1975, **11** (1), 37–41.

STEIN, H. B. A comparison of the effects of two kindergarten training programs on reading readiness and creativity. Unpublished master's thesis, Cornell University, 1972.

STENHOUSE, L. *Culture and Education.* New York: Weybright & Talley, 1967.

STEWART, G. R. *American Ways of Life.* Garden City, N.Y.: Doubleday, 1954.

STONE, L. J. and CHURCH, J. *Childhood and Adolescence.* New York: Random House, 1968.

SWERDLOW, J. A question of impact. *Wilson Quarterly,* 1981, **5** (1), 86–99.

TAUNTON, M. The influence of age on preferences for subject matter, realism, and spatial depth in painting reproductions. *Studies in Art Education,* 1980, **21** (3), 40–52.

TAYLOR, C. W. Questioning and creating: A model for curriculum reform. *The Journal of Creative Behavior,* 1967, **1** (1), 22.

TEMPLEMAN, K. D. A study of the relationship between the haptic and visual creative types and reading achievement in first and sixth grade children. Unpublished master's thesis, Cornell University, 1962.

THOMPSON, C. S. The effect of selected painting experiences on the self-concept, visual expression, and academic achievement of third and fourth grade underachievers. *Dissertation Abstracts International,* October 1970, **31** 1634–1635.

THOMPSON, L. S. *Manual of Drawing for Regents' Schools.* Boston: D.C. Heath, 1895.

TORRANCE, E. P. Career patterns and peak creative achievements of creative high school students twelve years

447

BIBLIOGRAPHY

later. *The Gifted Child Quarterly*, 1972, **16** (2), 75–88.

TORRANCE, E. P. *Guiding Creative Talent*. Englewood Cliffs, N.J.: Prentice-Hall, 1962.

TORRANCE, E. P. Non-test ways of identifying the creative child. In Gowan, J. C., Demos, G. D., and Torrance, E. P. (Eds.), *Creativity: Its Educational Implications*. New York: Wiley, 1967.

TRISDORFER, A. A study of the ability of pre-school children to copy triangles. Unpublished master's thesis, Cornell University, 1972.

TRIST, E. Adapting to a changing world. In *Readings on the Quality of Working Life*. Ottawa: The Labour Gazette, Labour Canada, 1978.

TROWBRIDGE, N. Creativity in children in the field of art: Criterion development study. *Studies in Art Education*, 1967, **9** (1), 2–17.

TROWBRIDGE, N. and CHARLES, D. C. Creativity in art students. *Journal of Genetic Psychology*, 1966, **109,** 281–289.

VERNON, M. D. *Perception Through Experience*. New York: Barnes and Noble, 1970.

VERNON, M. D. The development of perception in children. In Gordon, I. J. *Human Development*, Chicago: Scott, Foresman, 1965. Pp. 177–184.

WALL, J. The base line in children's drawings of self and its relationship to aspects of overt behavior. Unpublished doctoral dissertation, The Florida State University, 1959.

WALLACH, M. A. and KOGAN, N. *Modes of Thinking in Young Children*. New York: Holt, Rinehart & Winston, 1965.

WALLACH, M. A. and WING, C. W. *The Talented Student*. New York: Holt, Rinehart & Winston, 1969.

WALTER, W. G. *The Living Brain*. New York: Norton, 1963.

WAMPLER, J. *All Their Own*. New York: Schenckman Publishing Company, John Wiley and Sons, 1977.

WARD, W. Creativity and environmental cues in nursery school children. *Developmental Psychology*, 1969, **1** (5), 543–547.

WASHBURNE, C. and HEIL, L. M. What characteristics of teachers affect children's growth? In Glock, M. D. (Ed.), *Guiding Learning*. New York: Wiley, 1971.

WATSON, A. J. Multiple seriation and learning to read. *The Australian Journal of Education*, 1979, **23** (2), 171–180.

WEINSTOCK, R. *The Greening of the High School*. New York: Educational Facilities Laboratories, 1973.

WEISBERG, P. S. and SPRINGER, K. Environmental factors in creative function. In Mooney, R. and Razik, T. (Eds.), *Explorations in Creativity*. New York: Harper & Row, 1967. Pp. 120–134.

WHITE, B. L. and CASTLE, P. Visual exploratory behavior following postnatal handling of human infants. *Perceptual and Motor Skills*, 1964, **18,** 497–502.

WHITE, K. and ALLEN, R. Art counseling in an educational setting: Self-concept change among pre-adolescent boys. *Journal of School Psychology*, 1971, **9** (2), 218–225.

WHITESEL, L. S. Career attitudes of art students. *Studies in Art Education*, 1980, **22** (1), 36–41.

WIGGINTON, E. *Foxfire 1–6*. Garden City, New York: Anchor Press/ Doubleday, 1972–1980.

WILLATS, J. How children learn to draw realistic pictures. *Journal of Experimental Psychology*, 1977, **29**, 367–382.

WILLIAMS, A. J., POOLE, M. E., and LETT, W. R. The creativity/self-concept relationship reviewed: an Australian lon-

BIBLIOGRAPHY

gitudinal perspective. *Australian Psychologist,* 1977, **12** (3), 313–317.

WILLIAMS, F. E. *A Total Creativity Program for Individualizing and Humanizing the Learning Process.* Englewood Cliffs, N.J.: Educational Technology Publications, 1972.

WILSON, H. B. Toward industrial democracy. In *Readings on the Quality of Working Life.* Ottawa: The Labour Gazette, Labour Canada, 1978.

WILSON, L. L. *Picture Study in Elementary Schools.* New York: Macmillan, 1899.

WITKIN, H. A., et al. *Psychological Differentiation.* New York: Wiley, 1962.

WODTKE, K. H. and WALLEN, N. E. The effects of teacher control in the classroom on pupils' creativity-test gains. *American Educational Research Journal,* 1965, **2** (2), 75–82.

WORKMAN, E. A. and STILLION, J. M. The relationship between creativity and ego development. *The Journal of Psychology,* 1974, **88,** 191–195.

YOUNGBLOOD, M. S. The hemispherality wagon leaves laterality station at 12:45 for art superiority land. *Studies in Art Education,* 1979, **21** (1), 44–49.

ZAWACKI, A. An experimental study of analytic versus synthetic modelings and drawings of children. Unpublished doctoral dissertation, The Pennsylvania State University, 1956.

INDEX